DY KISS

VOLUME 1
BY KAZUKO FURUMIYA

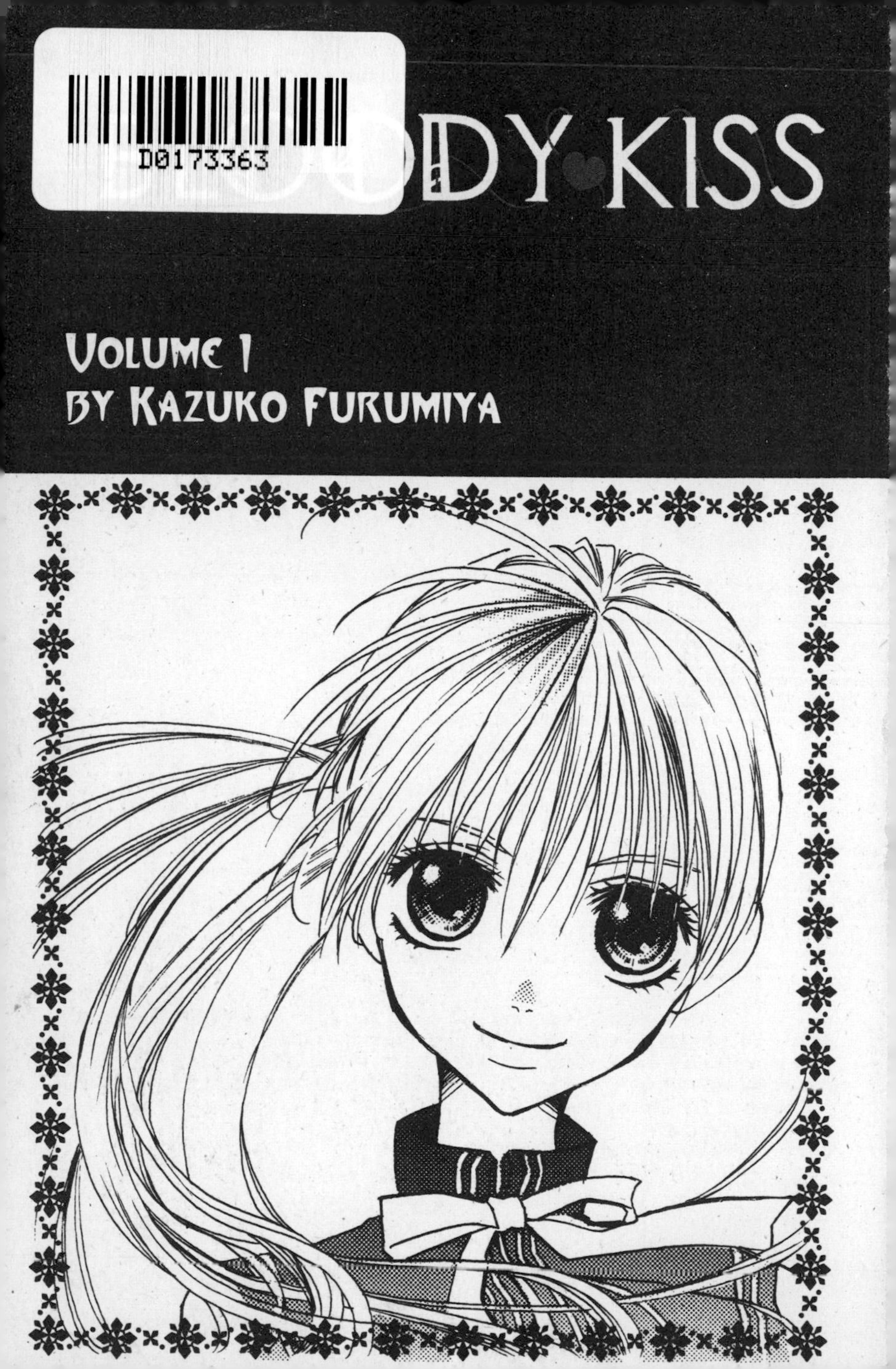

Bloody Kiss Volume 1
Created by Kazuko Furumiya

Translation - Monica Seya Chin
English Adaptation - Lianne Sentar
Retouch and Lettering - Star Print Brokers
Production Artist - Rui Kyo
Graphic Designer - Louis Csontos

Editor - Bryce P. Coleman
Print Production Manager - Lucas Rivera
Managing Editor - Vy Nguyen
Senior Designer - Louis Csontos
Director of Sales and Manufacturing - Allyson De Simone
Associate Publisher - Marco F. Pavia
President and C.O.O. - John Parker
C.E.O. and Chief Creative Officer - Stu Levy

A  Manga

TOKYOPOP and  are trademarks or registered trademarks of TOKYOPOP Inc.

TOKYOPOP Inc.
5900 Wilshire Blvd. Suite 2000
Los Angeles, CA 90036

E-mail: info@TOKYOPOP.com
Come visit us online at www.TOKYOPOP.com

ISBN: 978-1-4278-1579-8

First TOKYOPOP printing: August 2009
10 9 8 7 6 5 4 3 2
Printed in the USA

BLOODY KISS

VOLUME 1

CREATED BY
KAZUKO FURUMIYA

TOKYOPOP®

HAMBURG // LONDON // LOS ANGELES // TOKYO

BLOODY KISS

Contents

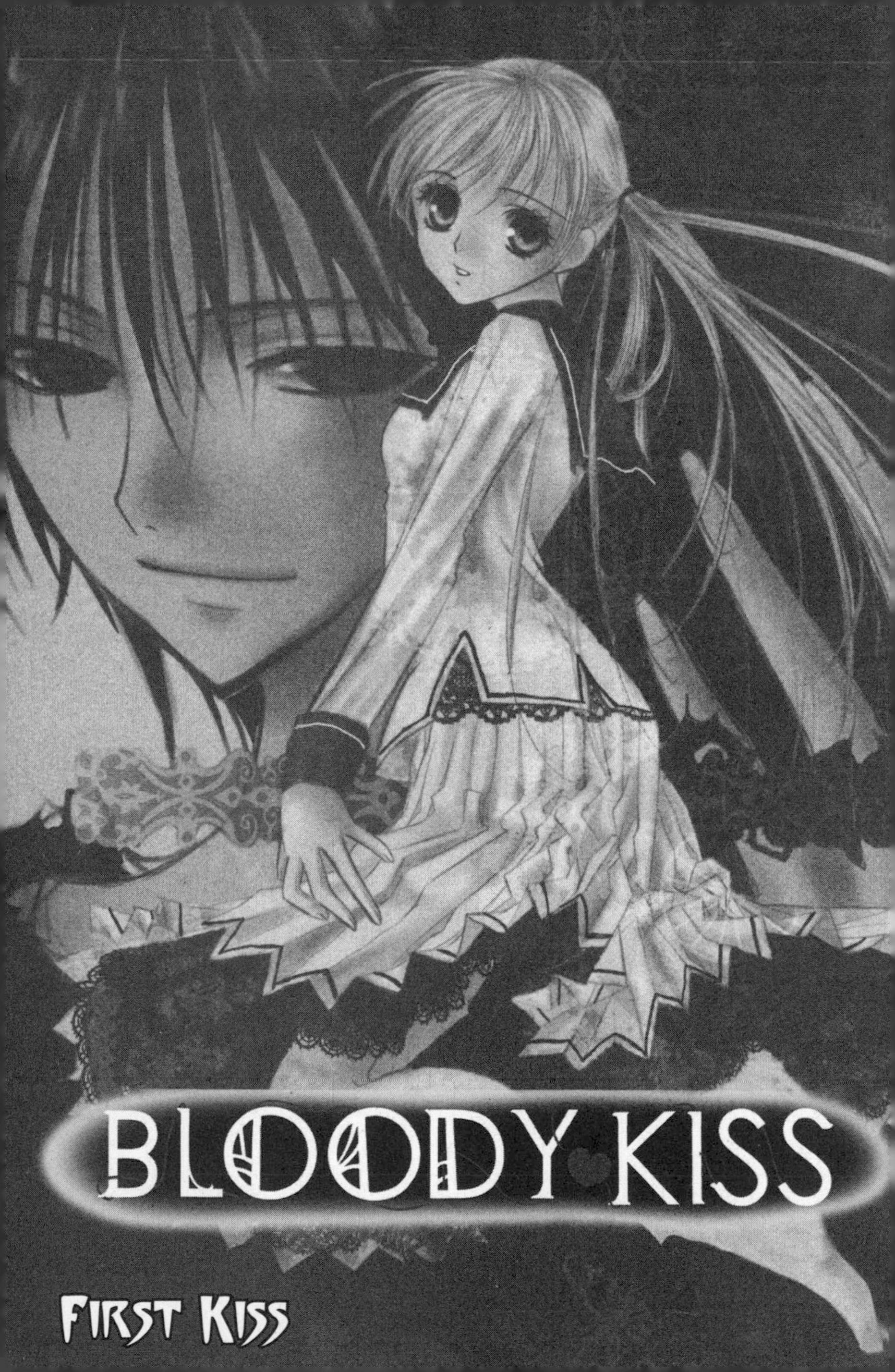
BLOODY KISS
FIRST KISS

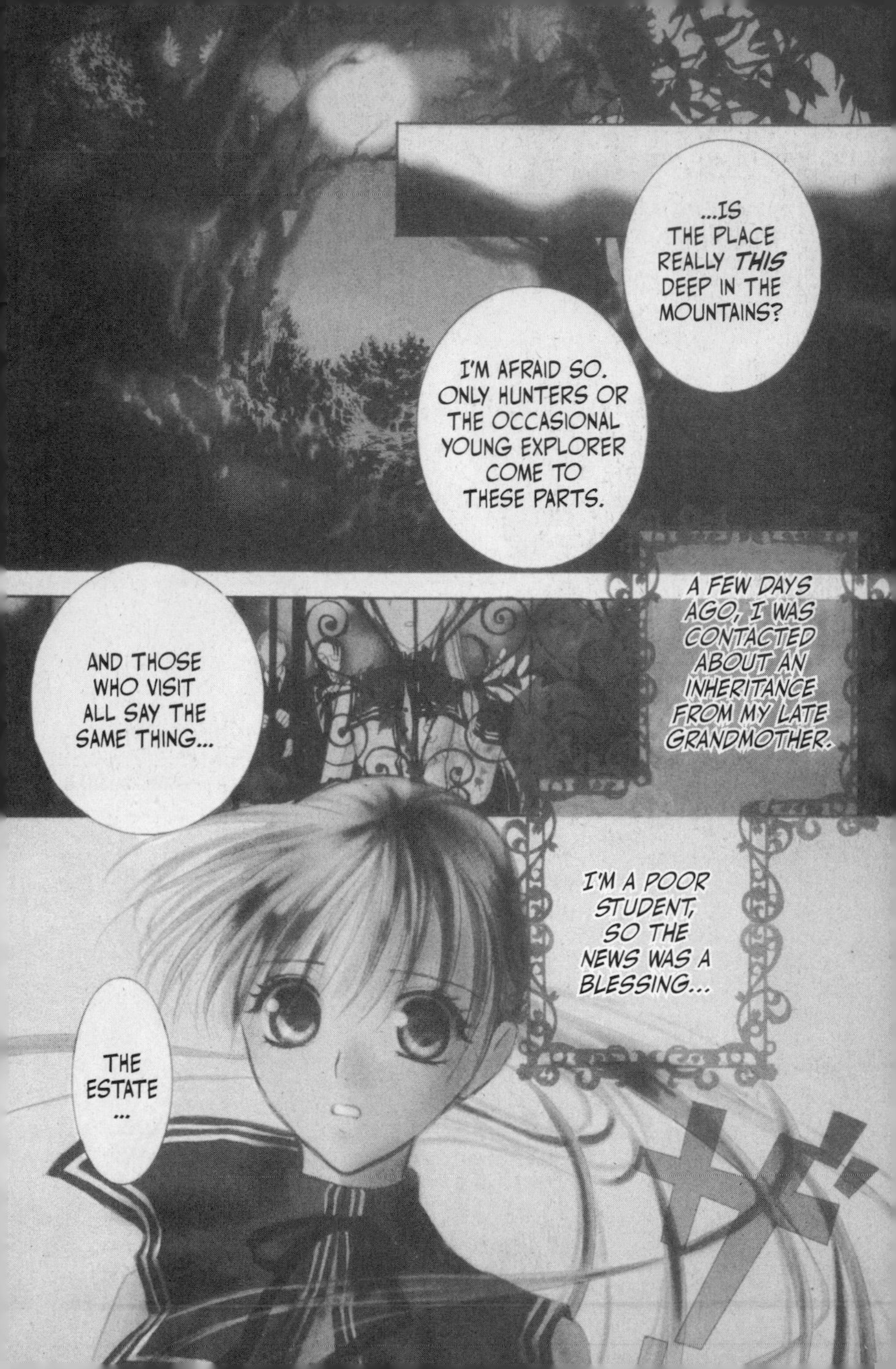

...IS THE PLACE REALLY *THIS* DEEP IN THE MOUNTAINS?
I'M AFRAID SO. ONLY HUNTERS OR THE OCCASIONAL YOUNG EXPLORER COME TO THESE PARTS.
A FEW DAYS AGO, I WAS CONTACTED ABOUT AN INHERITANCE FROM MY LATE GRANDMOTHER.
AND THOSE WHO VISIT ALL SAY THE SAME THING...
I'M A POOR STUDENT, SO THE NEWS WAS A BLESSING...
THE ESTATE ...

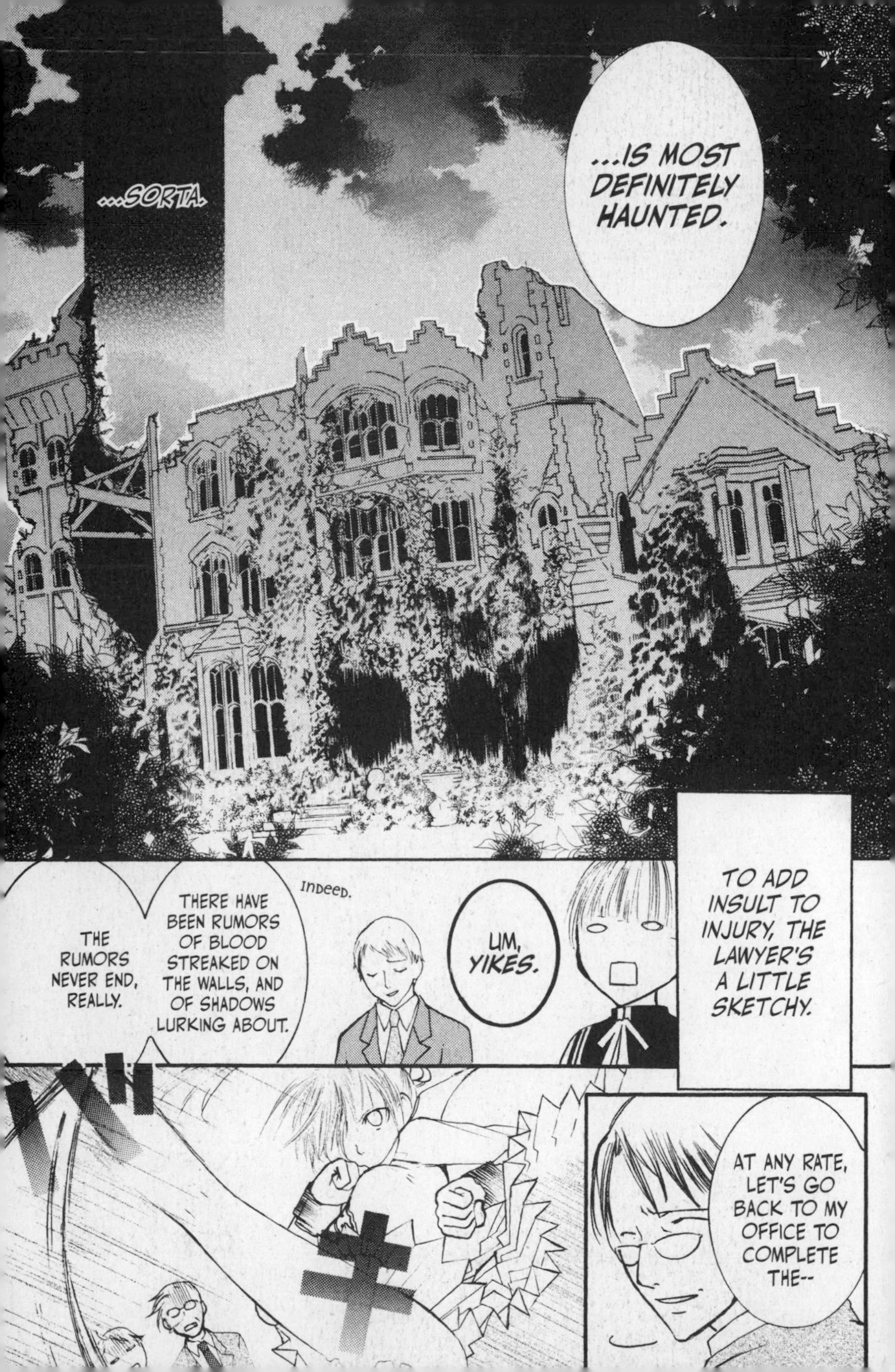
...IS MOST DEFINITELY HAUNTED.
...SORTA.
TO ADD INSULT TO INJURY, THE LAWYER'S A LITTLE SKETCHY.
UM, YIKES.
INDEED.
THERE HAVE BEEN RUMORS OF BLOOD STREAKED ON THE WALLS, AND OF SHADOWS LURKING ABOUT.
THE RUMORS NEVER END, REALLY.
AT ANY RATE, LET'S GO BACK TO MY OFFICE TO COMPLETE THE--

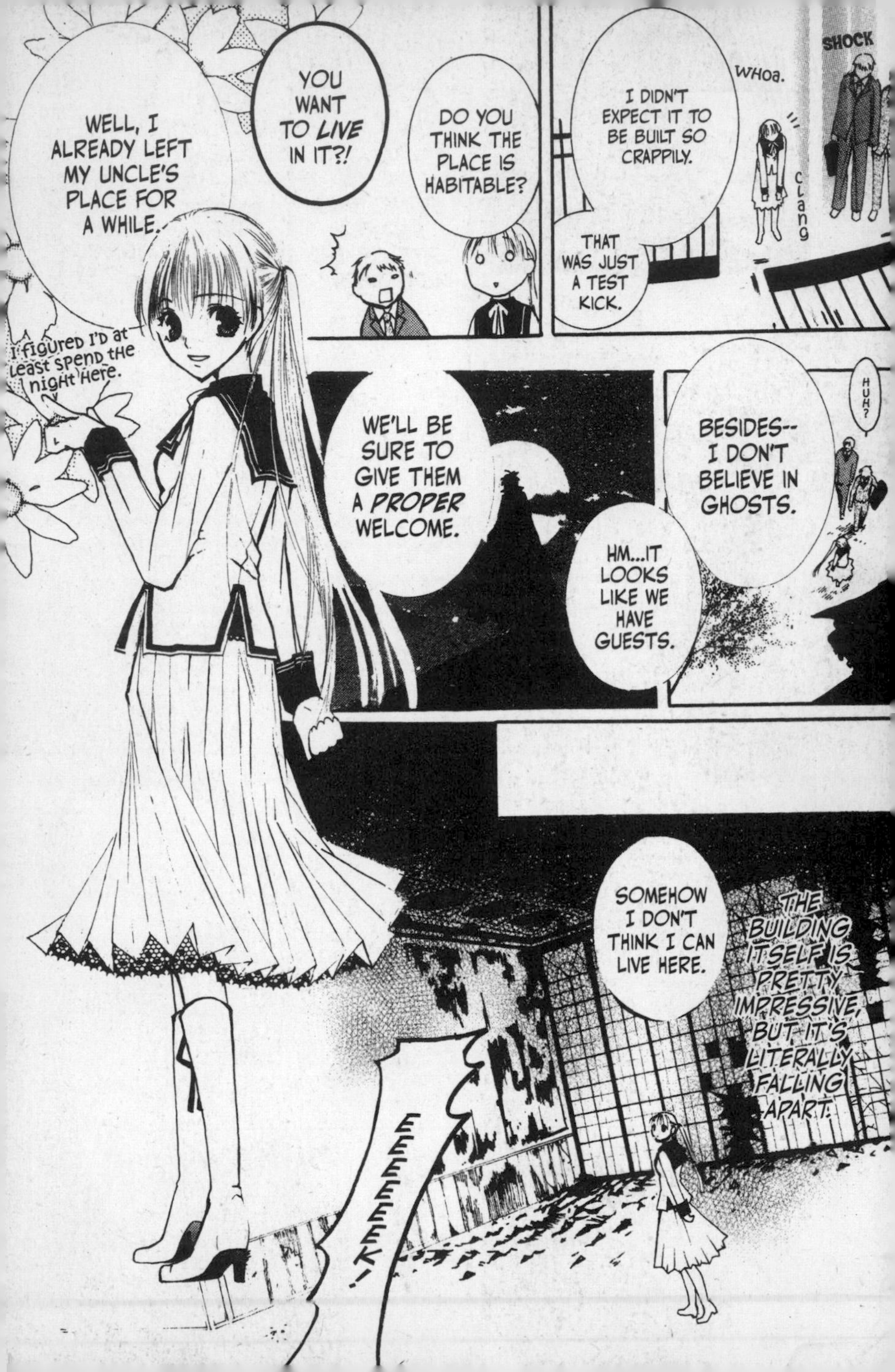
SHOCK
Whoa.
Clang
I DIDN'T EXPECT IT TO BE BUILT SO CRAPPILY.
THAT WAS JUST A TEST KICK.
DO YOU THINK THE PLACE IS HABITABLE?
YOU WANT TO *LIVE* IN IT?!
WELL, I ALREADY LEFT MY UNCLE'S PLACE FOR A WHILE.
I figured I'd at least spend the night here.
HUH?
BESIDES-- I DON'T BELIEVE IN GHOSTS.
HM...IT LOOKS LIKE WE HAVE GUESTS.
WE'LL BE SURE TO GIVE THEM A *PROPER* WELCOME.
THE BUILDING ITSELF IS PRETTY IMPRESSIVE, BUT IT'S LITERALLY FALLING APART.
SOMEHOW I DON'T THINK I CAN LIVE HERE.
EEEEEEK!

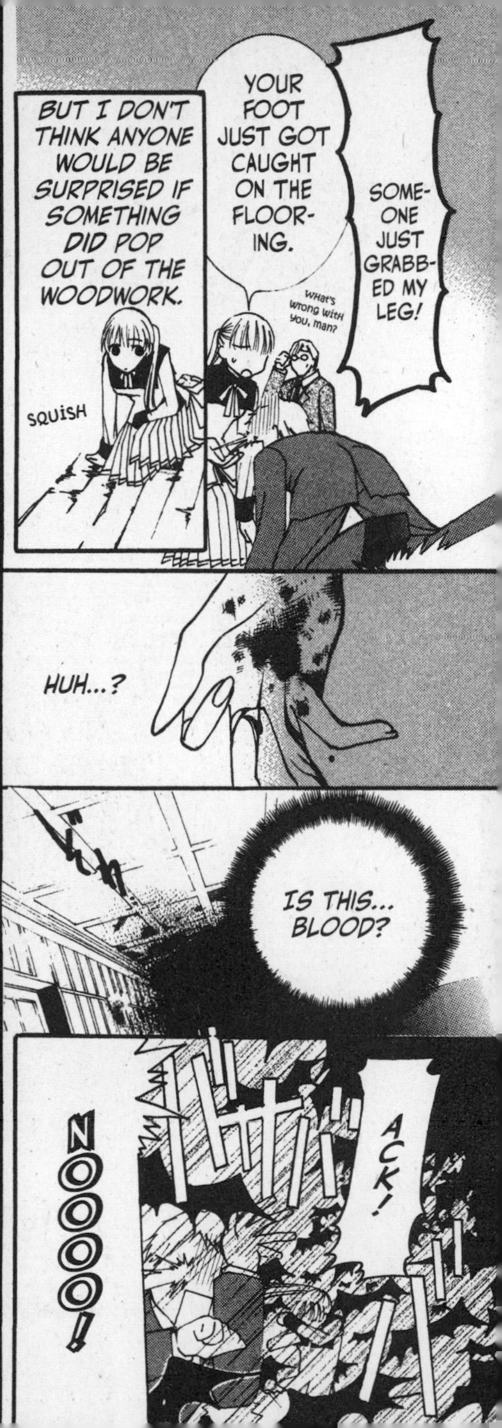
SOME-ONE JUST GRABB-ED MY LEG!
YOUR FOOT JUST GOT CAUGHT ON THE FLOOR-ING.
What's wrong with you, man?
BUT I DON'T THINK ANYONE WOULD BE SURPRISED IF SOMETHING DID POP OUT OF THE WOODWORK.
SQUISH
HUH...?
IS THIS... BLOOD?
ACK!
NOOOOO!
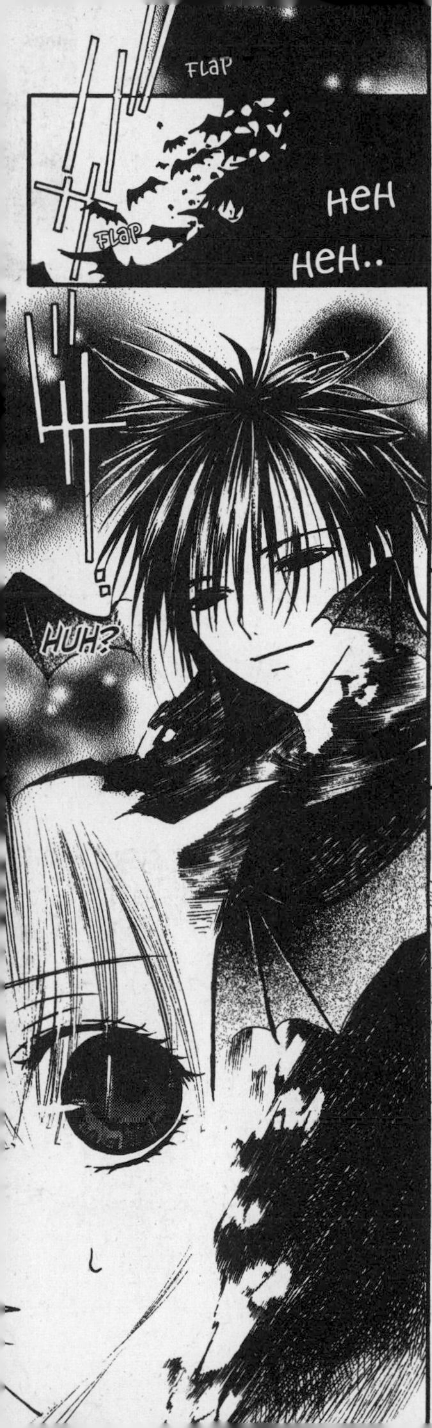
FLAP
HEH
HEH..
FLAP
HUH?

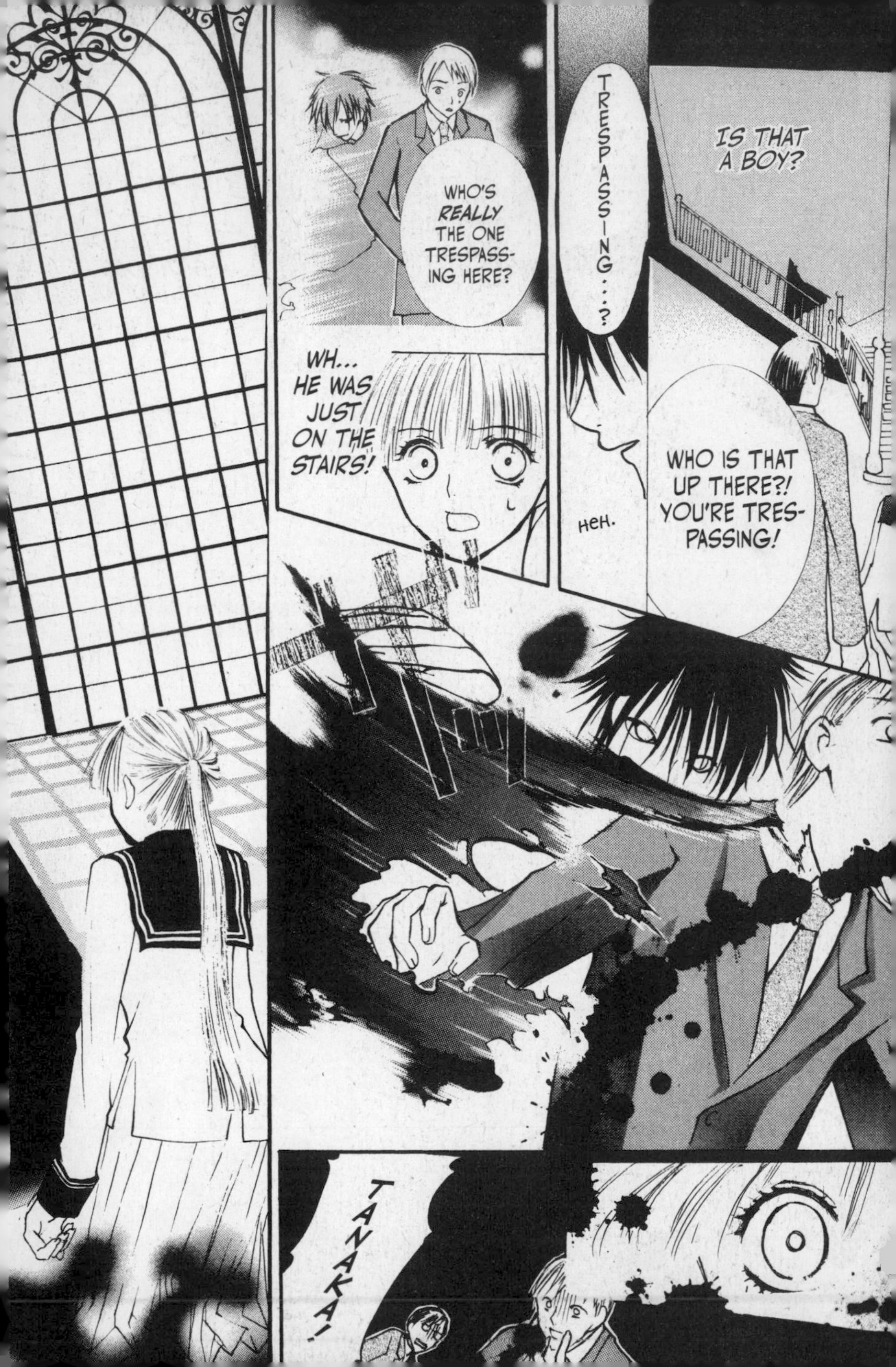
IS THAT A BOY?
WHO IS THAT UP THERE?! YOU'RE TRES-PASSING!
TRESPASSING...?
HEH.
WHO'S REALLY THE ONE TRESPASSING HERE?
WH... HE WAS JUST ON THE STAIRS!
TANAKA!

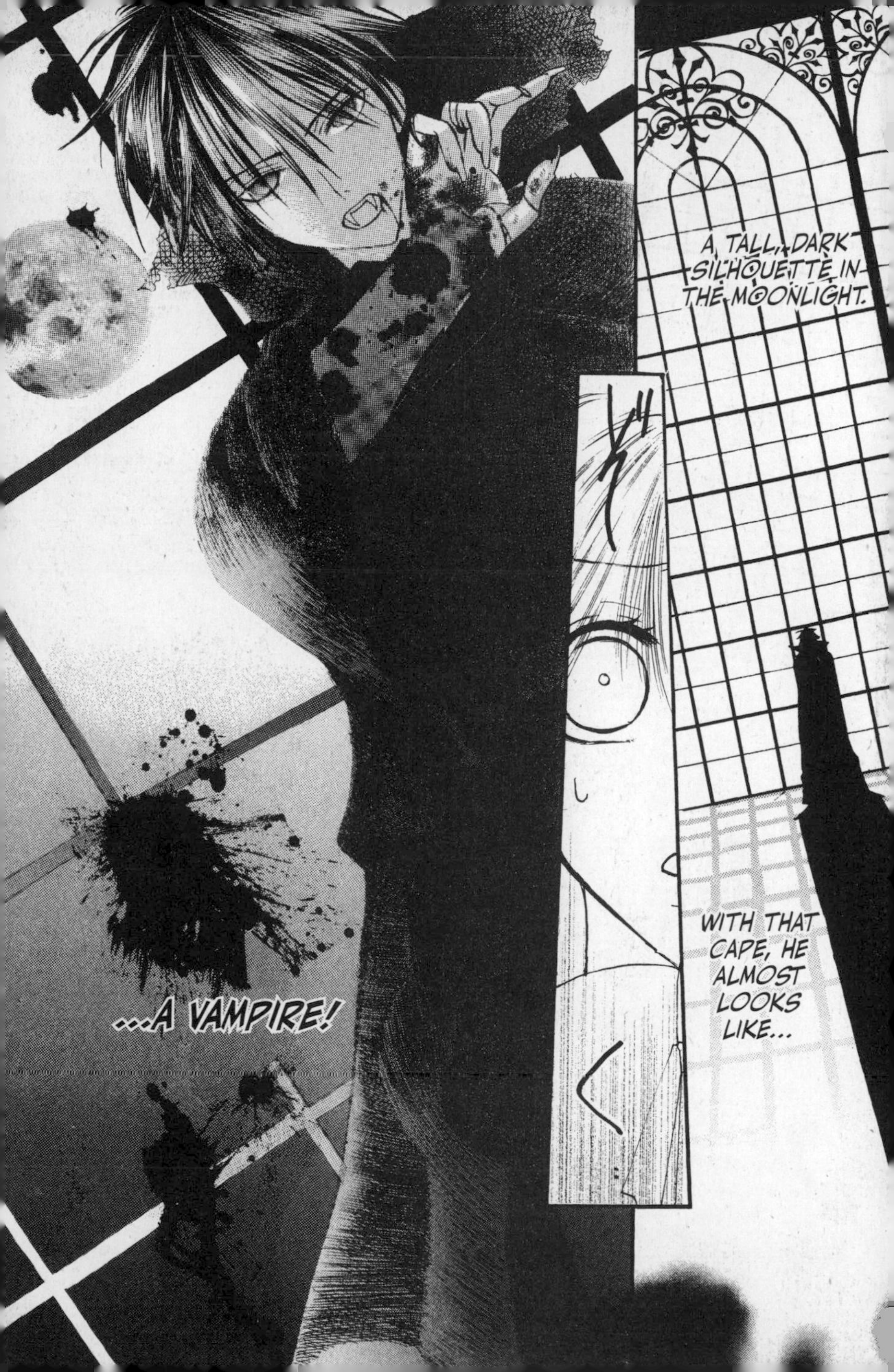
A TALL, DARK SILHOUETTE IN THE MOONLIGHT.
WITH THAT CAPE, HE ALMOST LOOKS LIKE...
...A VAMPIRE!

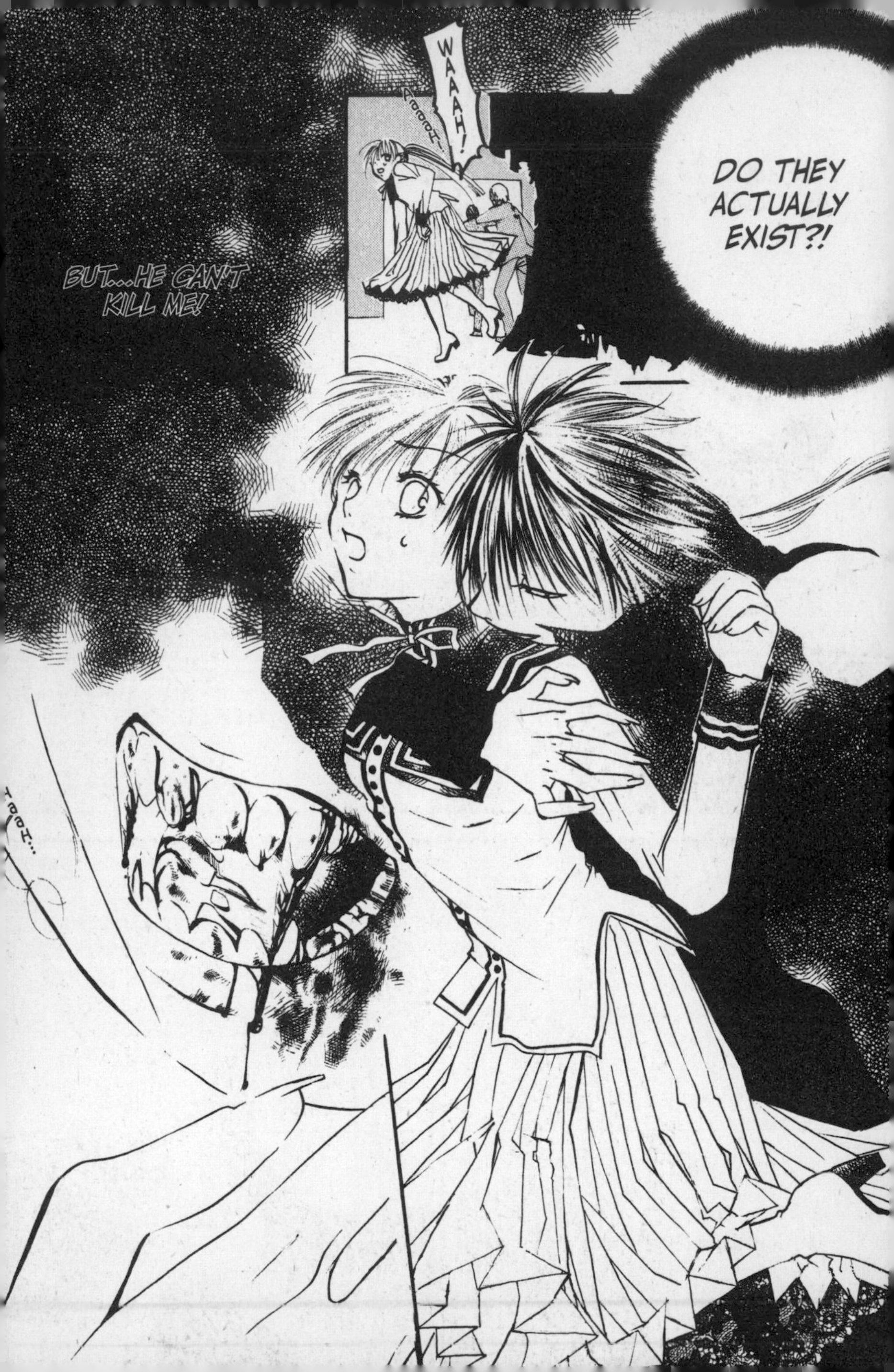
DO THEY ACTUALLY EXIST?!
WAAAH!
Aaaaah!
BUT...HE CAN'T KILL ME!

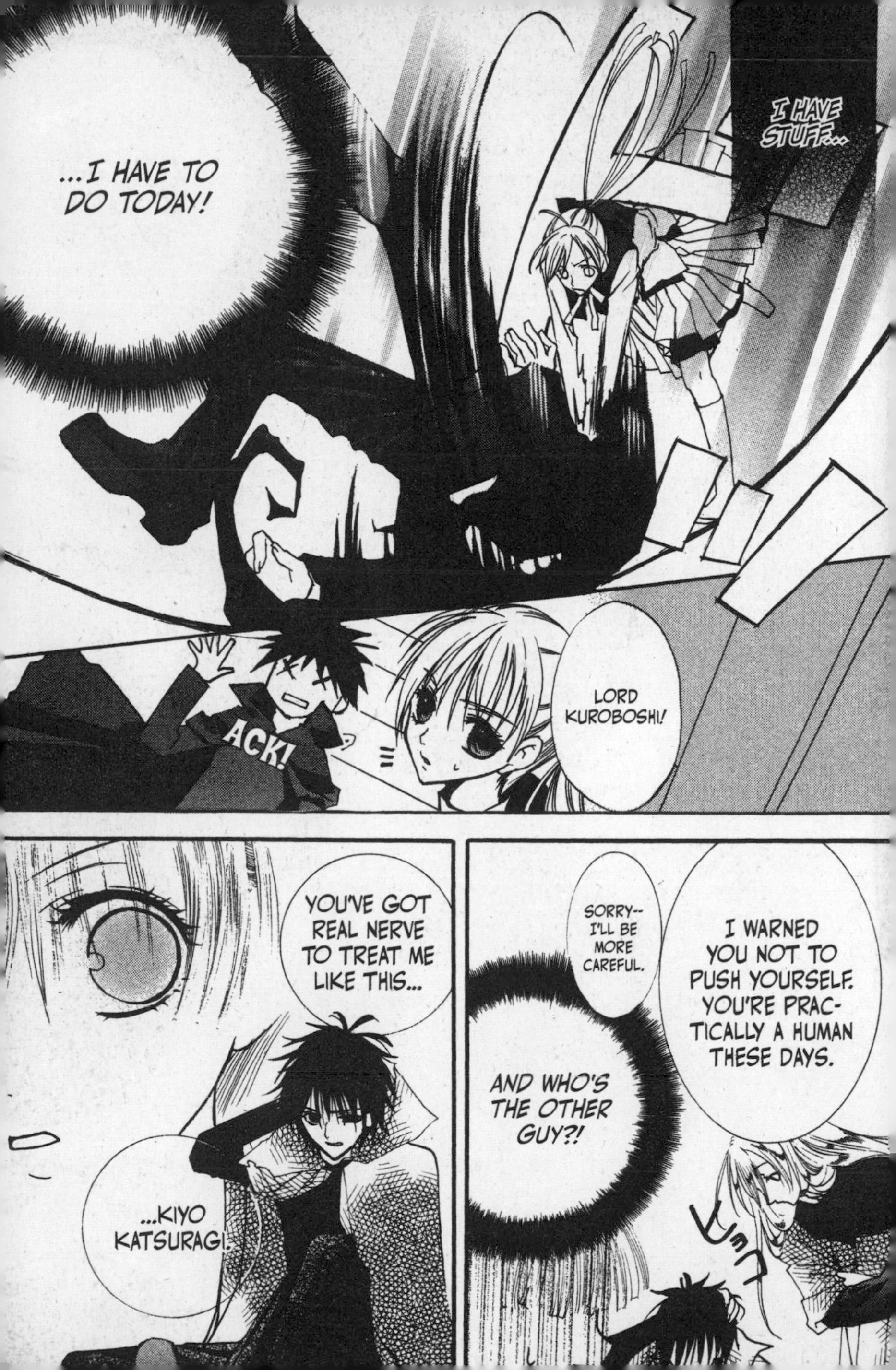
I HAVE STUFF...
...I HAVE TO DO TODAY!
LORD KUROBOSHI!
ACK!
I WARNED YOU NOT TO PUSH YOURSELF. YOU'RE PRAC-TICALLY A HUMAN THESE DAYS.
SORRY-- I'LL BE MORE CAREFUL.
AND WHO'S THE OTHER GUY?!
YOU'VE GOT REAL NERVE TO TREAT ME LIKE THIS...
...KIYO KATSURAGI.

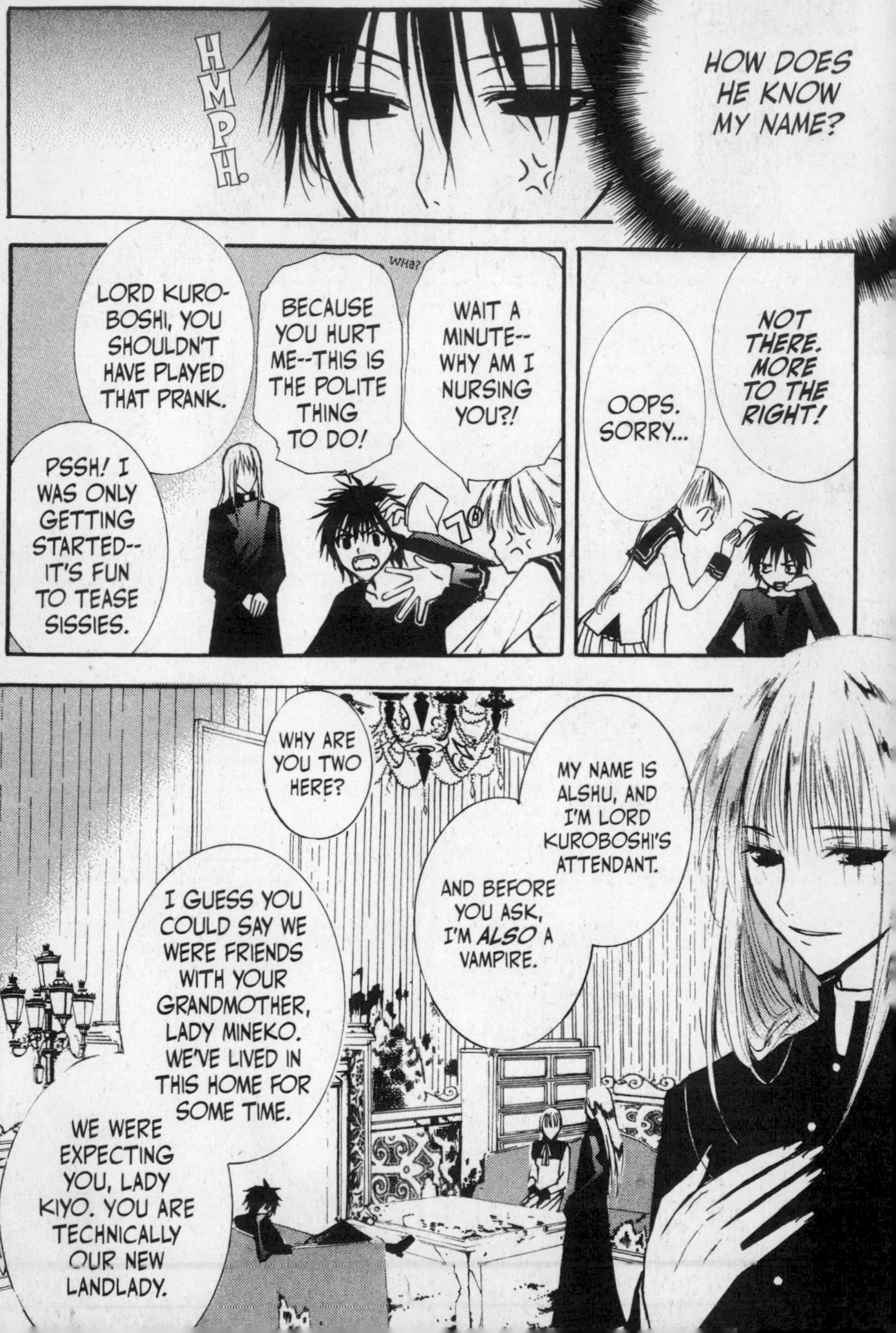
HOW DOES HE KNOW MY NAME?
HMPH.
NOT THERE. MORE TO THE RIGHT!
OOPS. SORRY...
WAIT A MINUTE-- WHY AM I NURSING YOU?!
WHA?
BECAUSE YOU HURT ME--THIS IS THE POLITE THING TO DO!
LORD KURO-BOSHI, YOU SHOULDN'T HAVE PLAYED THAT PRANK.
PSSH! I WAS ONLY GETTING STARTED-- IT'S FUN TO TEASE SISSIES.
WHY ARE YOU TWO HERE?
MY NAME IS ALSHU, AND I'M LORD KUROBOSHI'S ATTENDANT.
AND BEFORE YOU ASK, I'M *ALSO* A VAMPIRE.
I GUESS YOU COULD SAY WE WERE FRIENDS WITH YOUR GRANDMOTHER, LADY MINEKO. WE'VE LIVED IN THIS HOME FOR SOME TIME.
WE WERE EXPECTING YOU, LADY KIYO. YOU ARE TECHNICALLY OUR NEW LANDLADY.

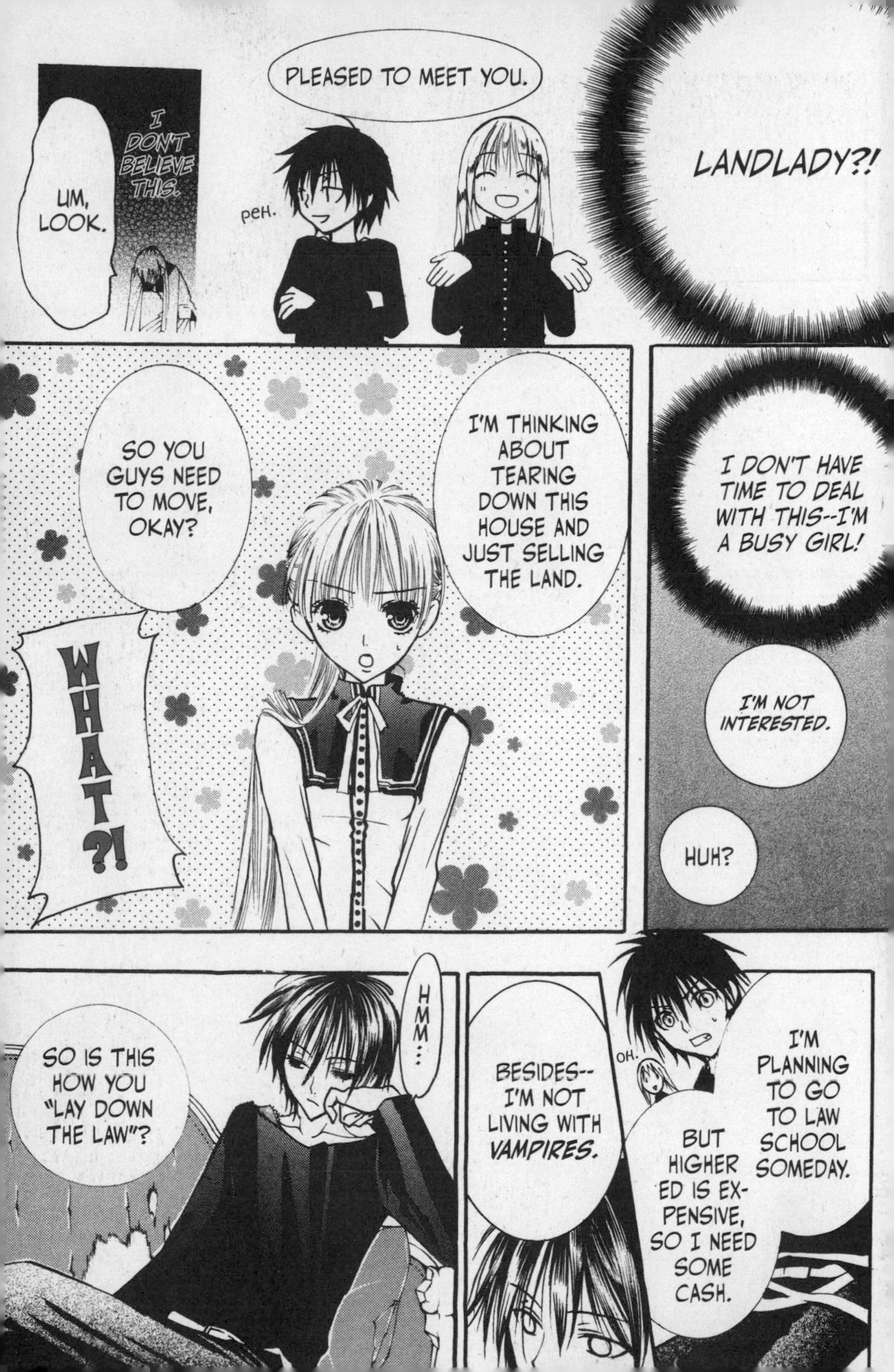
LANDLADY?!
PLEASED TO MEET YOU.
peH.
I DON'T BELIEVE THIS.
UM, LOOK.
I DON'T HAVE TIME TO DEAL WITH THIS--I'M A BUSY GIRL!
I'M NOT INTERESTED.
HUH?
I'M THINKING ABOUT TEARING DOWN THIS HOUSE AND JUST SELLING THE LAND.
SO YOU GUYS NEED TO MOVE, OKAY?
WHAT?!
I'M PLANNING TO GO TO LAW SCHOOL SOMEDAY.
OH.
BUT HIGHER ED IS EXPENSIVE, SO I NEED SOME CASH.
BESIDES--I'M NOT LIVING WITH *VAMPIRES.*
HMM...
SO IS THIS HOW YOU "LAY DOWN THE LAW"?

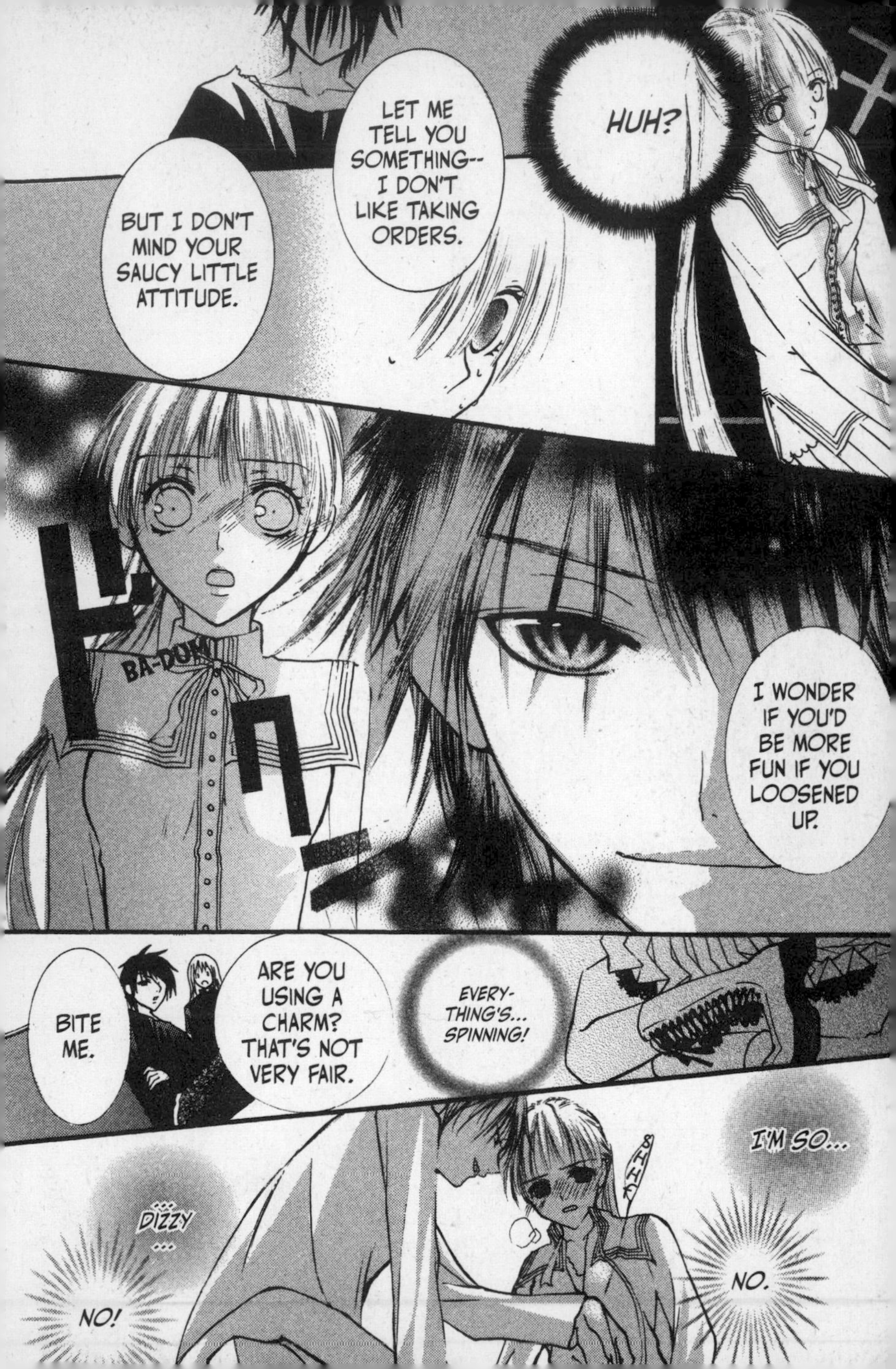
HUH?
LET ME TELL YOU SOMETHING-- I DON'T LIKE TAKING ORDERS.
BUT I DON'T MIND YOUR SAUCY LITTLE ATTITUDE.
I WONDER IF YOU'D BE MORE FUN IF YOU LOOSENED UP.
BA-DUM
EVERY-THING'S... SPINNING!
ARE YOU USING A CHARM? THAT'S NOT VERY FAIR.
BITE ME.
I'M SO...
NO.
SHHF
...DIZZY...
NO!

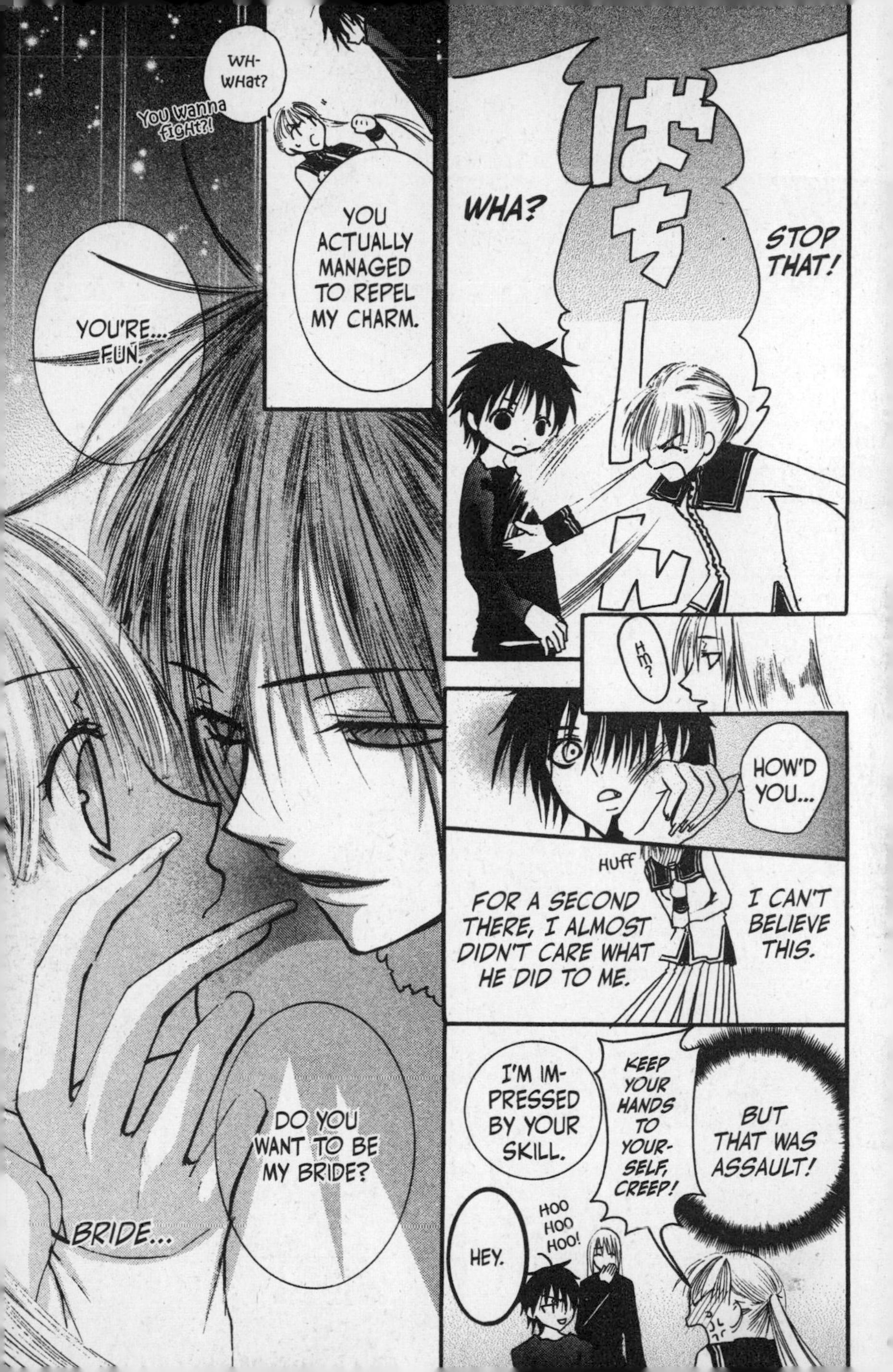

ぱちーん
STOP THAT!
WHA?
HM?
HOW'D YOU...
I CAN'T BELIEVE THIS.
HUFF
FOR A SECOND THERE, I ALMOST DIDN'T CARE WHAT HE DID TO ME.
BUT THAT WAS ASSAULT!
KEEP YOUR HANDS TO YOURSELF, CREEP!
I'M IMPRESSED BY YOUR SKILL.
HEY.
HOO HOO HOO!
YOU ACTUALLY MANAGED TO REPEL MY CHARM.
WH-WHat?
You wanna fight?!
YOU'RE... FUN.
DO YOU WANT TO BE MY BRIDE?
BRIDE...

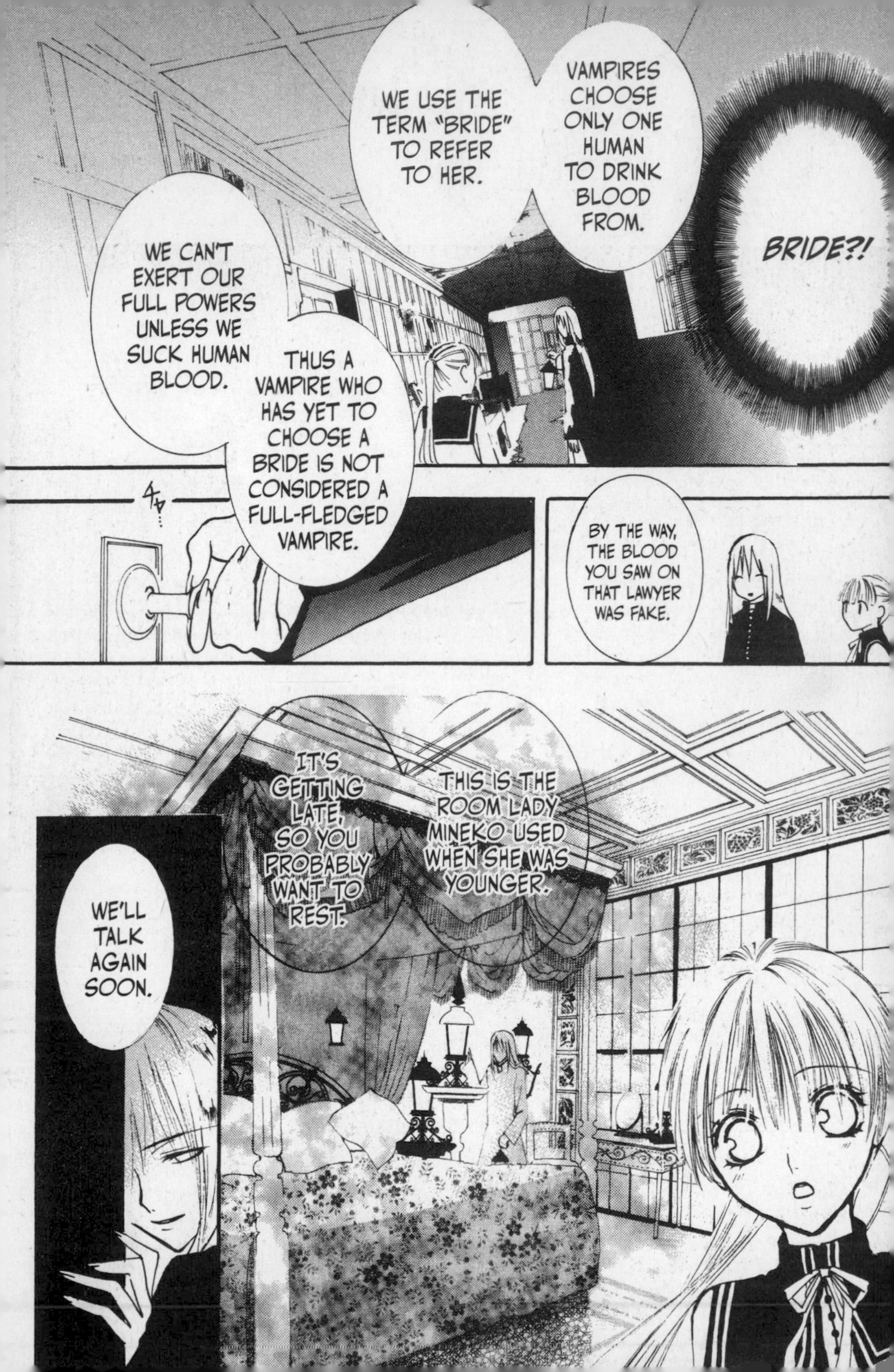
VAMPIRES CHOOSE ONLY ONE HUMAN TO DRINK BLOOD FROM.
WE USE THE TERM "BRIDE" TO REFER TO HER.
BRIDE?!
WE CAN'T EXERT OUR FULL POWERS UNLESS WE SUCK HUMAN BLOOD.
THUS A VAMPIRE WHO HAS YET TO CHOOSE A BRIDE IS NOT CONSIDERED A FULL-FLEDGED VAMPIRE.
BY THE WAY, THE BLOOD YOU SAW ON THAT LAWYER WAS FAKE.
THIS IS THE ROOM LADY MINEKO USED WHEN SHE WAS YOUNGER.
IT'S GETTING LATE, SO YOU PROBABLY WANT TO REST.
WE'LL TALK AGAIN SOON.

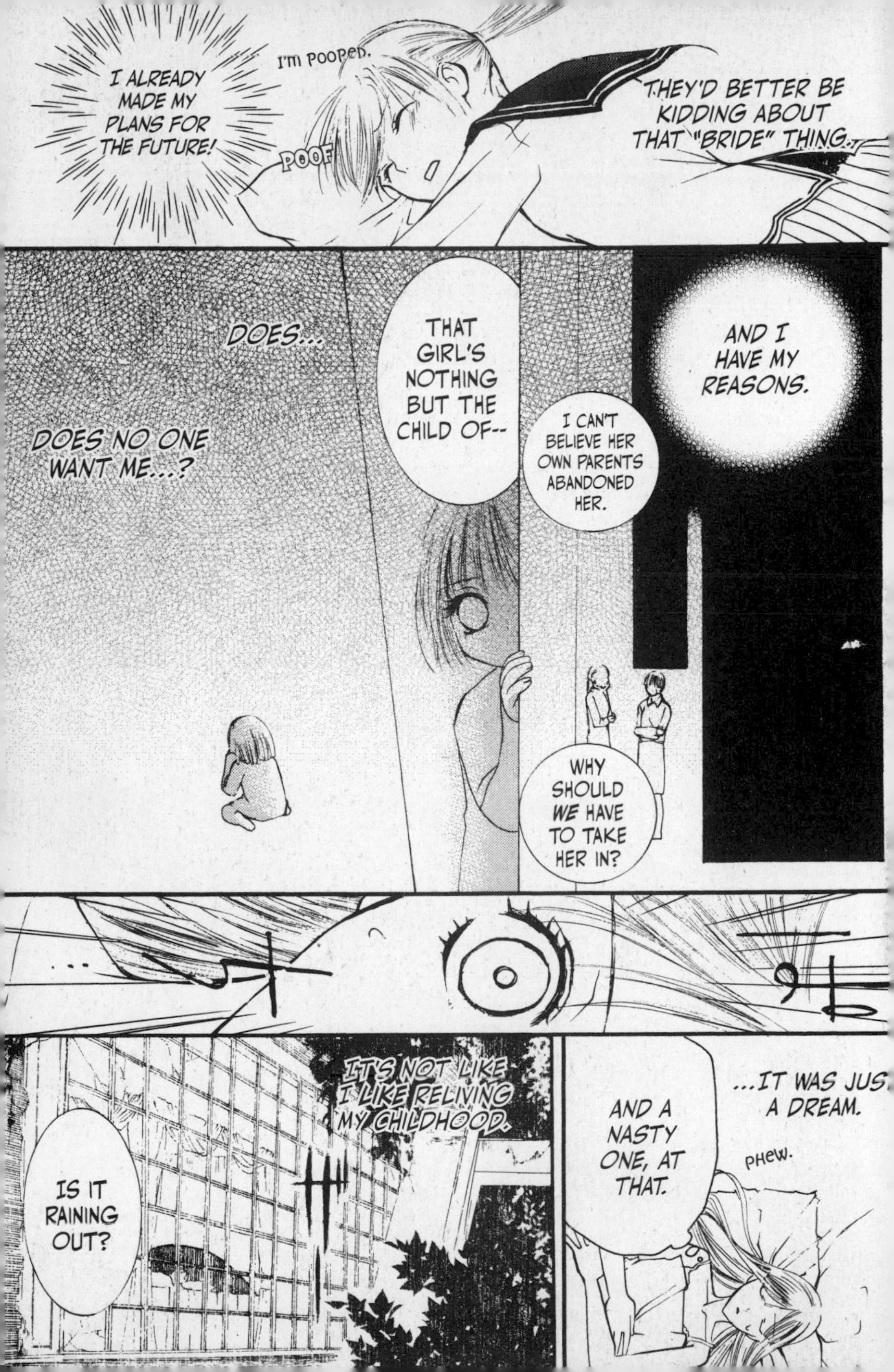
THEY'D BETTER BE KIDDING ABOUT THAT "BRIDE" THING.
I'M POOPED.
I ALREADY MADE MY PLANS FOR THE FUTURE!
POOF
AND I HAVE MY REASONS.
I CAN'T BELIEVE HER OWN PARENTS ABANDONED HER.
WHY SHOULD WE HAVE TO TAKE HER IN?
THAT GIRL'S NOTHING BUT THE CHILD OF--
DOES...
DOES NO ONE WANT ME...?
...
...IT WAS JUS. A DREAM.
PHEW.
AND A NASTY ONE, AT THAT.
IT'S NOT LIKE I LIKE RELIVING MY CHILDHOOD.
IS IT RAINING OUT?

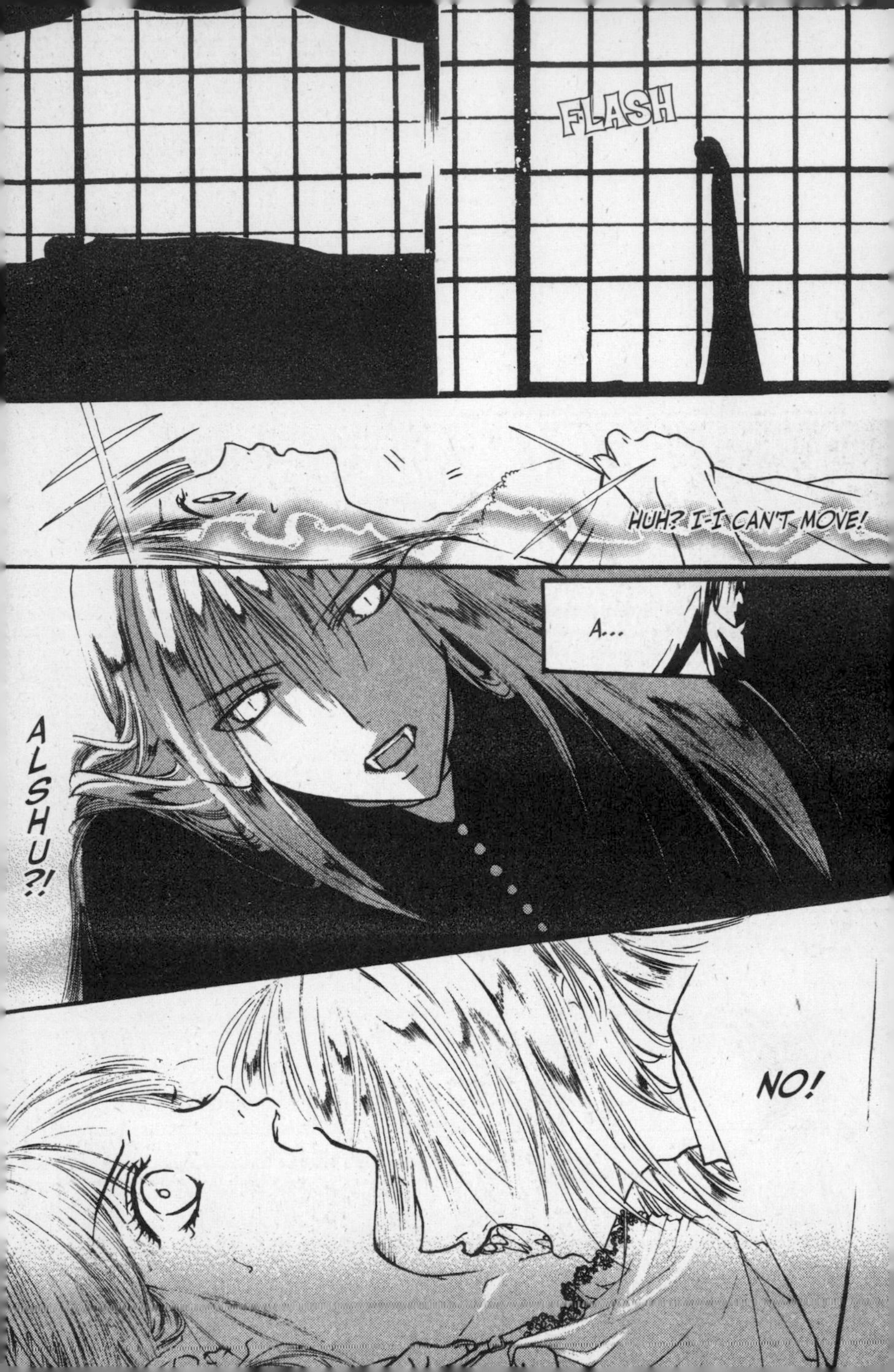
FLASH
HUH? I-I CAN'T MOVE!
A...
ALSHU?!
NO!

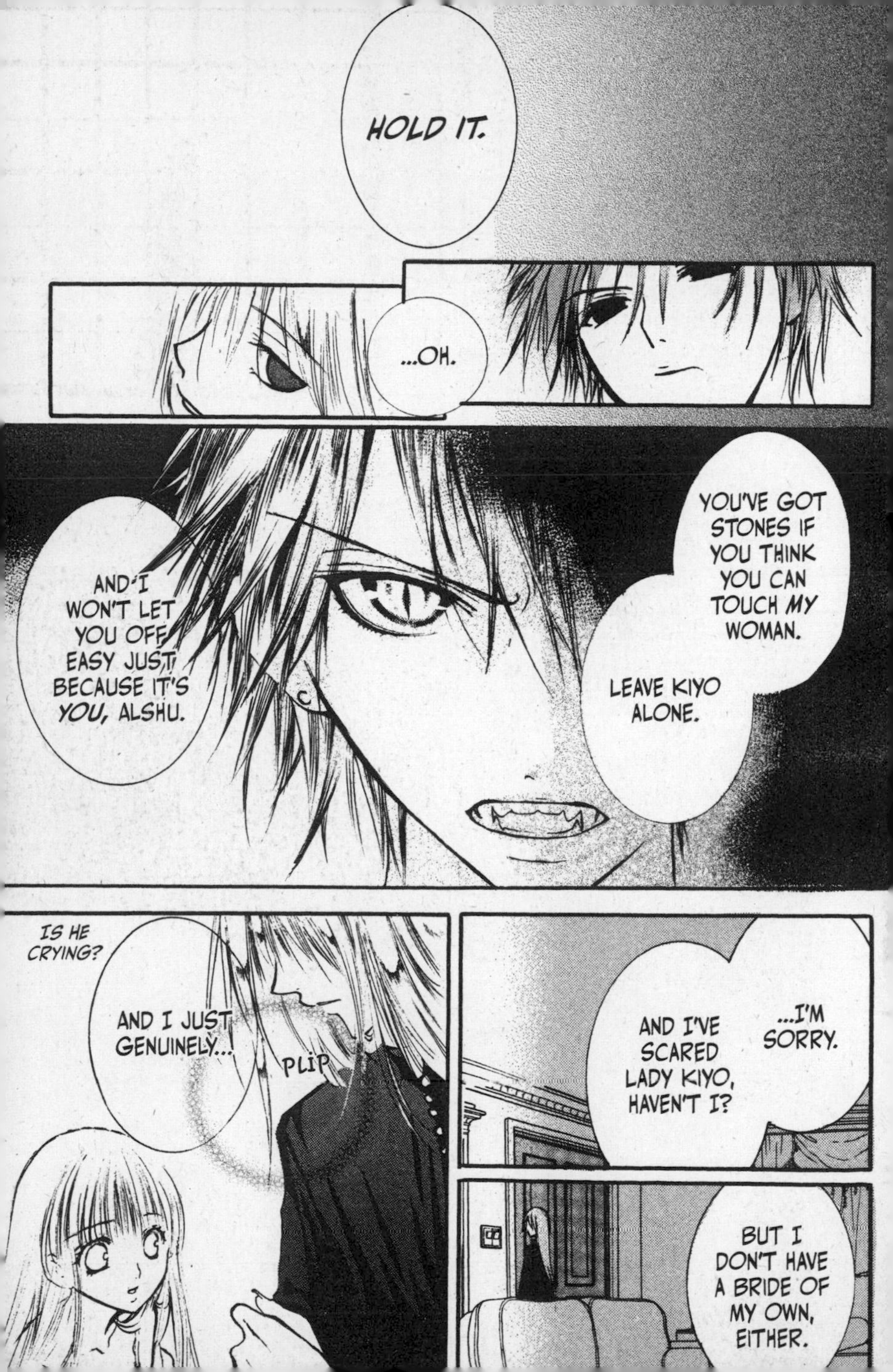

HOLD IT.
...OH.
YOU'VE GOT STONES IF YOU THINK YOU CAN TOUCH *MY* WOMAN.
LEAVE KIYO ALONE.
AND I WON'T LET YOU OFF EASY JUST BECAUSE IT'S *YOU*, ALSHU.
...I'M SORRY.
AND I'VE SCARED LADY KIYO, HAVEN'T I?
BUT I DON'T HAVE A BRIDE OF MY OWN, EITHER.
AND I JUST GENUINELY...!
PLIP
IS HE CRYING?

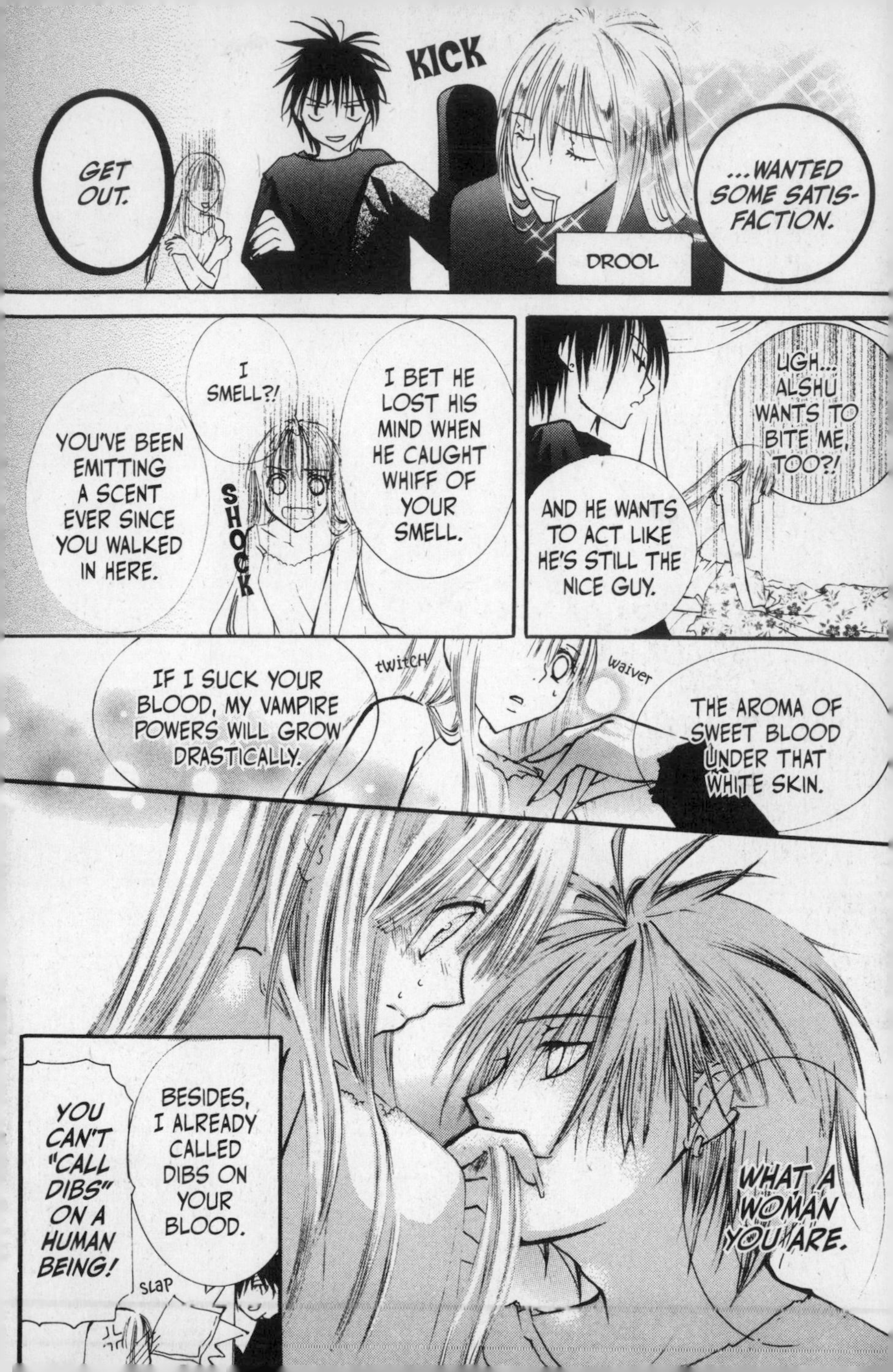
...WANTED SOME SATIS-FACTION.
DROOL
KICK
GET OUT.
UGH... ALSHU WANTS TO BITE ME, TOO?!
AND HE WANTS TO ACT LIKE HE'S STILL THE NICE GUY.
I BET HE LOST HIS MIND WHEN HE CAUGHT WHIFF OF YOUR SMELL.
I SMELL?!
SHOCK
YOU'VE BEEN EMITTING A SCENT EVER SINCE YOU WALKED IN HERE.
waiver
THE AROMA OF SWEET BLOOD UNDER THAT WHITE SKIN.
twitCH
IF I SUCK YOUR BLOOD, MY VAMPIRE POWERS WILL GROW DRASTICALLY.
WHAT A WOMAN YOU ARE.
BESIDES, I ALREADY CALLED DIBS ON YOUR BLOOD.
YOU CAN'T "CALL DIBS" ON A HUMAN BEING!
SLAP

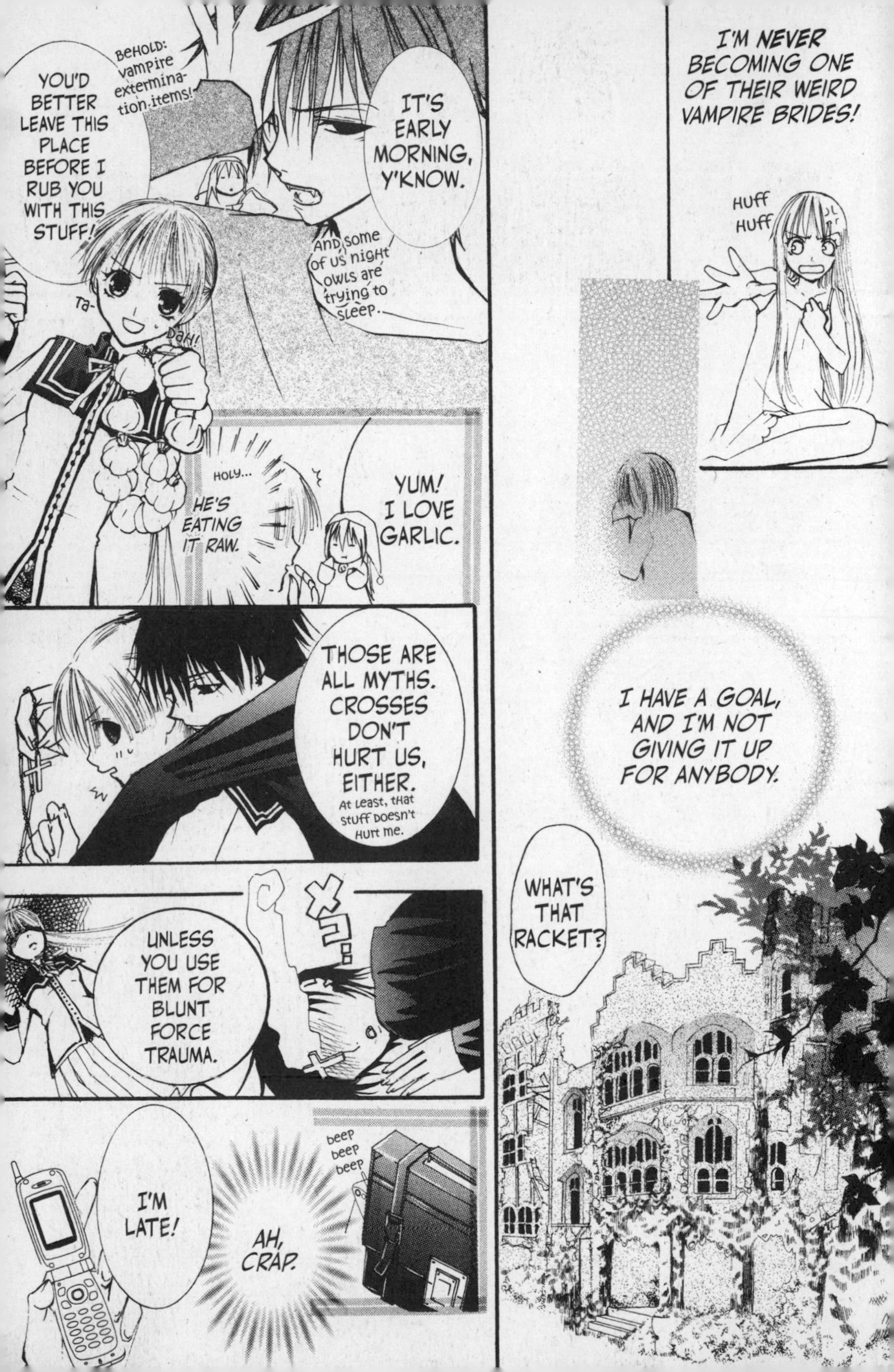
I'M NEVER BECOMING ONE OF THEIR WEIRD VAMPIRE BRIDES!
HUFF HUFF
I HAVE A GOAL, AND I'M NOT GIVING IT UP FOR ANYBODY.
WHAT'S THAT RACKET?
IT'S EARLY MORNING, Y'KNOW.
And some of us night owls are trying to sleep.
BEHOLD: vampire extermination items!
YOU'D BETTER LEAVE THIS PLACE BEFORE I RUB YOU WITH THIS STUFF!
Ta-DAH!
YUM! I LOVE GARLIC.
HOLY...
HE'S EATING IT RAW.
THOSE ARE ALL MYTHS. CROSSES DON'T HURT US, EITHER.
At least, that stuff doesn't hurt me.
UNLESS YOU USE THEM FOR BLUNT FORCE TRAUMA.
beep beep beep
AH, CRAP.
I'M LATE!

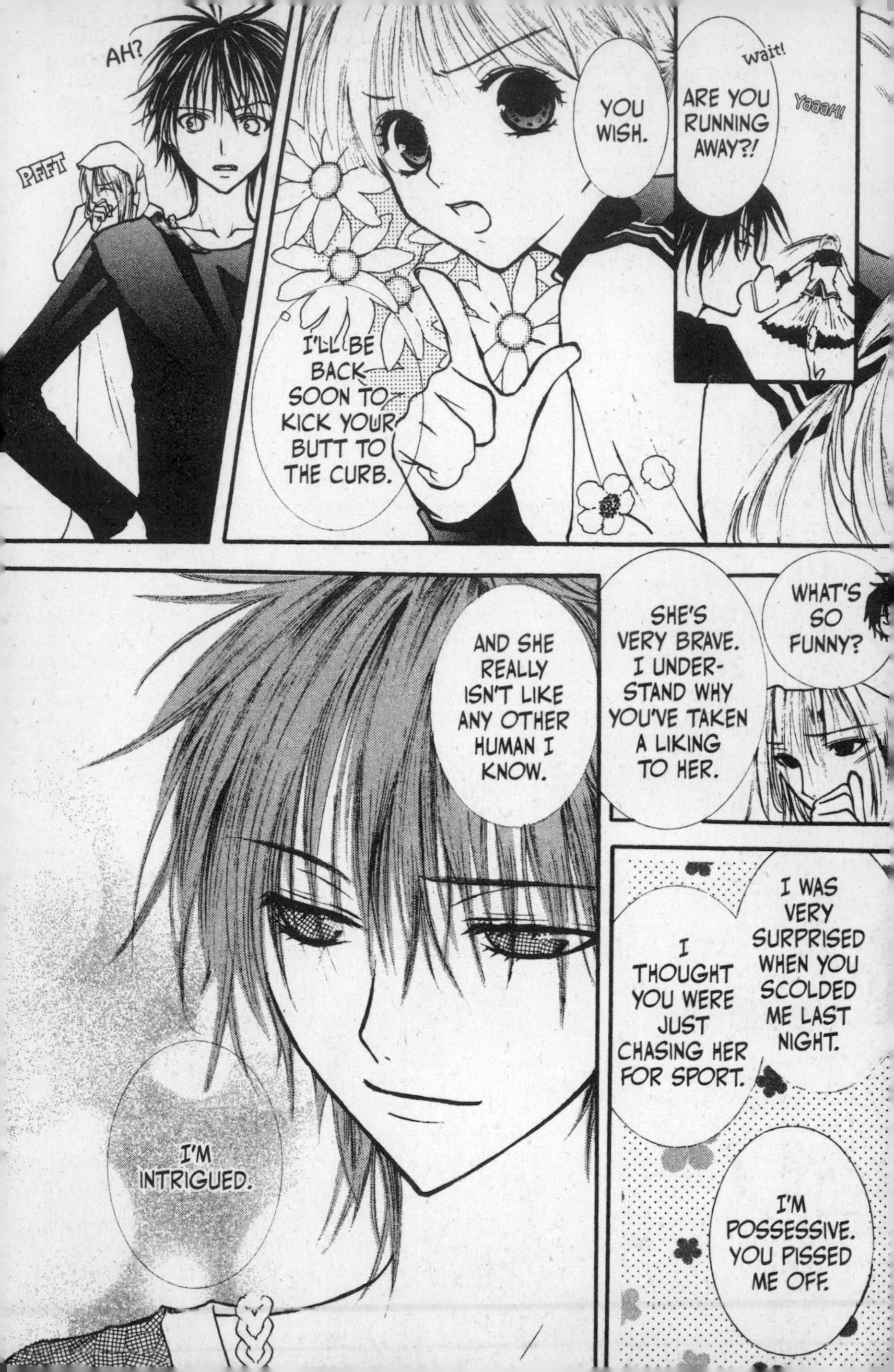
Yaaah!
wait!
ARE YOU RUNNING AWAY?!
YOU WISH.
I'LL BE BACK SOON TO KICK YOUR BUTT TO THE CURB.
AH?
PFFT
WHAT'S SO FUNNY?
SHE'S VERY BRAVE. I UNDER-STAND WHY YOU'VE TAKEN A LIKING TO HER.
I WAS VERY SURPRISED WHEN YOU SCOLDED ME LAST NIGHT.
I THOUGHT YOU WERE JUST CHASING HER FOR SPORT.
I'M POSSESSIVE. YOU PISSED ME OFF.
AND SHE REALLY ISN'T LIKE ANY OTHER HUMAN I KNOW.
I'M INTRIGUED.

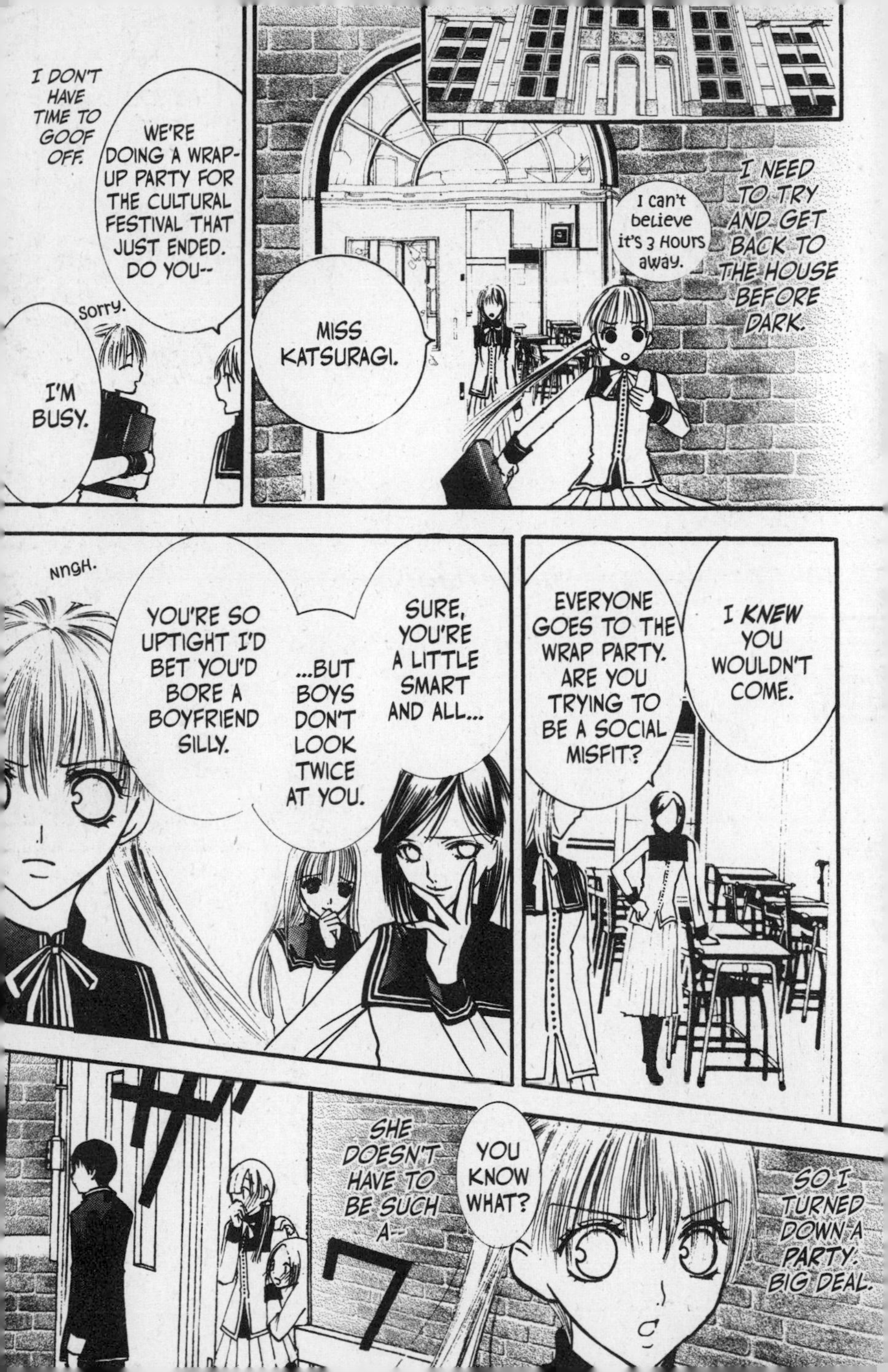
I NEED TO TRY AND GET BACK TO THE HOUSE BEFORE DARK.
I can't believe it's 3 Hours away.
MISS KATSURAGI.
WE'RE DOING A WRAP-UP PARTY FOR THE CULTURAL FESTIVAL THAT JUST ENDED. DO YOU--
Sorry.
I'M BUSY.
I DON'T HAVE TIME TO GOOF OFF.
I KNEW YOU WOULDN'T COME.
EVERYONE GOES TO THE WRAP PARTY. ARE YOU TRYING TO BE A SOCIAL MISFIT?
SURE, YOU'RE A LITTLE SMART AND ALL...
...BUT BOYS DON'T LOOK TWICE AT YOU.
YOU'RE SO UPTIGHT I'D BET YOU'D BORE A BOYFRIEND SILLY.
Nngh.
SO I TURNED DOWN A PARTY. BIG DEAL.
YOU KNOW WHAT?
SHE DOESN'T HAVE TO BE SUCH A-

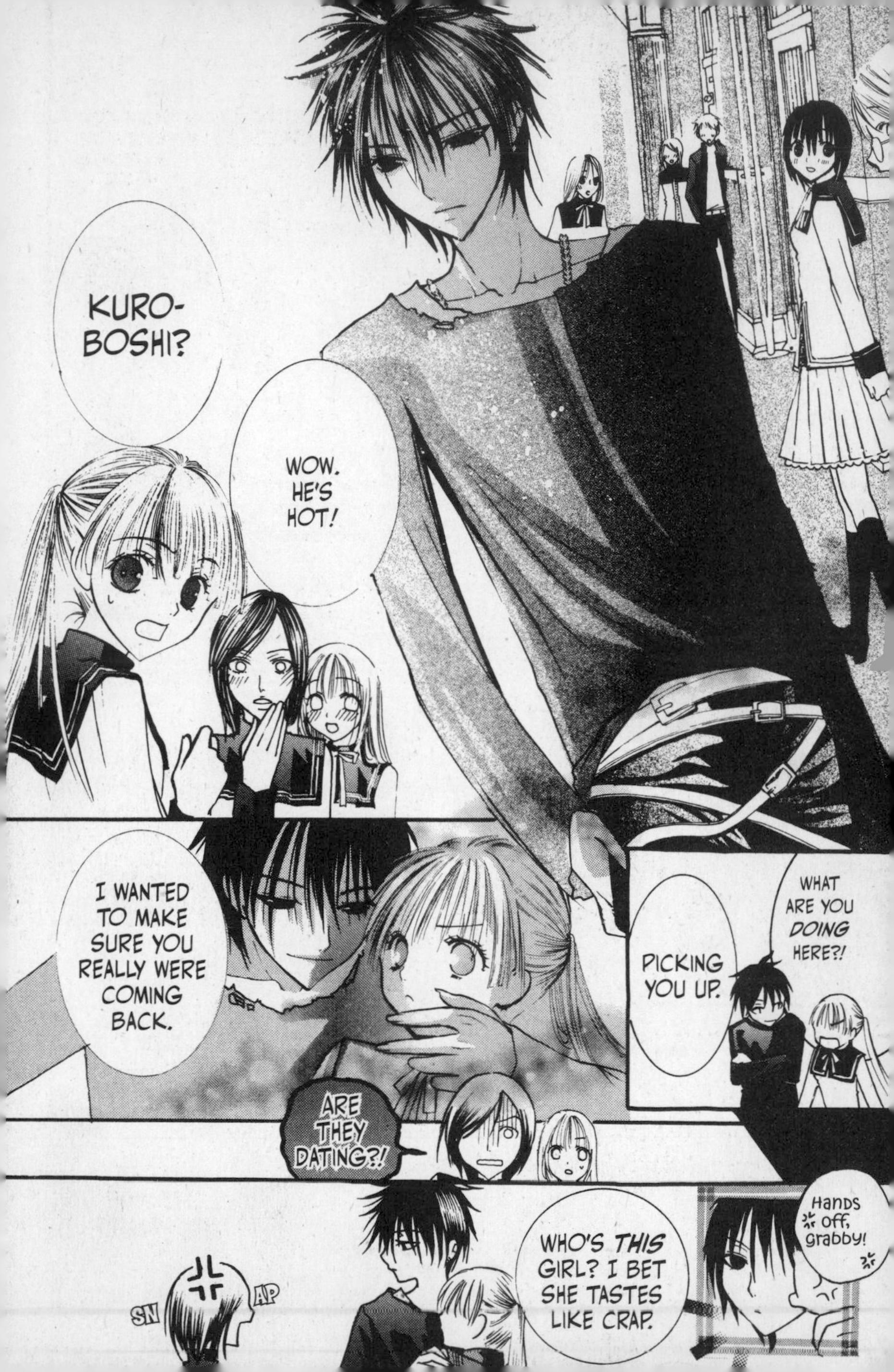
KURO-BOSHI?
WOW. HE'S HOT!
WHAT ARE YOU *DOING* HERE?!
PICKING YOU UP.
I WANTED TO MAKE SURE YOU REALLY WERE COMING BACK.
ARE THEY DATING?!
Hands off, grabby!
WHO'S *THIS* GIRL? I BET SHE TASTES LIKE CRAP.
SN
AP

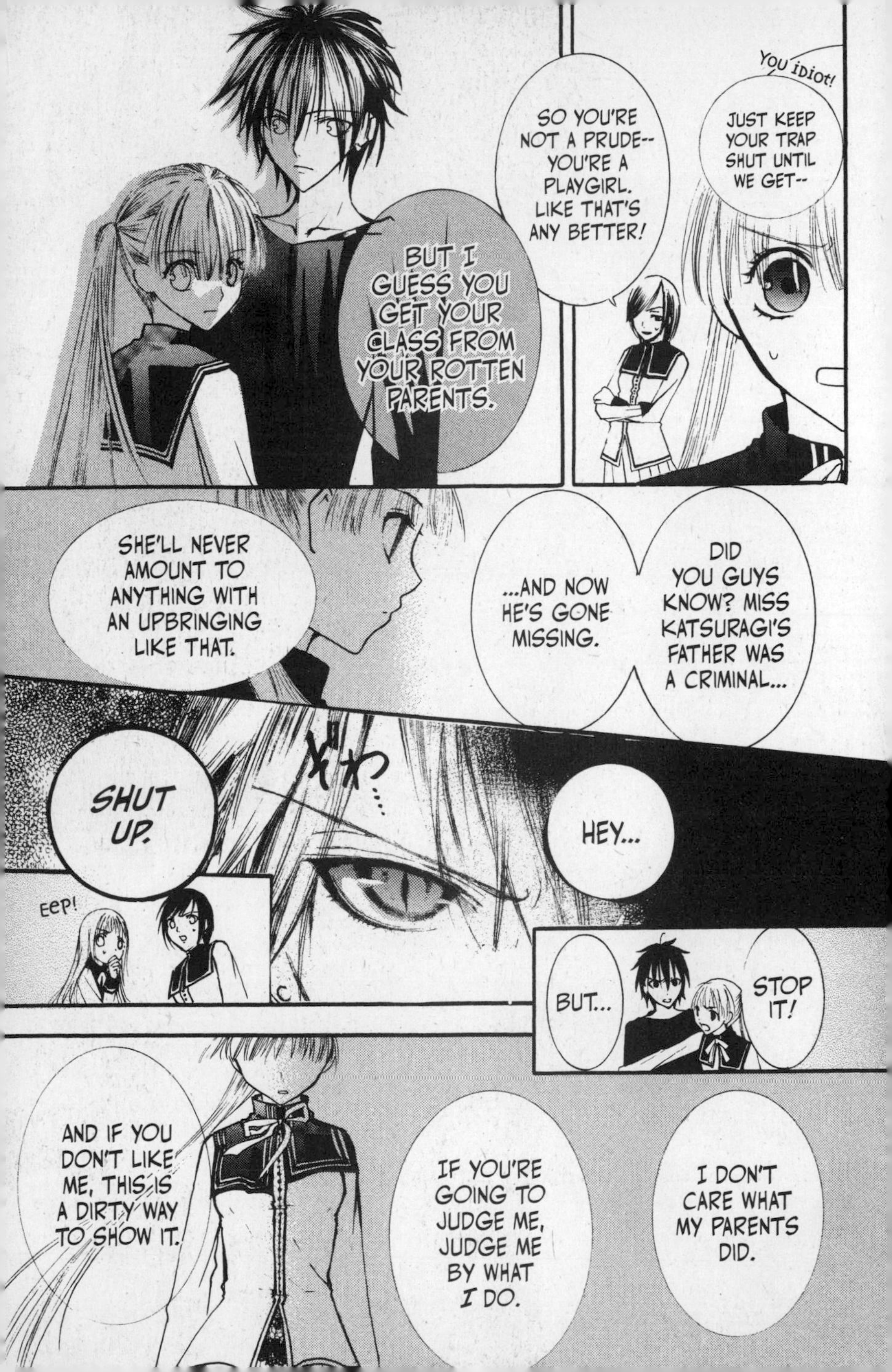

YOU IDIOT!
JUST KEEP YOUR TRAP SHUT UNTIL WE GET--
SO YOU'RE NOT A PRUDE-- YOU'RE A PLAYGIRL. LIKE THAT'S ANY BETTER!
BUT I GUESS YOU GET YOUR CLASS FROM YOUR ROTTEN PARENTS.
DID YOU GUYS KNOW? MISS KATSURAGI'S FATHER WAS A CRIMINAL...
...AND NOW HE'S GONE MISSING.
SHE'LL NEVER AMOUNT TO ANYTHING WITH AN UPBRINGING LIKE THAT.
HEY...
SHUT UP.
STOP IT!
BUT...
EEP!
I DON'T CARE WHAT MY PARENTS DID.
IF YOU'RE GOING TO JUDGE ME, JUDGE ME BY WHAT I DO.
AND IF YOU DON'T LIKE ME, THIS IS A DIRTY WAY TO SHOW IT.

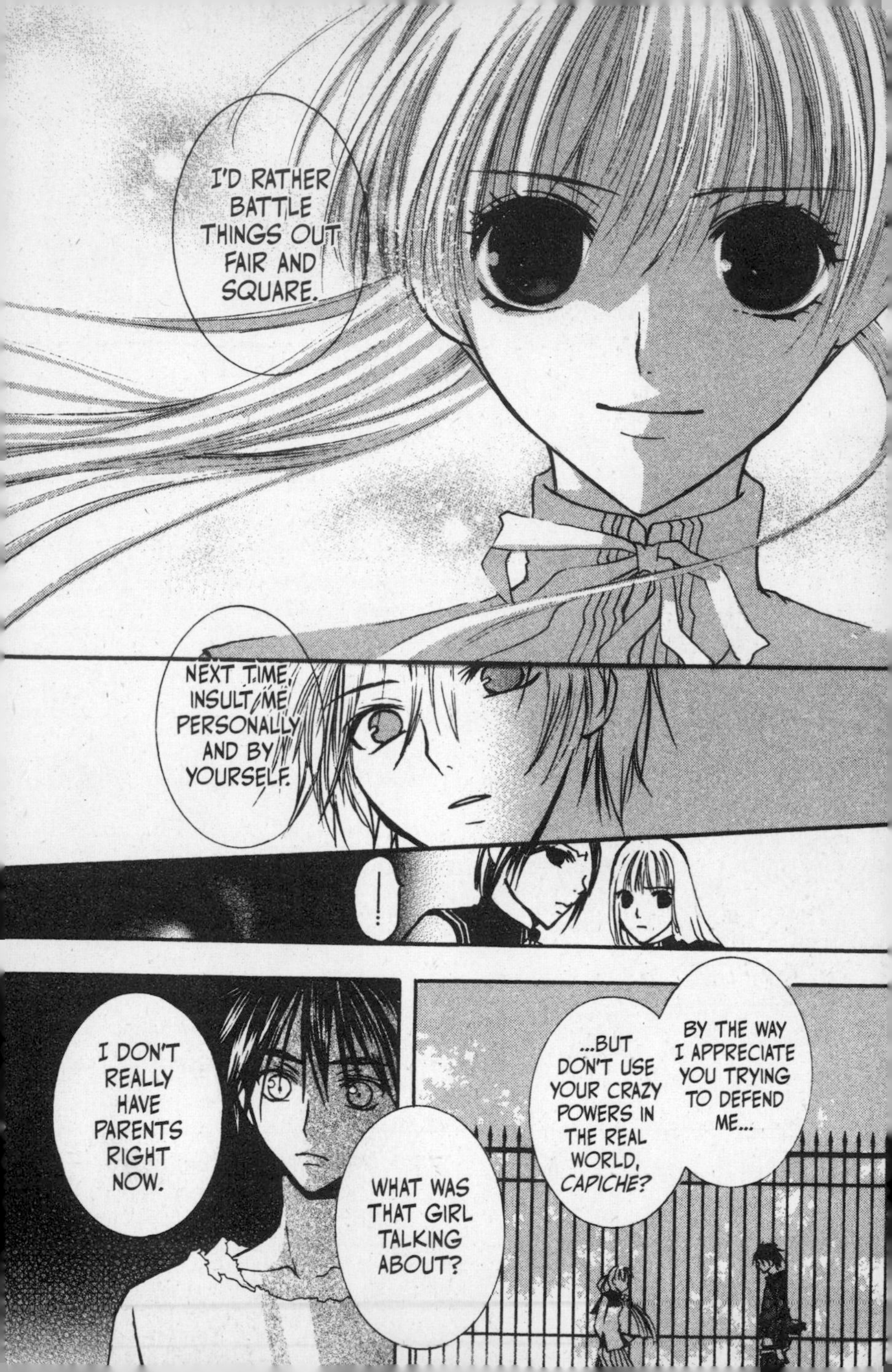
I'D RATHER BATTLE THINGS OUT FAIR AND SQUARE.
NEXT TIME, INSULT ME PERSONALLY AND BY YOURSELF.
!
BY THE WAY I APPRECIATE YOU TRYING TO DEFEND ME...
...BUT DON'T USE YOUR CRAZY POWERS IN THE REAL WORLD, *CAPICHE?*
WHAT WAS THAT GIRL TALKING ABOUT?
I DON'T REALLY HAVE PARENTS RIGHT NOW.

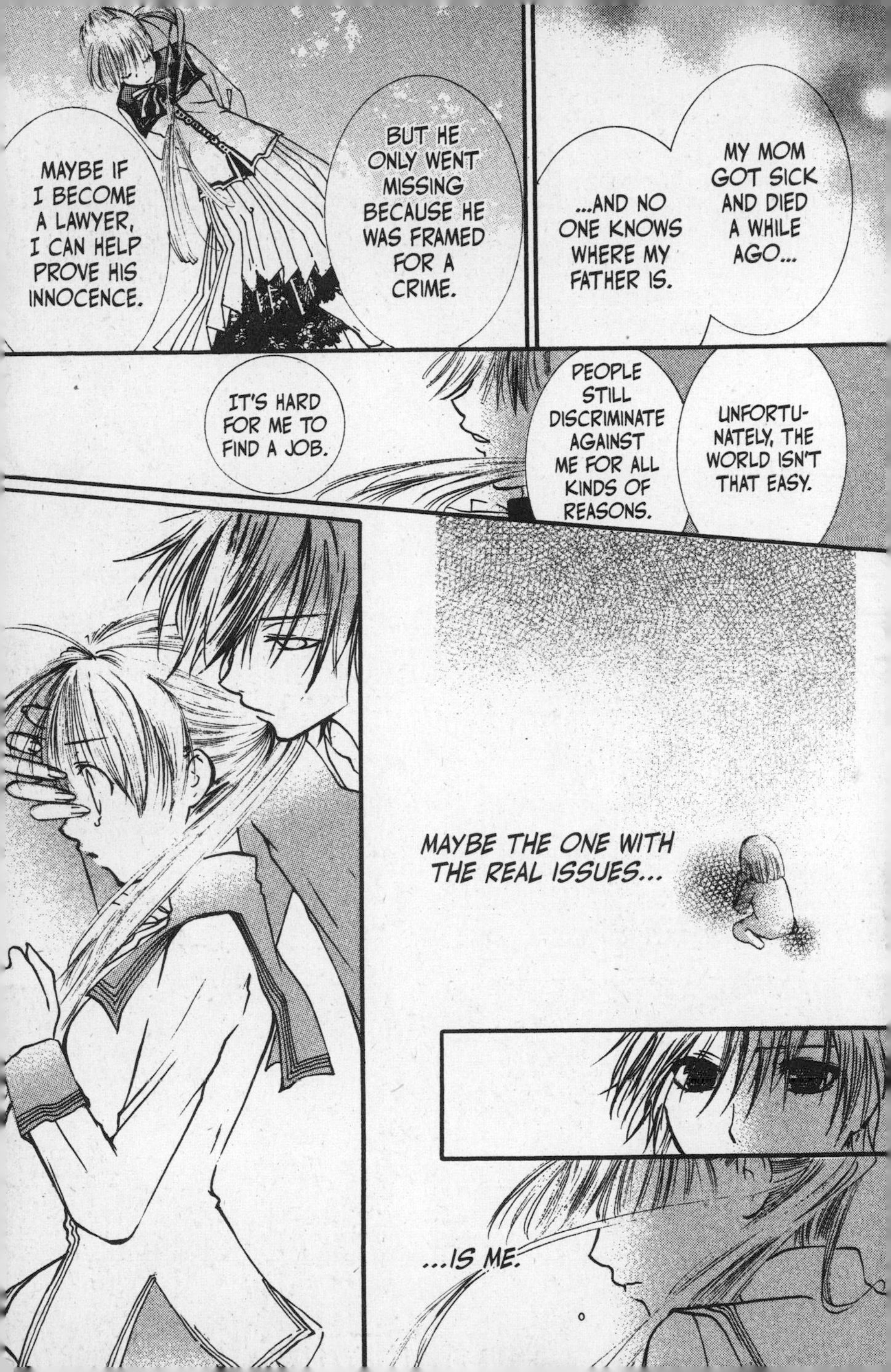
MY MOM GOT SICK AND DIED A WHILE AGO...
...AND NO ONE KNOWS WHERE MY FATHER IS.
BUT HE ONLY WENT MISSING BECAUSE HE WAS FRAMED FOR A CRIME.
MAYBE IF I BECOME A LAWYER, I CAN HELP PROVE HIS INNOCENCE.
UNFORTU-NATELY, THE WORLD ISN'T THAT EASY.
PEOPLE STILL DISCRIMINATE AGAINST ME FOR ALL KINDS OF REASONS.
IT'S HARD FOR ME TO FIND A JOB.
MAYBE THE ONE WITH THE REAL ISSUES...
...IS ME.

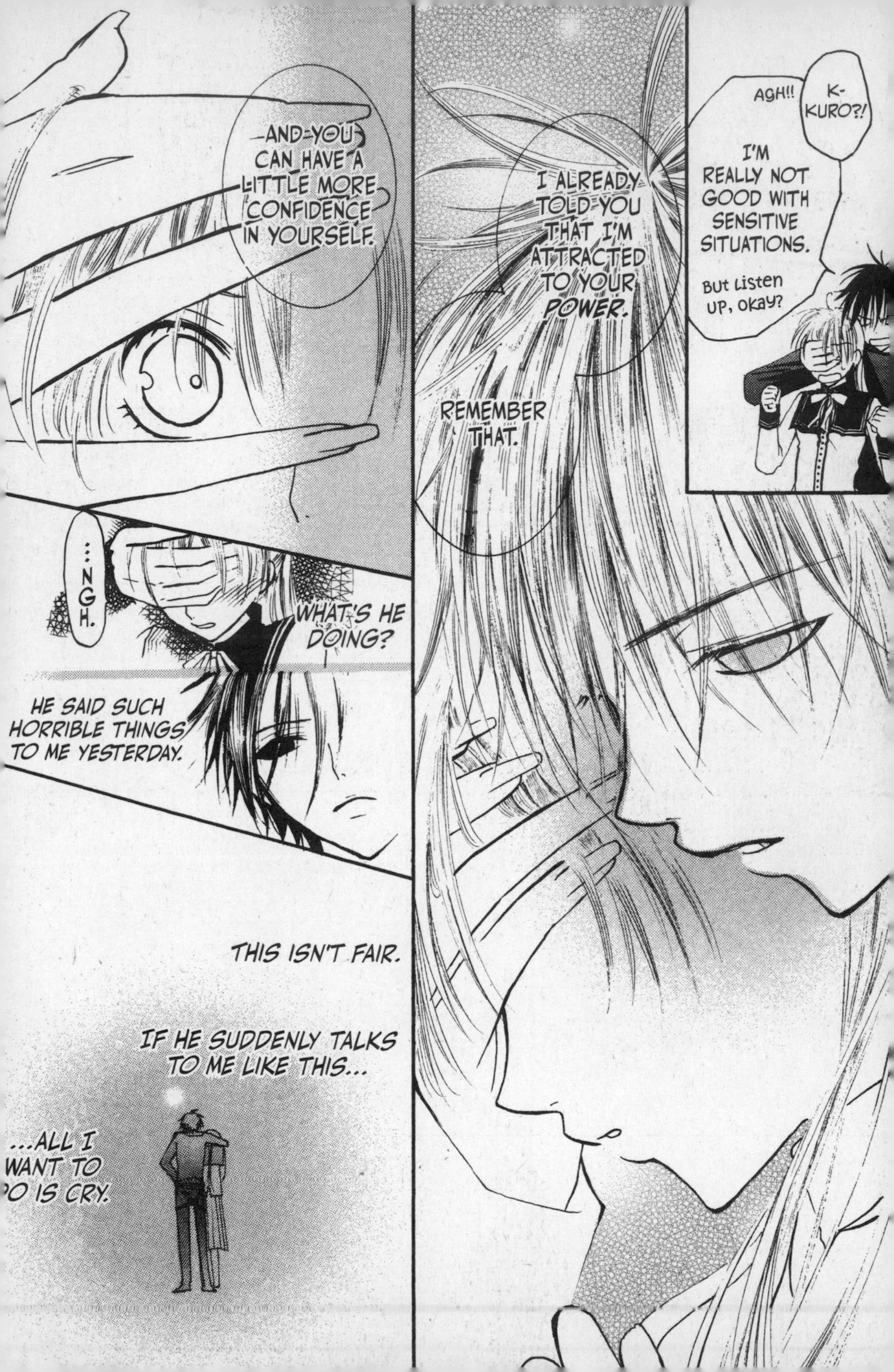
K-KURO?!
AGH!!
I'M REALLY NOT GOOD WITH SENSITIVE SITUATIONS.
But listen up, okay?
I ALREADY TOLD YOU THAT I'M ATTRACTED TO YOUR POWER.
REMEMBER THAT.
AND YOU CAN HAVE A LITTLE MORE CONFIDENCE IN YOURSELF.
...NGH.
WHAT'S HE DOING?
HE SAID SUCH HORRIBLE THINGS TO ME YESTERDAY.
THIS ISN'T FAIR.
IF HE SUDDENLY TALKS TO ME LIKE THIS...
...ALL I WANT TO DO IS CRY.

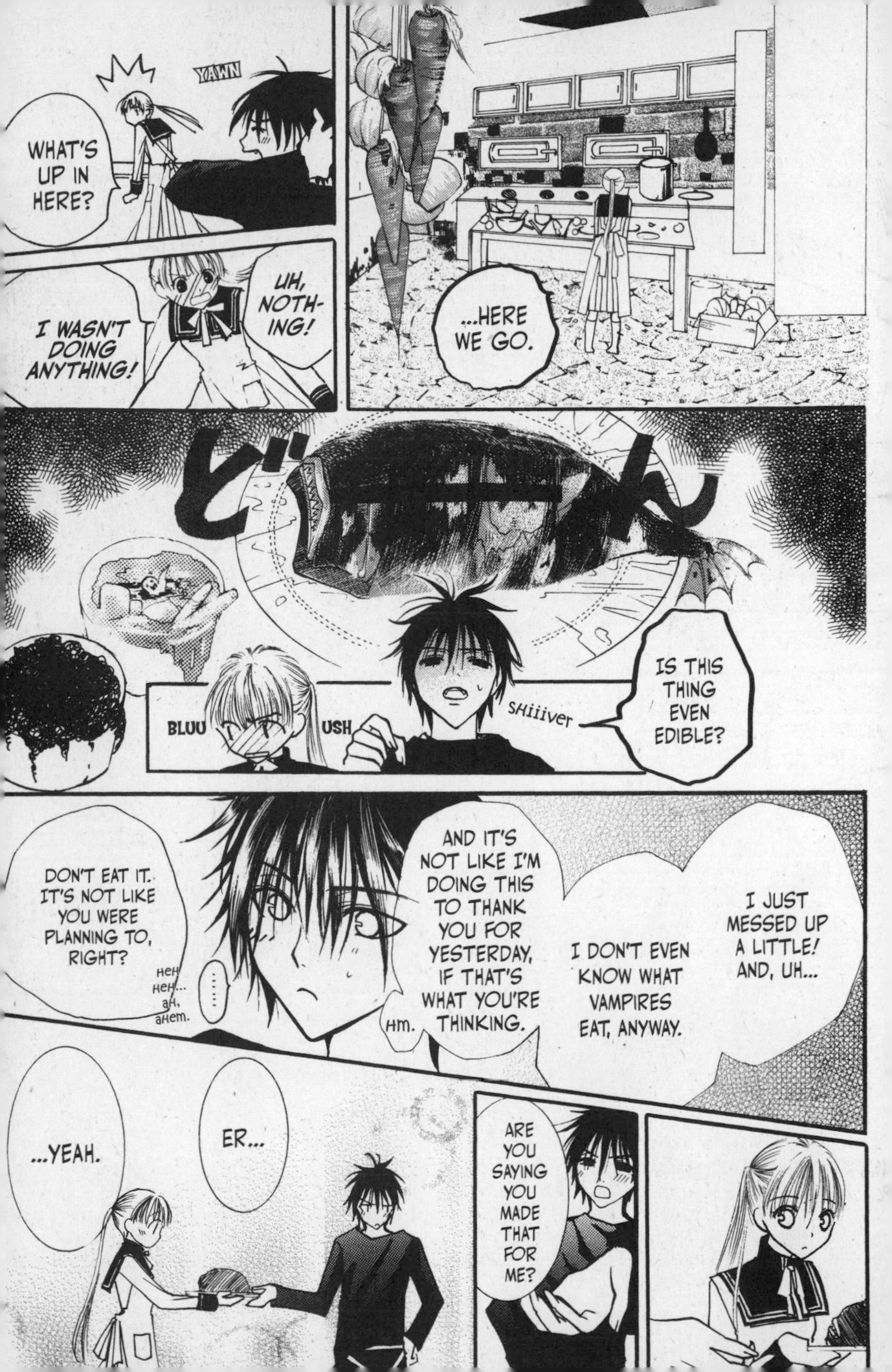
...HERE WE GO.
YAWN
WHAT'S UP IN HERE?
UH, NOTHING!
I WASN'T DOING ANYTHING!
IS THIS THING EVEN EDIBLE?
SHiiiver
BLUU USH
I JUST MESSED UP A LITTLE! AND, UH...
I DON'T EVEN KNOW WHAT VAMPIRES EAT, ANYWAY.
AND IT'S NOT LIKE I'M DOING THIS TO THANK YOU FOR YESTERDAY, IF THAT'S WHAT YOU'RE THINKING.
HM.
......
HEH HEH... AH, AHEM.
DON'T EAT IT. IT'S NOT LIKE YOU WERE PLANNING TO, RIGHT?
ARE YOU SAYING YOU MADE THAT FOR ME?
ER...
...YEAH.

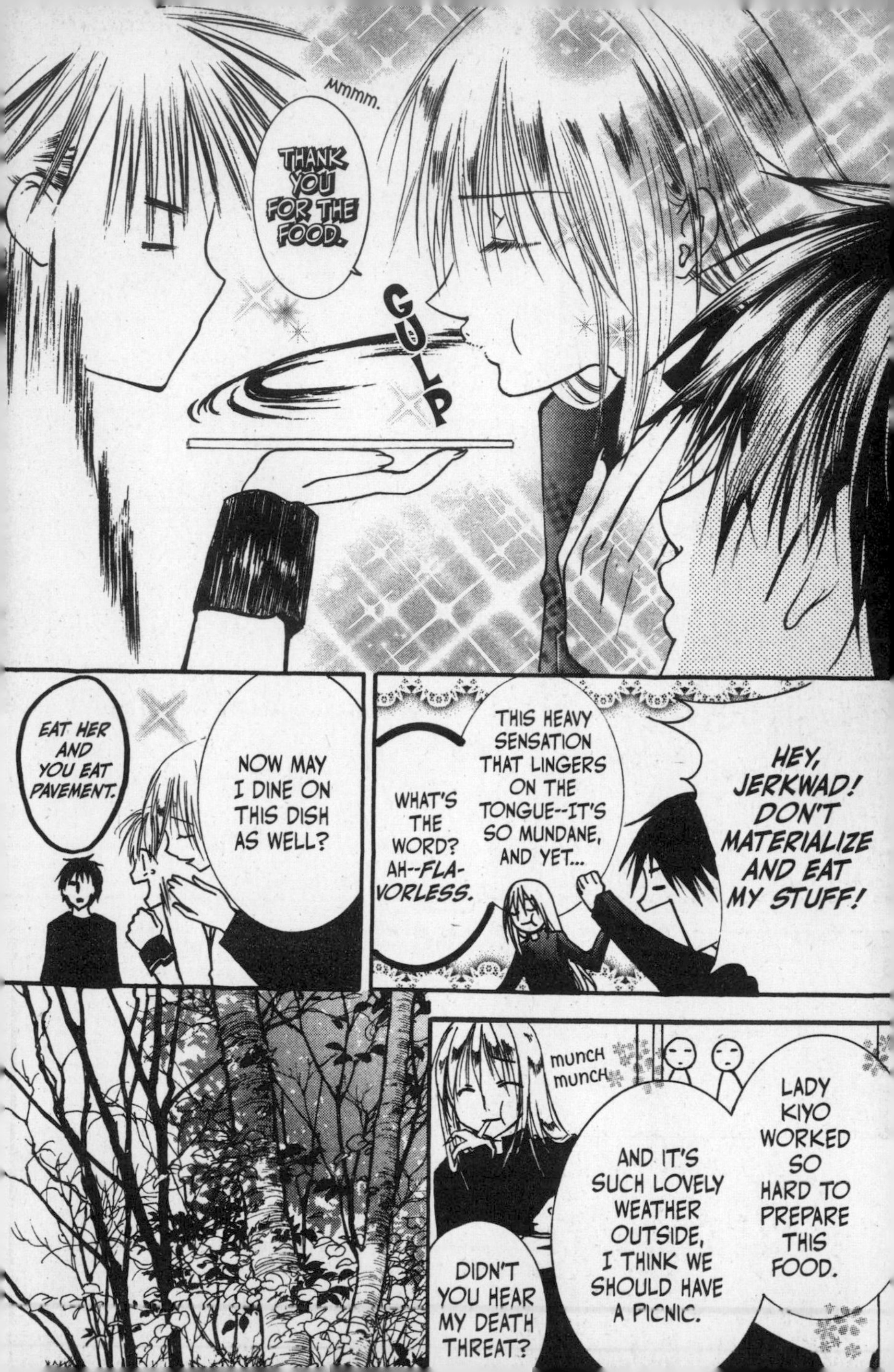
Mmmm.
THANK YOU FOR THE FOOD.
GULP
HEY, JERKWAD! DON'T MATERIALIZE AND EAT MY STUFF!
THIS HEAVY SENSATION THAT LINGERS ON THE TONGUE--IT'S SO MUNDANE, AND YET...
WHAT'S THE WORD? AH--FLAVORLESS.
NOW MAY I DINE ON THIS DISH AS WELL?
EAT HER AND YOU EAT PAVEMENT.
munch munch
LADY KIYO WORKED SO HARD TO PREPARE THIS FOOD.
AND IT'S SUCH LOVELY WEATHER OUTSIDE, I THINK WE SHOULD HAVE A PICNIC.
DIDN'T YOU HEAR MY DEATH THREAT?

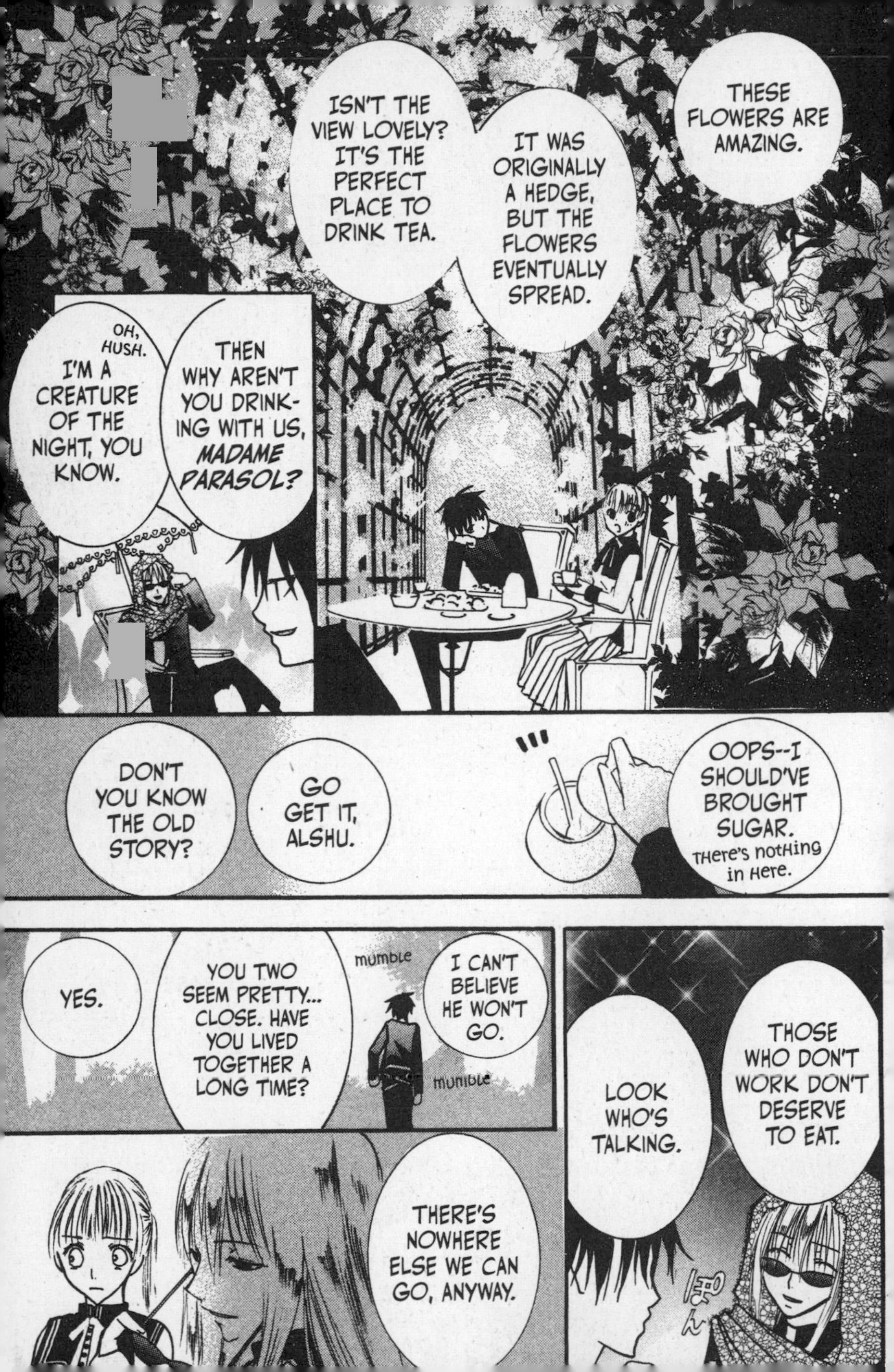
THESE FLOWERS ARE AMAZING.
IT WAS ORIGINALLY A HEDGE, BUT THE FLOWERS EVENTUALLY SPREAD.
ISN'T THE VIEW LOVELY? IT'S THE PERFECT PLACE TO DRINK TEA.
THEN WHY AREN'T YOU DRINKING WITH US, *MADAME PARASOL?*
OH, HUSH. I'M A CREATURE OF THE NIGHT, YOU KNOW.
OOPS--I SHOULD'VE BROUGHT SUGAR. There's nothing in here.
GO GET IT, ALSHU.
DON'T YOU KNOW THE OLD STORY?
THOSE WHO DON'T WORK DON'T DESERVE TO EAT.
LOOK WHO'S TALKING.
ぽん
I CAN'T BELIEVE HE WON'T GO.
mumble
mumble
YOU TWO SEEM PRETTY... CLOSE. HAVE YOU LIVED TOGETHER A LONG TIME?
YES.
THERE'S NOWHERE ELSE WE CAN GO, ANYWAY.

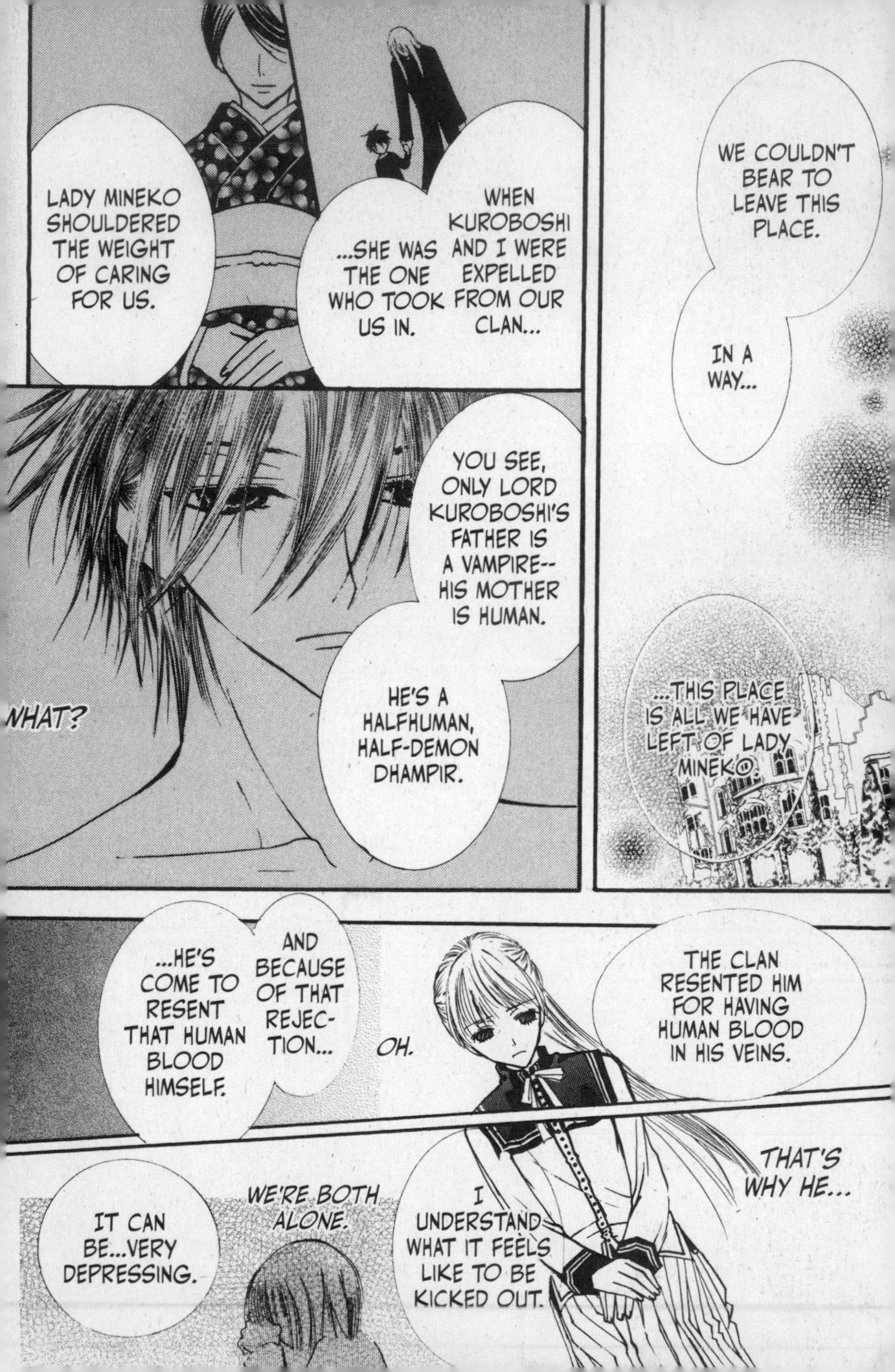
WE COULDN'T BEAR TO LEAVE THIS PLACE.
IN A WAY...
...THIS PLACE IS ALL WE HAVE LEFT OF LADY MINEKO.
WHEN KUROBOSHI AND I WERE EXPELLED FROM OUR CLAN...
...SHE WAS THE ONE WHO TOOK US IN.
LADY MINEKO SHOULDERED THE WEIGHT OF CARING FOR US.
YOU SEE, ONLY LORD KUROBOSHI'S FATHER IS A VAMPIRE--HIS MOTHER IS HUMAN.
HE'S A HALFHUMAN, HALF-DEMON DHAMPIR.
WHAT?
THE CLAN RESENTED HIM FOR HAVING HUMAN BLOOD IN HIS VEINS.
OH.
AND BECAUSE OF THAT REJECTION...
...HE'S COME TO RESENT THAT HUMAN BLOOD HIMSELF.
THAT'S WHY HE...
I UNDERSTAND WHAT IT FEELS LIKE TO BE KICKED OUT.
WE'RE BOTH ALONE.
IT CAN BE...VERY DEPRESSING.

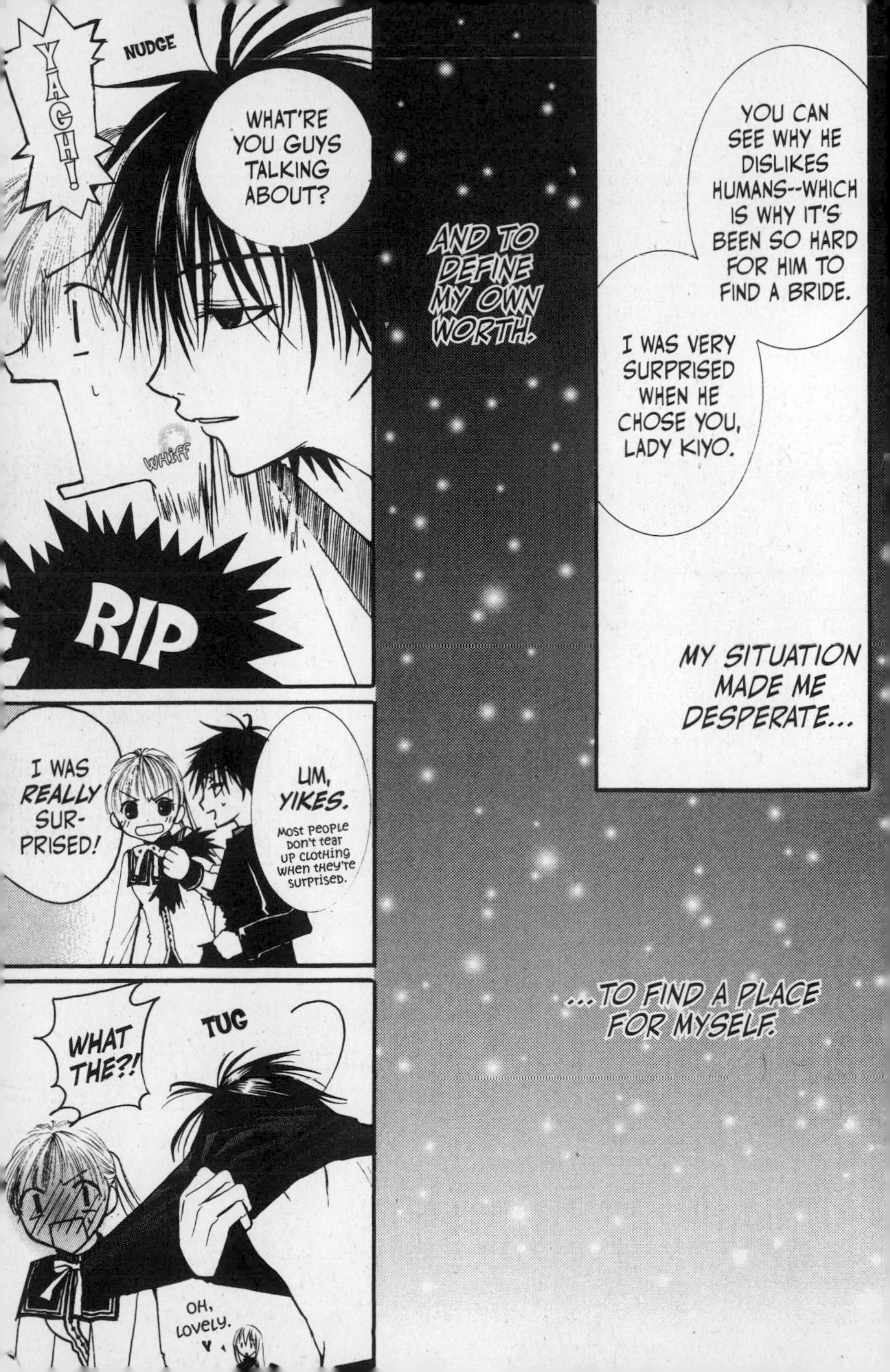
YOU CAN SEE WHY HE DISLIKES HUMANS--WHICH IS WHY IT'S BEEN SO HARD FOR HIM TO FIND A BRIDE.
I WAS VERY SURPRISED WHEN HE CHOSE YOU, LADY KIYO.
AND TO DEFINE MY OWN WORTH.
MY SITUATION MADE ME DESPERATE...
...TO FIND A PLACE FOR MYSELF.
NUDGE
WHAT'RE YOU GUYS TALKING ABOUT?
YAGH!
WHIFF
RIP
UM, YIKES.
Most people don't tear up clothing when they're surprised.
I WAS REALLY SUR-PRISED!
TUG
WHAT THE?!
OH, LOVELY.

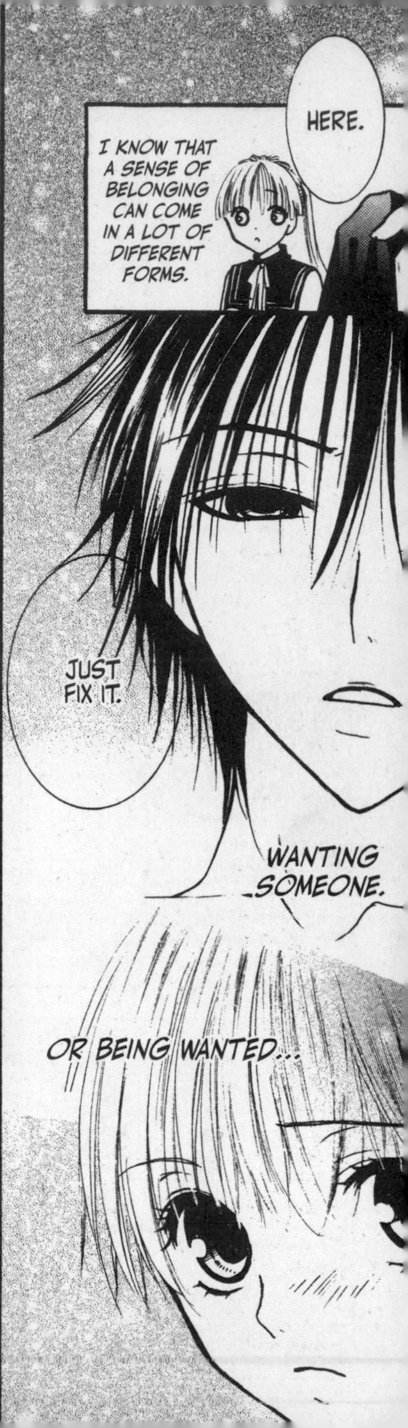
HERE.
I KNOW THAT A SENSE OF BELONGING CAN COME IN A LOT OF DIFFERENT FORMS.
JUST FIX IT.
WANTING SOMEONE.
OR BEING WANTED...

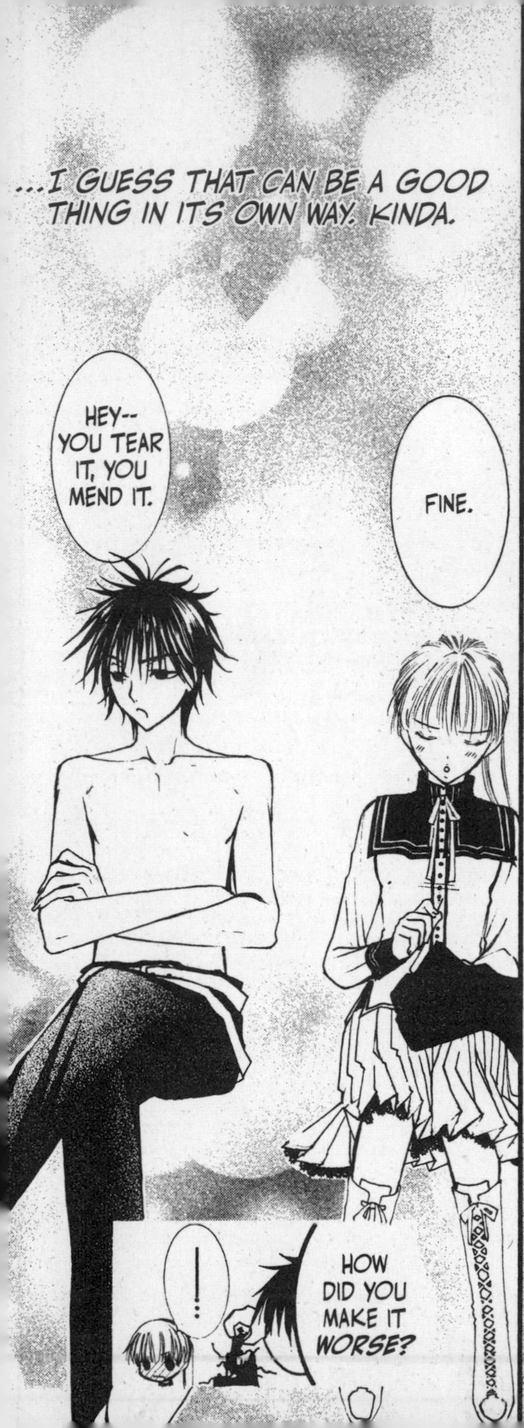
...I GUESS THAT CAN BE A GOOD THING IN ITS OWN WAY. KINDA.
HEY-- YOU TEAR IT, YOU MEND IT.
FINE.
HOW DID YOU MAKE IT WORSE?
!

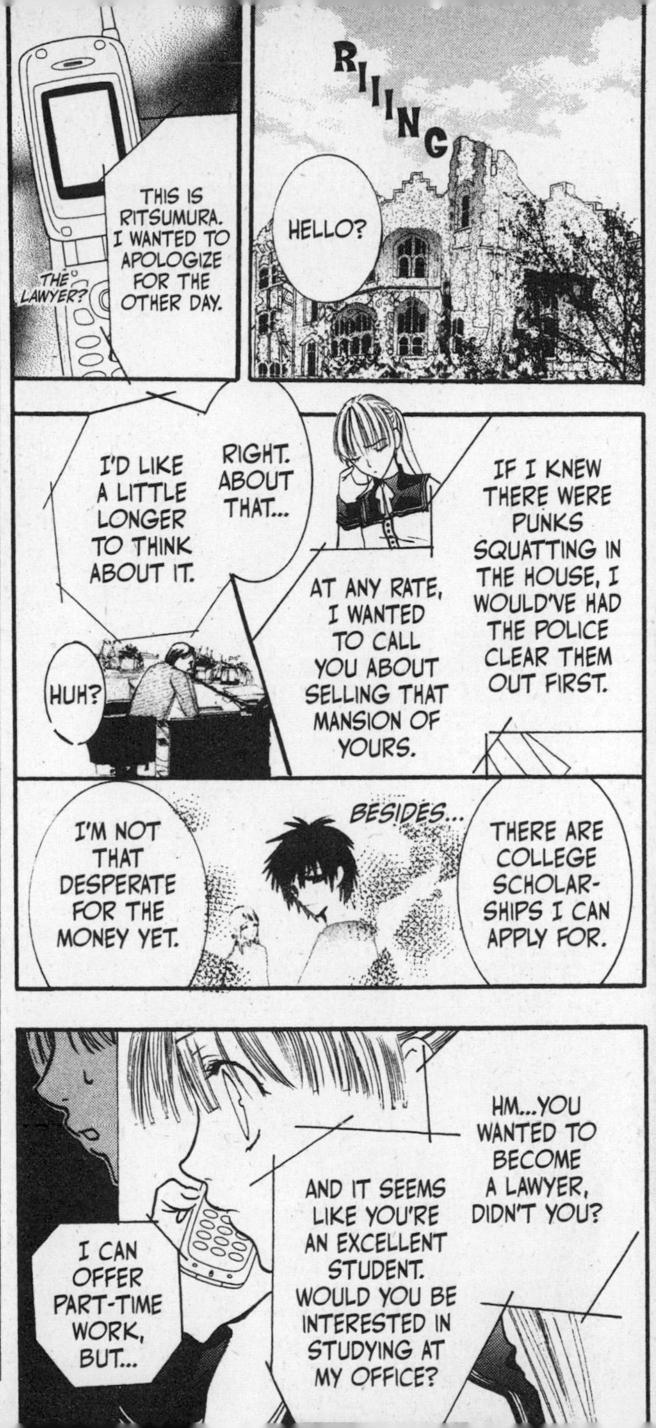
RIIING
HELLO?
THIS IS RITSUMURA. I WANTED TO APOLOGIZE FOR THE OTHER DAY.
THE LAWYER?
IF I KNEW THERE WERE PUNKS SQUATTING IN THE HOUSE, I WOULD'VE HAD THE POLICE CLEAR THEM OUT FIRST.
AT ANY RATE, I WANTED TO CALL YOU ABOUT SELLING THAT MANSION OF YOURS.
RIGHT. ABOUT THAT...
I'D LIKE A LITTLE LONGER TO THINK ABOUT IT.
HUH?
THERE ARE COLLEGE SCHOLAR-SHIPS I CAN APPLY FOR.
BESIDES...
I'M NOT THAT DESPERATE FOR THE MONEY YET.
HM...YOU WANTED TO BECOME A LAWYER, DIDN'T YOU?
AND IT SEEMS LIKE YOU'RE AN EXCELLENT STUDENT. WOULD YOU BE INTERESTED IN STUDYING AT MY OFFICE?
I CAN OFFER PART-TIME WORK, BUT...

Hello, folks. This is Kazuko Furumiya. Thanks for picking up "Chi-Chu"* (christened by fellow manga author Nakamura Seiko-san). I hope you enjoy reading it.

This manga is a one-shot story that was turned into a series. But all the art for the chapters is just so...ugly. Especially First Kiss. It was really bad when it was published in the magazine, but I hope it's gotten a little better for the book version. Actually, Kiyo's school uniform was originally different in the first chapter, although I think it's been fixed to be consistent in the comic book. (I need to fix more...) I feel that drawing uniforms is tedious, but I still like it. Designing and drawing girls' clothes, especially uniforms, is fun! (Pervert...) On the other hand, when it comes to men...I have no interest in designing their clothes whatsoever... (But uniforms are a different story.)

↑Definitely a pervert.

*Note: "Chi-Chu" is the Japanese-form for "Bloody Kiss." Chi=blood, chu=kiss.

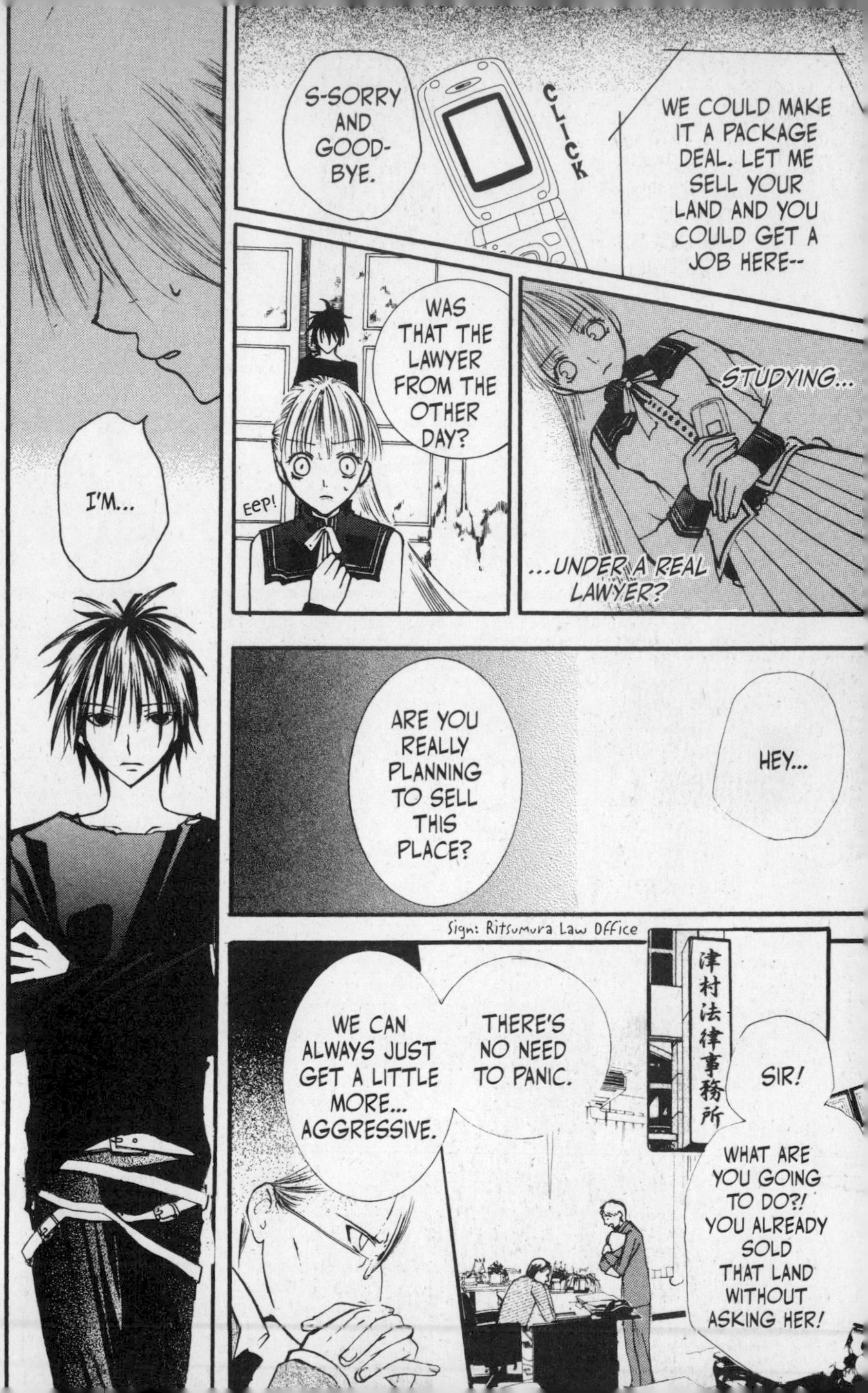
WE COULD MAKE IT A PACKAGE DEAL. LET ME SELL YOUR LAND AND YOU COULD GET A JOB HERE--
CLICK
S-SORRY AND GOOD-BYE.
STUDYING...
...UNDER A REAL LAWYER?
WAS THAT THE LAWYER FROM THE OTHER DAY?
EEP!
HEY...
ARE YOU REALLY PLANNING TO SELL THIS PLACE?
Sign: Ritsumura Law Office
津村法律事務所
SIR!
WHAT ARE YOU GOING TO DO?! YOU ALREADY SOLD THAT LAND WITHOUT ASKING HER!
THERE'S NO NEED TO PANIC.
WE CAN ALWAYS JUST GET A LITTLE MORE... AGGRESSIVE.
I'M...

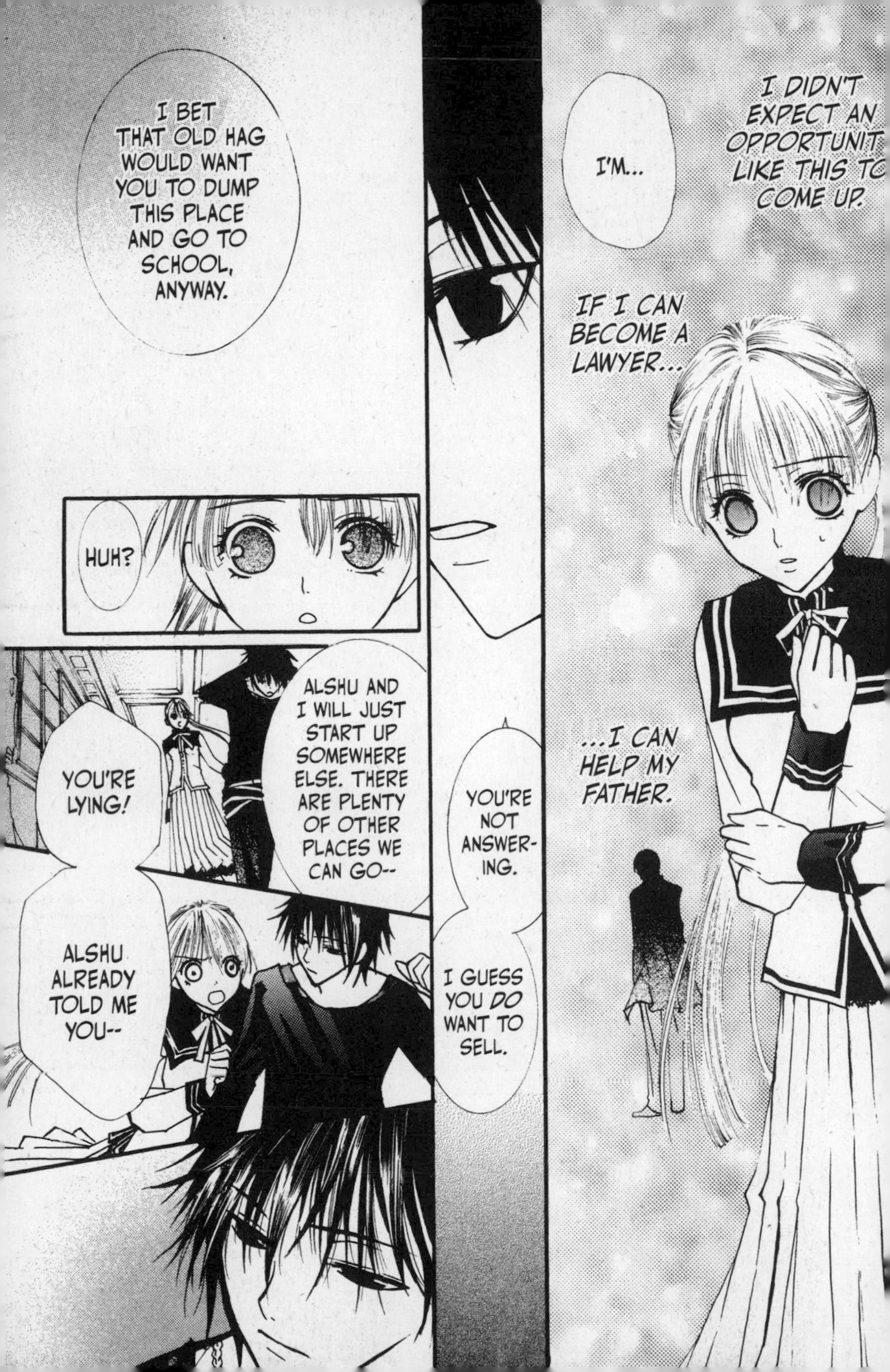
I DIDN'T EXPECT AN OPPORTUNIT LIKE THIS TO COME UP.
I'M...
IF I CAN BECOME A LAWYER...
...I CAN HELP MY FATHER.
I BET THAT OLD HAG WOULD WANT YOU TO DUMP THIS PLACE AND GO TO SCHOOL, ANYWAY.
HUH?
YOU'RE NOT ANSWER-ING.
I GUESS YOU *DO* WANT TO SELL.
ALSHU AND I WILL JUST START UP SOMEWHERE ELSE. THERE ARE PLENTY OF OTHER PLACES WE CAN GO--
YOU'RE LYING!
ALSHU ALREADY TOLD ME YOU--

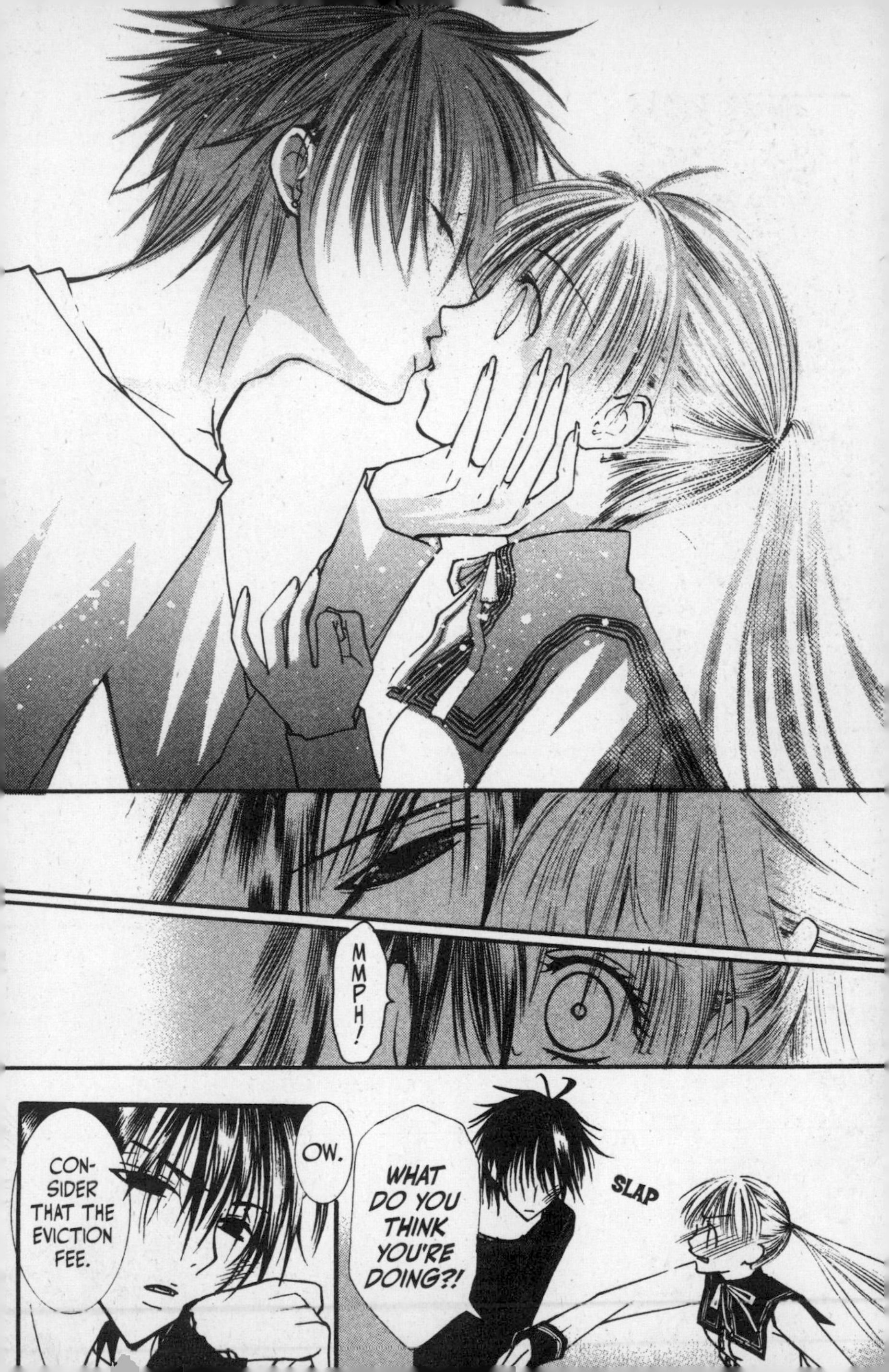
MMPH!
SLAP
OW.
WHAT DO YOU THINK YOU'RE DOING?!
CON-SIDER THAT THE EVICTION FEE.

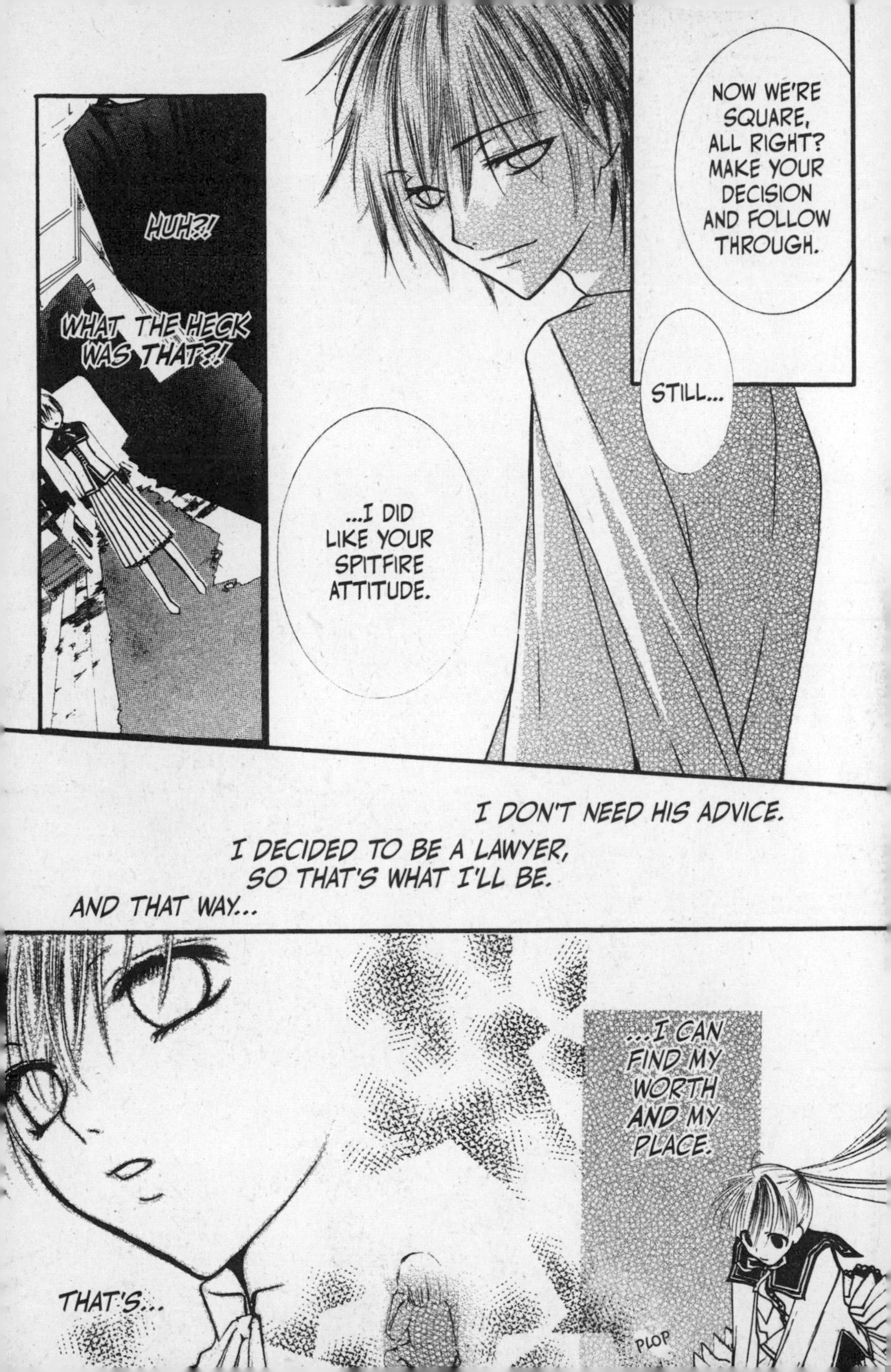
NOW WE'RE SQUARE, ALL RIGHT? MAKE YOUR DECISION AND FOLLOW THROUGH.
STILL...
...I DID LIKE YOUR SPITFIRE ATTITUDE.
HUH?!
WHAT THE HECK WAS THAT?!
I DON'T NEED HIS ADVICE.
I DECIDED TO BE A LAWYER, SO THAT'S WHAT I'LL BE.
AND THAT WAY...
...I CAN FIND MY WORTH AND MY PLACE.
PLOP
THAT'S...

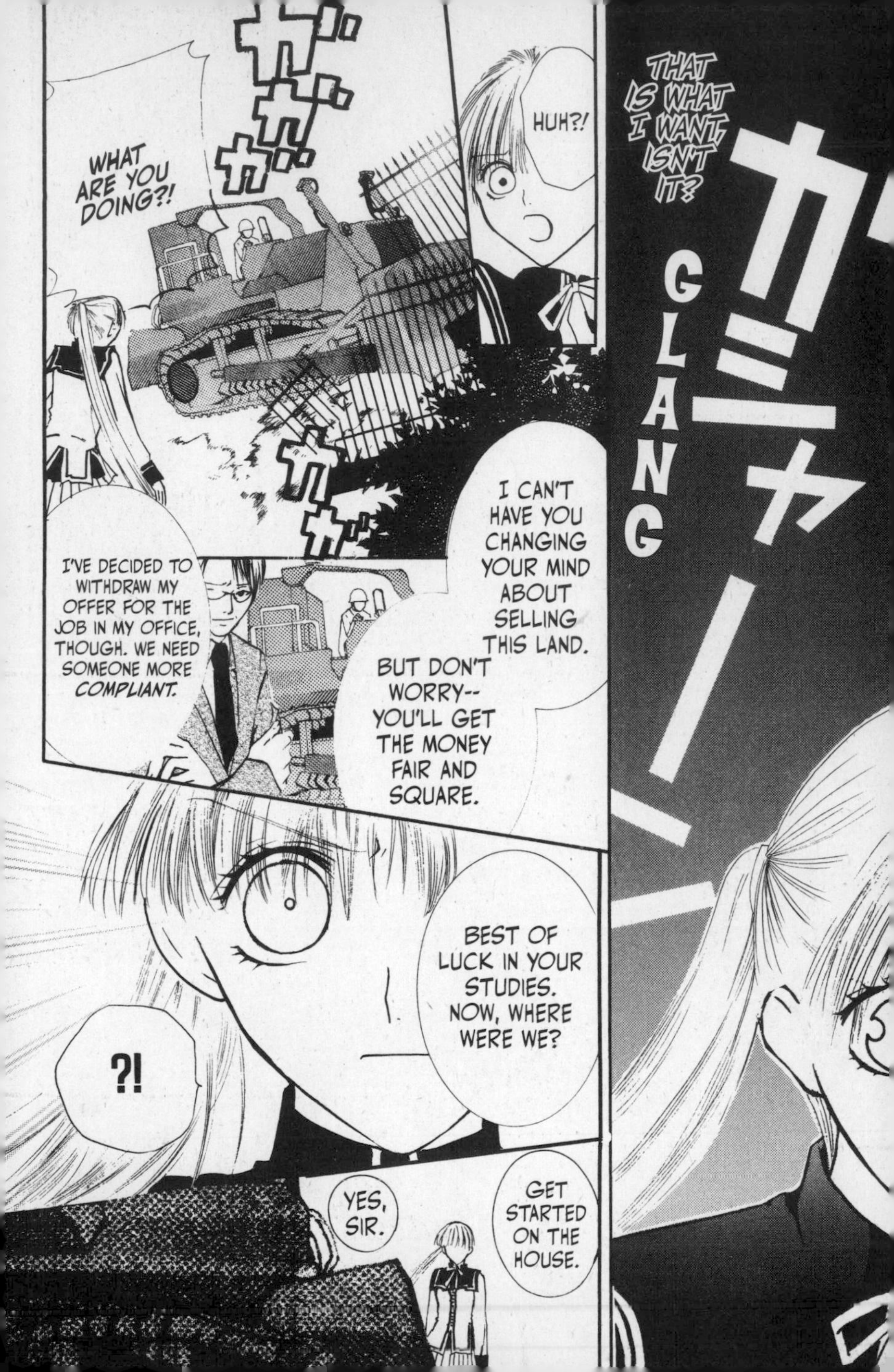
THAT IS WHAT I WANT, ISN'T IT?
カシャー
GLANG
HUH?!
ガガガ
WHAT ARE YOU DOING?!
ガガ
I CAN'T HAVE YOU CHANGING YOUR MIND ABOUT SELLING THIS LAND.
BUT DON'T WORRY-- YOU'LL GET THE MONEY FAIR AND SQUARE.
I'VE DECIDED TO WITHDRAW MY OFFER FOR THE JOB IN MY OFFICE, THOUGH. WE NEED SOMEONE MORE *COMPLIANT.*
BEST OF LUCK IN YOUR STUDIES. NOW, WHERE WERE WE?
?!
GET STARTED ON THE HOUSE.
YES, SIR.

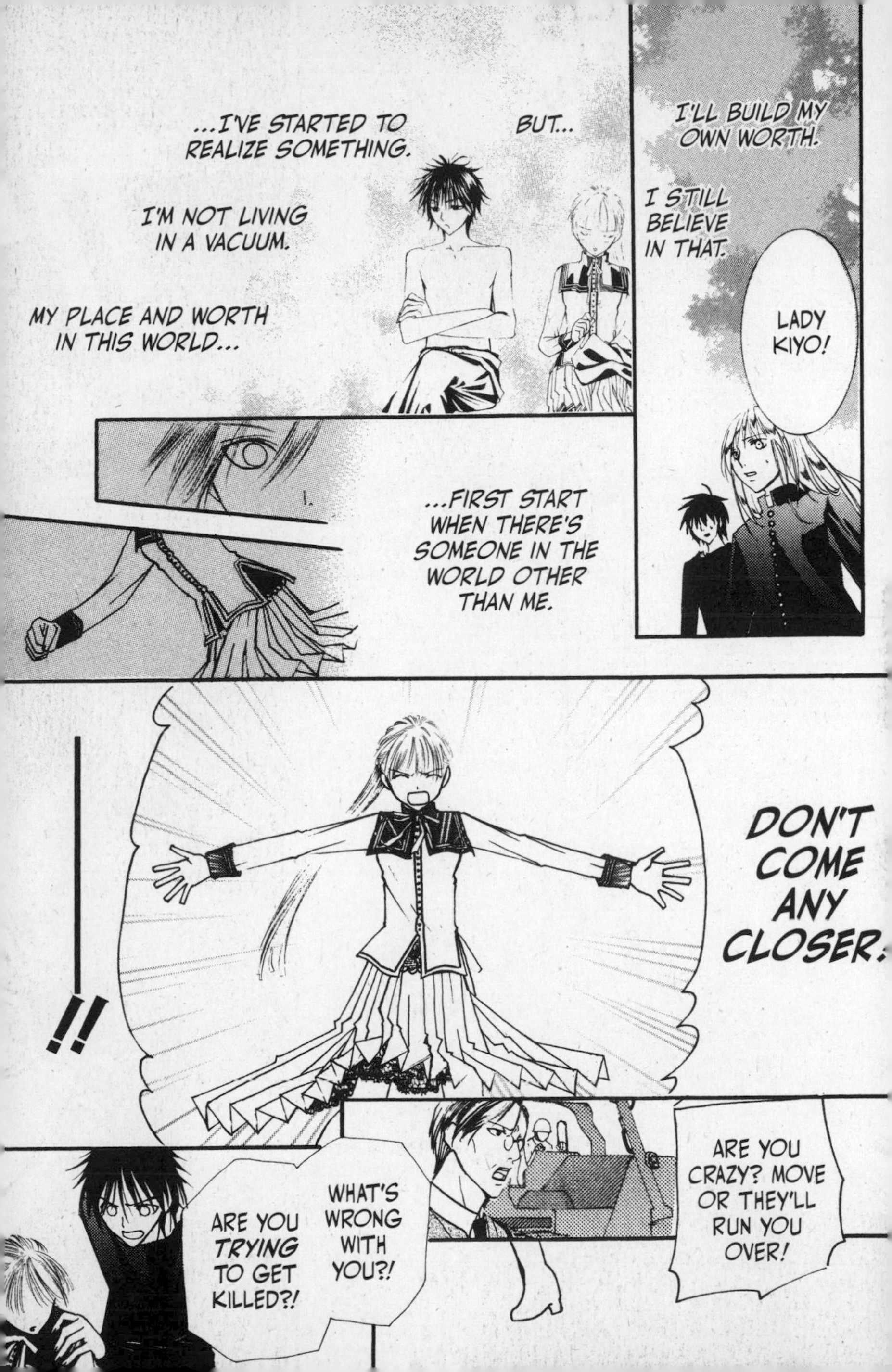
I'LL BUILD MY OWN WORTH.
I STILL BELIEVE IN THAT.
LADY KIYO!
BUT...
...I'VE STARTED TO REALIZE SOMETHING.
I'M NOT LIVING IN A VACUUM.
MY PLACE AND WORTH IN THIS WORLD...
...FIRST START WHEN THERE'S SOMEONE IN THE WORLD OTHER THAN ME.
DON'T COME ANY CLOSER.
!!
ARE YOU CRAZY? MOVE OR THEY'LL RUN YOU OVER!
WHAT'S WRONG WITH YOU?!
ARE YOU *TRYING* TO GET KILLED?!

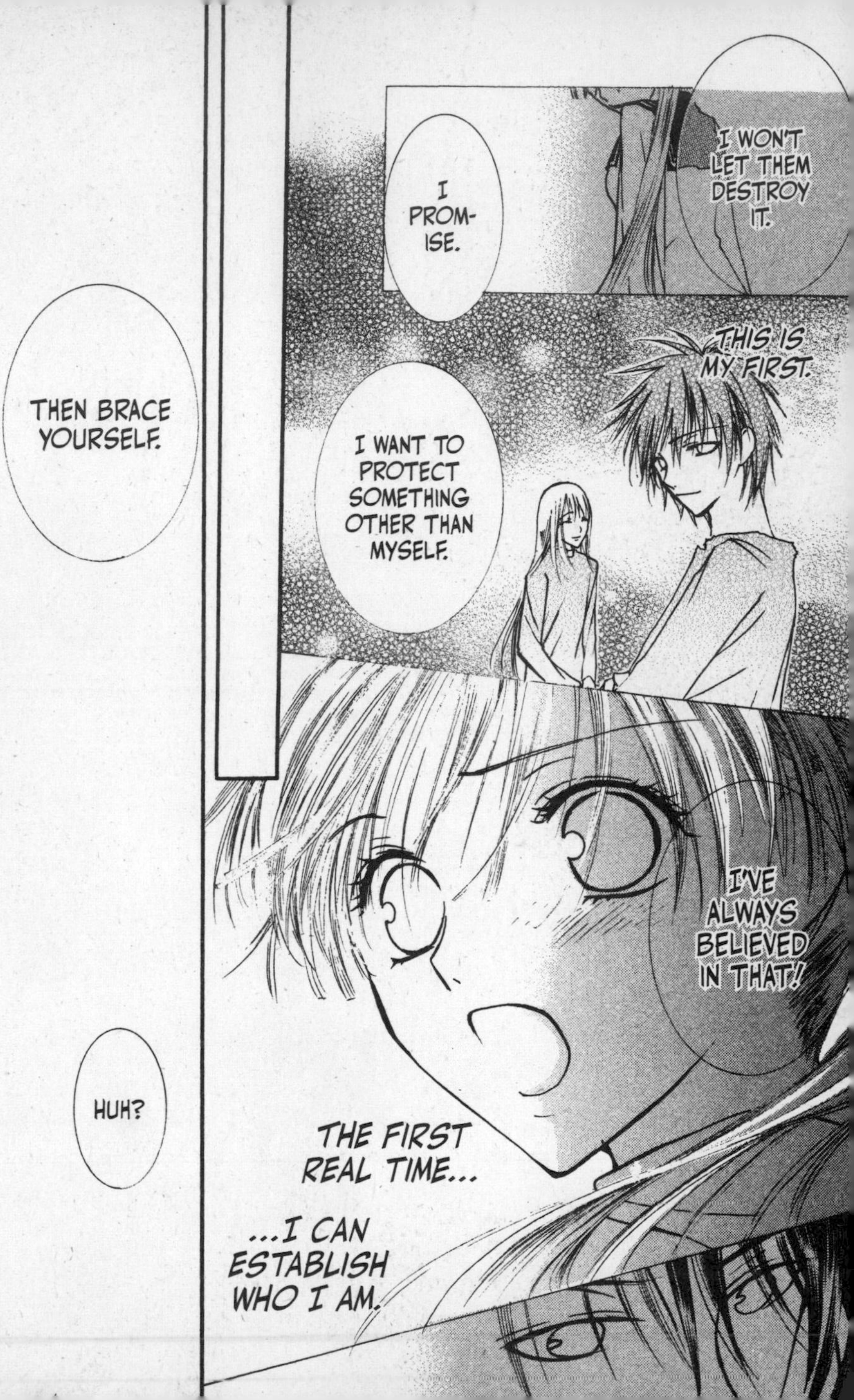
I WON'T LET THEM DESTROY IT.
I PROMISE.
THIS IS MY FIRST.
I WANT TO PROTECT SOMETHING OTHER THAN MYSELF.
I'VE ALWAYS BELIEVED IN THAT!
THE FIRST REAL TIME...
...I CAN ESTABLISH WHO I AM.
THEN BRACE YOURSELF.
HUH?

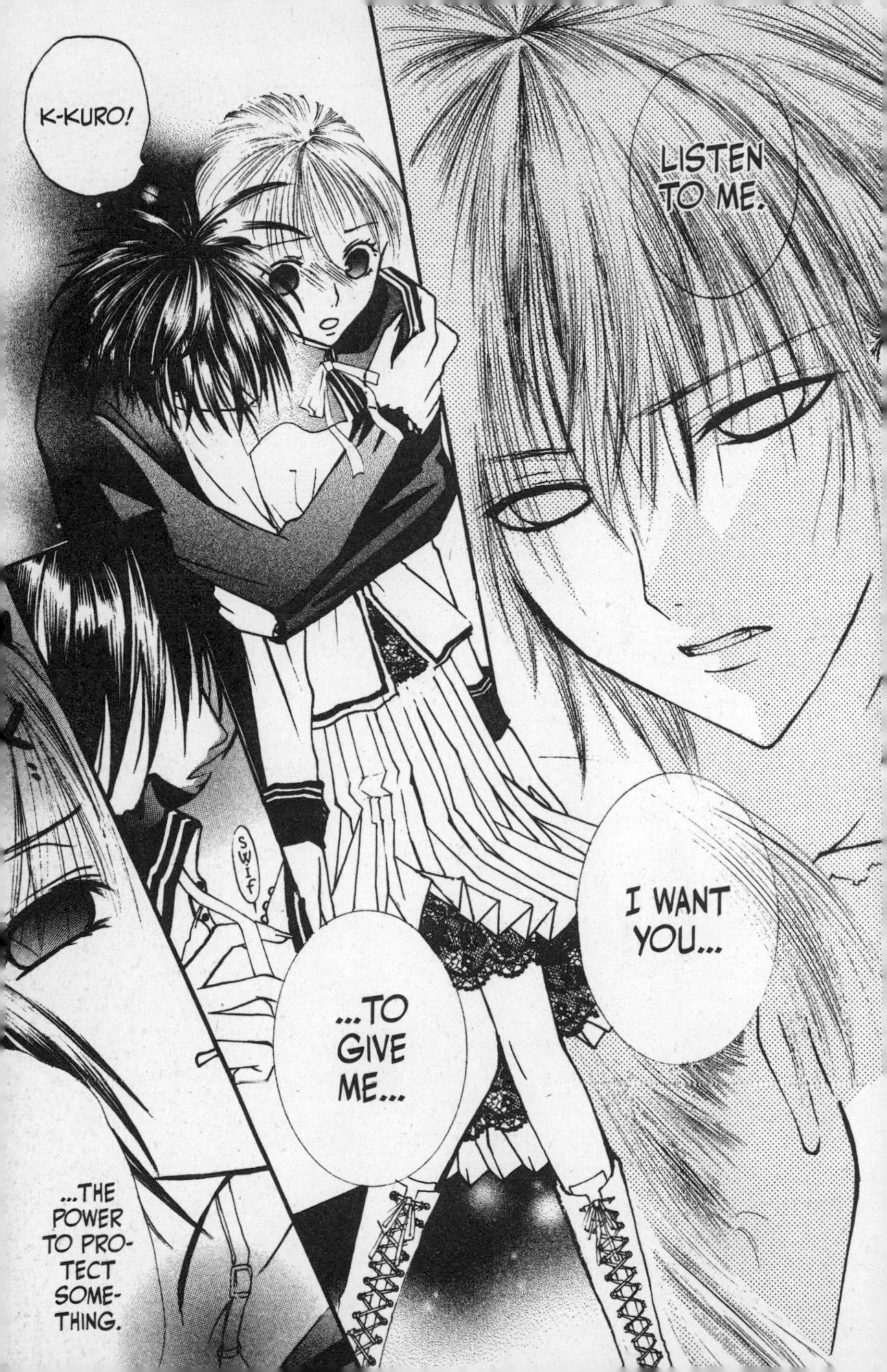
LISTEN TO ME.
I WANT YOU...
...TO GIVE ME...
K-KURO!
SWIF
...THE POWER TO PRO-TECT SOME-THING.

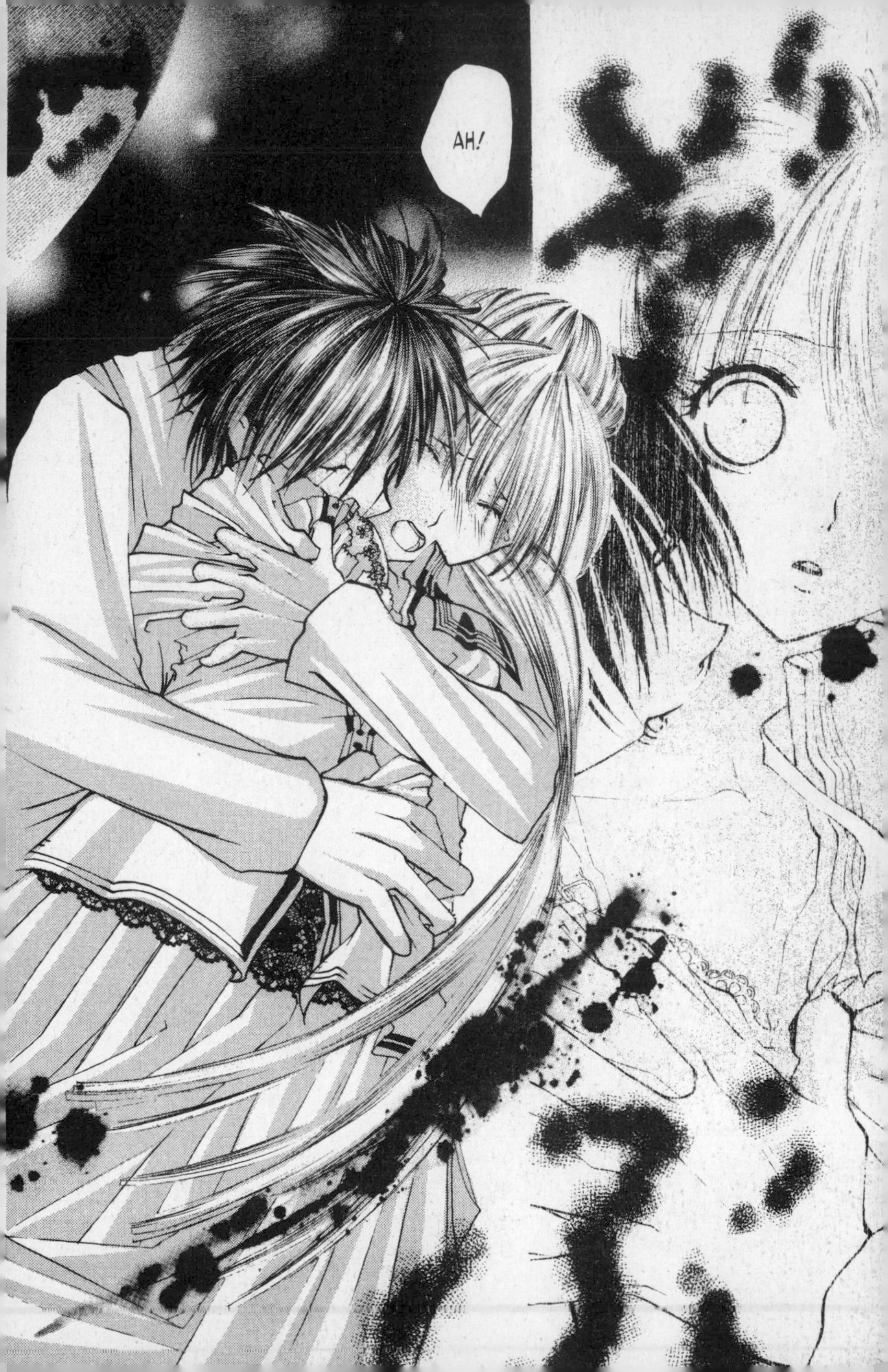
AH!

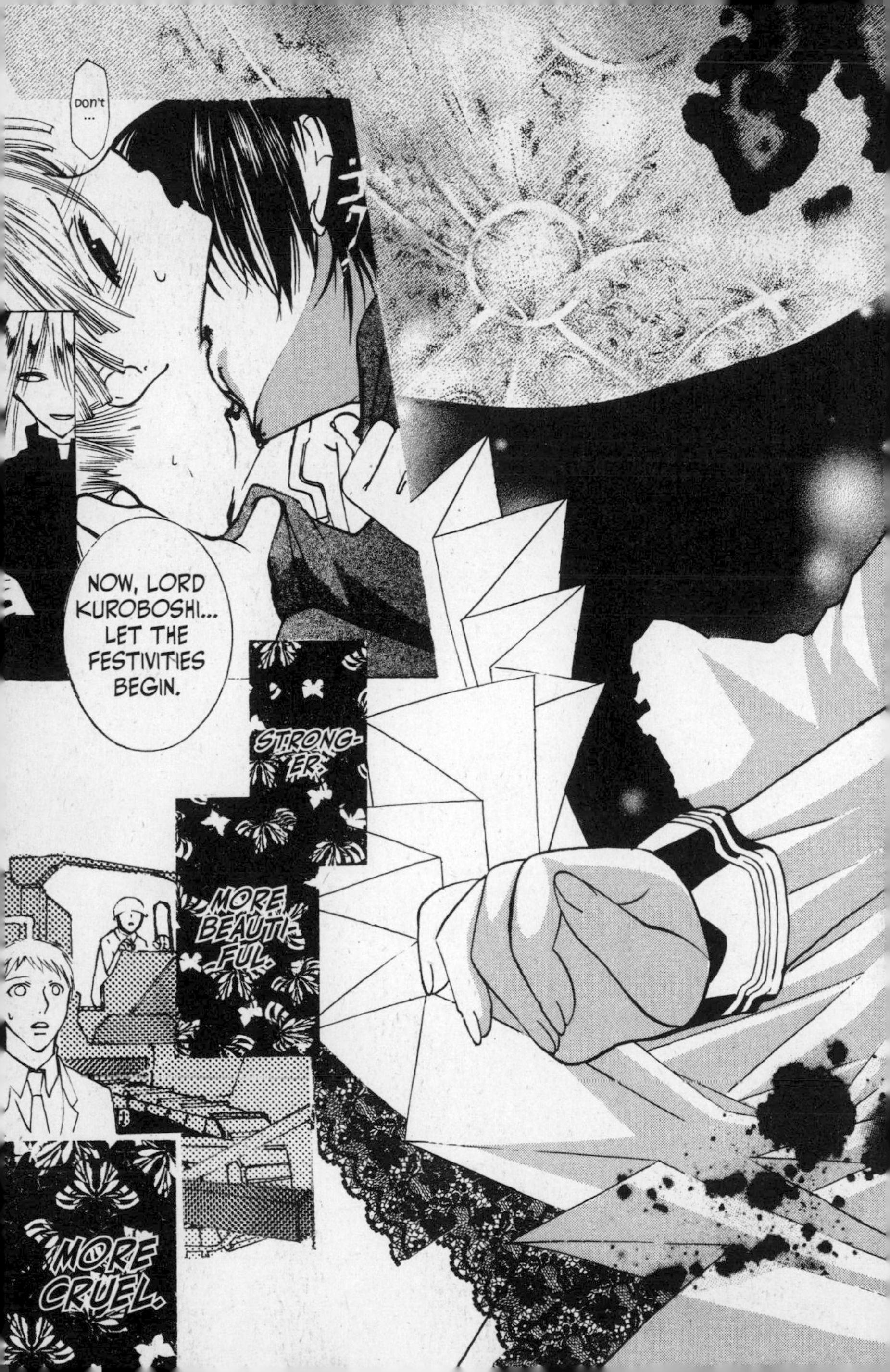
Don't ...
NOW, LORD KUROBOSHI... LET THE FESTIVITIES BEGIN.
STRONG-ER.
MORE BEAUTI-FUL.
MORE CRUEL.

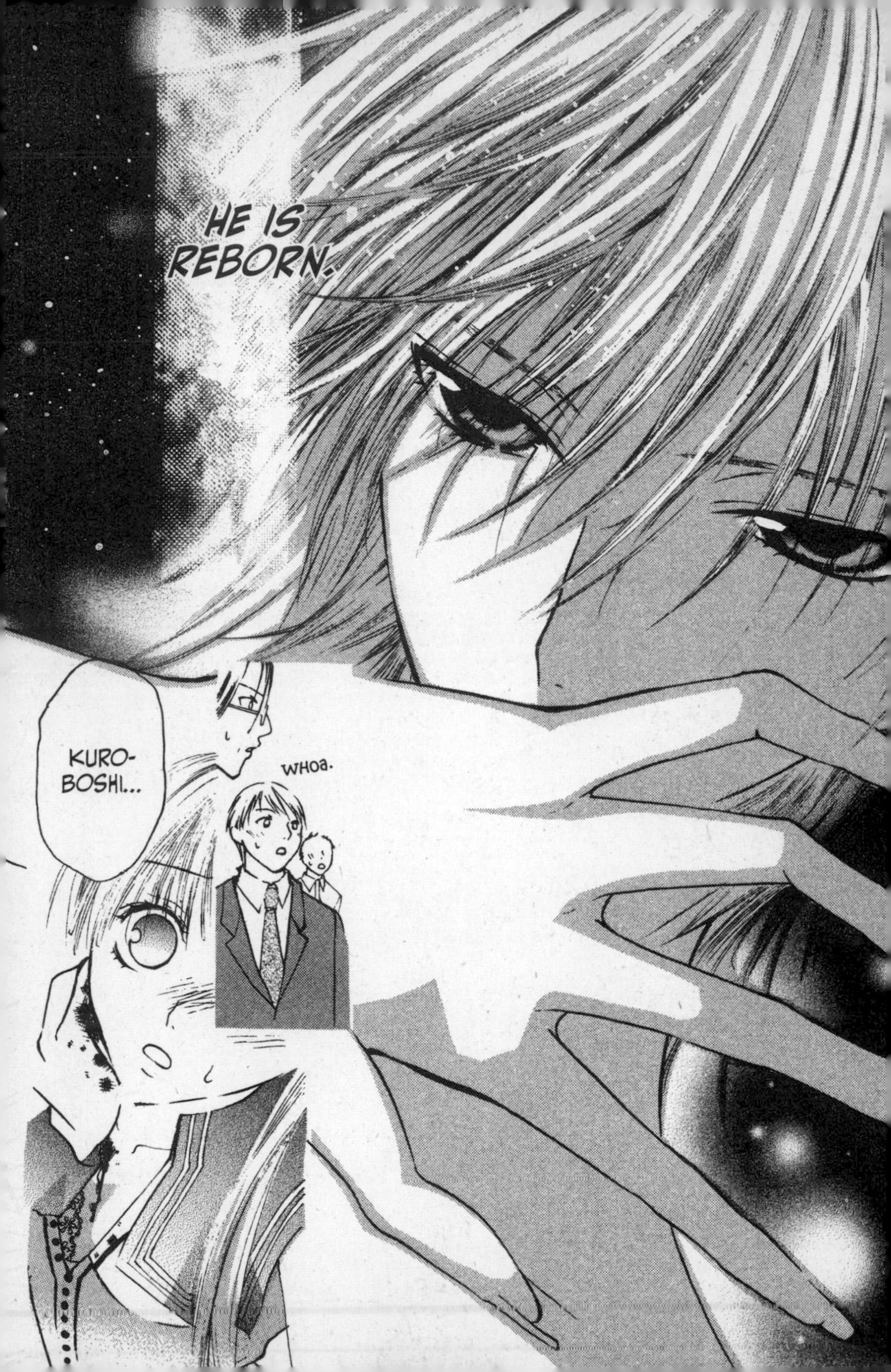
HE IS REBORN.
WHOA.
KURO-BOSHI...

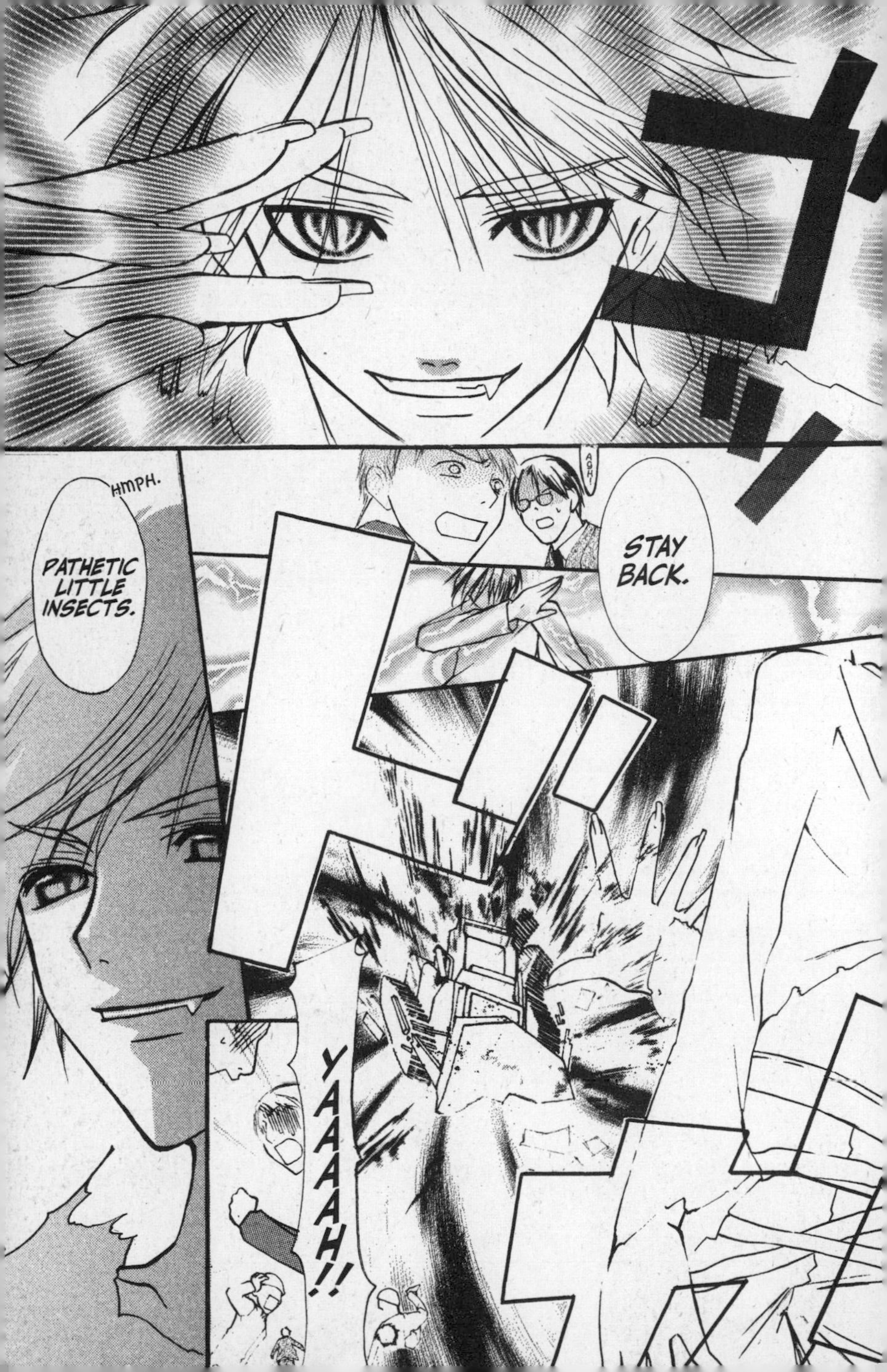
AGH!
STAY BACK.
HMPH.
PATHETIC LITTLE INSECTS.
YAAAAAH!!

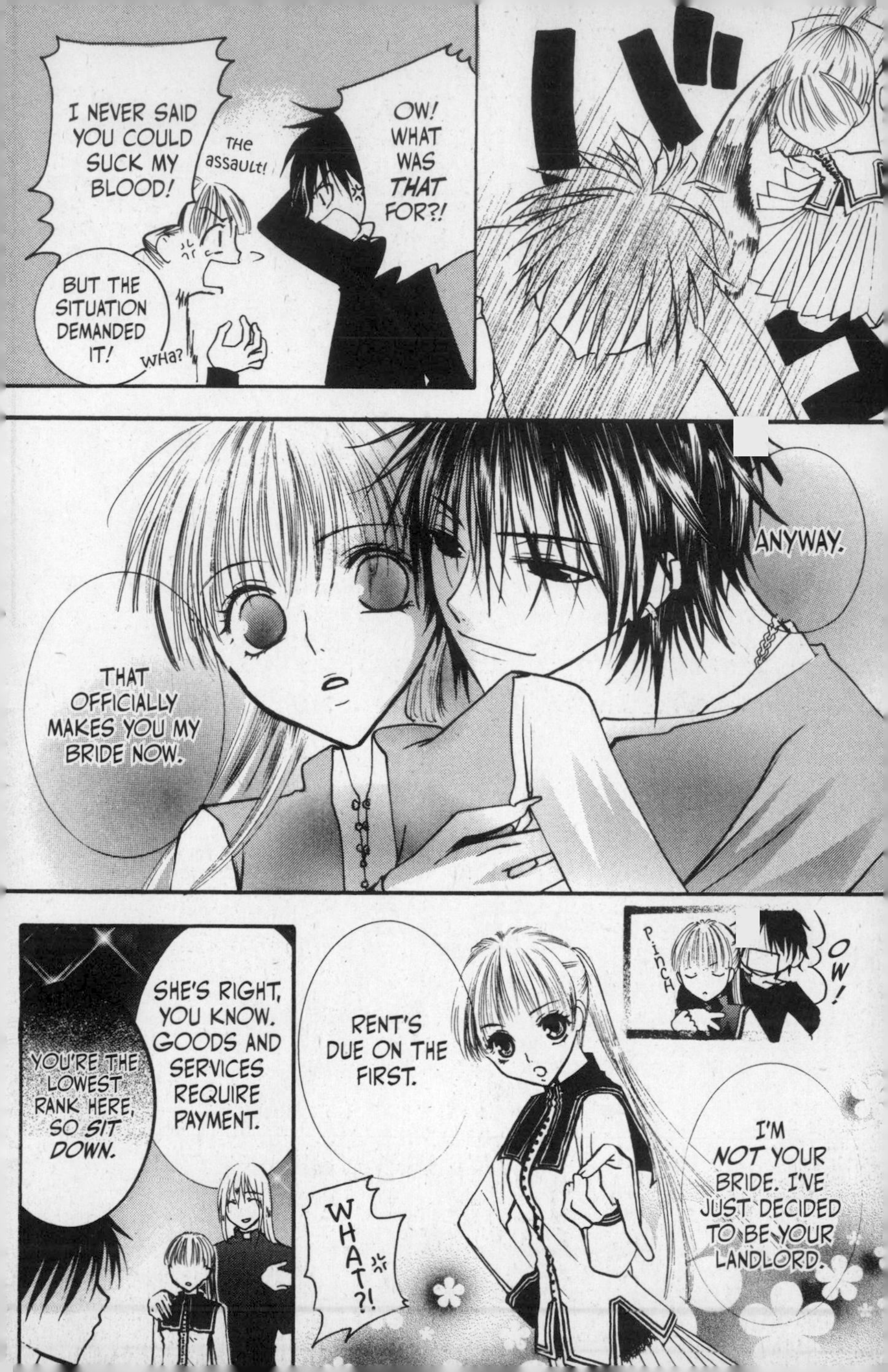
OW! WHAT WAS THAT FOR?!
The assault!
I NEVER SAID YOU COULD SUCK MY BLOOD!
BUT THE SITUATION DEMANDED IT!
WHa?
ANYWAY.
THAT OFFICIALLY MAKES YOU MY BRIDE NOW.
OW!
PINCH
I'M NOT YOUR BRIDE. I'VE JUST DECIDED TO BE YOUR LANDLORD.
RENT'S DUE ON THE FIRST.
WHAT?!
SHE'S RIGHT, YOU KNOW. GOODS AND SERVICES REQUIRE PAYMENT.
YOU'RE THE LOWEST RANK HERE, SO SIT DOWN.

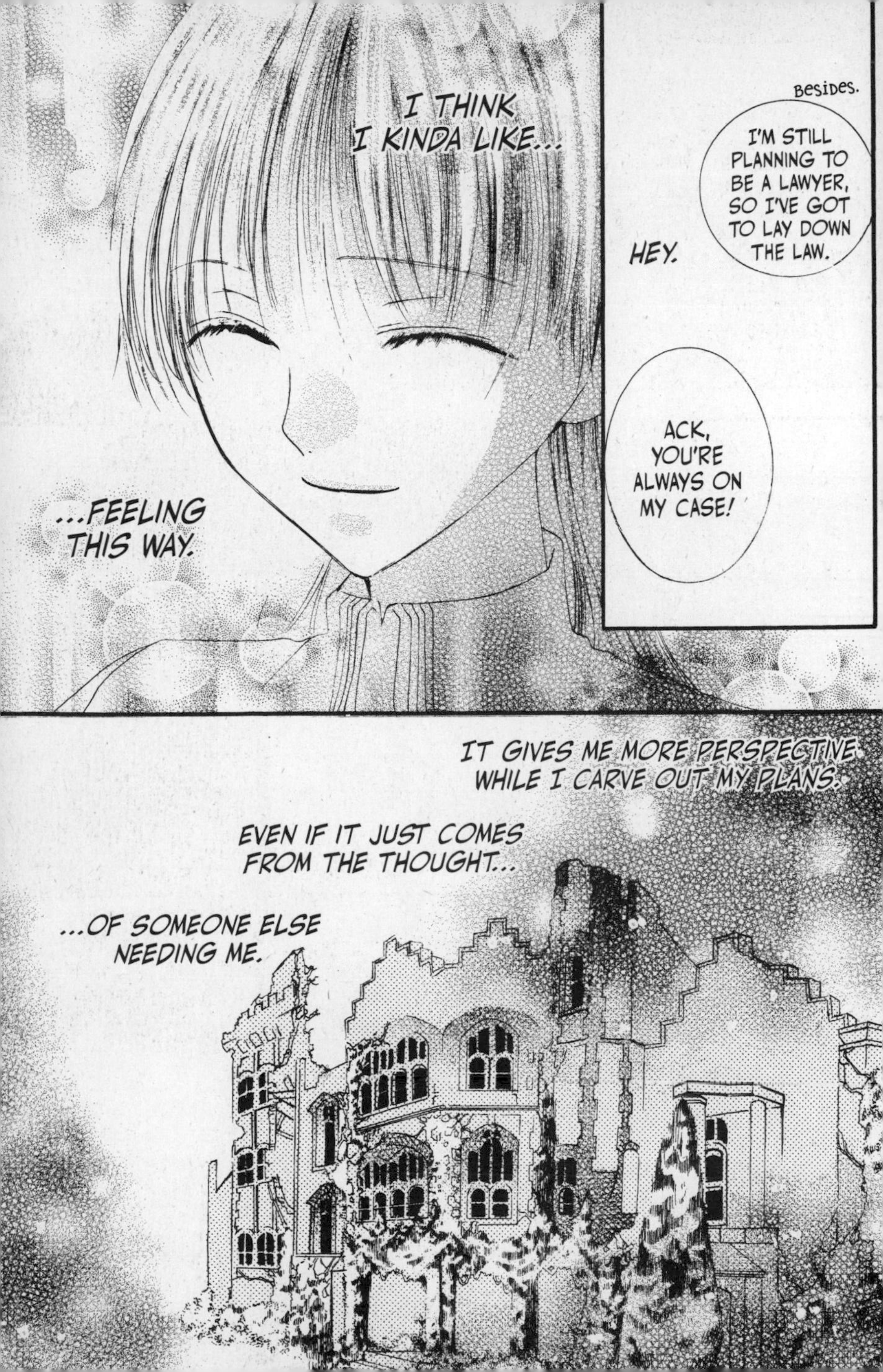
Besides.
I'M STILL PLANNING TO BE A LAWYER, SO I'VE GOT TO LAY DOWN THE LAW.
HEY.
ACK, YOU'RE ALWAYS ON MY CASE!
I THINK I KINDA LIKE...
...FEELING THIS WAY.
IT GIVES ME MORE PERSPECTIVE WHILE I CARVE OUT MY PLANS.
EVEN IF IT JUST COMES FROM THE THOUGHT...
...OF SOMEONE ELSE NEEDING ME.

I re-draw things like a crazy woman. Not only do I go through re-dos on my storylines, but I also re-do rough drafts and even inking.

For example, in the third panel on page 68... those re-dos almost made me cry.

Continued on page 104.

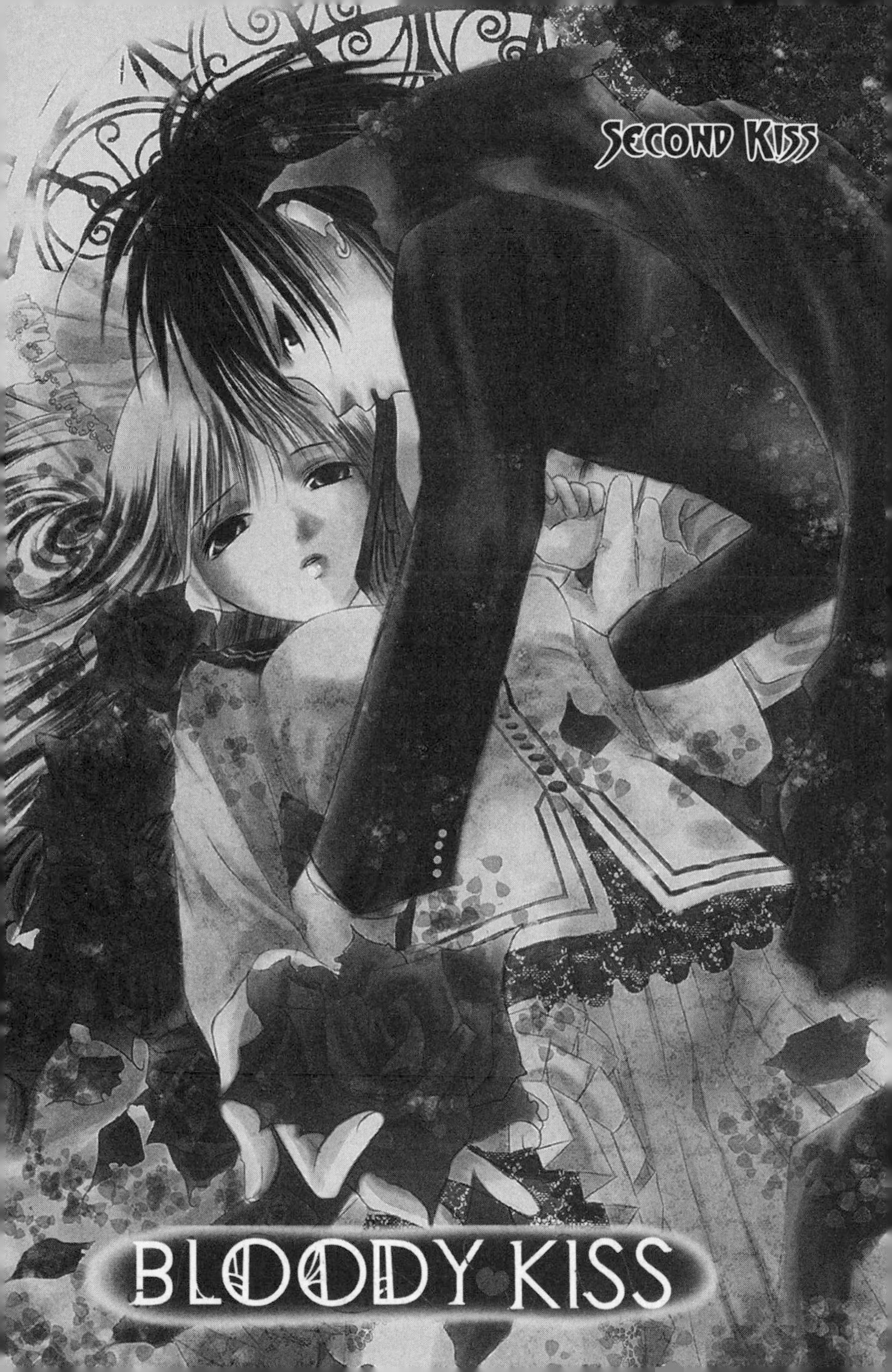

SECOND KISS
BLOODY KISS

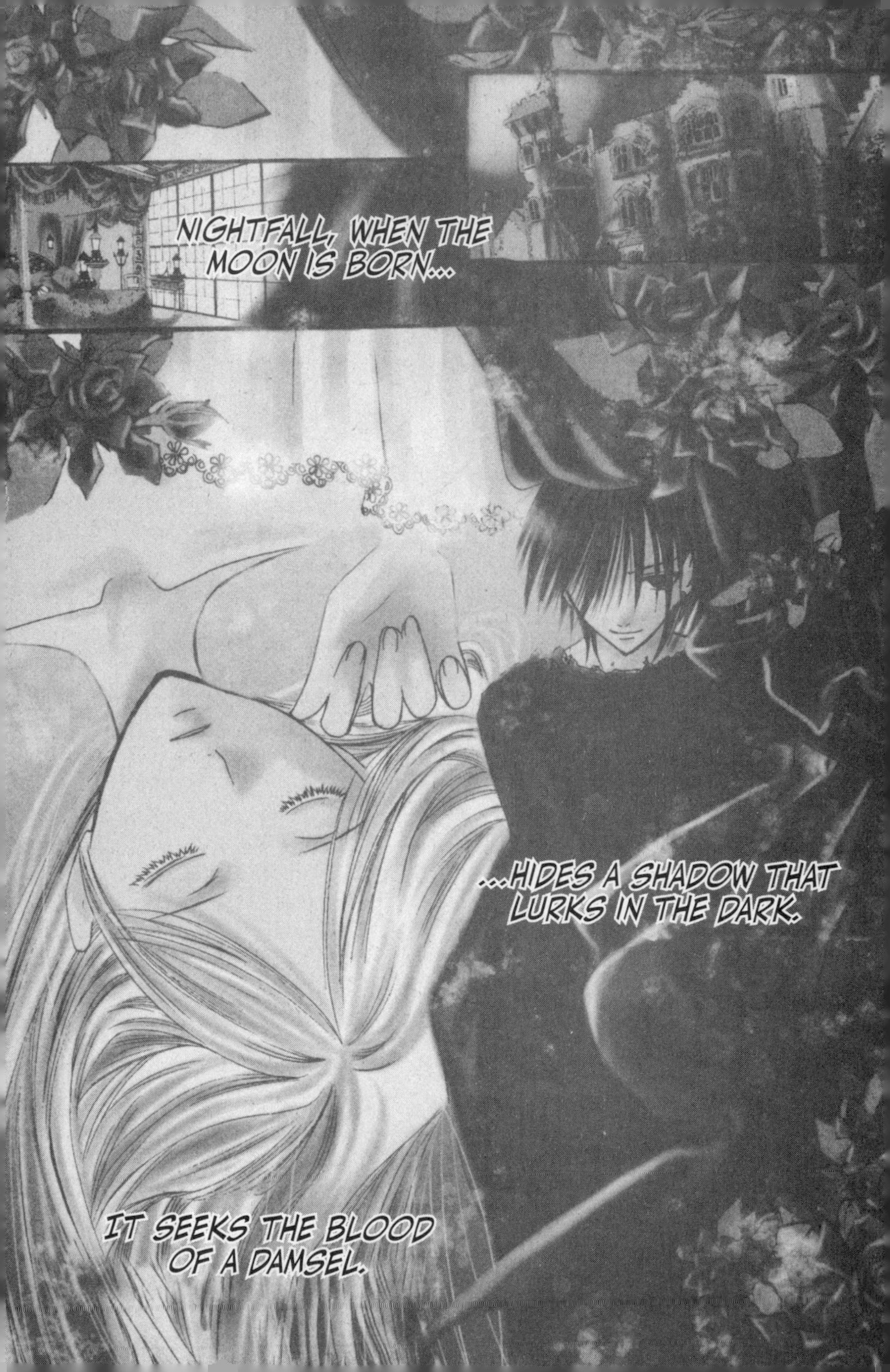
NIGHTFALL, WHEN THE MOON IS BORN...
...HIDES A SHADOW THAT LURKS IN THE DARK.
IT SEEKS THE BLOOD OF A DAMSEL.

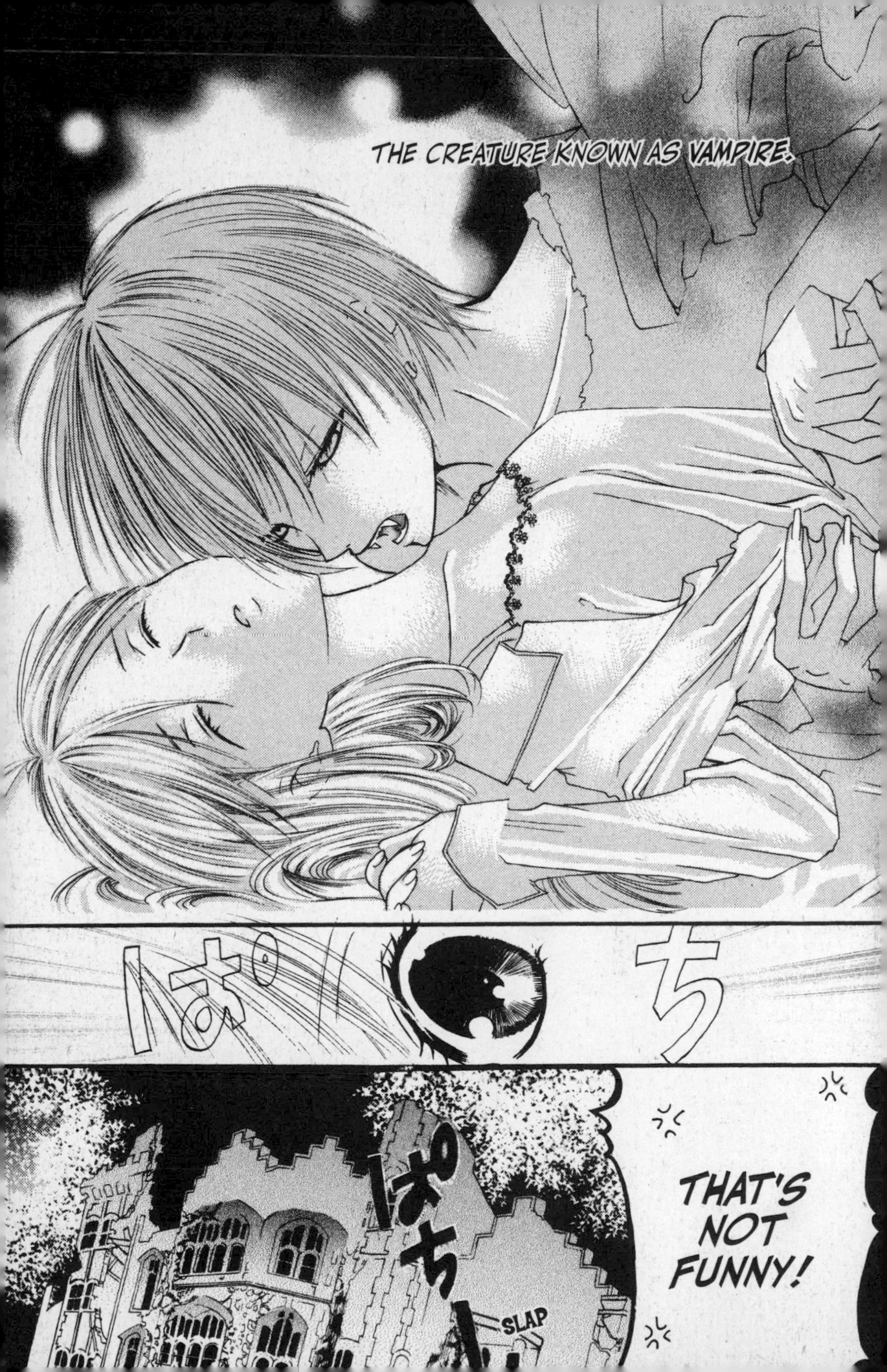
THE CREATURE KNOWN AS VAMPIRE.
ぱち
THAT'S NOT FUNNY!
ぱち
SLAP

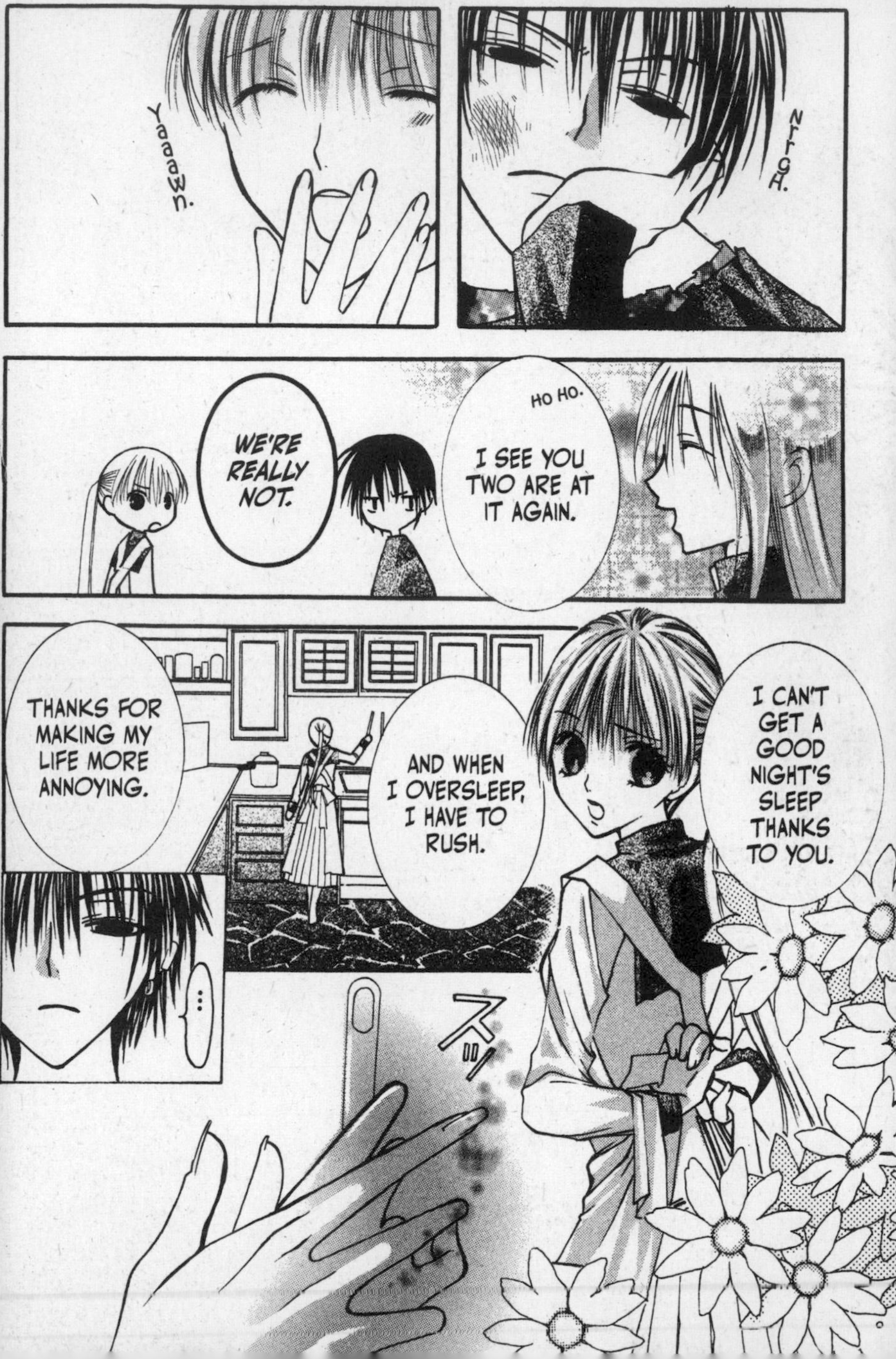
Nrrgh.
Yaaawn.
HO HO.
I SEE YOU TWO ARE AT IT AGAIN.
WE'RE REALLY NOT.
I CAN'T GET A GOOD NIGHT'S SLEEP THANKS TO YOU.
AND WHEN I OVERSLEEP, I HAVE TO RUSH.
THANKS FOR MAKING MY LIFE MORE ANNOYING.
...

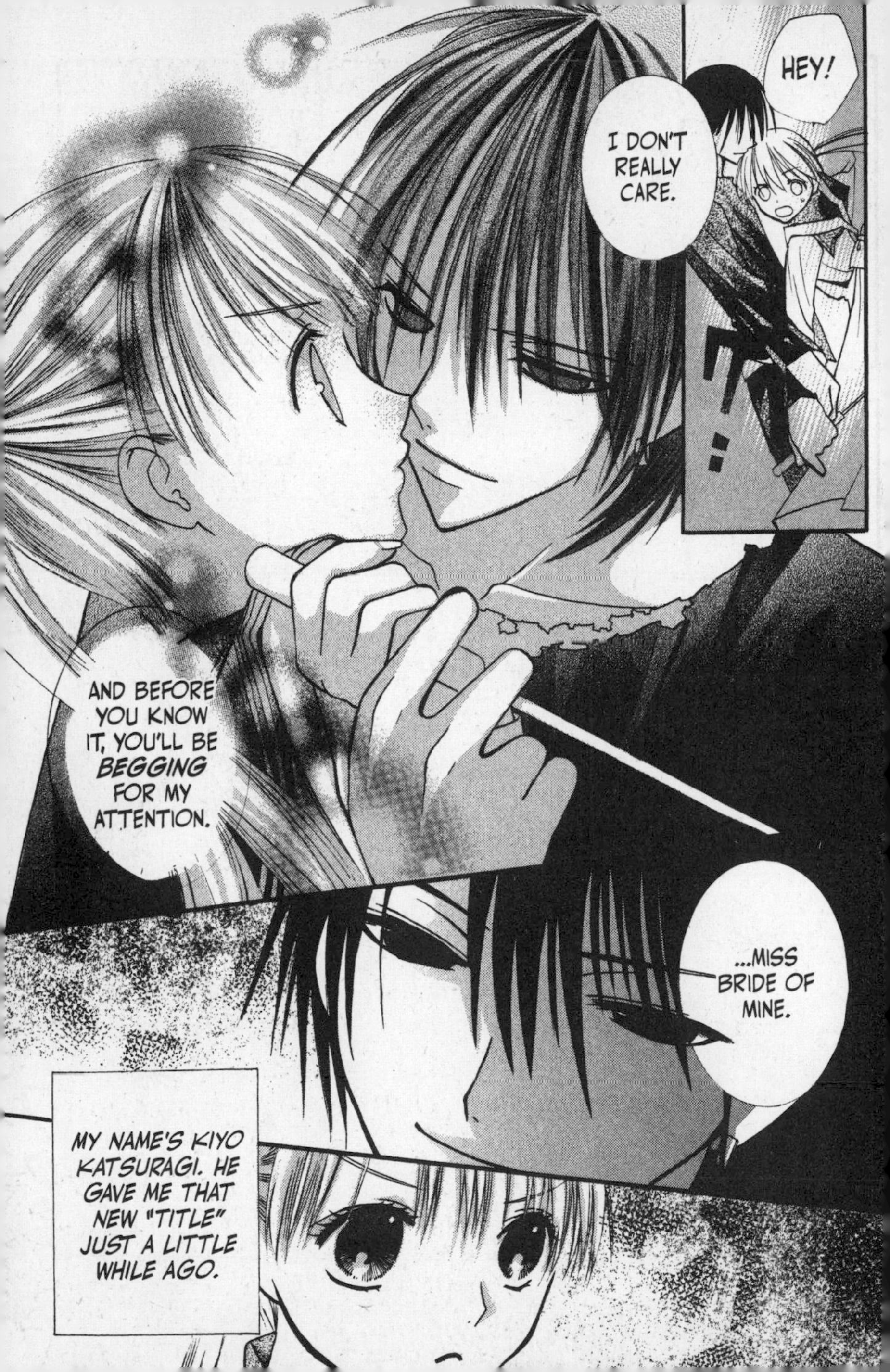
HEY!
I DON'T REALLY CARE.
AND BEFORE YOU KNOW IT, YOU'LL BE *BEGGING* FOR MY ATTENTION.
...MISS BRIDE OF MINE.
MY NAME'S KIYO KATSURAGI. HE GAVE ME THAT NEW "TITLE" JUST A LITTLE WHILE AGO.

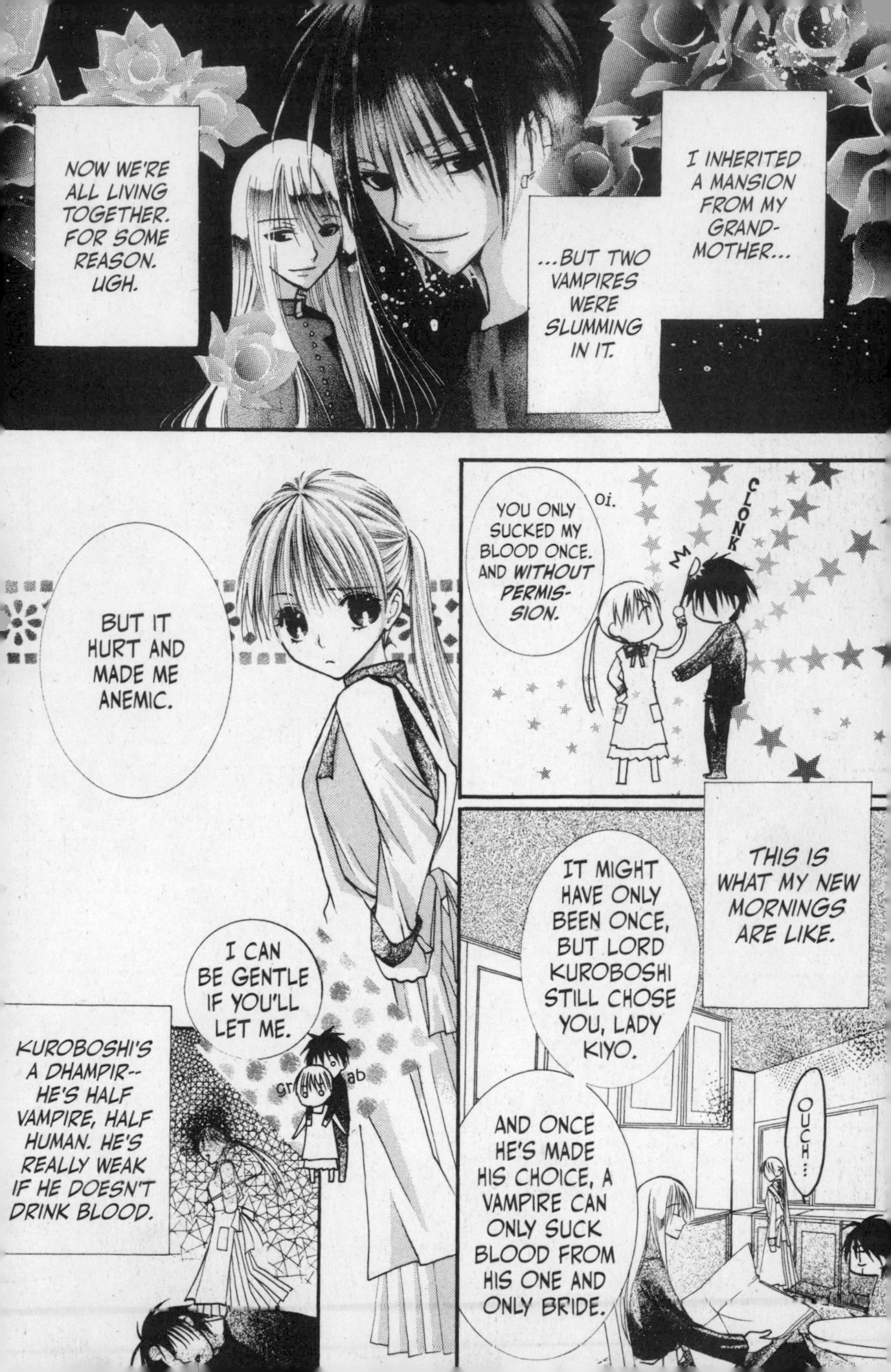
I INHERITED A MANSION FROM MY GRAND-MOTHER...
...BUT TWO VAMPIRES WERE SLUMMING IN IT.
NOW WE'RE ALL LIVING TOGETHER. FOR SOME REASON. UGH.
CLONK
oi.
YOU ONLY SUCKED MY BLOOD ONCE. AND *WITHOUT* PERMIS-SION.
THIS IS WHAT MY NEW MORNINGS ARE LIKE.
IT MIGHT HAVE ONLY BEEN ONCE, BUT LORD KUROBOSHI STILL CHOSE YOU, LADY KIYO.
OUCH...
AND ONCE HE'S MADE HIS CHOICE, A VAMPIRE CAN ONLY SUCK BLOOD FROM HIS ONE AND ONLY BRIDE.
BUT IT HURT AND MADE ME ANEMIC.
I CAN BE GENTLE IF YOU'LL LET ME.
Grab
KUROBOSHI'S A DHAMPIR-- HE'S HALF VAMPIRE, HALF HUMAN. HE'S REALLY WEAK IF HE DOESN'T DRINK BLOOD.

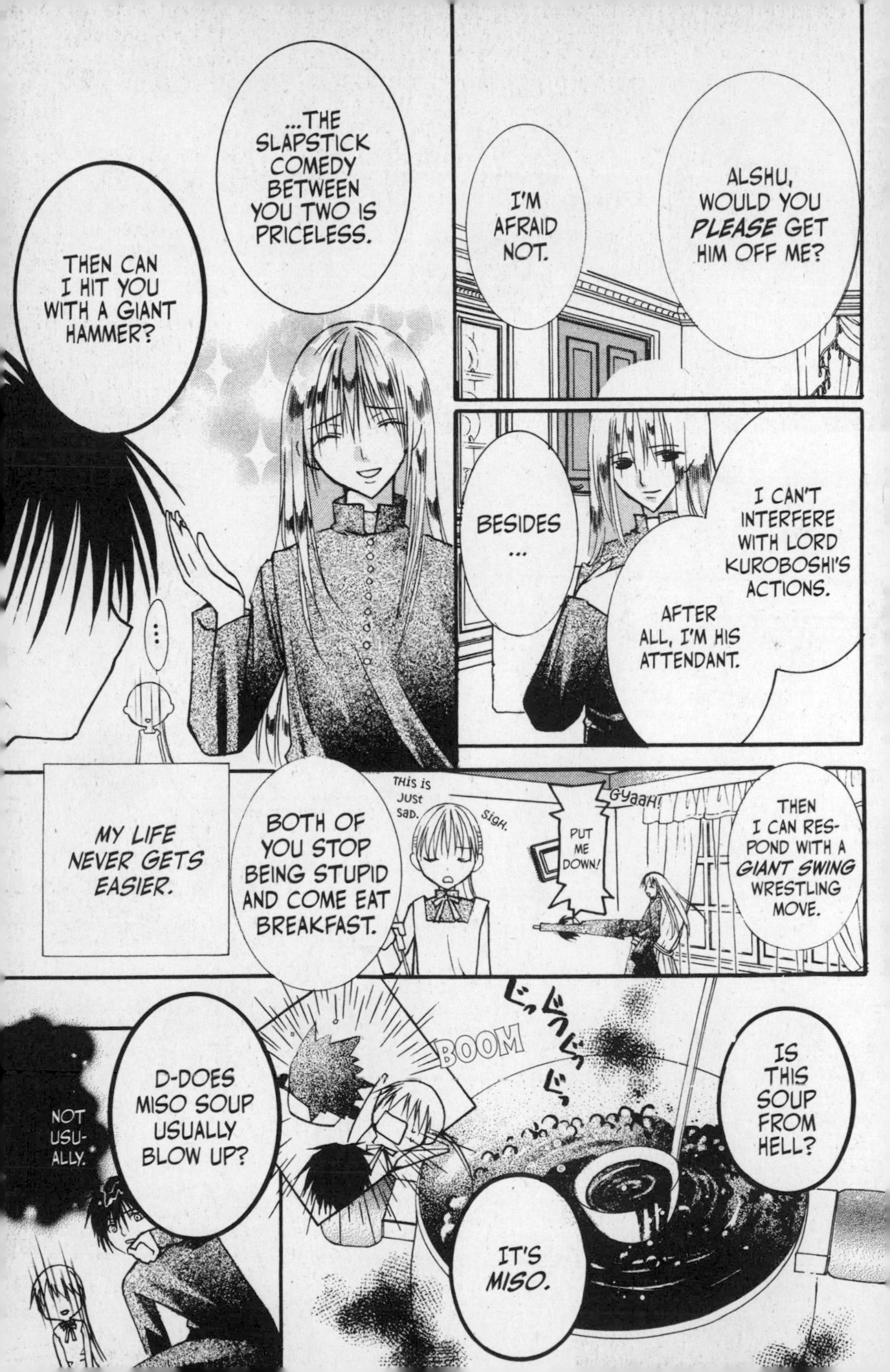
ALSHU, WOULD YOU PLEASE GET HIM OFF ME?
I'M AFRAID NOT.
I CAN'T INTERFERE WITH LORD KUROBOSHI'S ACTIONS.
AFTER ALL, I'M HIS ATTENDANT.
BESIDES...
...THE SLAPSTICK COMEDY BETWEEN YOU TWO IS PRICELESS.
THEN CAN I HIT YOU WITH A GIANT HAMMER?
...
THEN I CAN RESPOND WITH A GIANT SWING WRESTLING MOVE.
GYAAH!
PUT ME DOWN!
THIS IS JUST SAD.
SIGH.
BOTH OF YOU STOP BEING STUPID AND COME EAT BREAKFAST.
MY LIFE NEVER GETS EASIER.
IS THIS SOUP FROM HELL?
BOOM
IT'S MISO.
D-DOES MISO SOUP USUALLY BLOW UP?
NOT USUALLY.

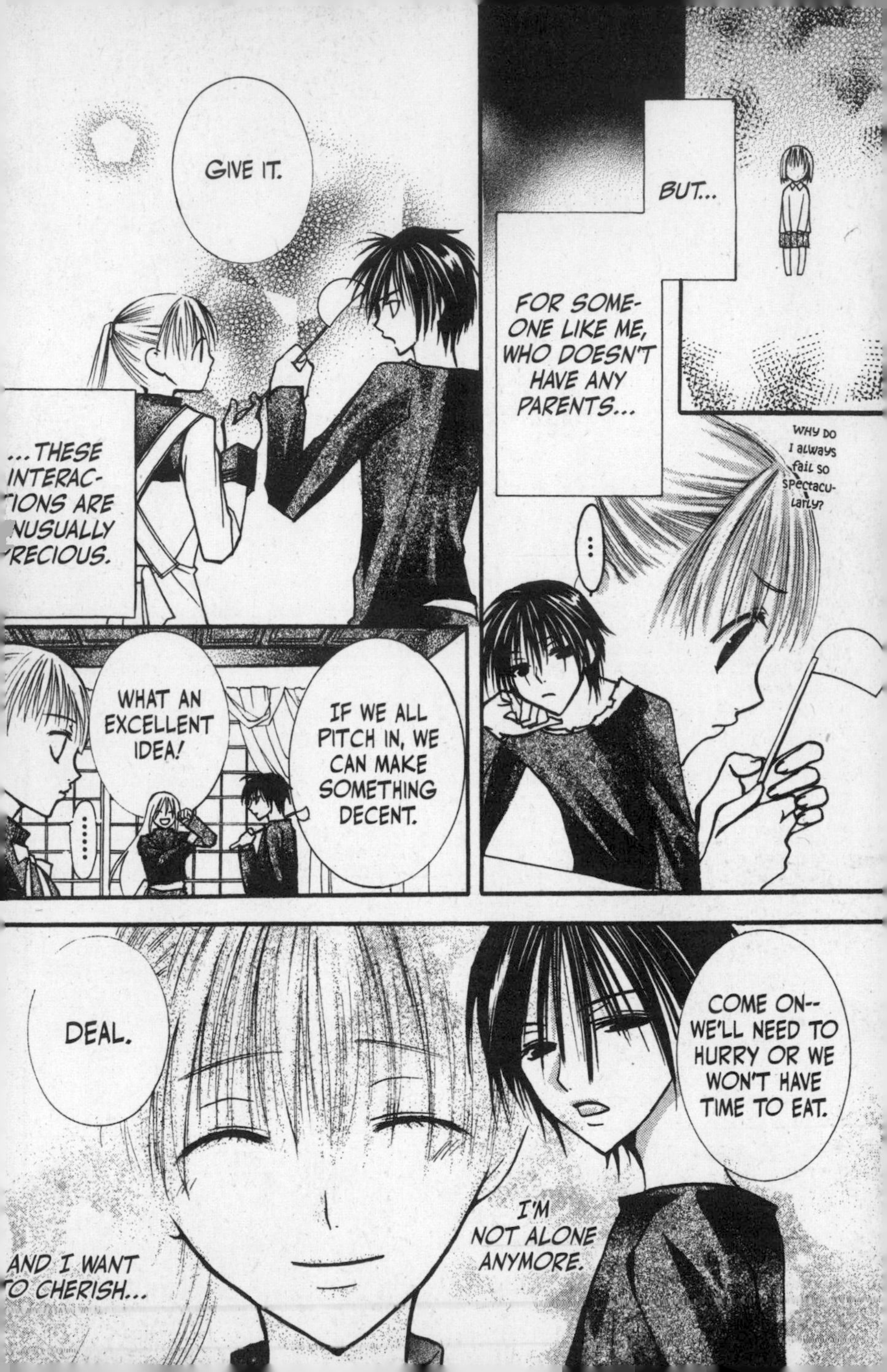
BUT...
FOR SOME-ONE LIKE ME, WHO DOESN'T HAVE ANY PARENTS...
GIVE IT.
...THESE INTERAC-TIONS ARE UNUSUALLY PRECIOUS.
...
WHY DO I ALWAYS FAIL SO SPECTACU-LARLY?
IF WE ALL PITCH IN, WE CAN MAKE SOMETHING DECENT.
WHAT AN EXCELLENT IDEA!
......
COME ON-- WE'LL NEED TO HURRY OR WE WON'T HAVE TIME TO EAT.
DEAL.
I'M NOT ALONE ANYMORE.
AND I WANT TO CHERISH...

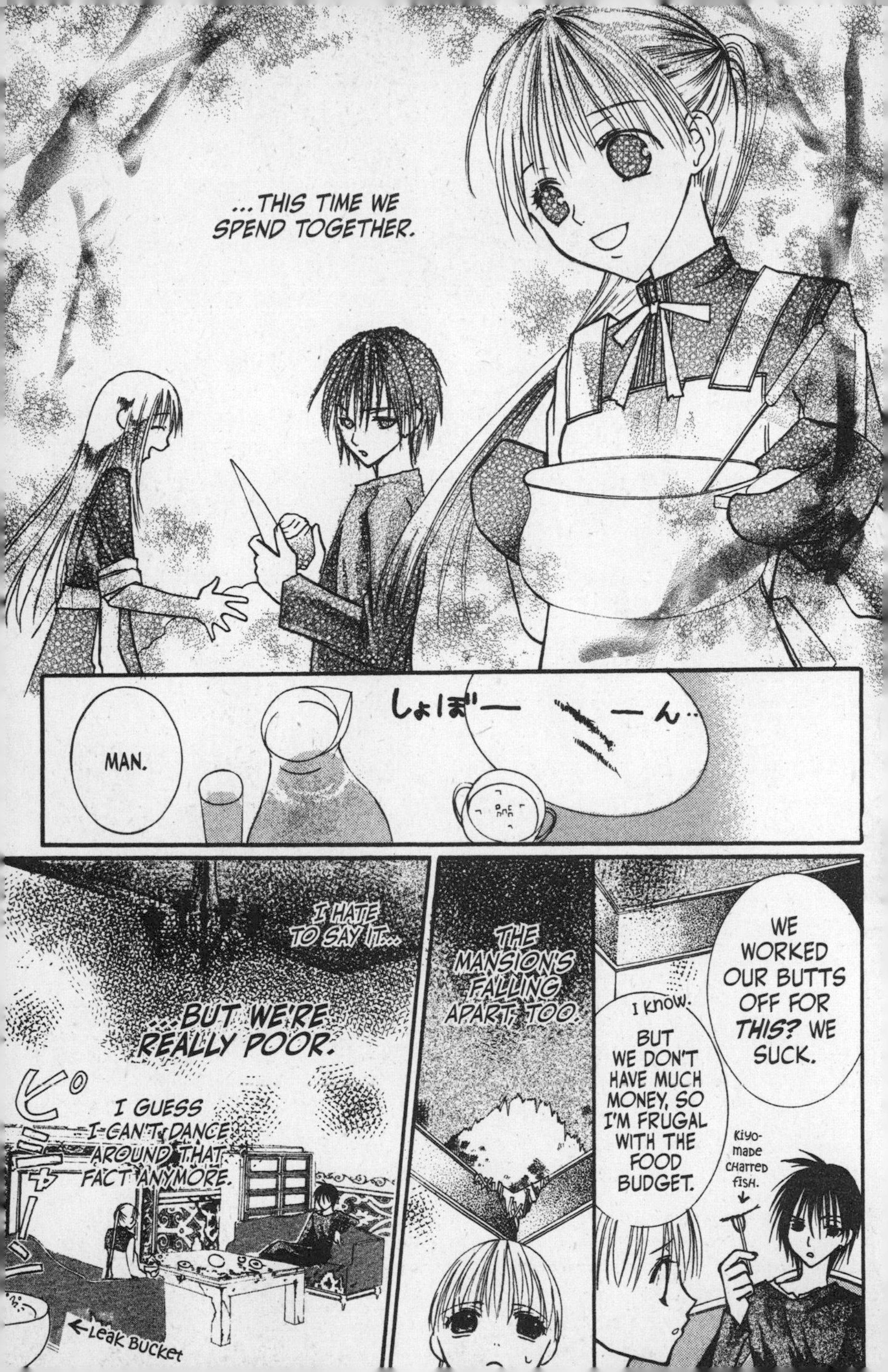
...THIS TIME WE SPEND TOGETHER.
しょぼーーーん…
MAN.
WE WORKED OUR BUTTS OFF FOR THIS? WE SUCK.
I know.
BUT WE DON'T HAVE MUCH MONEY, SO I'M FRUGAL WITH THE FOOD BUDGET.
Kiyo-made charred fish.
THE MANSION'S FALLING APART, TOO.
I HATE TO SAY IT...
...BUT WE'RE REALLY POOR.
I GUESS I CAN'T DANCE AROUND THAT FACT ANYMORE.
←Leak Bucket

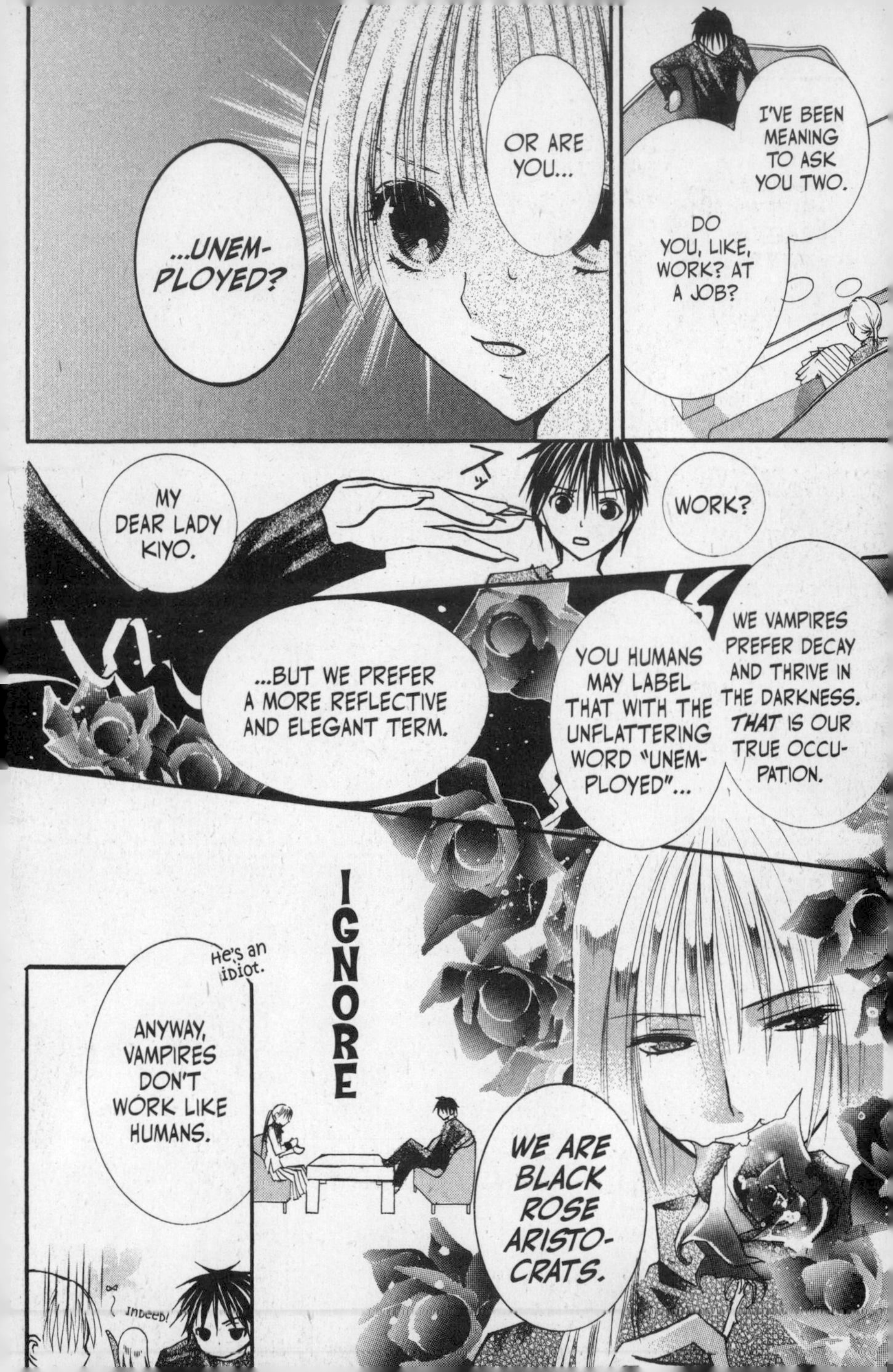
I'VE BEEN MEANING TO ASK YOU TWO.
DO YOU, LIKE, WORK? AT A JOB?
OR ARE YOU...
...UNEM-PLOYED?
WORK?
スッ
MY DEAR LADY KIYO.
WE VAMPIRES PREFER DECAY AND THRIVE IN THE DARKNESS. *THAT* IS OUR TRUE OCCU-PATION.
YOU HUMANS MAY LABEL THAT WITH THE UNFLATTERING WORD "UNEM-PLOYED"...
...BUT WE PREFER A MORE REFLECTIVE AND ELEGANT TERM.
WE ARE BLACK ROSE ARISTO-CRATS.
IGNORE
He's an idiot.
ANYWAY, VAMPIRES DON'T WORK LIKE HUMANS.
Indeed!

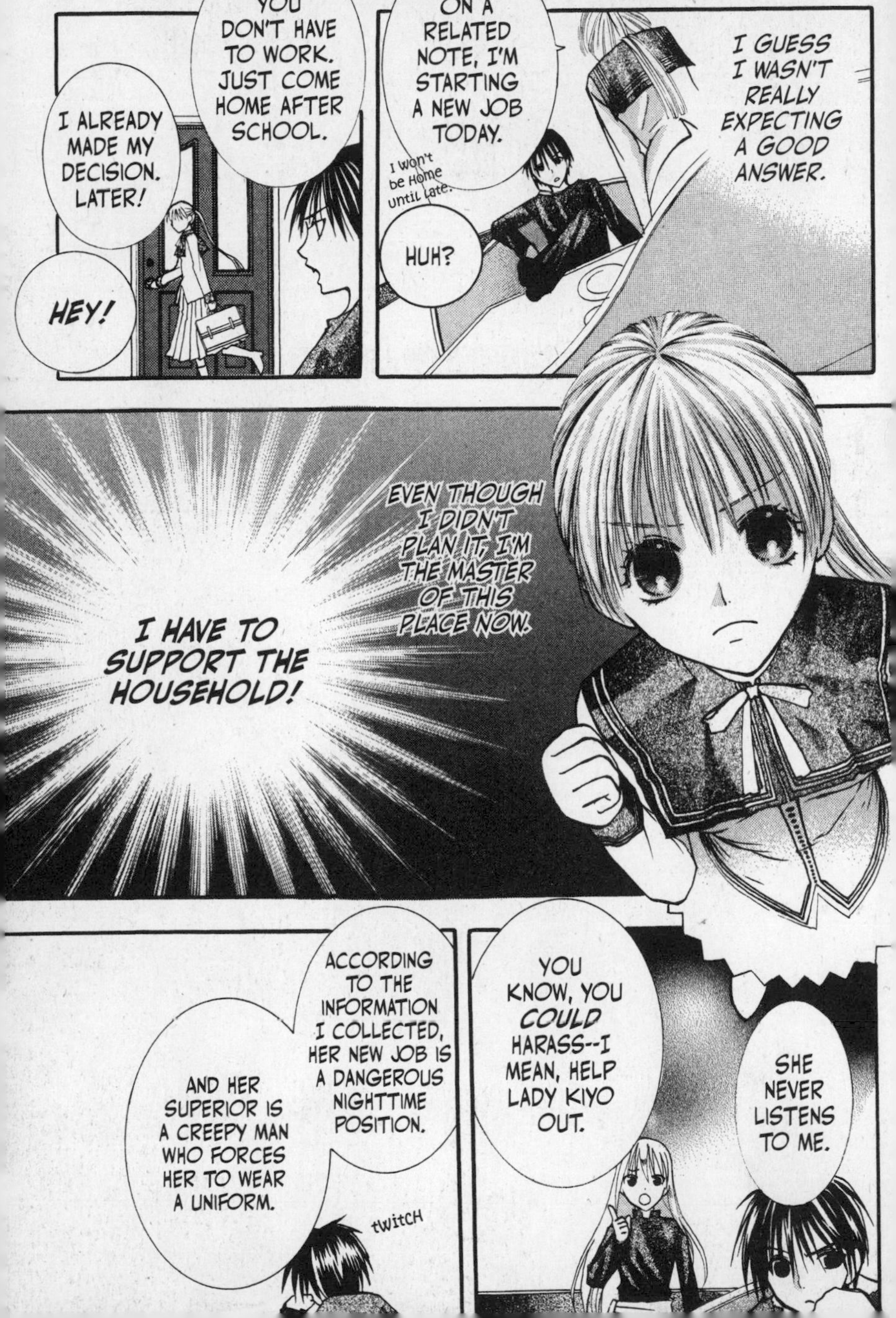

I GUESS I WASN'T REALLY EXPECTING A GOOD ANSWER.
ON A RELATED NOTE, I'M STARTING A NEW JOB TODAY.
I won't be Home Until late.
HUH?
YOU DON'T HAVE TO WORK. JUST COME HOME AFTER SCHOOL.
I ALREADY MADE MY DECISION. LATER!
HEY!
EVEN THOUGH I DIDN'T PLAN IT, I'M THE MASTER OF THIS PLACE NOW.
I HAVE TO SUPPORT THE HOUSEHOLD!
SHE NEVER LISTENS TO ME.
YOU KNOW, YOU COULD HARASS--I MEAN, HELP LADY KIYO OUT.
ACCORDING TO THE INFORMATION I COLLECTED, HER NEW JOB IS A DANGEROUS NIGHTTIME POSITION.
AND HER SUPERIOR IS A CREEPY MAN WHO FORCES HER TO WEAR A UNIFORM.
twitCH

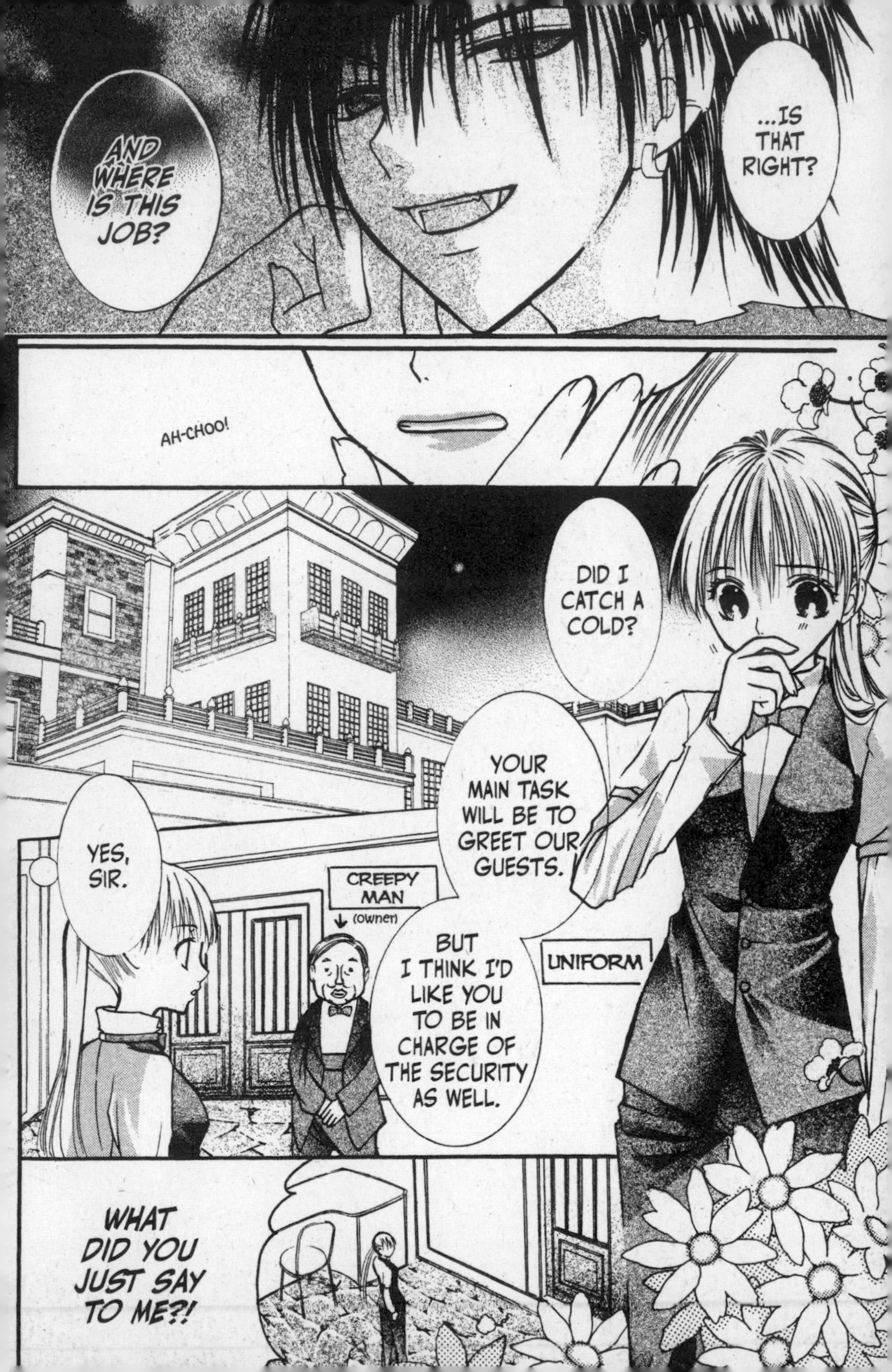
...IS THAT RIGHT?
AND WHERE IS THIS JOB?
AH-CHOO!
DID I CATCH A COLD?
YOUR MAIN TASK WILL BE TO GREET OUR GUESTS.
UNIFORM
BUT I THINK I'D LIKE YOU TO BE IN CHARGE OF THE SECURITY AS WELL.
CREEPY MAN
(Owner)
YES, SIR.
WHAT DID YOU JUST SAY TO ME?!

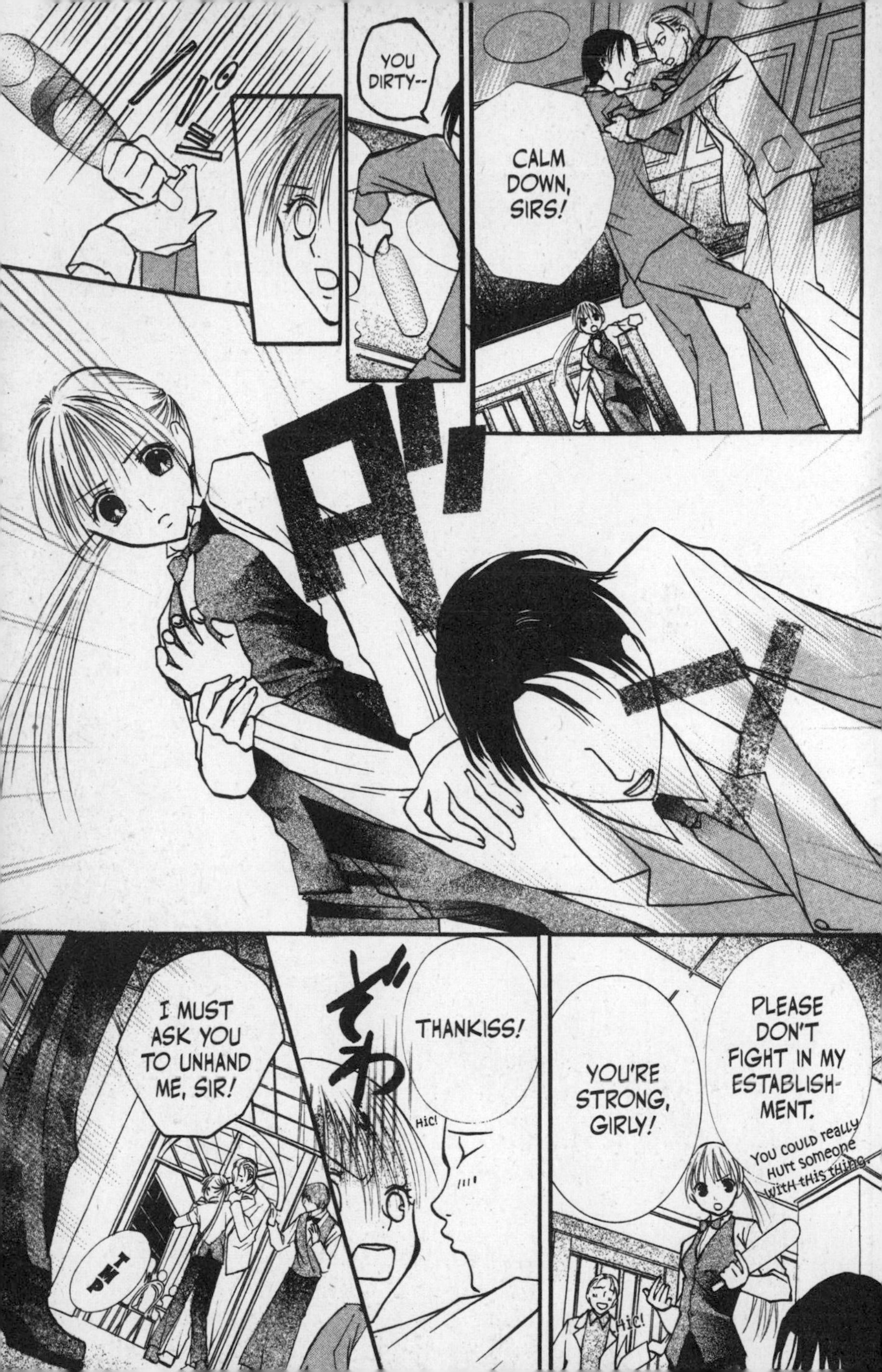
CALM DOWN, SIRS!
YOU DIRTY--
PLEASE DON'T FIGHT IN MY ESTABLISHMENT.
YOU'RE STRONG, GIRLY!
You could really hurt someone with this thing.
Hic!
THANKISS!
Hic!
I MUST ASK YOU TO UNHAND ME, SIR!
THMP

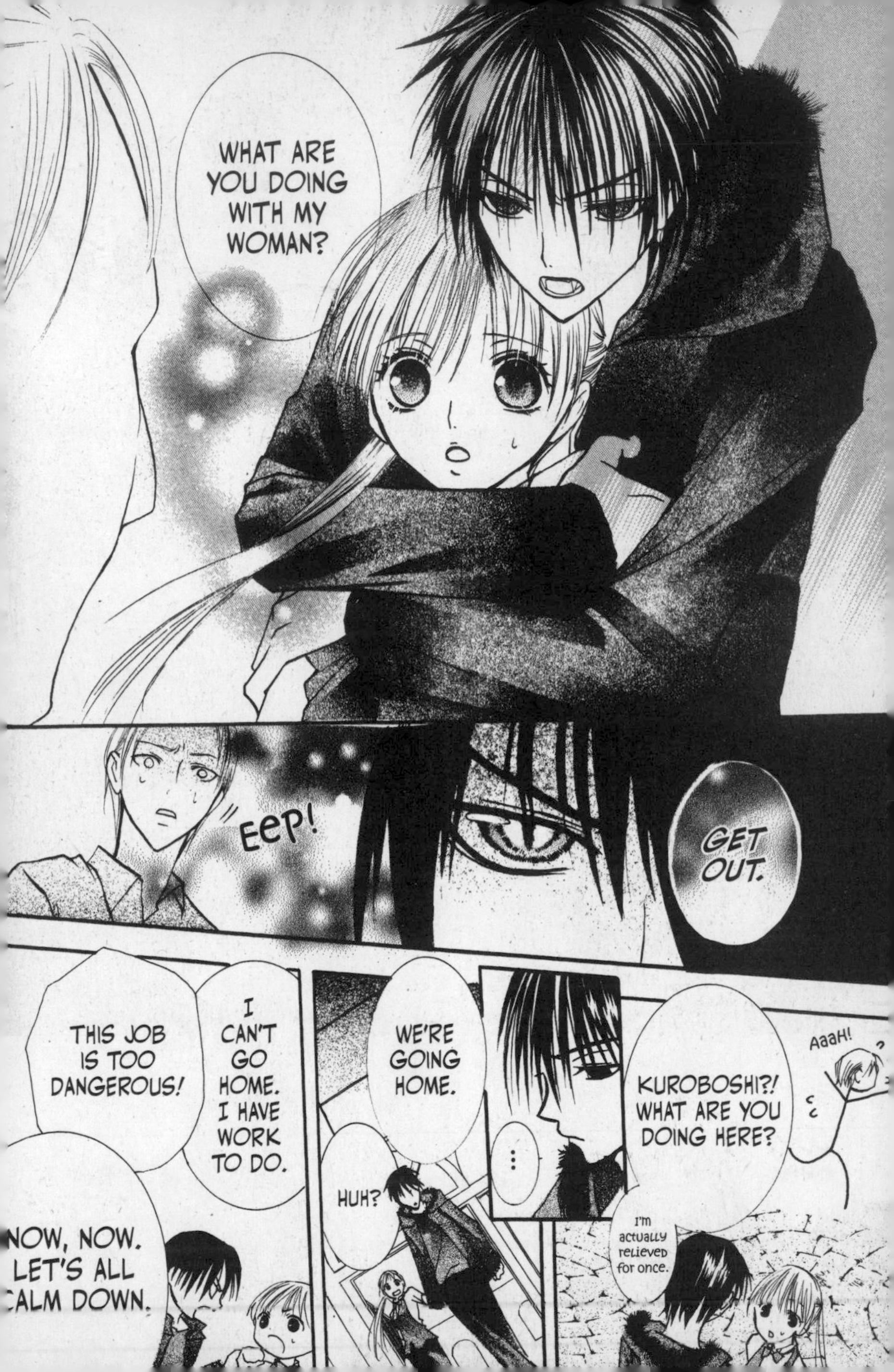
WHAT ARE YOU DOING WITH MY WOMAN?
GET OUT.
EEP!
AaaH!
KUROBOSHI?! WHAT ARE YOU DOING HERE?
I'm actually relieved for once.
...
WE'RE GOING HOME.
HUH?
I CAN'T GO HOME. I HAVE WORK TO DO.
THIS JOB IS TOO DANGEROUS!
NOW, NOW. LET'S ALL CALM DOWN.

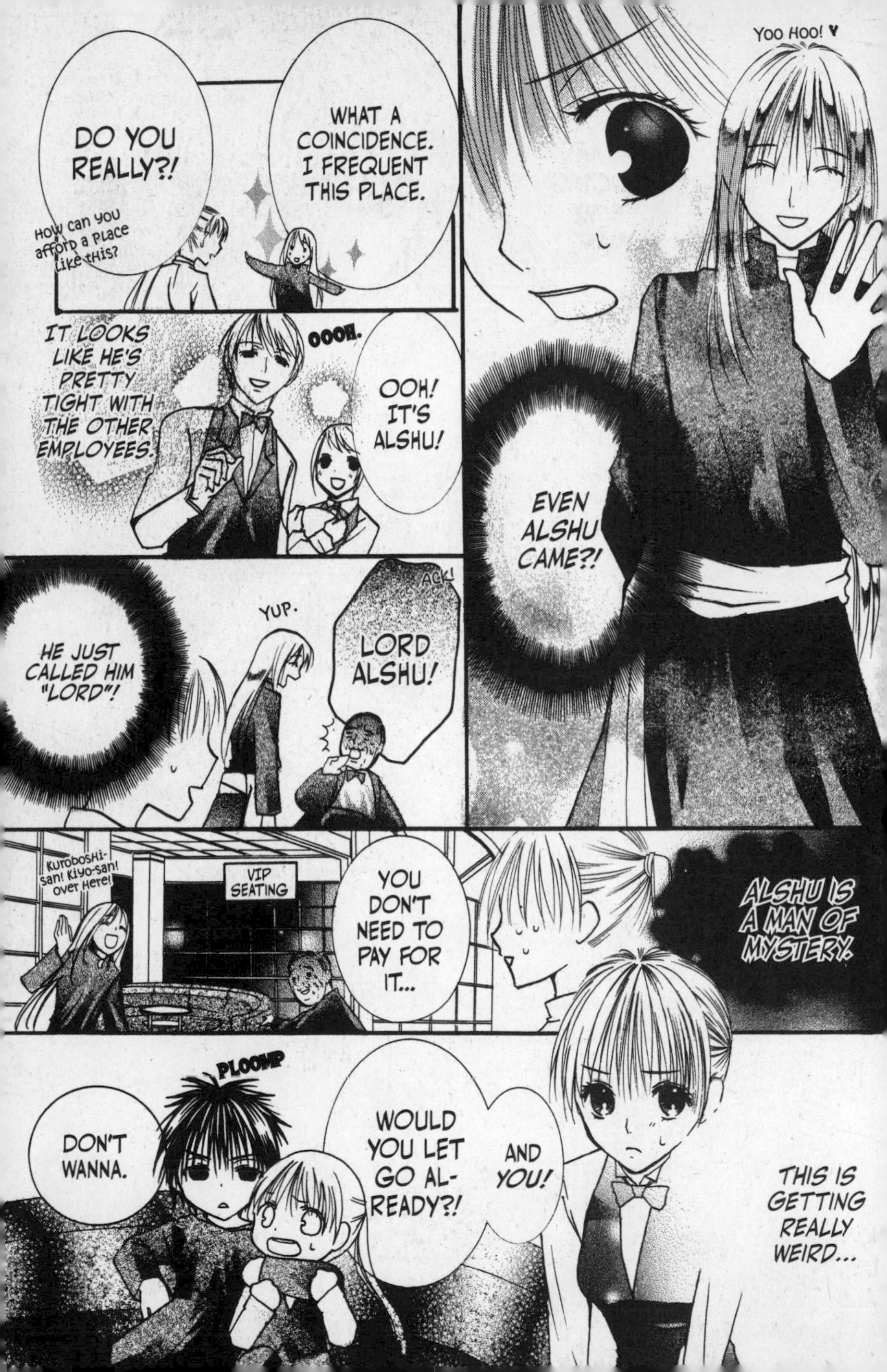
YOO HOO! ♥
EVEN ALSHU CAME?!
WHAT A COINCIDENCE. I FREQUENT THIS PLACE.
DO YOU REALLY?!
How can you afford a place like this?
OOH! IT'S ALSHU!
OOOH.
IT LOOKS LIKE HE'S PRETTY TIGHT WITH THE OTHER EMPLOYEES.
ACK!
LORD ALSHU!
YUP.
HE JUST CALLED HIM "LORD"!
ALSHU IS A MAN OF MYSTERY.
YOU DON'T NEED TO PAY FOR IT...
VIP SEATING
Kuroboshi-san! Kiyo-san! Over here!
THIS IS GETTING REALLY WEIRD...
AND YOU!
WOULD YOU LET GO AL-READY?!
PLOOMP
DON'T WANNA.

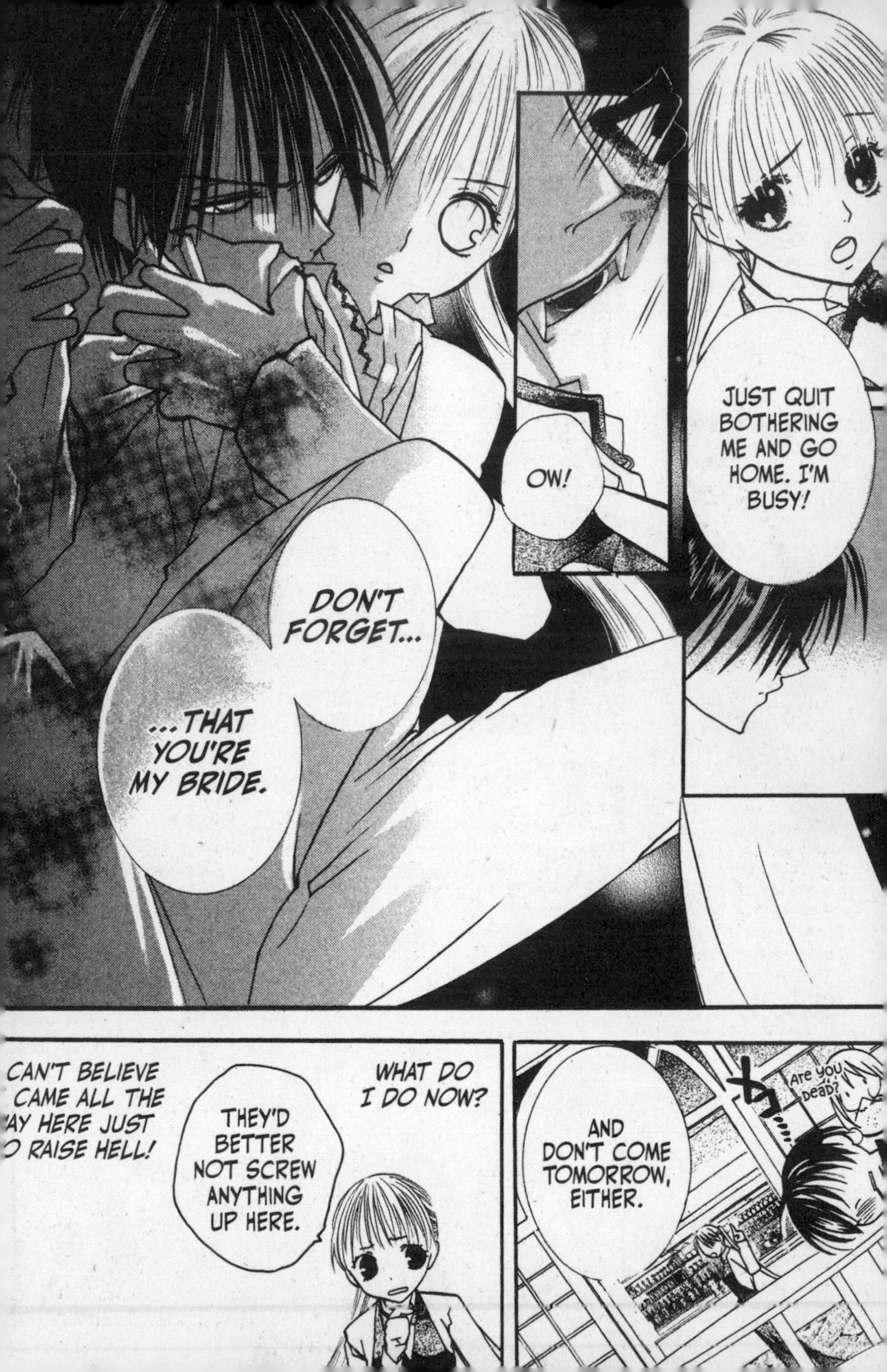
JUST QUIT BOTHERING ME AND GO HOME. I'M BUSY!
OW!
DON'T FORGET...
...THAT YOU'RE MY BRIDE.
Are you Dead?
AND DON'T COME TOMORROW, EITHER.
WHAT DO I DO NOW?
THEY'D BETTER NOT SCREW ANYTHING UP HERE.
CAN'T BELIEVE
CAME ALL THE
AY HERE JUST
O RAISE HELL!

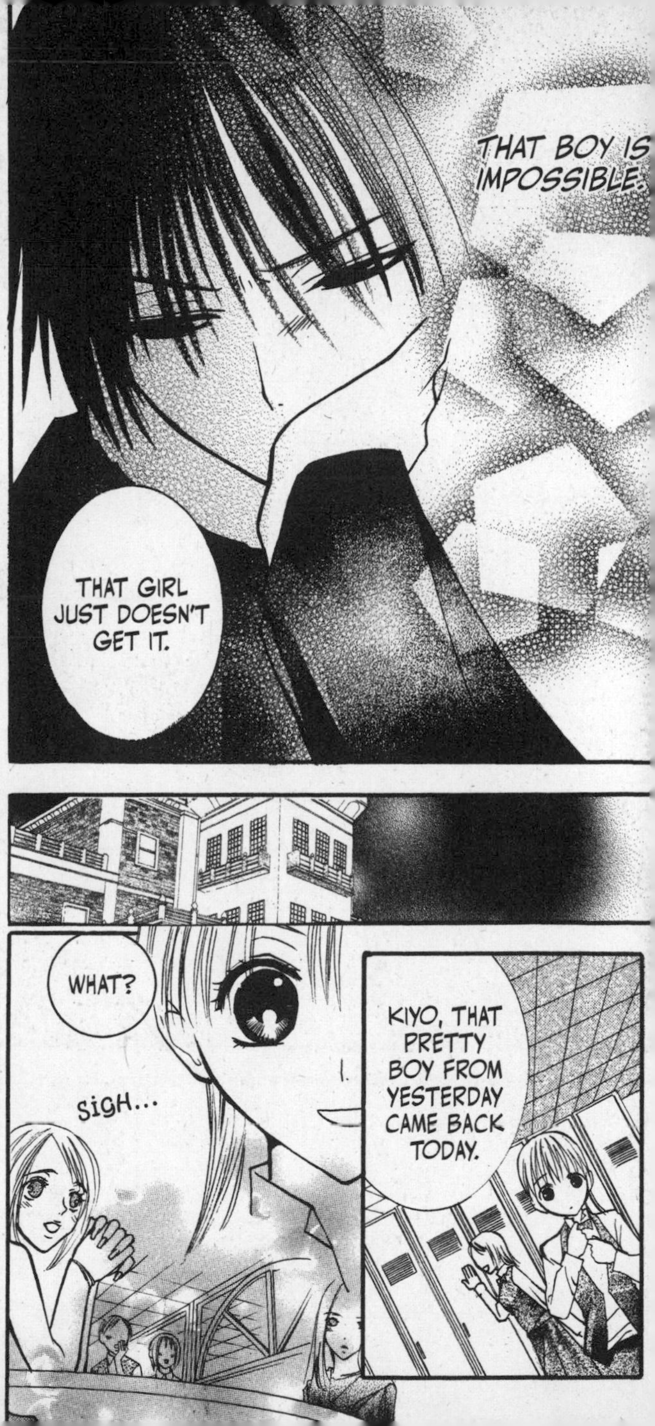
THAT BOY IS IMPOSSIBLE.
THAT GIRL JUST DOESN'T GET IT.
KIYO, THAT PRETTY BOY FROM YESTERDAY CAME BACK TODAY.
WHAT?
!
SIGH...

Lookie here! Kuroboshi's wardrobe... It's like he's wearing a unitard. That reminds me of a certain someone.

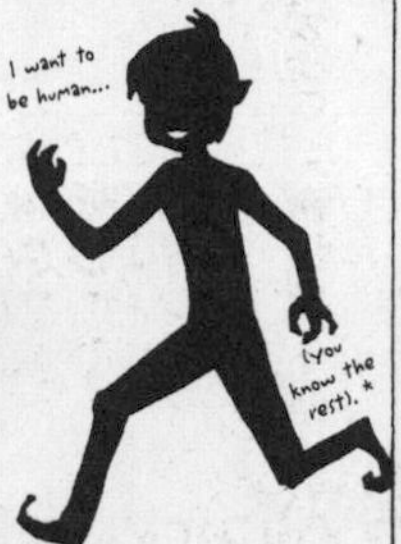
I want to be human...
(you know the rest). *

Kuroboshi has joined the undisclosed humanoid team. I really can't think of anything else clever to dress the boys in. I'm totally not interested in men's fashion. But I figured it was too cruel to keep Kuroboshi in a unitard, and so I tried my best after Third Kiss. Still, my agonizing over clothes is finally ending. Kuroboshi will transform into a uniform-wearing character! (That makes no sense.) That's right--Kuroboshi will be wearing uniforms after Fourth Kiss. I was so excited, I designed the uniform myself. I even went ahead and made colored cover art.

...However, even this solution had its downfall...

* Note: This is a reference to a Japanese anime "Humanoid Monster Bem." The ongoing theme/motto of this anime is "I want to be human soon."

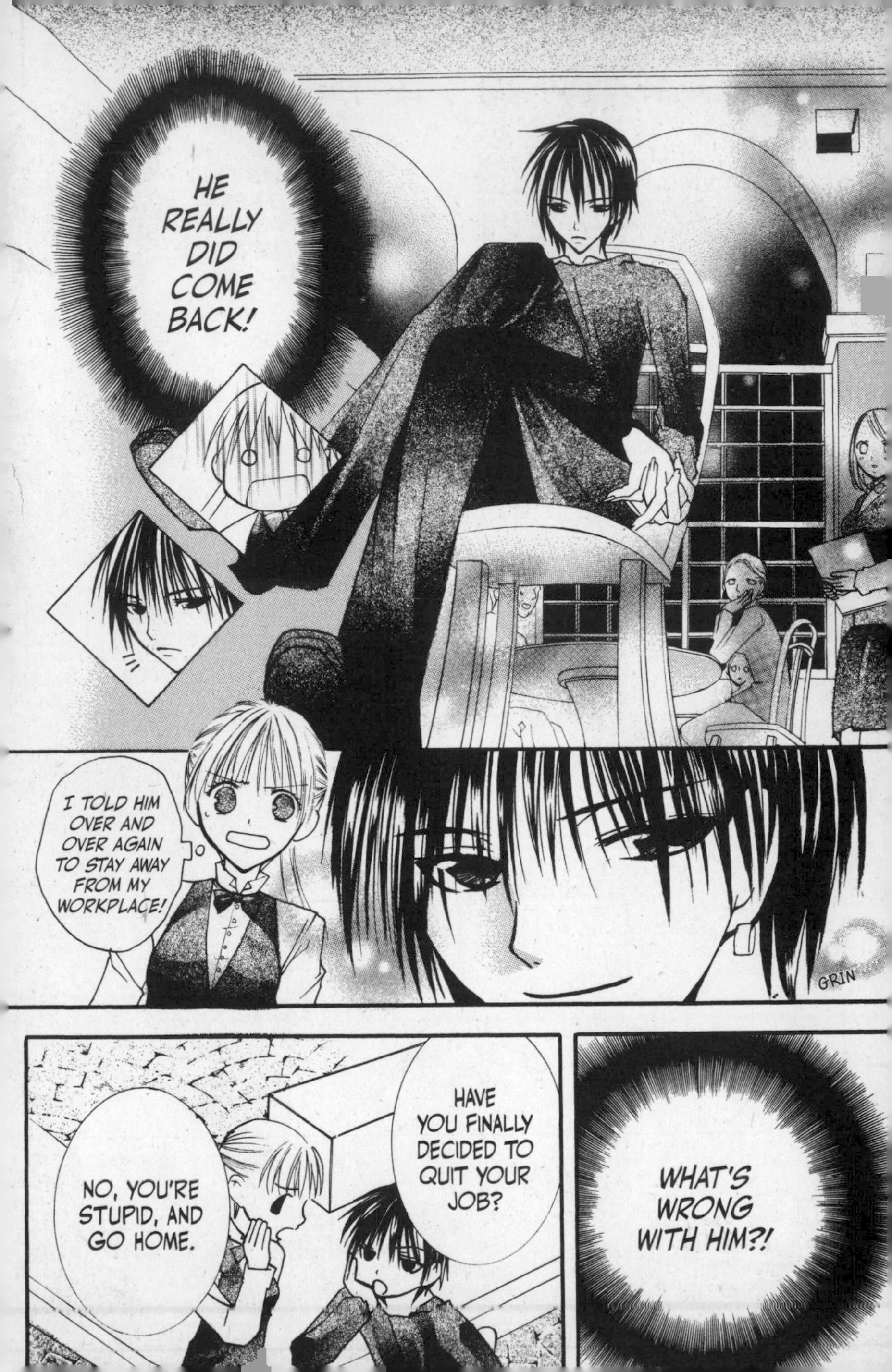
HE REALLY DID COME BACK!
I TOLD HIM OVER AND OVER AGAIN TO STAY AWAY FROM MY WORKPLACE!
GRIN
WHAT'S WRONG WITH HIM?!
HAVE YOU FINALLY DECIDED TO QUIT YOUR JOB?
NO, YOU'RE STUPID, AND GO HOME.

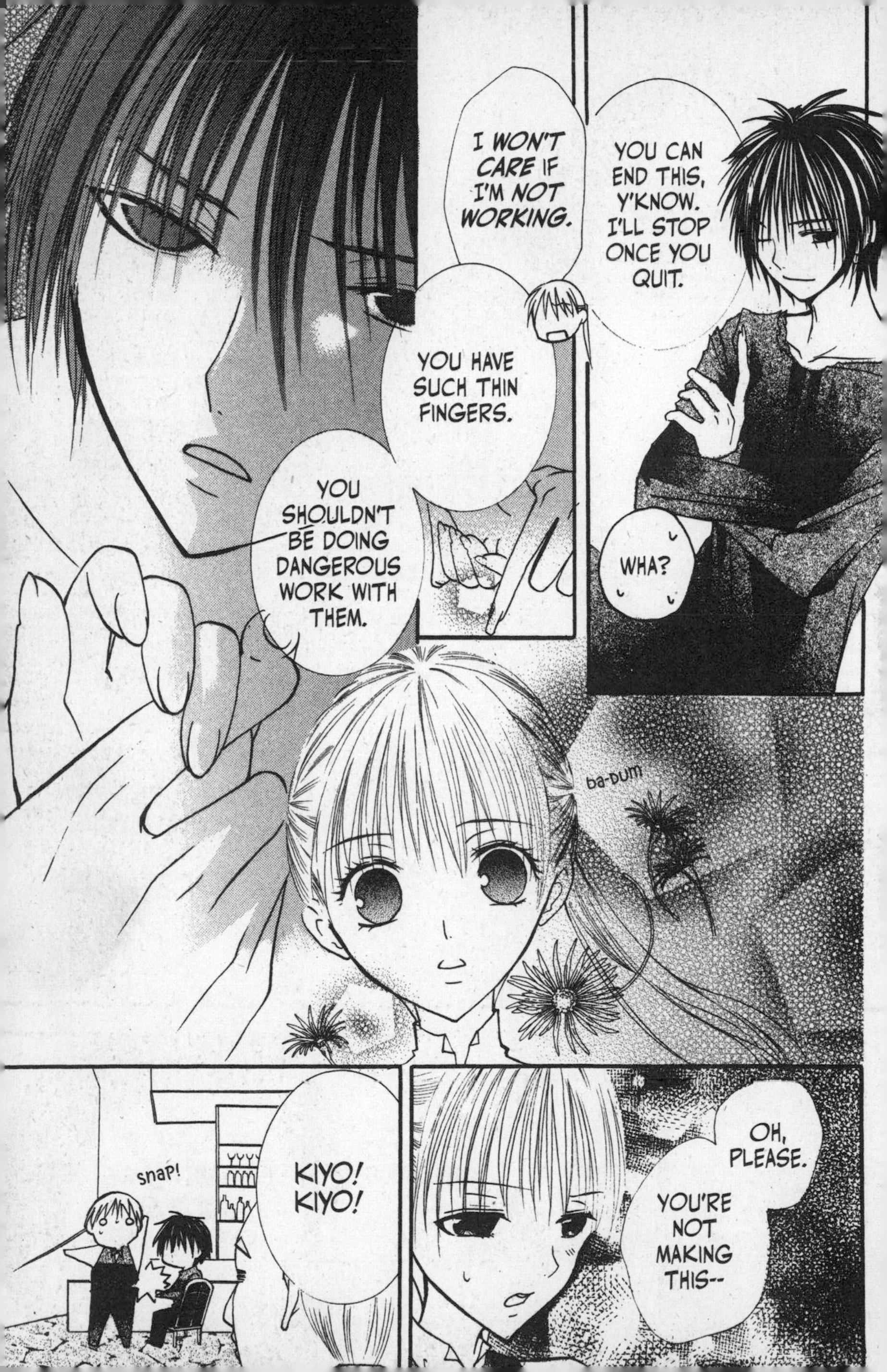
YOU CAN END THIS, Y'KNOW. I'LL STOP ONCE YOU QUIT.
WHA?
I *WON'T CARE* IF I'M *NOT WORKING.*
YOU HAVE SUCH THIN FINGERS.
YOU SHOULDN'T BE DOING DANGEROUS WORK WITH THEM.
ba-dum
OH, PLEASE.
YOU'RE NOT MAKING THIS--
KIYO! KIYO!
snap!

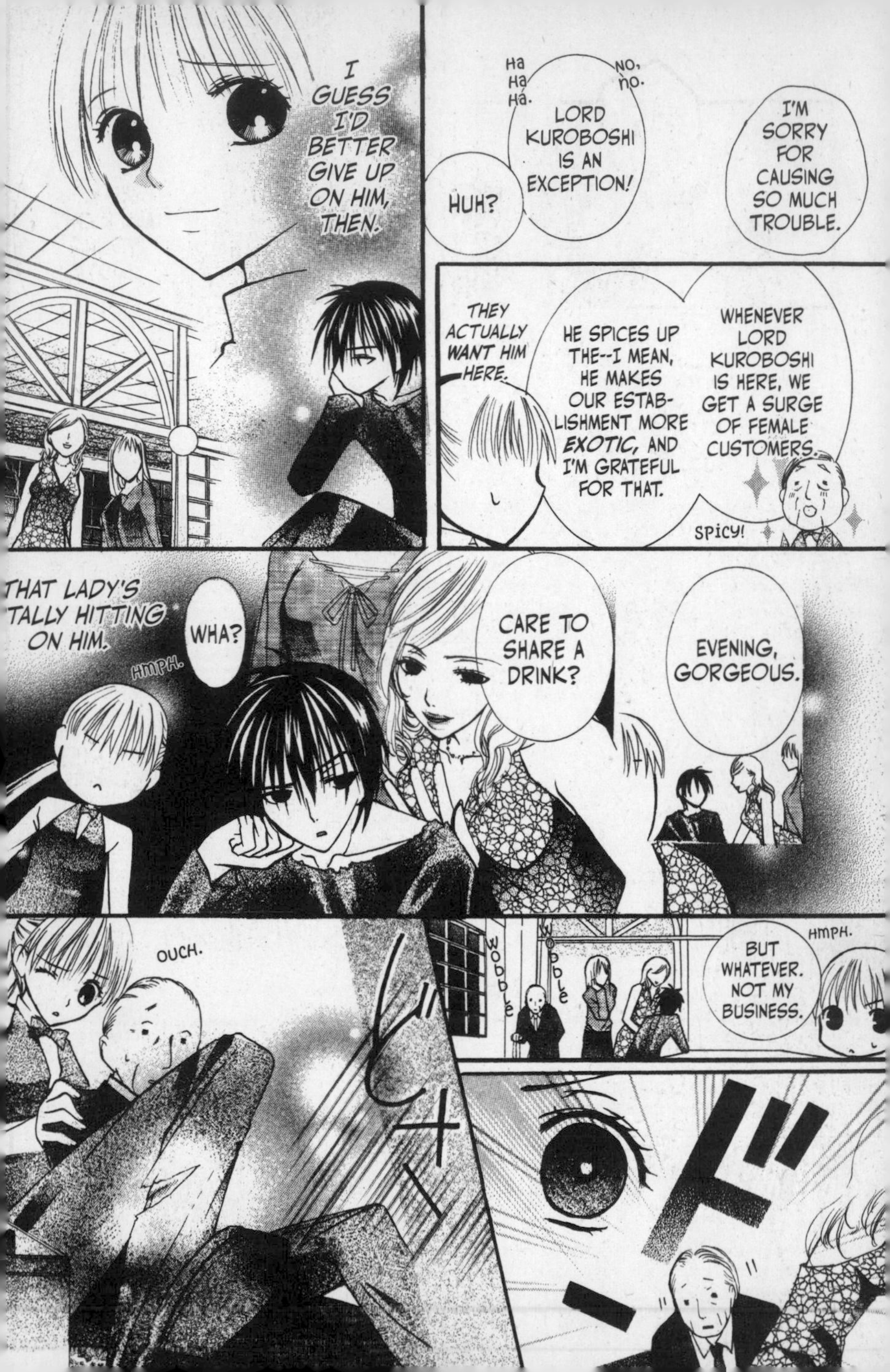
I'M SORRY FOR CAUSING SO MUCH TROUBLE.
NO, NO.
HA HA HA.
LORD KUROBOSHI IS AN EXCEPTION!
HUH?
WHENEVER LORD KUROBOSHI IS HERE, WE GET A SURGE OF FEMALE CUSTOMERS.
SPICY!
HE SPICES UP THE--I MEAN, HE MAKES OUR ESTAB-LISHMENT MORE *EXOTIC,* AND I'M GRATEFUL FOR THAT.
THEY ACTUALLY *WANT* HIM HERE.
I GUESS I'D BETTER GIVE UP ON HIM, THEN.
EVENING, GORGEOUS.
CARE TO SHARE A DRINK?
WHA?
HMPH.
THAT LADY'S TALLY HITTING ON HIM.
HMPH.
BUT WHATEVER. NOT MY BUSINESS.
WOBBLE
WOBBLE
OUCH.
ド

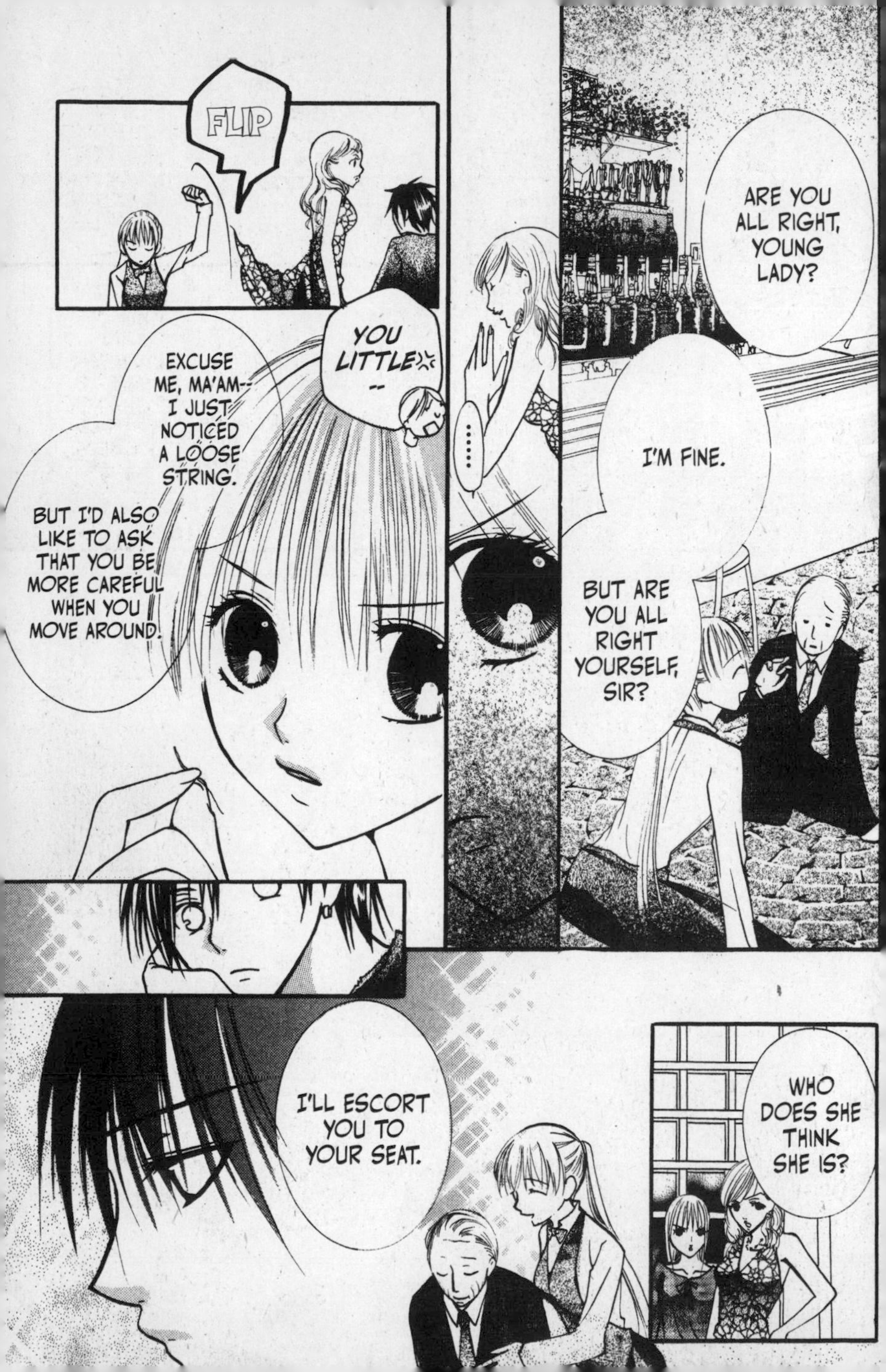
ARE YOU ALL RIGHT, YOUNG LADY?
I'M FINE.
BUT ARE YOU ALL RIGHT YOURSELF, SIR?
......
FLIP
YOU LITTLE--
EXCUSE ME, MA'AM-- I JUST NOTICED A LOOSE STRING.
BUT I'D ALSO LIKE TO ASK THAT YOU BE MORE CAREFUL WHEN YOU MOVE AROUND.
WHO DOES SHE THINK SHE IS?
I'LL ESCORT YOU TO YOUR SEAT.

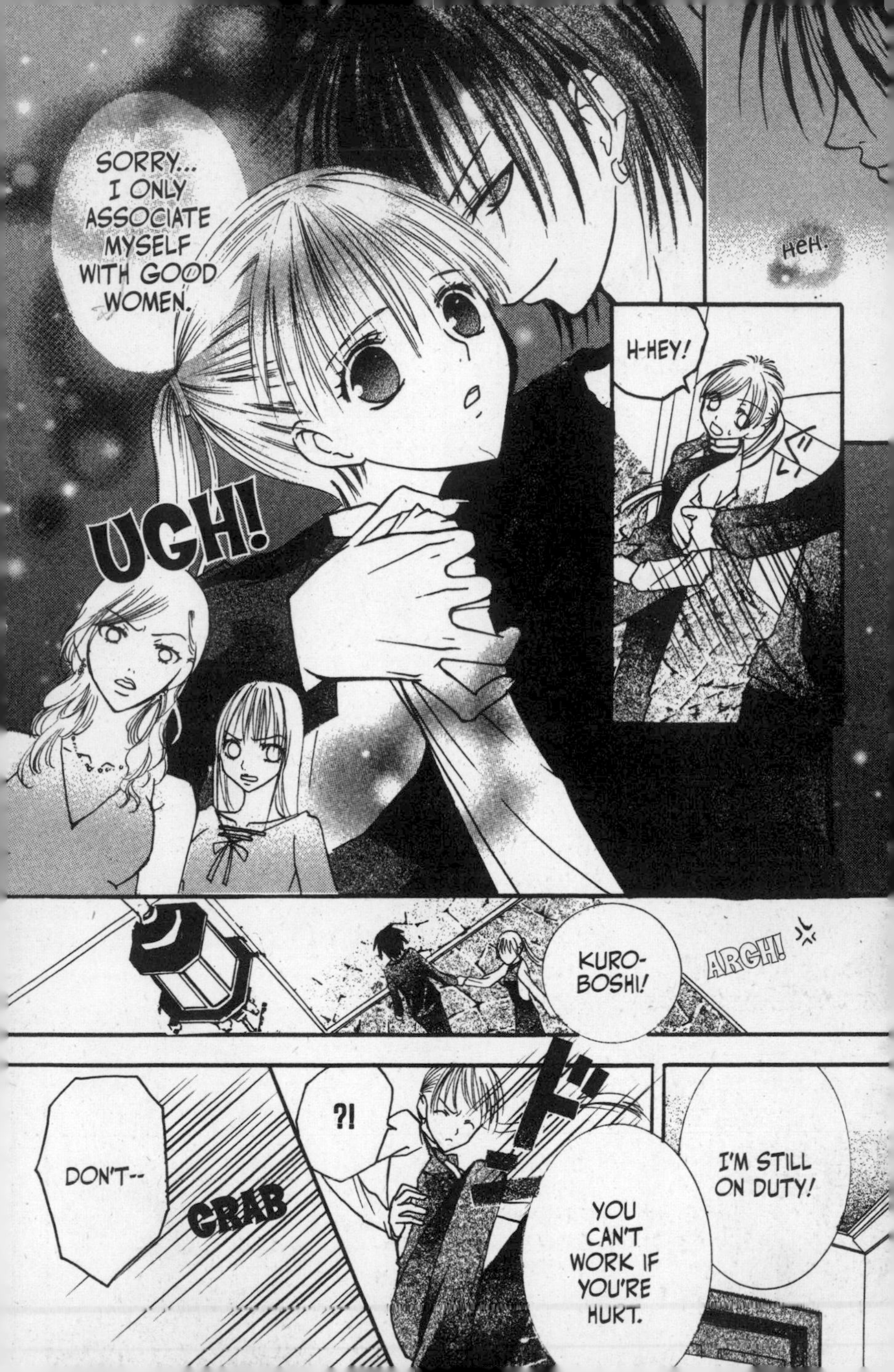
HEH.
SORRY... I ONLY ASSOCIATE MYSELF WITH GOOD WOMEN.
UGH!
H-HEY!
ARGH!
KURO-BOSHI!
I'M STILL ON DUTY!
YOU CAN'T WORK IF YOU'RE HURT.
?!
GRAB
DON'T--

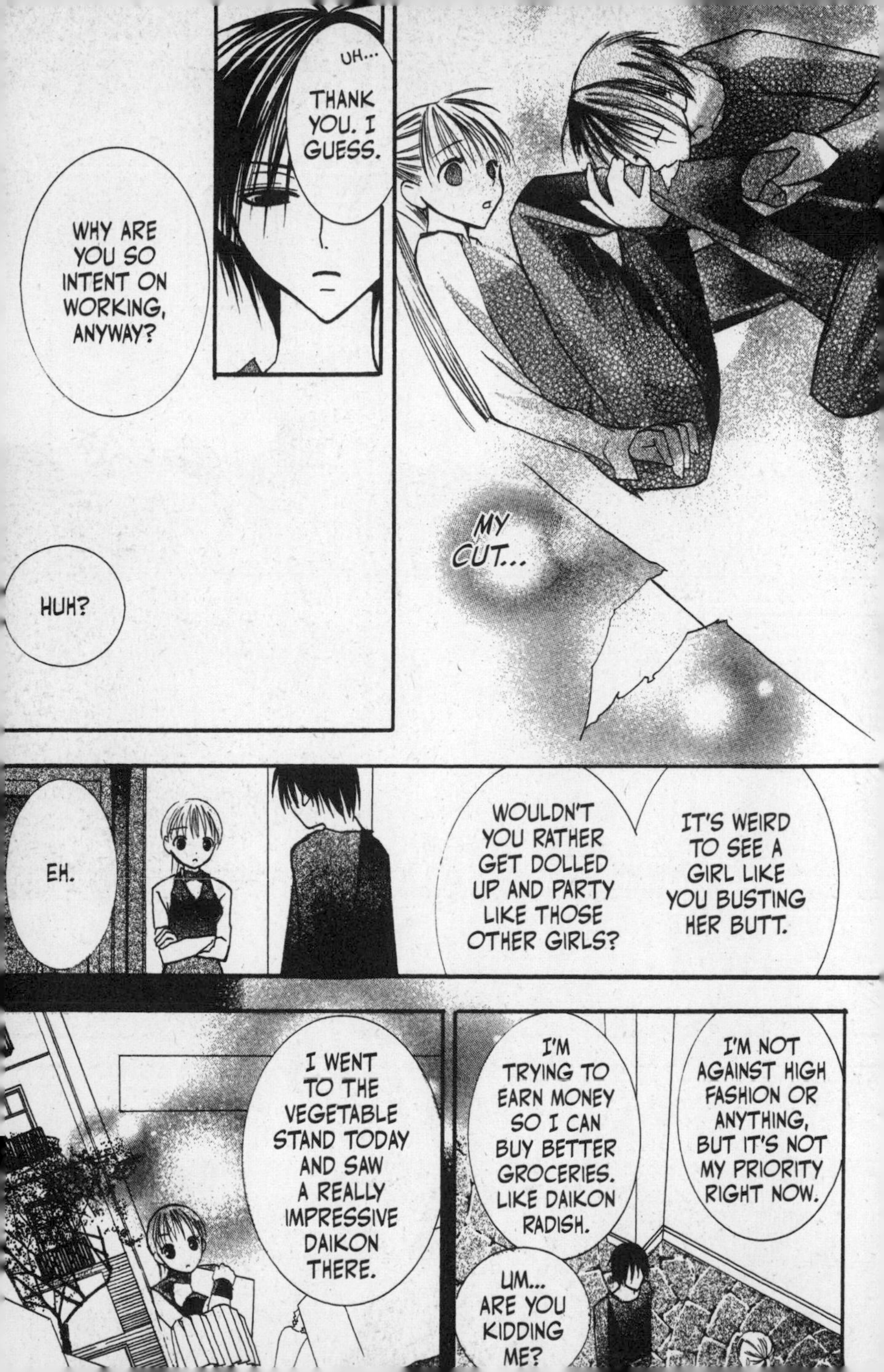
MY CUT...
UH...
THANK YOU. I GUESS.
WHY ARE YOU SO INTENT ON WORKING, ANYWAY?
HUH?
IT'S WEIRD TO SEE A GIRL LIKE YOU BUSTING HER BUTT.
WOULDN'T YOU RATHER GET DOLLED UP AND PARTY LIKE THOSE OTHER GIRLS?
EH.
I'M NOT AGAINST HIGH FASHION OR ANYTHING, BUT IT'S NOT MY PRIORITY RIGHT NOW.
I'M TRYING TO EARN MONEY SO I CAN BUY BETTER GROCERIES. LIKE DAIKON RADISH.
UM... ARE YOU KIDDING ME?
I WENT TO THE VEGETABLE STAND TODAY AND SAW A REALLY IMPRESSIVE DAIKON THERE.

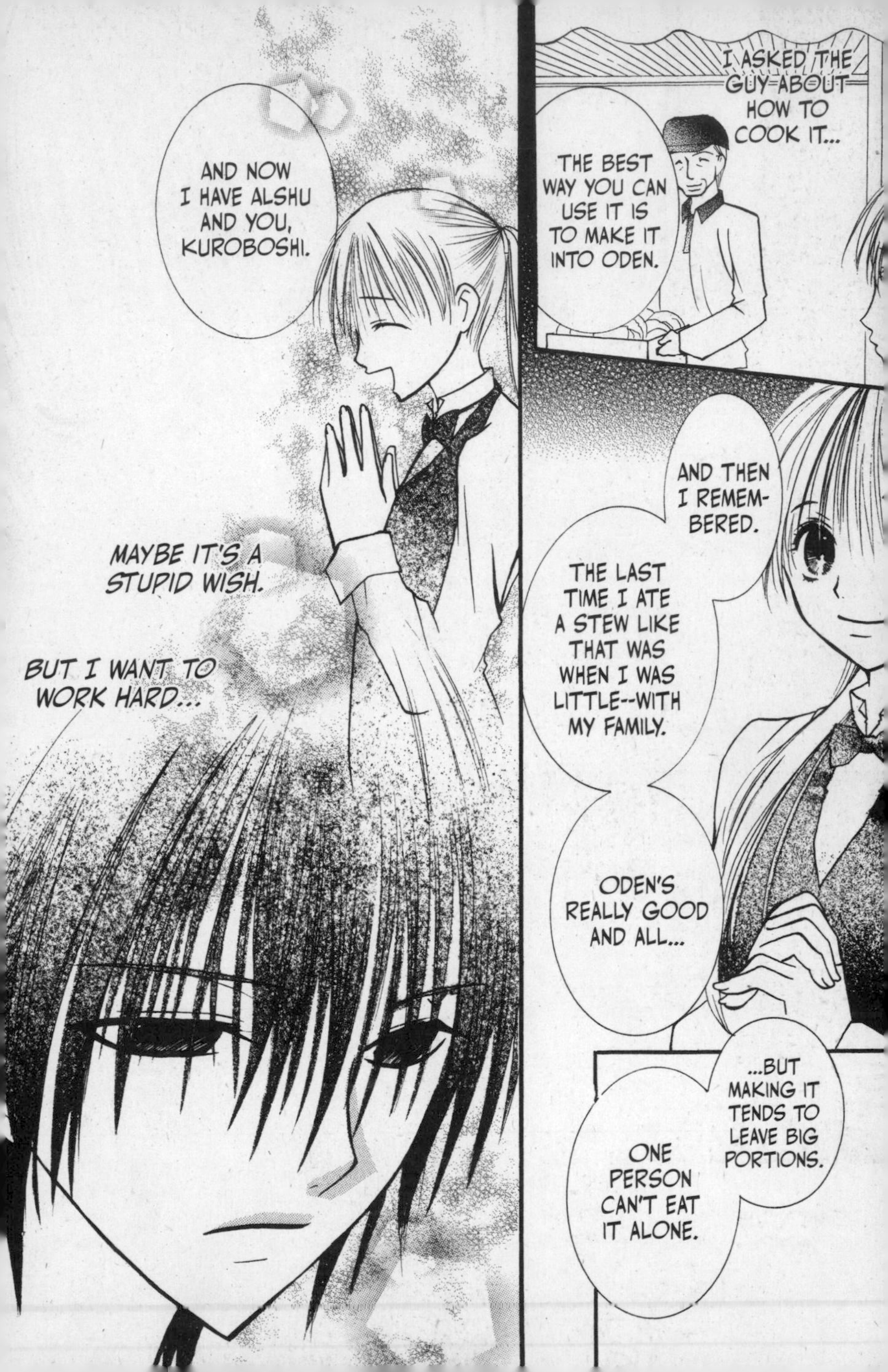
I ASKED THE GUY ABOUT HOW TO COOK IT...
THE BEST WAY YOU CAN USE IT IS TO MAKE IT INTO ODEN.
AND THEN I REMEMBERED.
THE LAST TIME I ATE A STEW LIKE THAT WAS WHEN I WAS LITTLE--WITH MY FAMILY.
ODEN'S REALLY GOOD AND ALL...
...BUT MAKING IT TENDS TO LEAVE BIG PORTIONS.
ONE PERSON CAN'T EAT IT ALONE.
AND NOW I HAVE ALSHU AND YOU, KUROBOSHI.
MAYBE IT'S A STUPID WISH.
BUT I WANT TO WORK HARD...

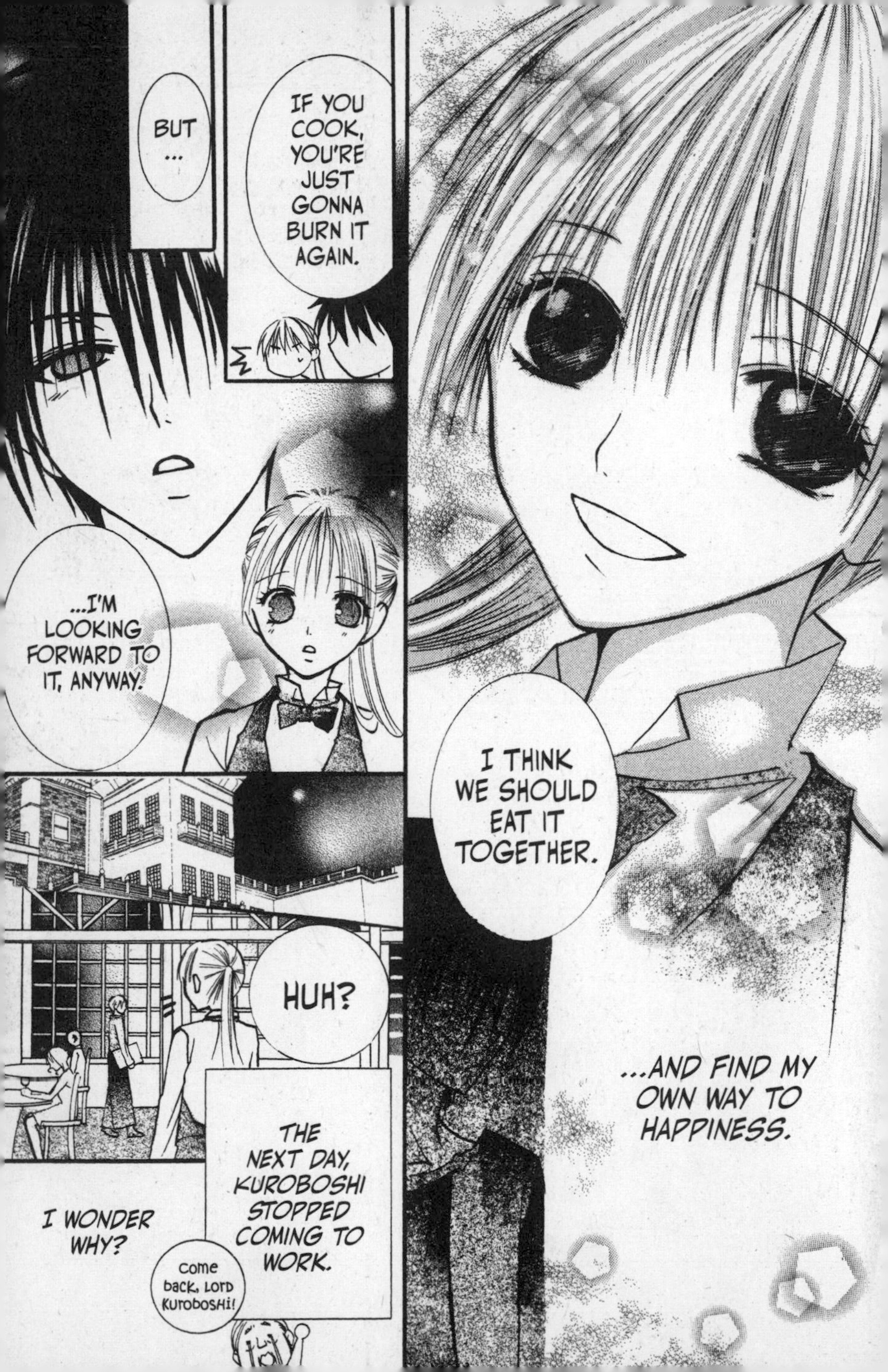
I THINK WE SHOULD EAT IT TOGETHER.
...AND FIND MY OWN WAY TO HAPPINESS.
IF YOU COOK, YOU'RE JUST GONNA BURN IT AGAIN.
BUT ...
...I'M LOOKING FORWARD TO IT, ANYWAY.
HUH?
THE NEXT DAY, KUROBOSHI STOPPED COMING TO WORK.
I WONDER WHY?
Come back, Lord Kuroboshi!

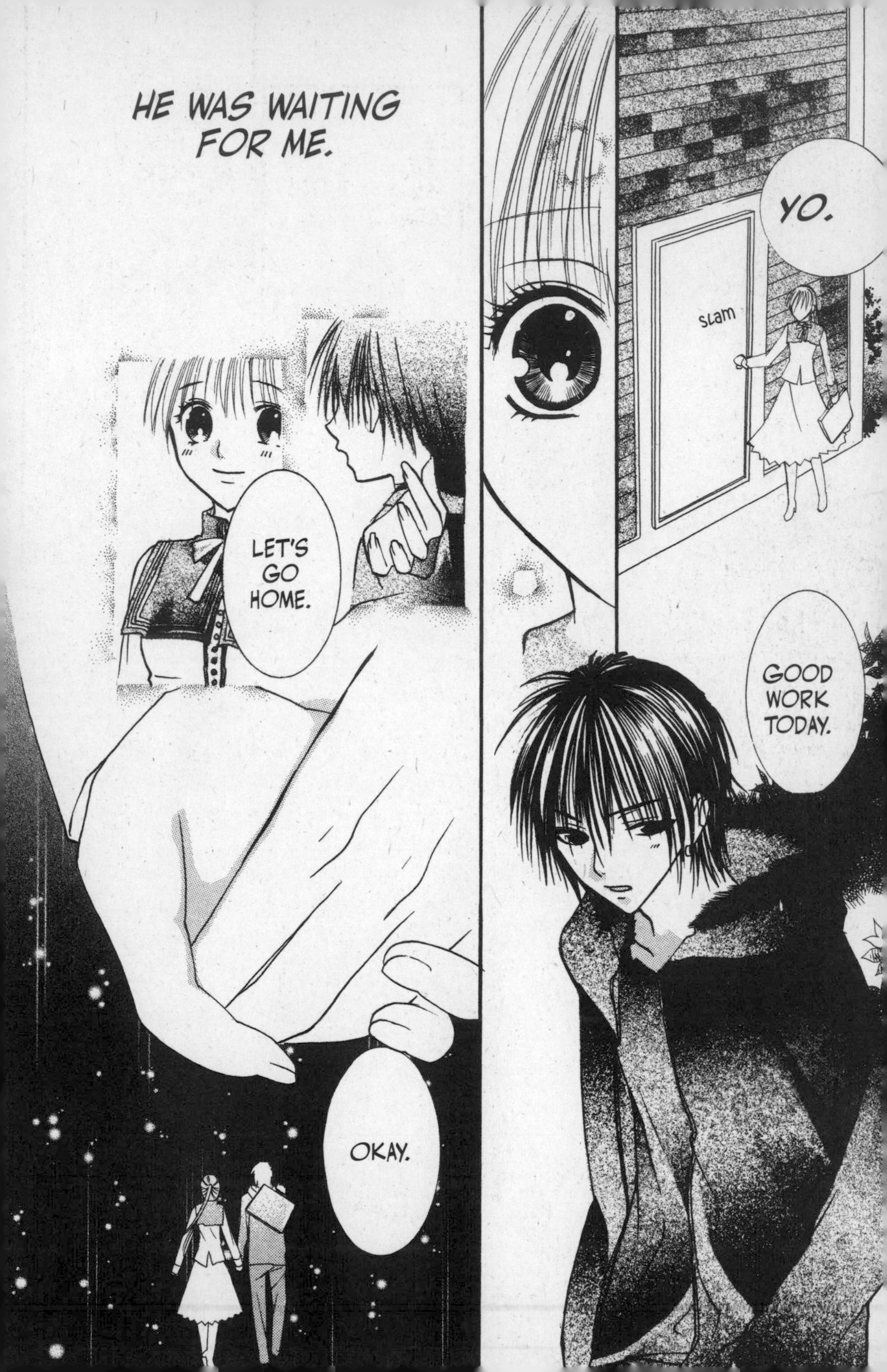
YO.
slam
GOOD WORK TODAY.
HE WAS WAITING FOR ME.
LET'S GO HOME.
OKAY.

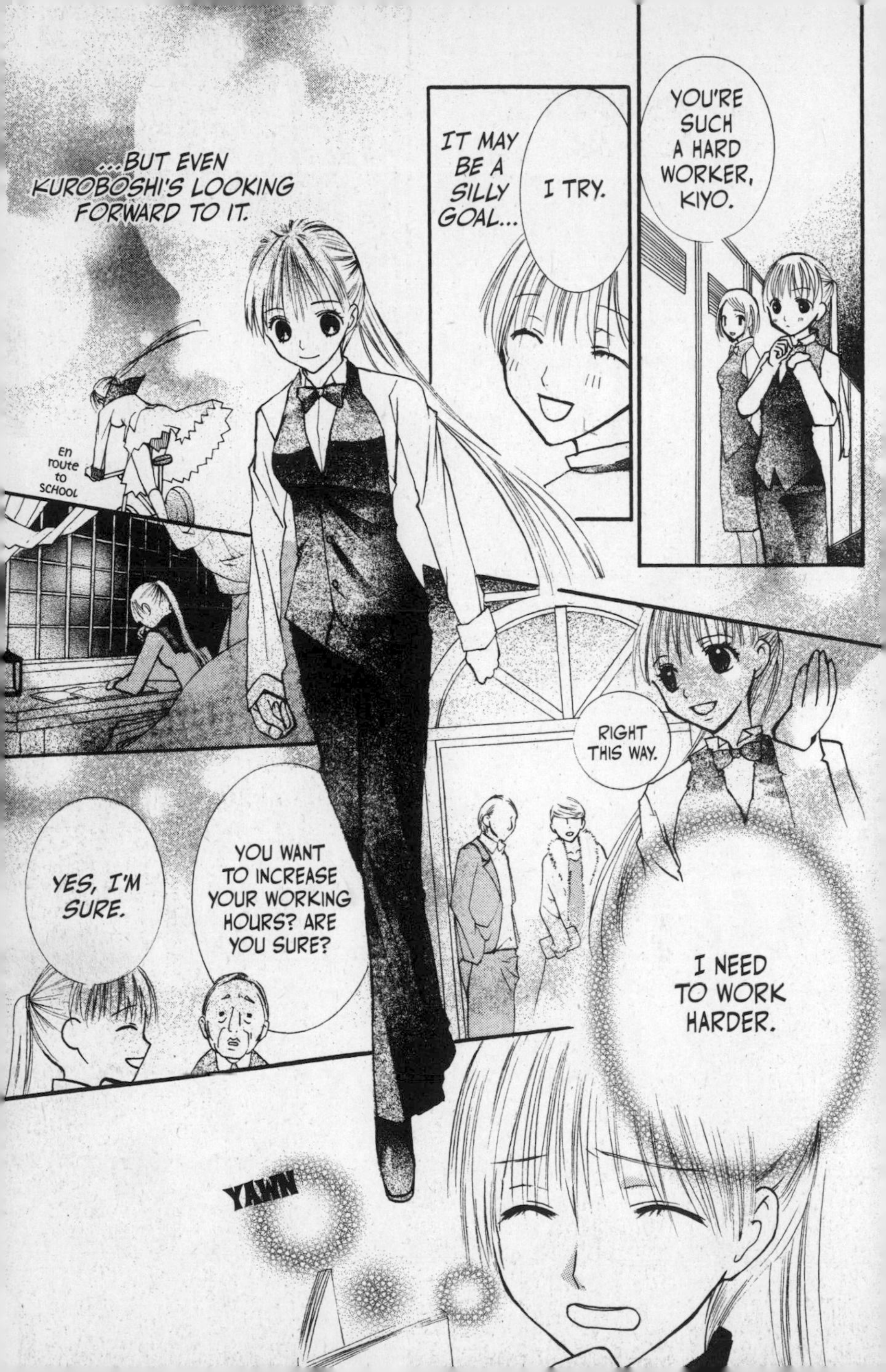
YOU'RE SUCH A HARD WORKER, KIYO.
I TRY.
IT MAY BE A SILLY GOAL...
...BUT EVEN KUROBOSHI'S LOOKING FORWARD TO IT.
En route to SCHOOL
RIGHT THIS WAY.
YOU WANT TO INCREASE YOUR WORKING HOURS? ARE YOU SURE?
YES, I'M SURE.
I NEED TO WORK HARDER.
YAWN

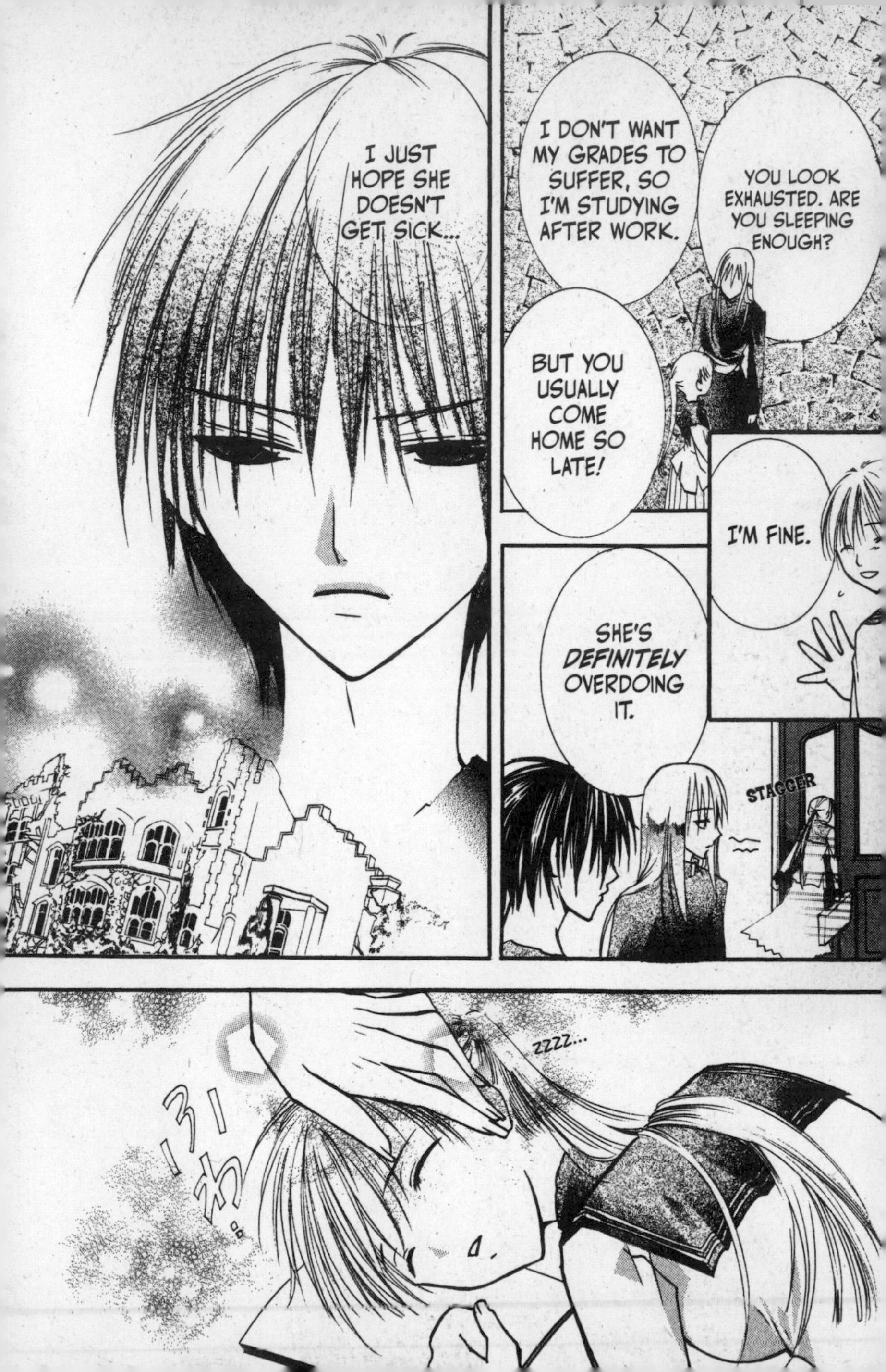
YOU LOOK EXHAUSTED. ARE YOU SLEEPING ENOUGH?
I DON'T WANT MY GRADES TO SUFFER, SO I'M STUDYING AFTER WORK.
BUT YOU USUALLY COME HOME SO LATE!
I'M FINE.
SHE'S DEFINITELY OVERDOING IT.
STAGGER
I JUST HOPE SHE DOESN'T GET SICK...
ZZZZ...

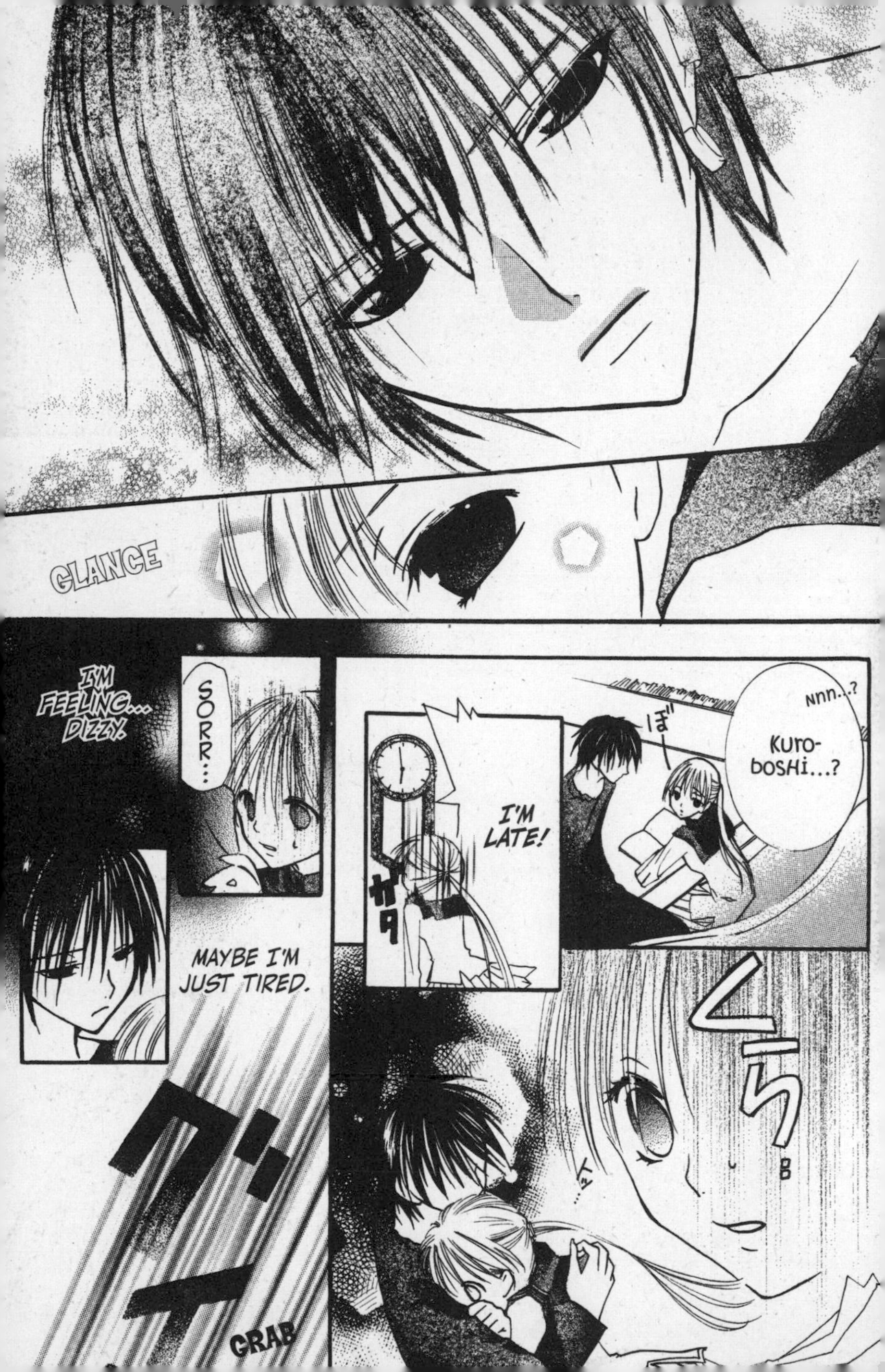
GLANCE
Nnn...?
Kuro-boshi...?
ぼー
I'M LATE!
ガタ
SORR...
I'M FEELING... DIZZY.
MAYBE I'M JUST TIRED.
くら
GRAB

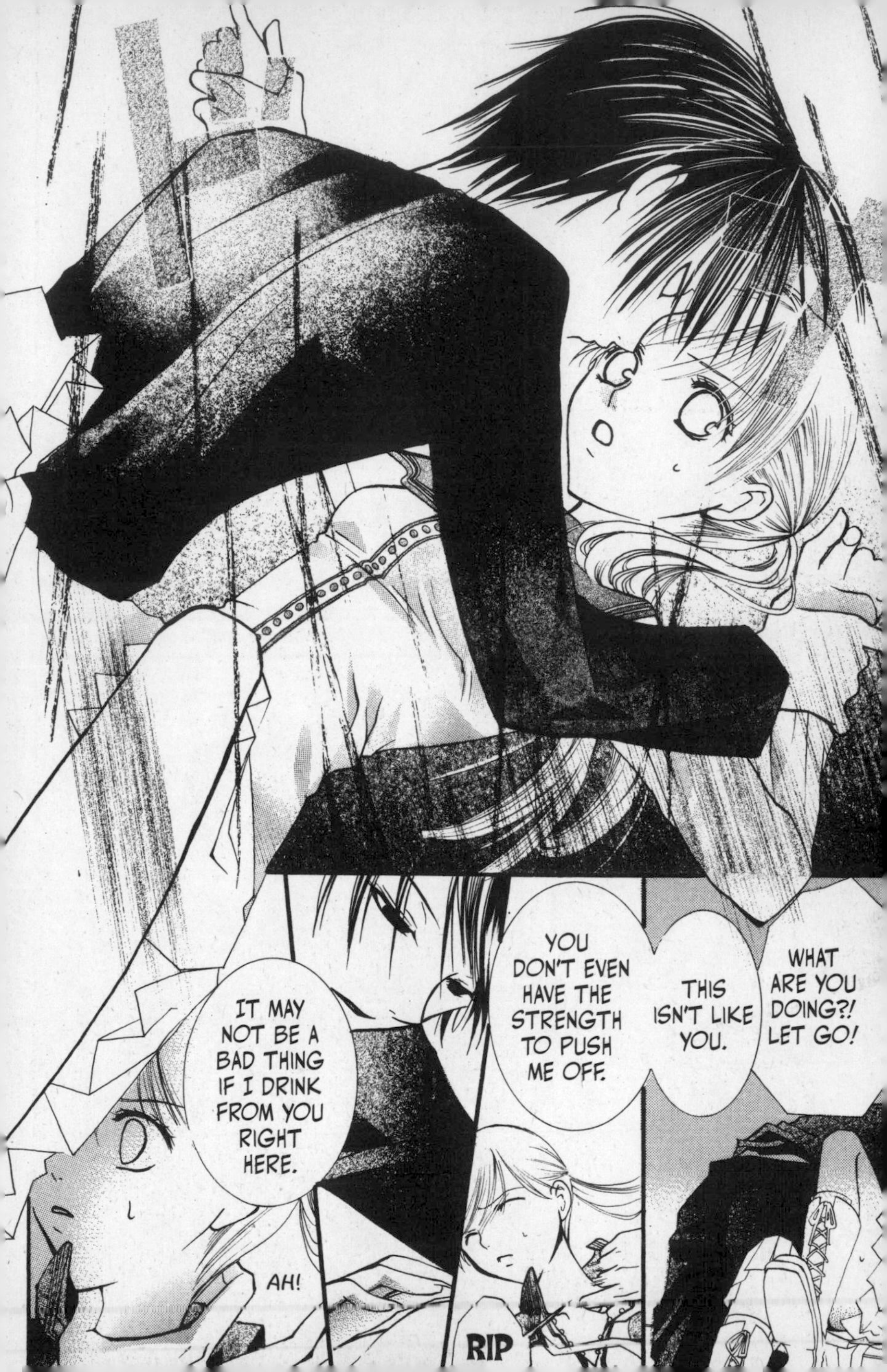
WHAT ARE YOU DOING?! LET GO!
THIS ISN'T LIKE YOU.
YOU DON'T EVEN HAVE THE STRENGTH TO PUSH ME OFF.
RIP
IT MAY NOT BE A BAD THING IF I DRINK FROM YOU RIGHT HERE.
AH!

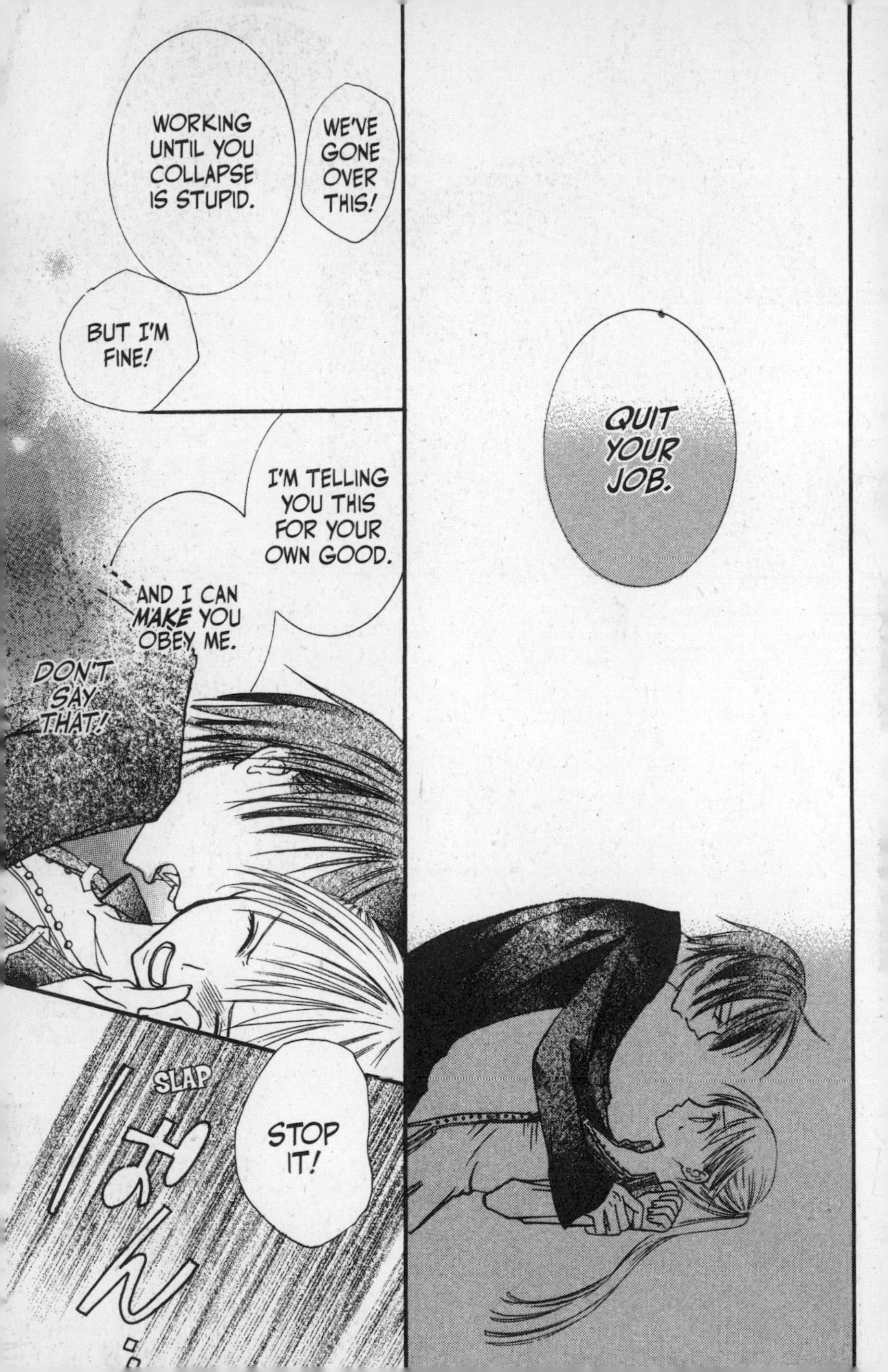
QUIT YOUR JOB.
WE'VE GONE OVER THIS!
WORKING UNTIL YOU COLLAPSE IS STUPID.
BUT I'M FINE!
I'M TELLING YOU THIS FOR YOUR OWN GOOD.
AND I CAN *MAKE* YOU OBEY ME.
DON'T SAY THAT!
STOP IT!
SLAP
ぱん

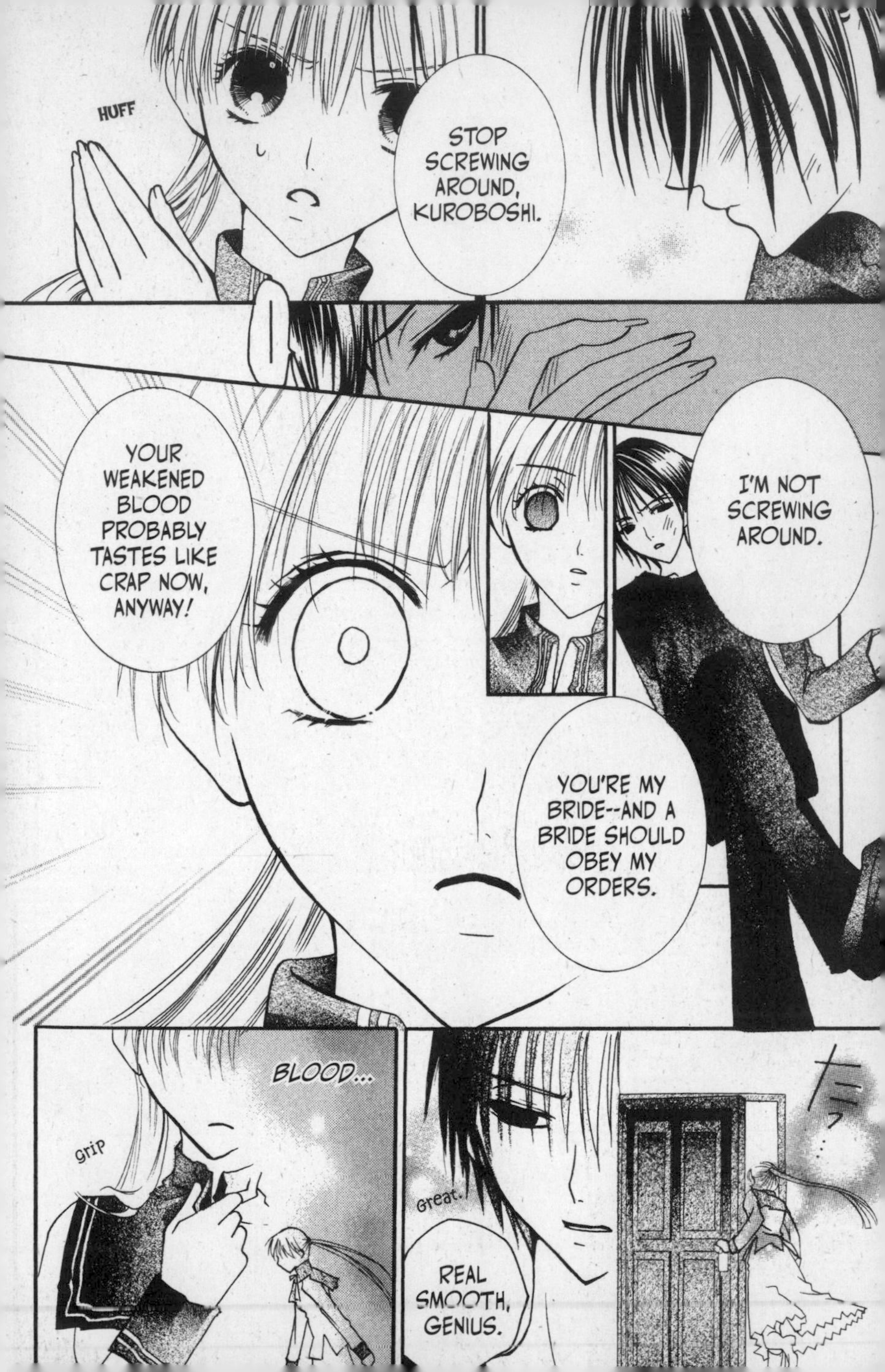
STOP SCREWING AROUND, KUROBOSHI.
HUFF
I'M NOT SCREWING AROUND.
YOU'RE MY BRIDE--AND A BRIDE SHOULD OBEY MY ORDERS.
YOUR WEAKENED BLOOD PROBABLY TASTES LIKE CRAP NOW, ANYWAY!
Great.
REAL SMOOTH, GENIUS.
BLOOD...
grip

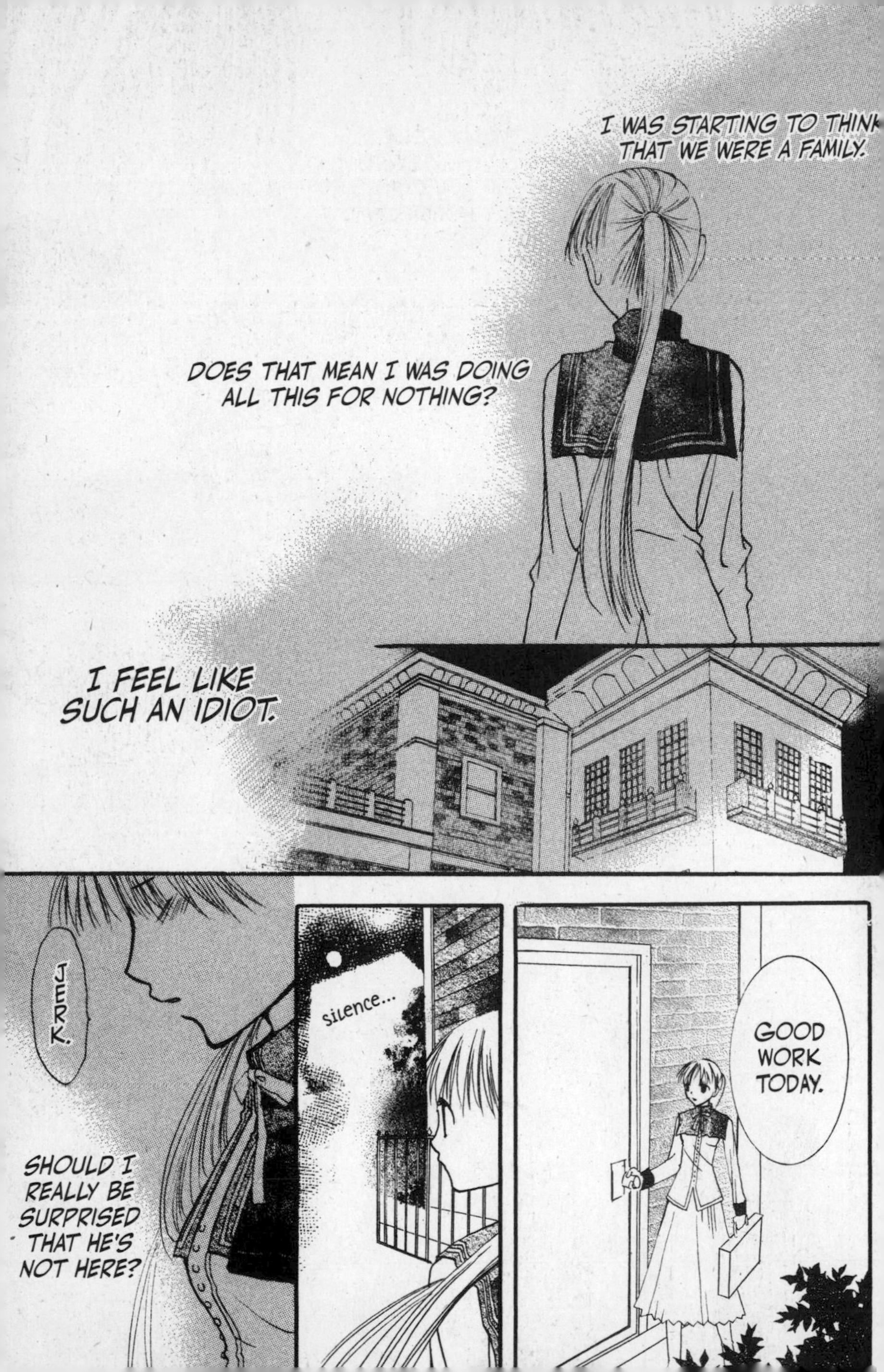
I WAS STARTING TO THINK THAT WE WERE A FAMILY.
DOES THAT MEAN I WAS DOING ALL THIS FOR NOTHING?
I FEEL LIKE SUCH AN IDIOT.
GOOD WORK TODAY.
silence...
JERK.
SHOULD I REALLY BE SURPRISED THAT HE'S NOT HERE?

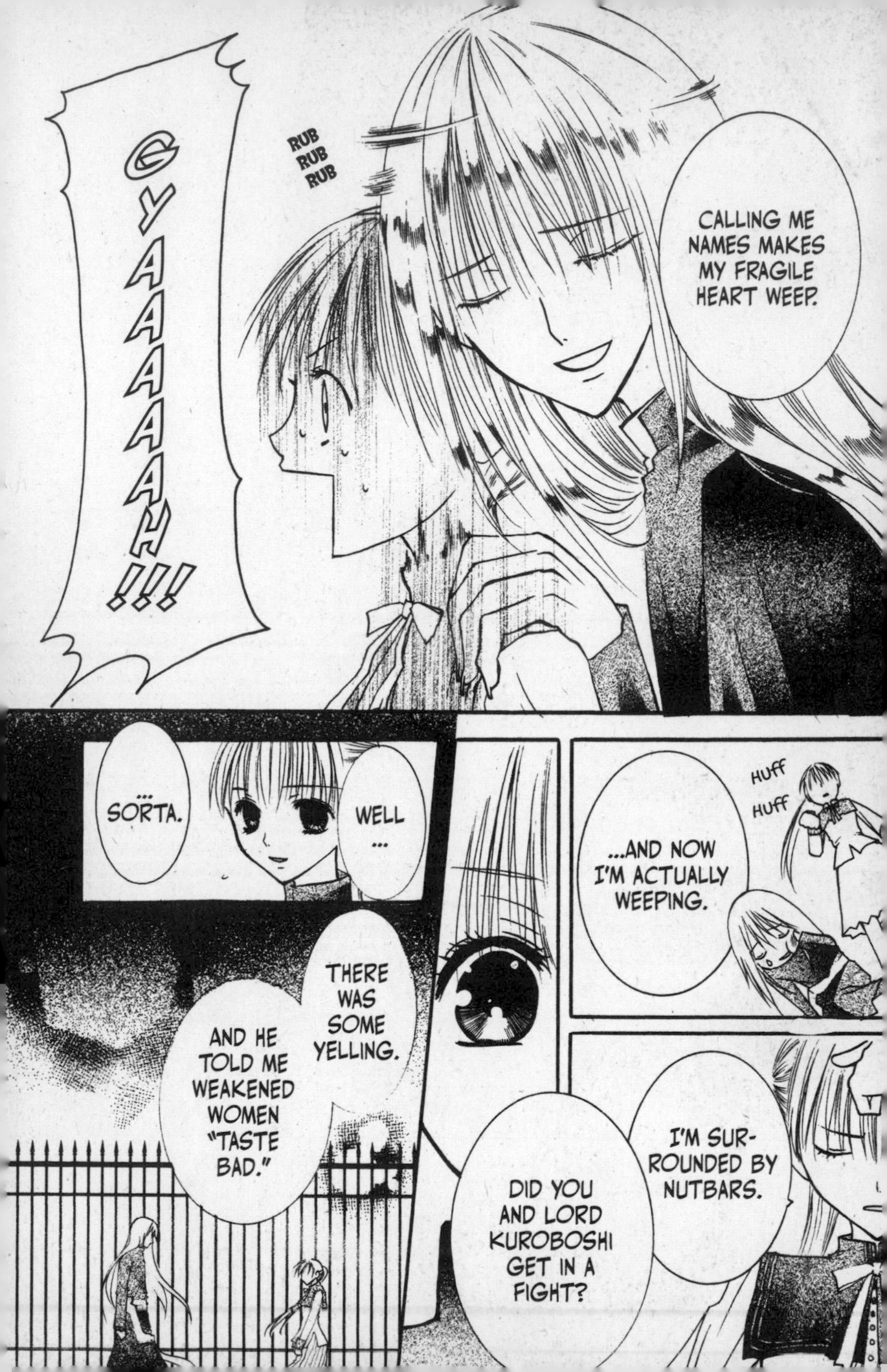
CALLING ME NAMES MAKES MY FRAGILE HEART WEEP.
RUB RUB RUB
GYAAAAAH!!!
...AND NOW I'M ACTUALLY WEEPING.
HUFF HUFF
I'M SUR-ROUNDED BY NUTBARS.
DID YOU AND LORD KUROBOSHI GET IN A FIGHT?
WELL ...
... SORTA.
THERE WAS SOME YELLING.
AND HE TOLD ME WEAKENED WOMEN "TASTE BAD."

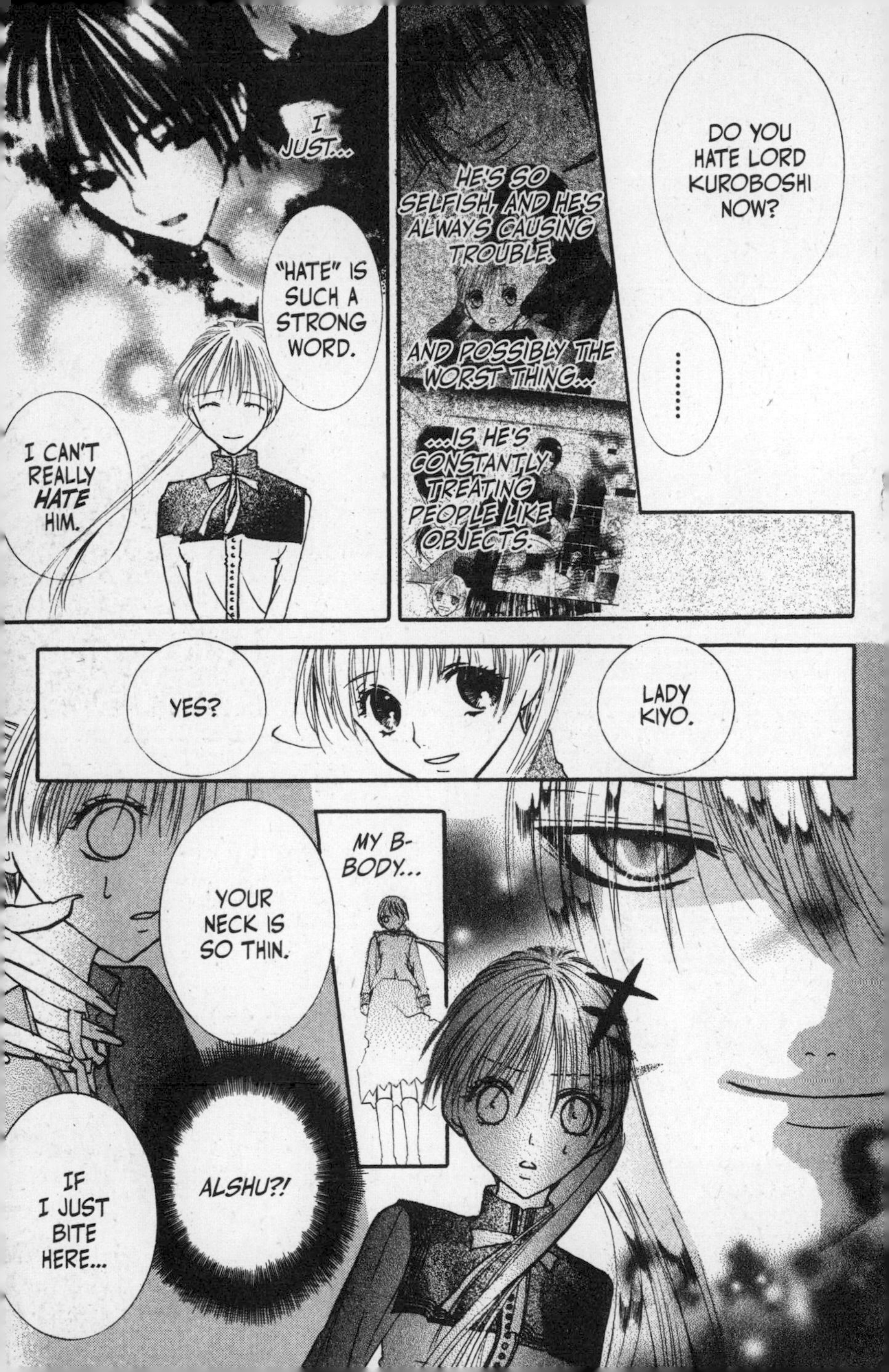
DO YOU HATE LORD KUROBOSHI NOW?
......
HE'S SO SELFISH, AND HE'S ALWAYS CAUSING TROUBLE.
AND POSSIBLY THE WORST THING...
...IS HE'S CONSTANTLY TREATING PEOPLE LIKE OBJECTS.
I JUST...
"HATE" IS SUCH A STRONG WORD.
I CAN'T REALLY *HATE* HIM.
LADY KIYO.
YES?
MY B-BODY...
YOUR NECK IS SO THIN.
ALSHU?!
IF I JUST BITE HERE...

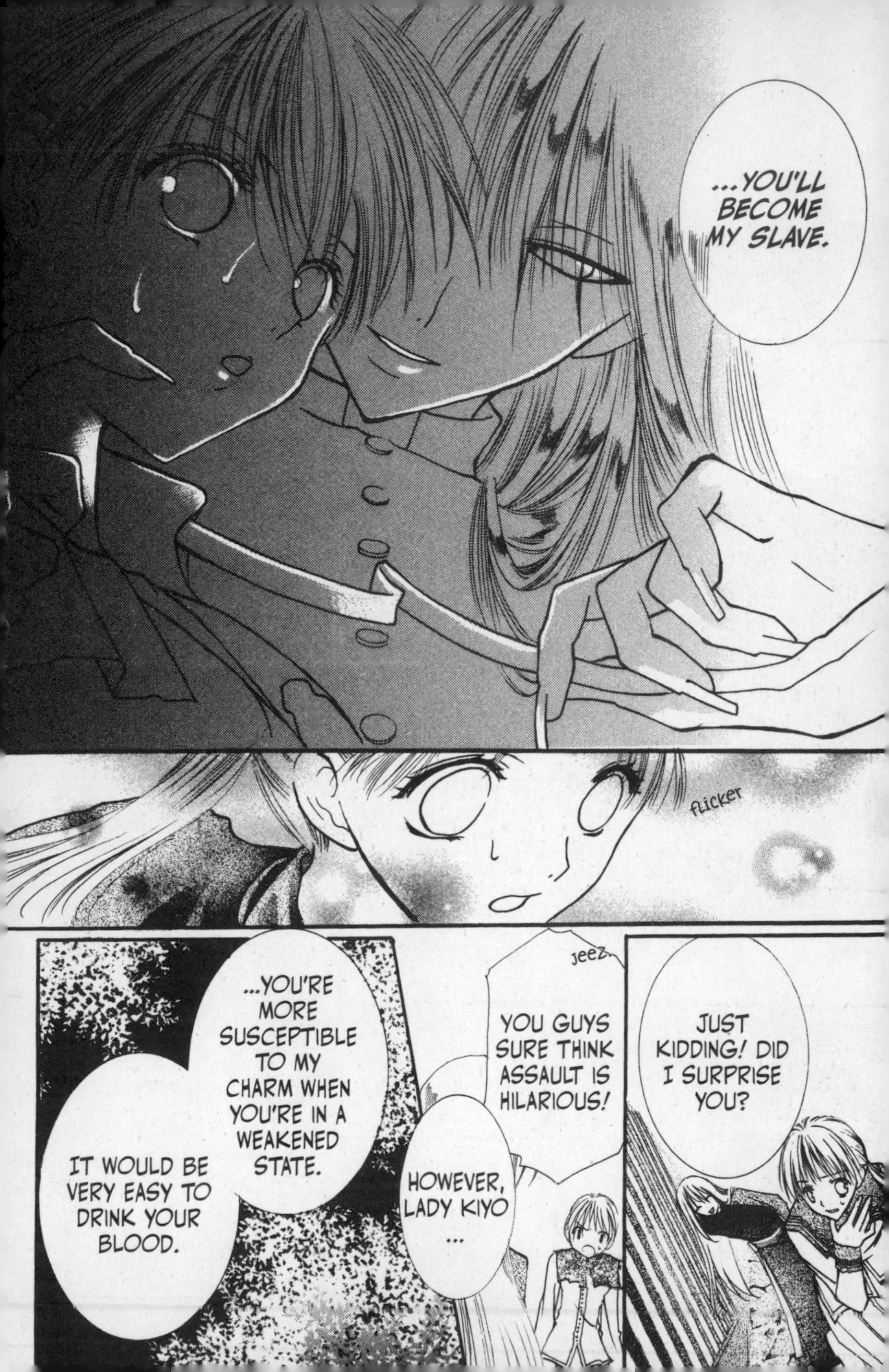
...YOU'LL BECOME MY SLAVE.
flicker
JUST KIDDING! DID I SURPRISE YOU?
JEEZ.
YOU GUYS SURE THINK ASSAULT IS HILARIOUS!
HOWEVER, LADY KIYO ...
...YOU'RE MORE SUSCEPTIBLE TO MY CHARM WHEN YOU'RE IN A WEAKENED STATE.
IT WOULD BE VERY EASY TO DRINK YOUR BLOOD.

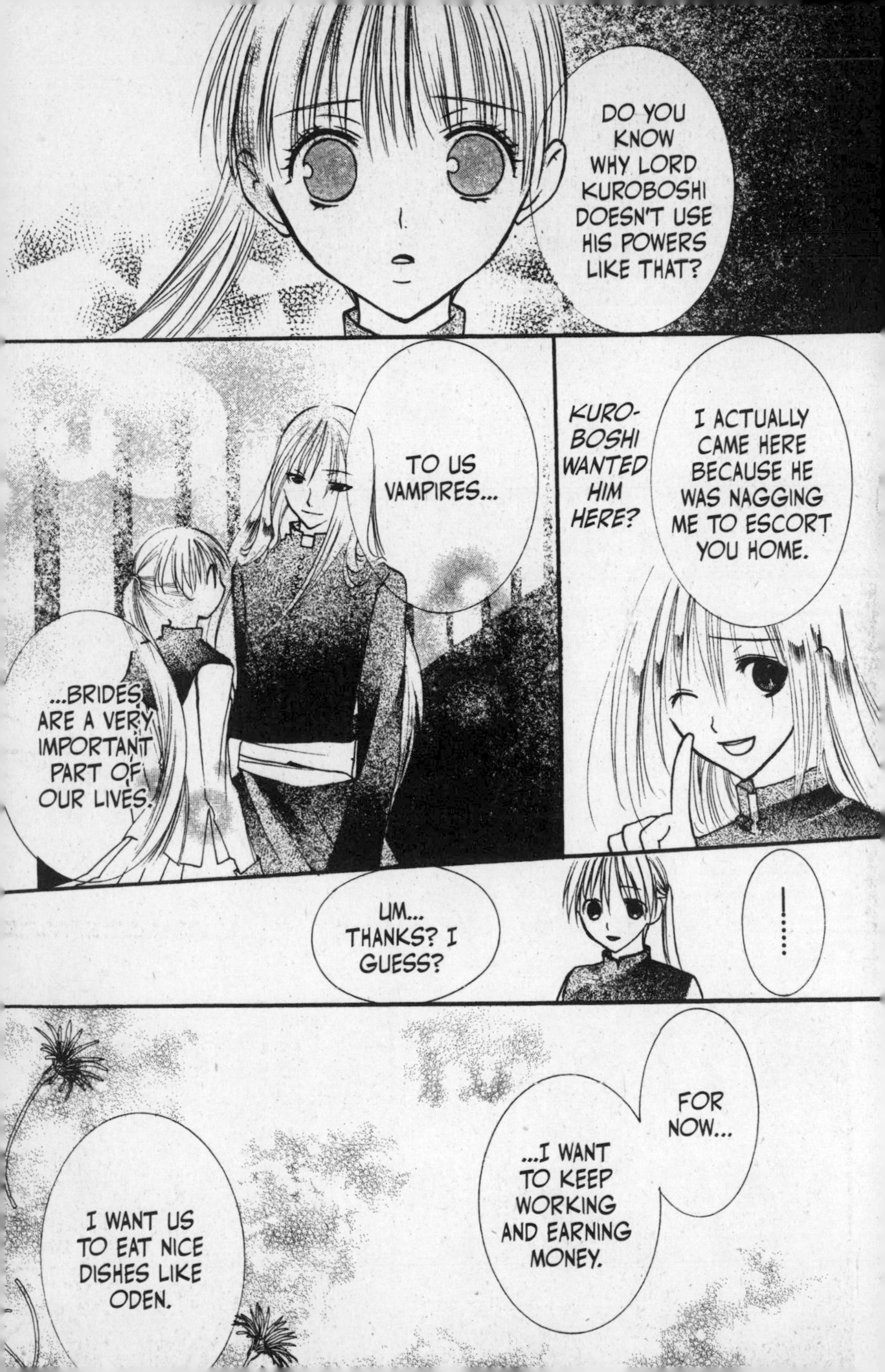
DO YOU KNOW WHY LORD KUROBOSHI DOESN'T USE HIS POWERS LIKE THAT?
I ACTUALLY CAME HERE BECAUSE HE WAS NAGGING ME TO ESCORT YOU HOME.
KURO-BOSHI WANTED HIM HERE?
TO US VAMPIRES...
...BRIDES ARE A VERY IMPORTANT PART OF OUR LIVES.
......!
UM... THANKS? I GUESS?
FOR NOW...
...I WANT TO KEEP WORKING AND EARNING MONEY.
I WANT US TO EAT NICE DISHES LIKE ODEN.

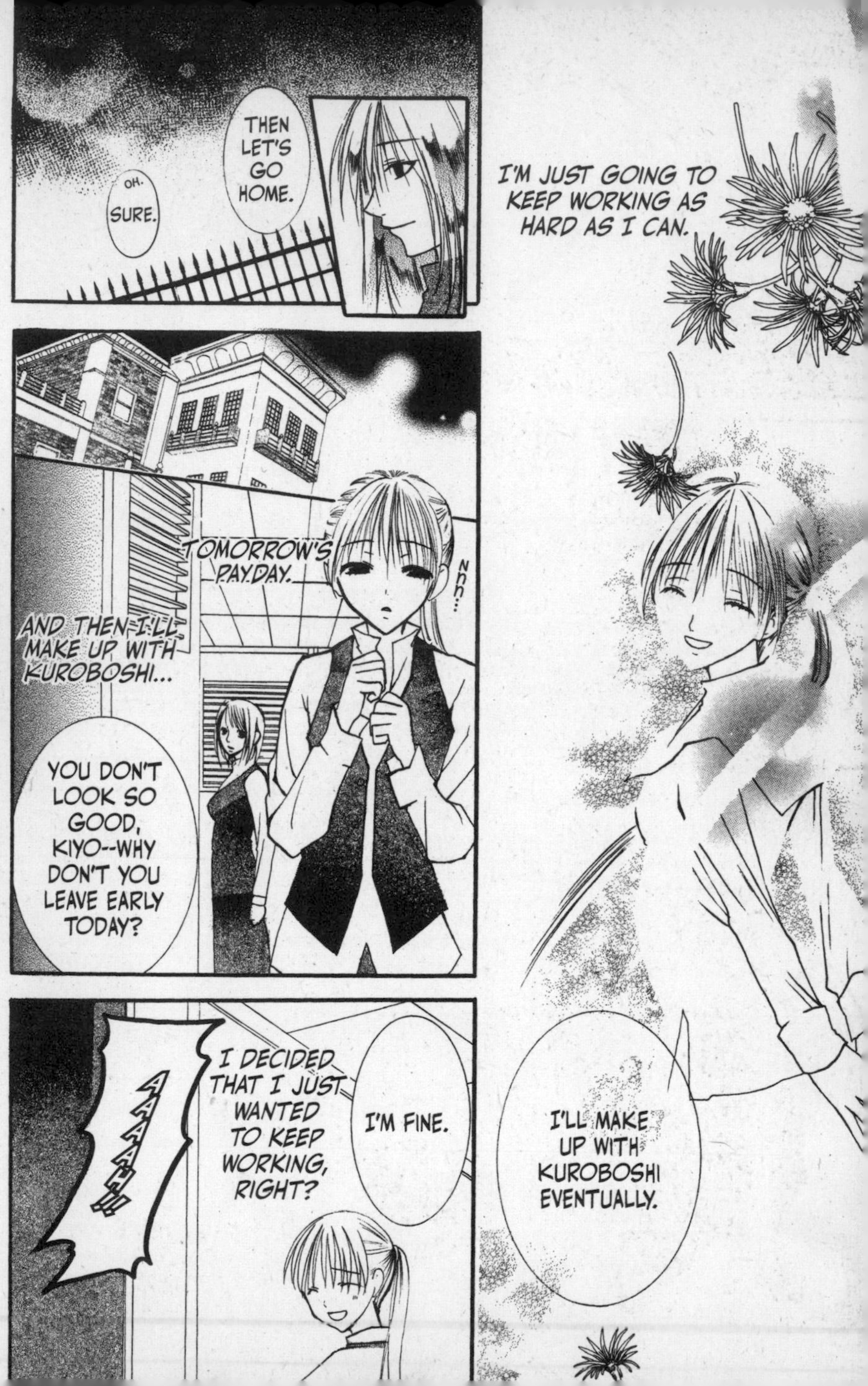
I'M JUST GOING TO KEEP WORKING AS HARD AS I CAN.
I'LL MAKE UP WITH KUROBOSHI EVENTUALLY.
THEN LET'S GO HOME.
OH. SURE.
TOMORROW'S PAYDAY.
NNN...
AND THEN I'LL MAKE UP WITH KUROBOSHI...
YOU DON'T LOOK SO GOOD, KIYO--WHY DON'T YOU LEAVE EARLY TODAY?
I'M FINE.
I DECIDED THAT I JUST WANTED TO KEEP WORKING, RIGHT?
AAAAH!!

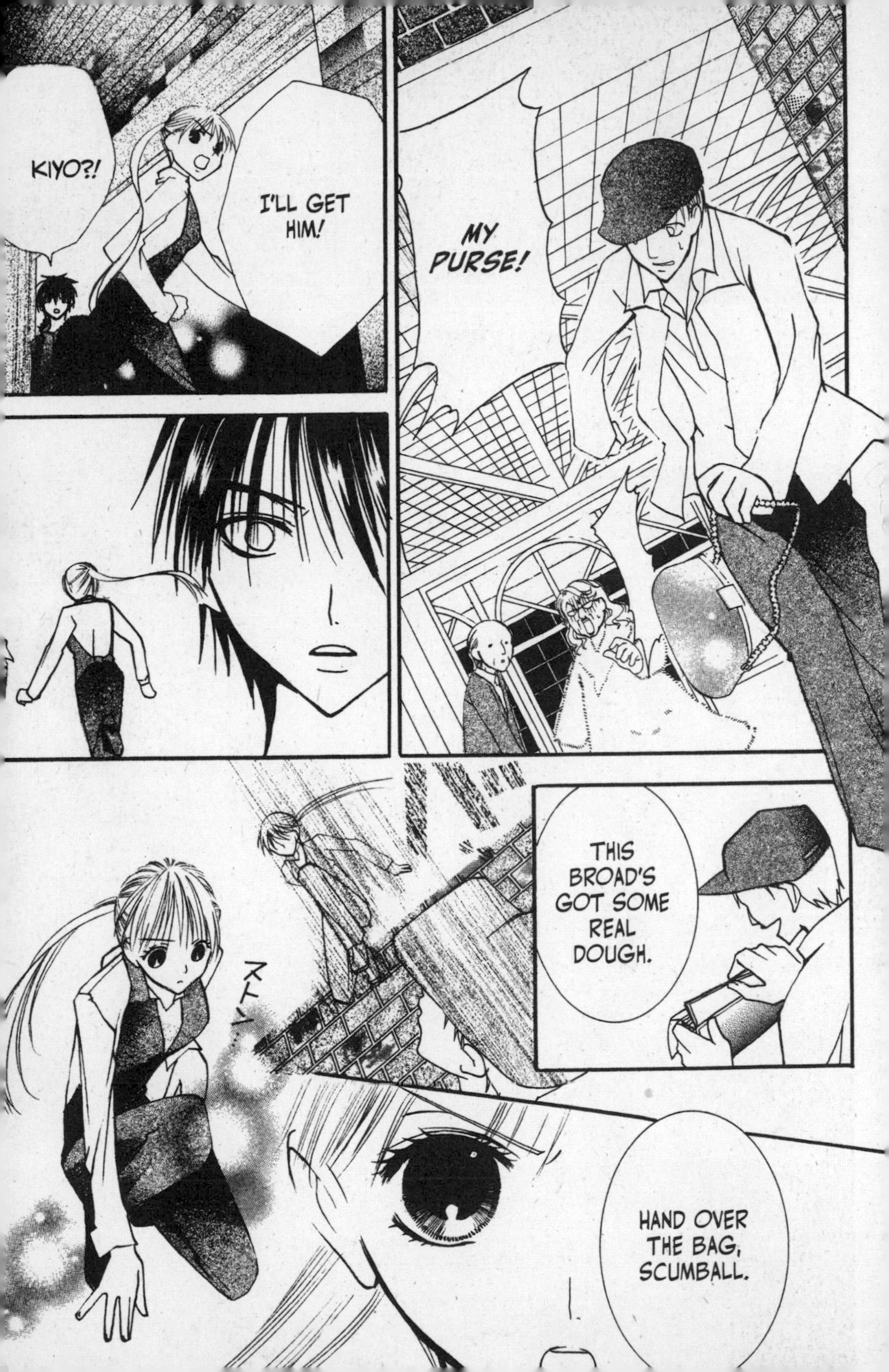
MY PURSE!
I'LL GET HIM!
KIYO?!
THIS BROAD'S GOT SOME REAL DOUGH.
ストン
HAND OVER THE BAG, SCUMBALL.

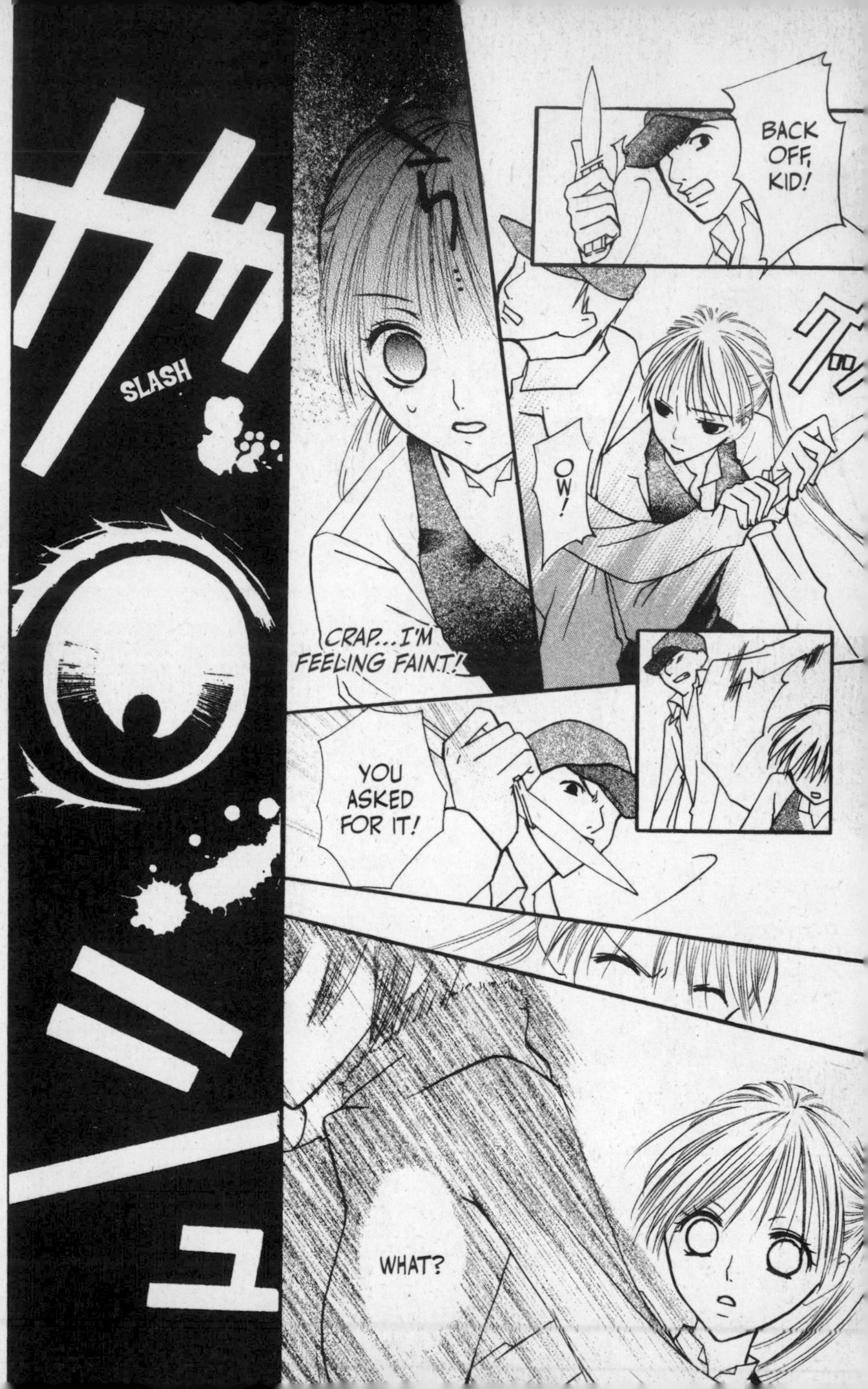
BACK OFF, KID!
OW!
CRAP...I'M FEELING FAINT!
YOU ASKED FOR IT!
WHAT?
SLASH

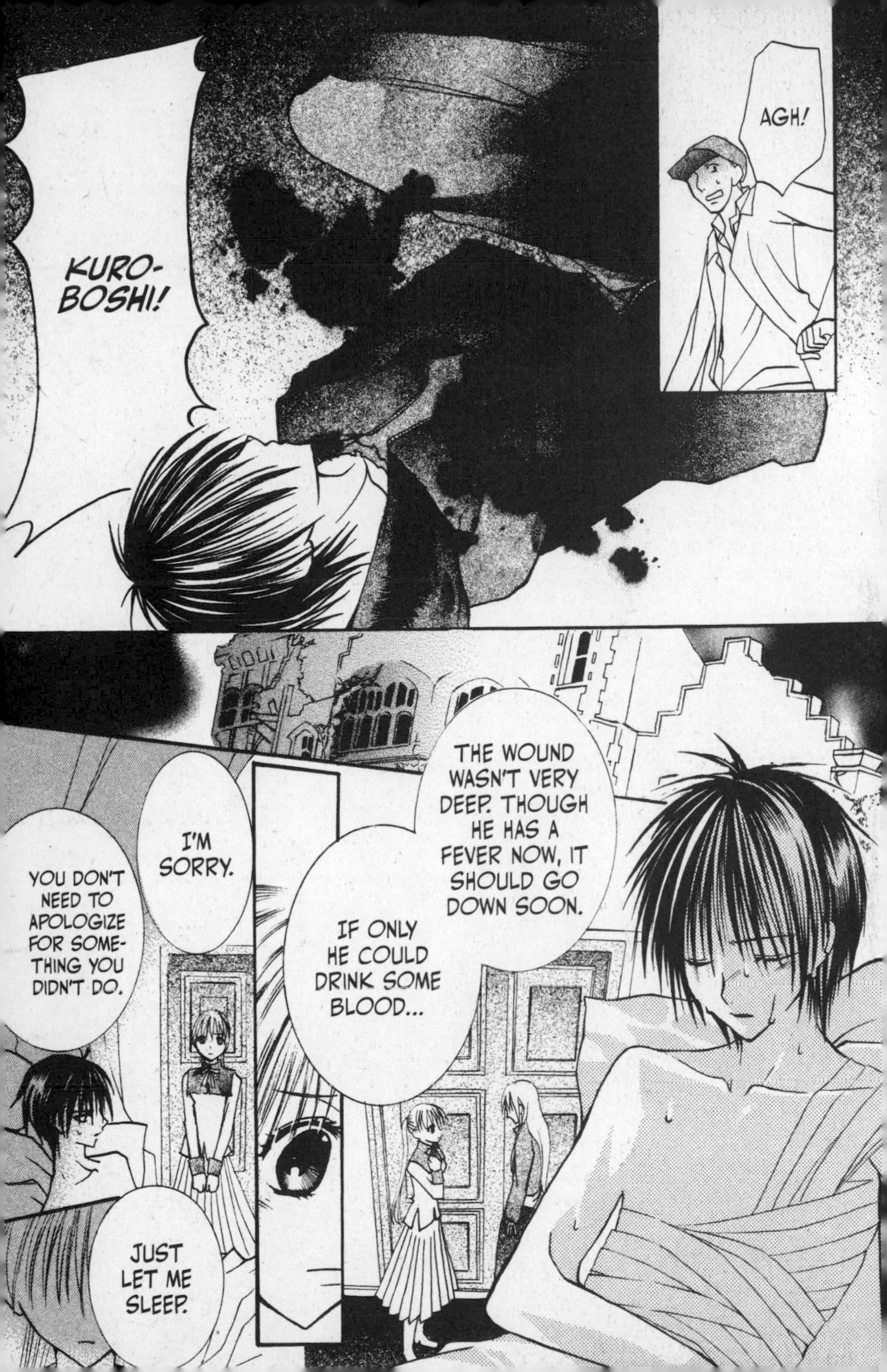
AGH!
KURO-BOSHI!
THE WOUND WASN'T VERY DEEP. THOUGH HE HAS A FEVER NOW, IT SHOULD GO DOWN SOON.
IF ONLY HE COULD DRINK SOME BLOOD...
I'M SORRY.
YOU DON'T NEED TO APOLOGIZE FOR SOME-THING YOU DIDN'T DO.
JUST LET ME SLEEP.

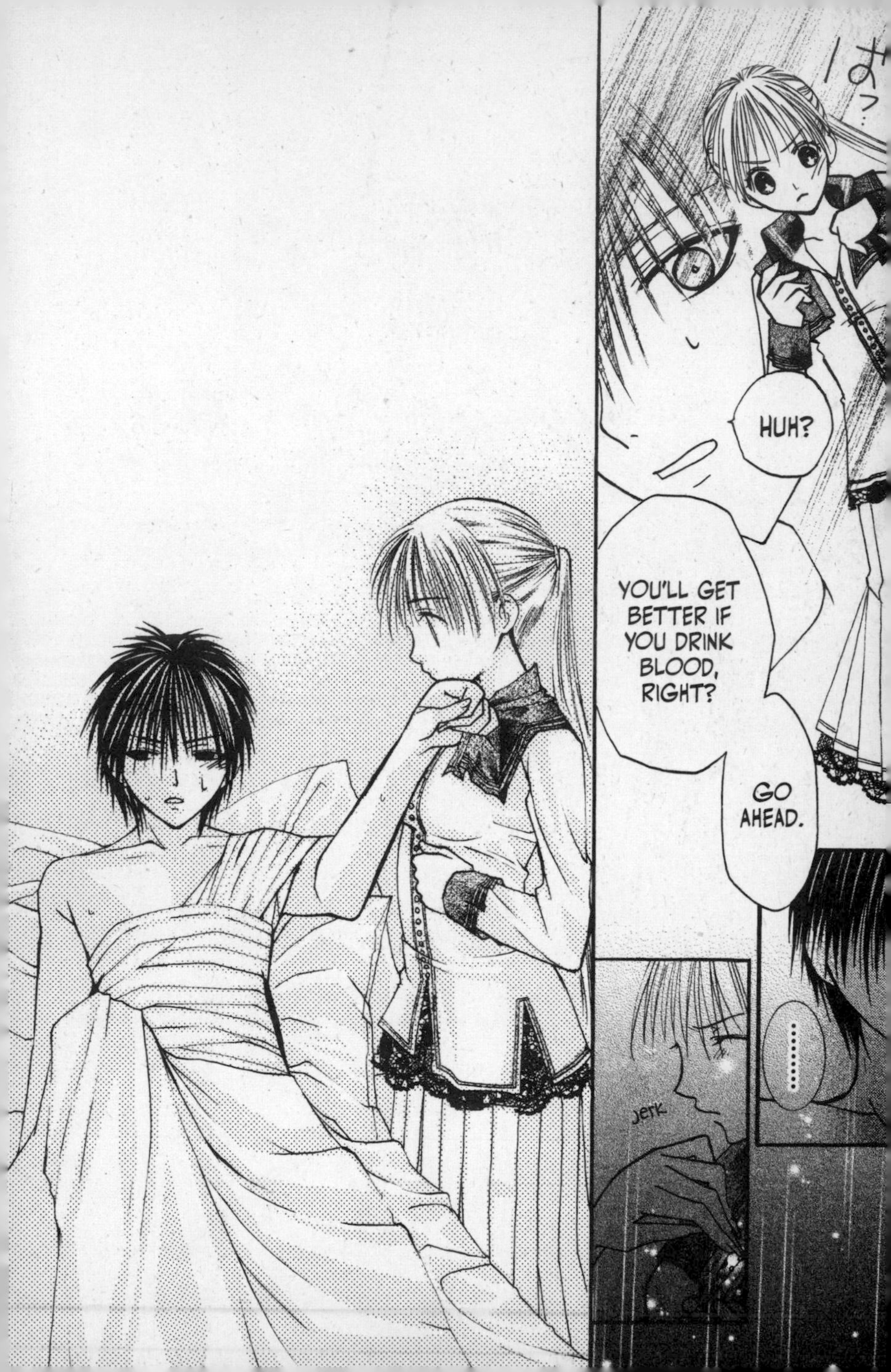
はっ…
HUH?
YOU'LL GET BETTER IF YOU DRINK BLOOD, RIGHT?
GO AHEAD.
......
JERK

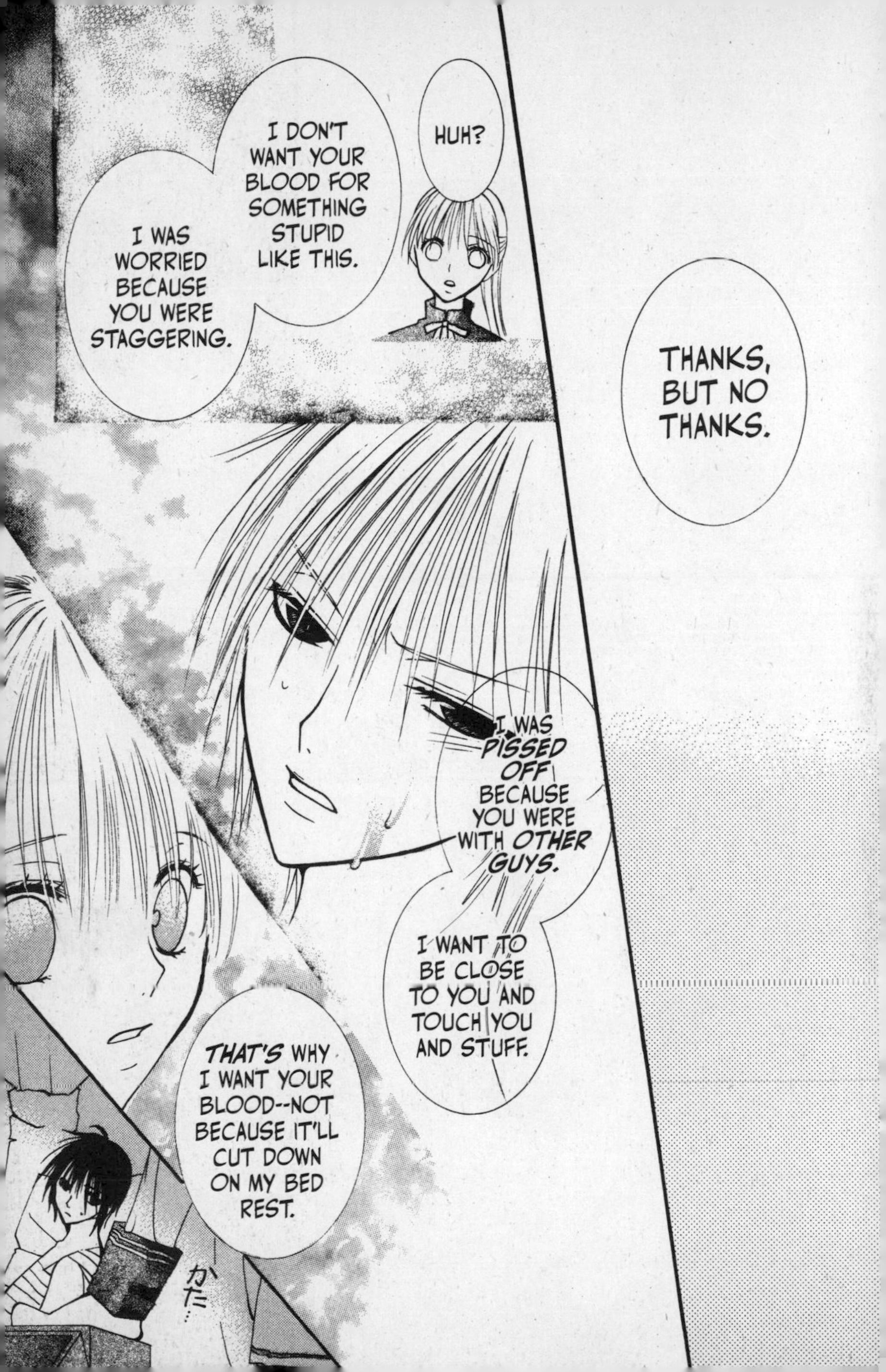
THANKS, BUT NO THANKS.
HUH?
I DON'T WANT YOUR BLOOD FOR SOMETHING STUPID LIKE THIS.
I WAS WORRIED BECAUSE YOU WERE STAGGERING.
I WAS PISSED OFF BECAUSE YOU WERE WITH OTHER GUYS.
I WANT TO BE CLOSE TO YOU AND TOUCH YOU AND STUFF.
THAT'S WHY I WANT YOUR BLOOD--NOT BECAUSE IT'LL CUT DOWN ON MY BED REST.
かた…

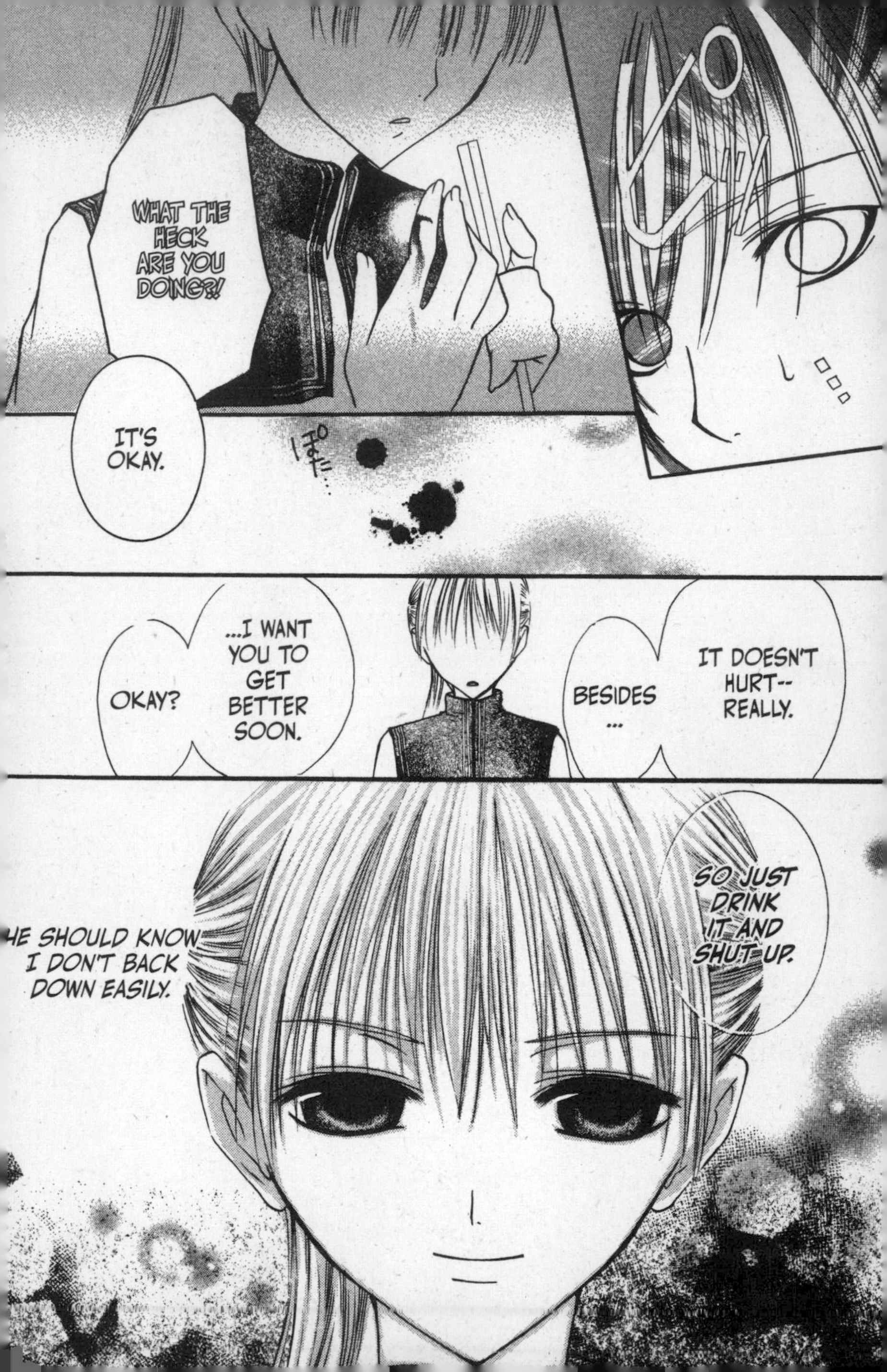
WHAT THE HECK ARE YOU DOING?!
IT'S OKAY.
ぽた…
IT DOESN'T HURT-- REALLY.
BESIDES ...
...I WANT YOU TO GET BETTER SOON.
OKAY?
SO JUST DRINK IT AND SHUT UP.
HE SHOULD KNOW I DON'T BACK DOWN EASILY.

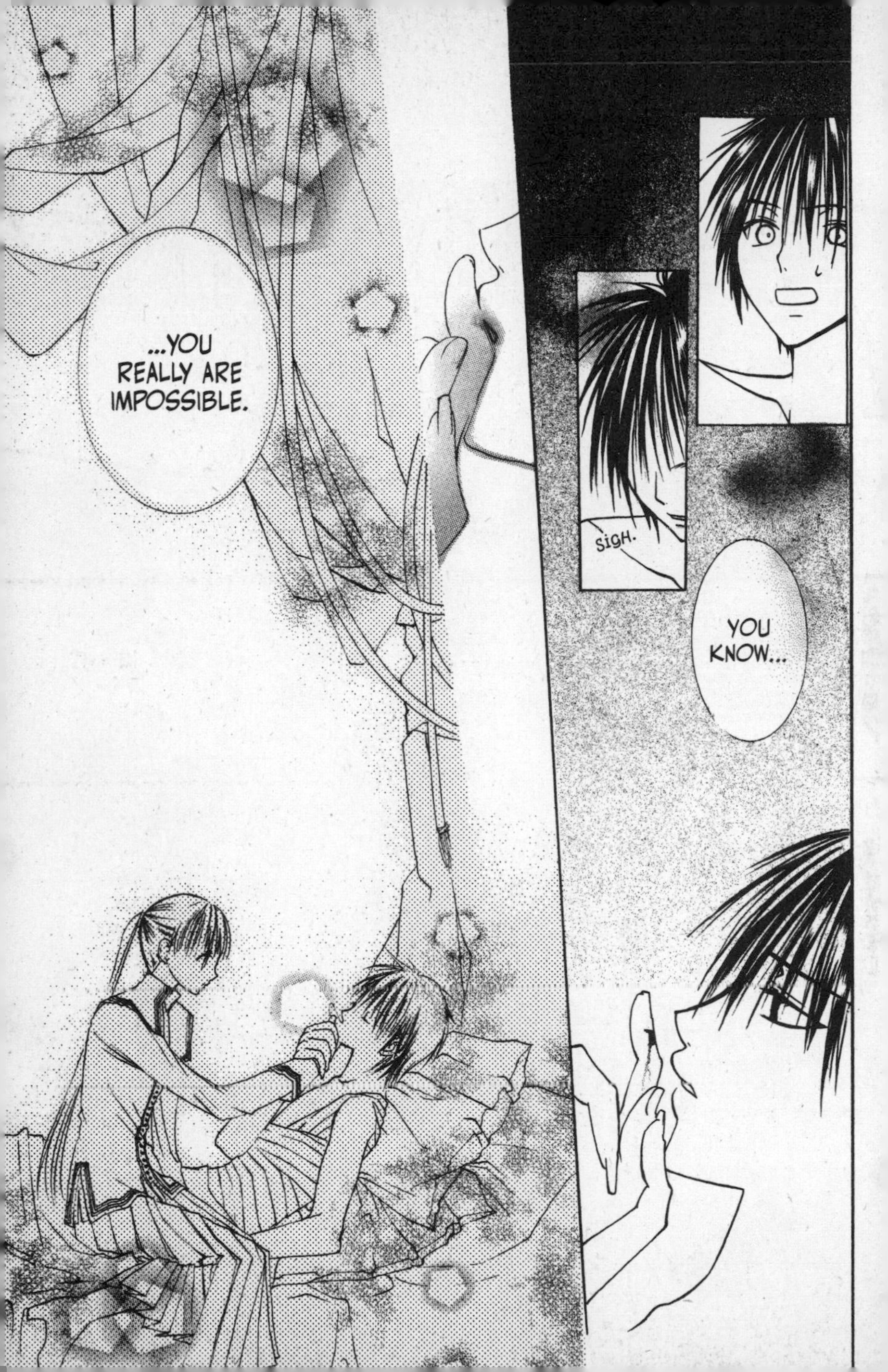
SIGH.
YOU KNOW...
...YOU REALLY ARE IMPOSSIBLE.

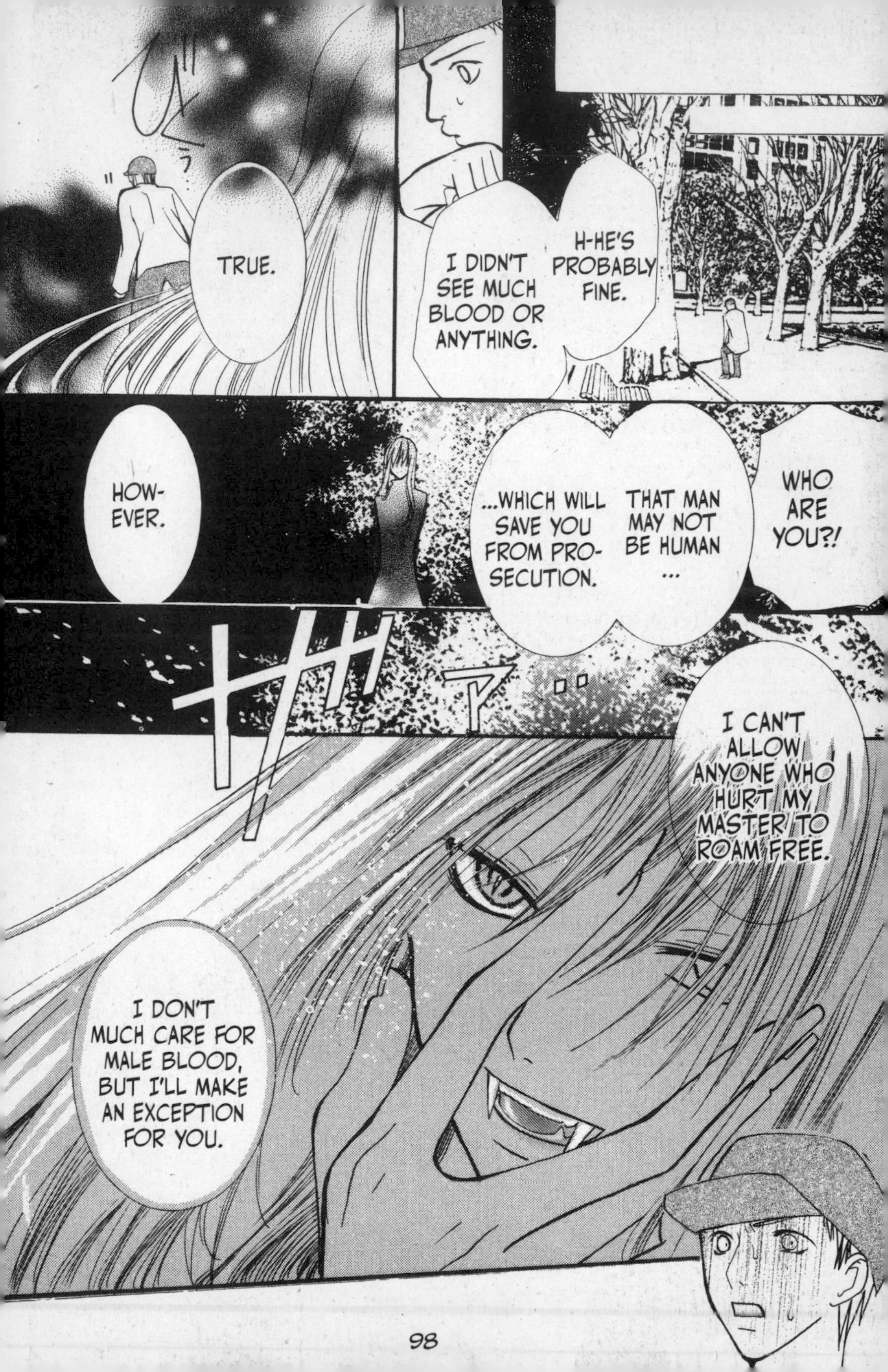
H-HE'S PROBABLY FINE.
I DIDN'T SEE MUCH BLOOD OR ANYTHING.
TRUE.
WHO ARE YOU?!
THAT MAN MAY NOT BE HUMAN ...
...WHICH WILL SAVE YOU FROM PRO-SECUTION.
HOW-EVER.
I CAN'T ALLOW ANYONE WHO HURT MY MASTER TO ROAM FREE.
I DON'T MUCH CARE FOR MALE BLOOD, BUT I'LL MAKE AN EXCEPTION FOR YOU.

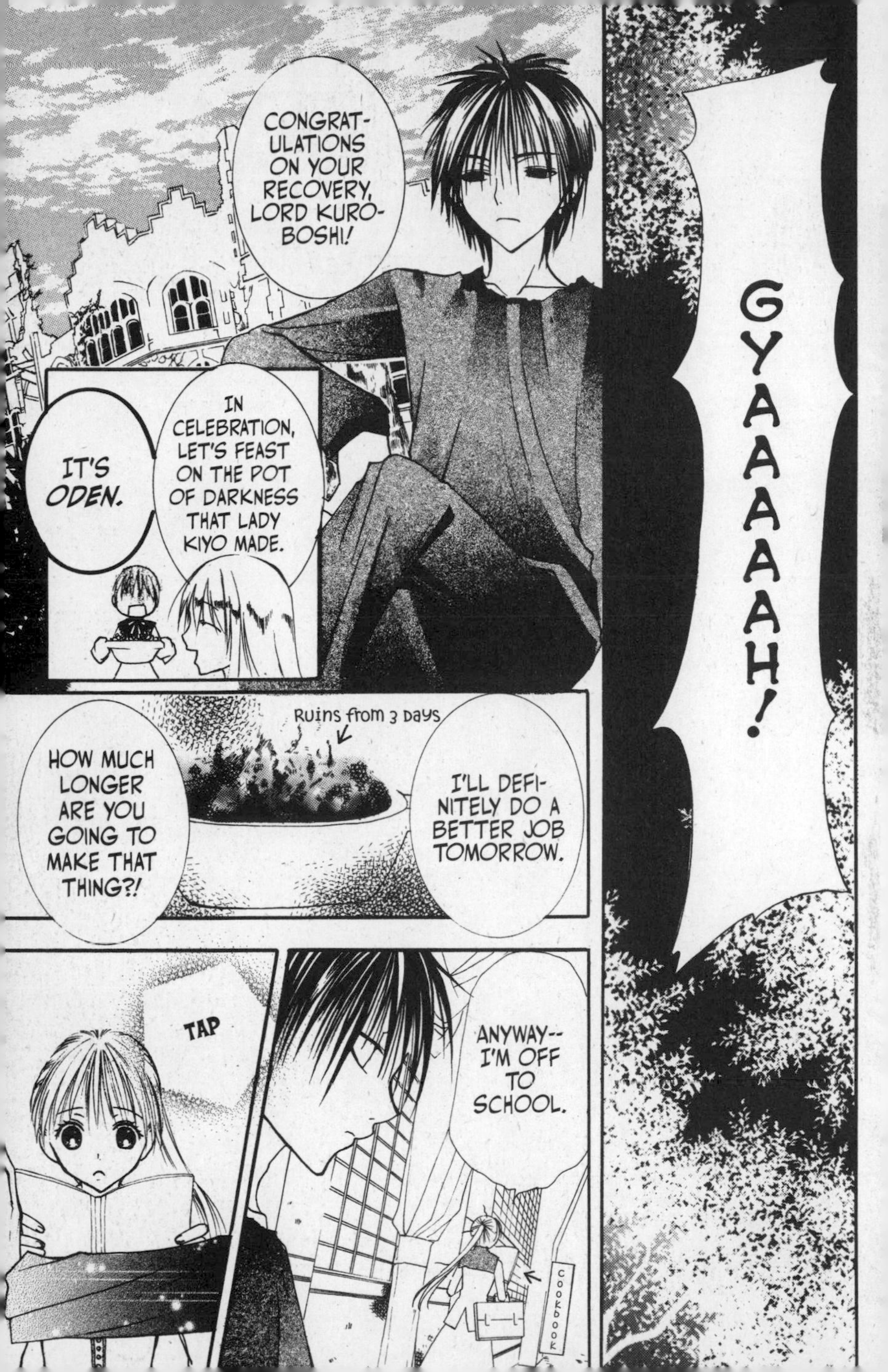
GYAAAAAH!
CONGRAT-ULATIONS ON YOUR RECOVERY, LORD KURO-BOSHI!
IN CELEBRATION, LET'S FEAST ON THE POT OF DARKNESS THAT LADY KIYO MADE.
IT'S ODEN.
I'LL DEFI-NITELY DO A BETTER JOB TOMORROW.
Ruins from 3 days
HOW MUCH LONGER ARE YOU GOING TO MAKE THAT THING?!
ANYWAY-- I'M OFF TO SCHOOL.
COOKBOOK
TAP

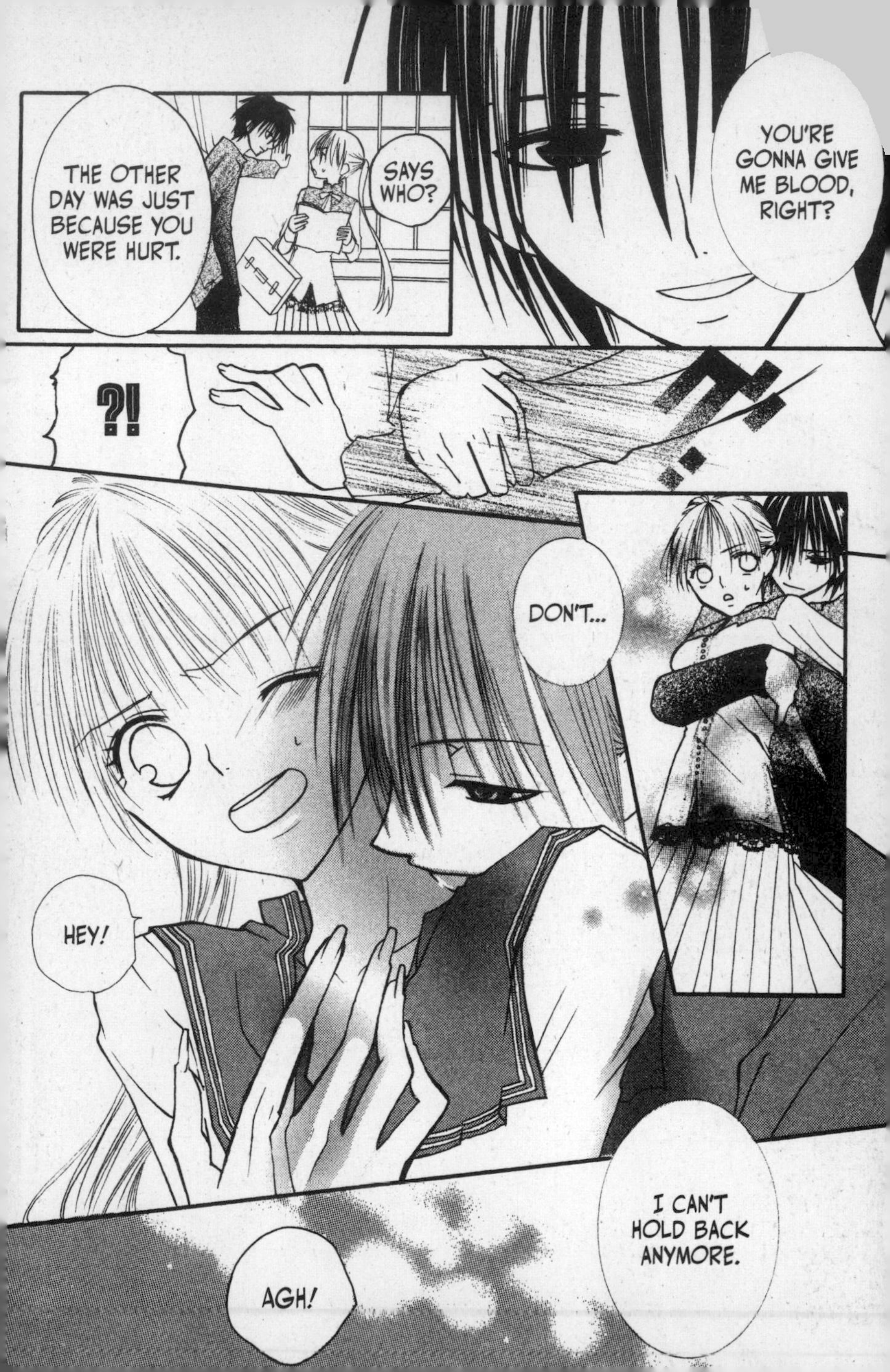
YOU'RE GONNA GIVE ME BLOOD, RIGHT?
THE OTHER DAY WAS JUST BECAUSE YOU WERE HURT.
SAYS WHO?
?!
DON'T...
HEY!
I CAN'T HOLD BACK ANYMORE.
AGH!

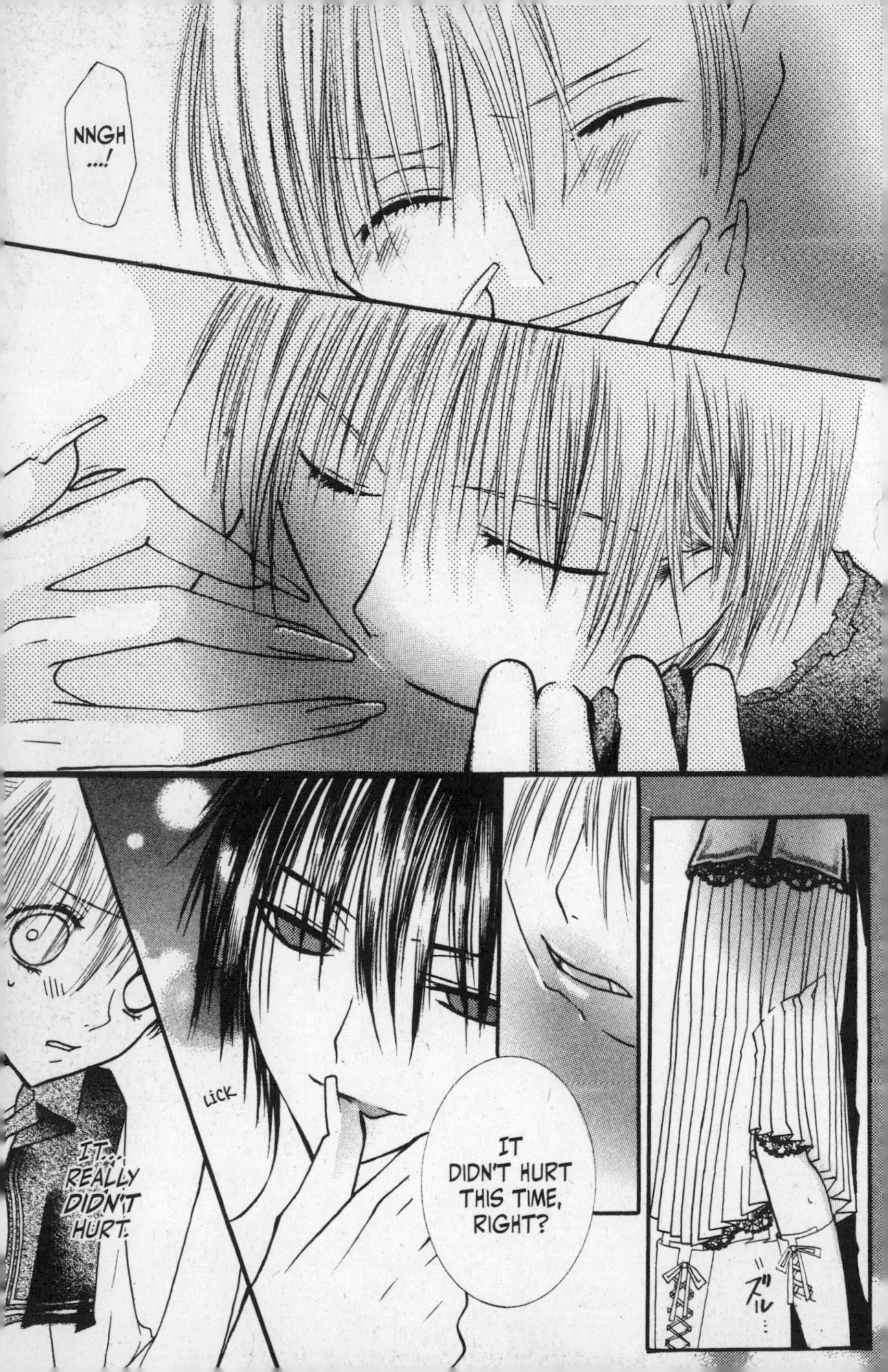
NNGH ...!
ズル…
LICK
IT DIDN'T HURT THIS TIME, RIGHT?
IT... REALLY DIDN'T HURT.

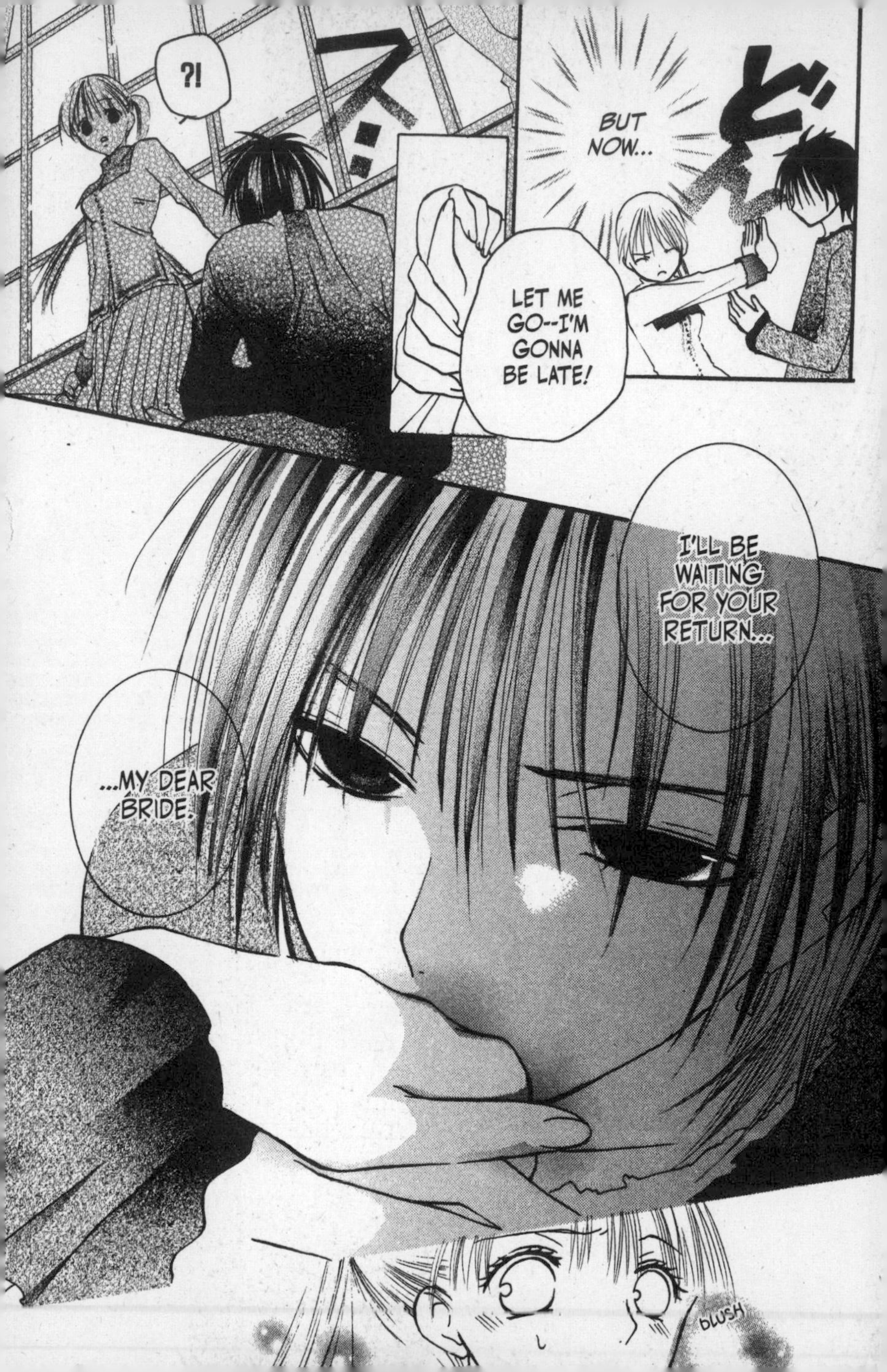
BUT NOW...
LET ME GO--I'M GONNA BE LATE!
?!
I'LL BE WAITING FOR YOUR RETURN...
...MY DEAR BRIDE.
BLUSH

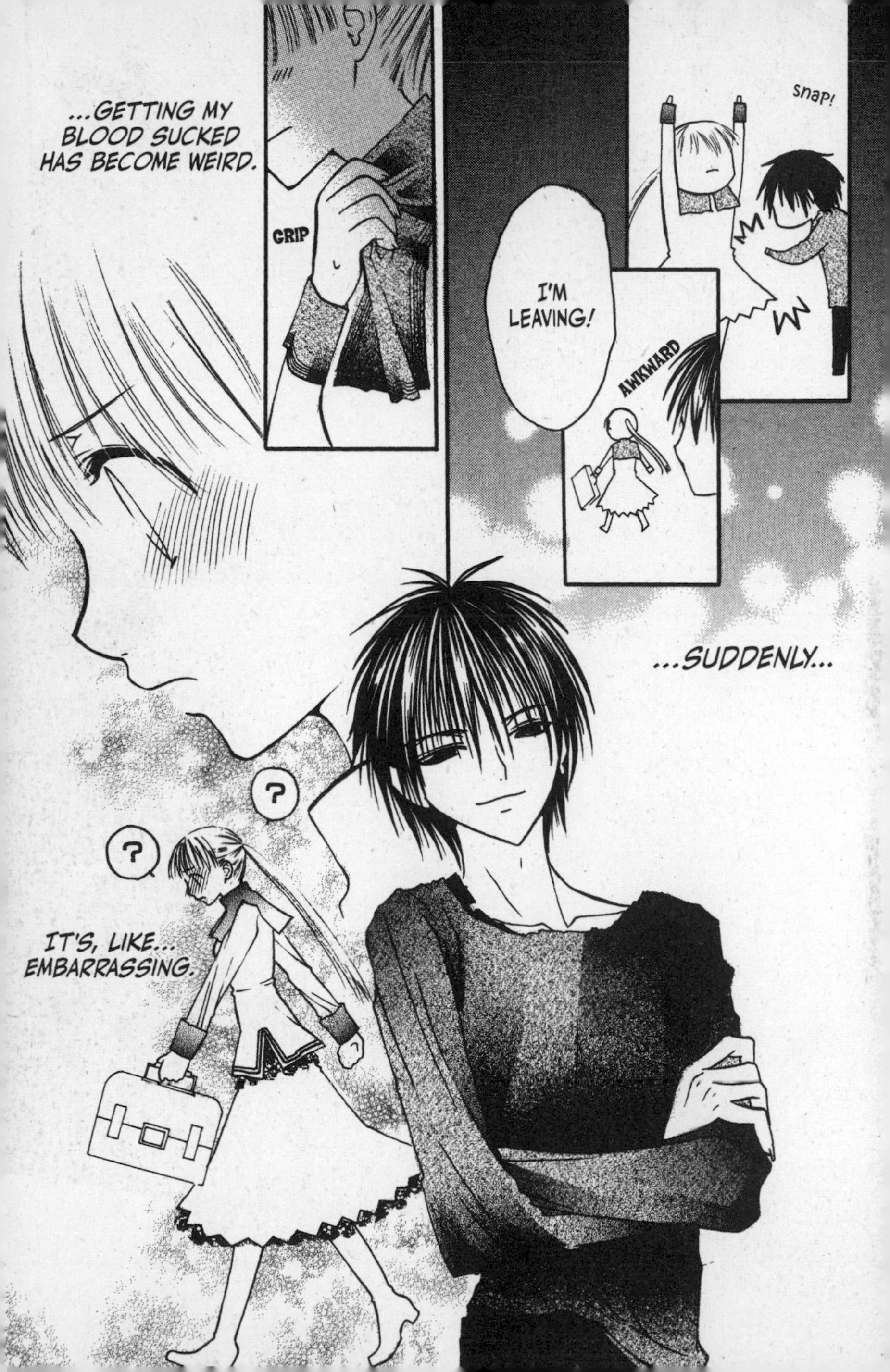
Snap!
I'M LEAVING!
AWKWARD
...SUDDENLY...
GRIP
...GETTING MY BLOOD SUCKED HAS BECOME WEIRD.
?
?
IT'S, LIKE... EMBARRASSING.

Rejected Draft of Page 66

Part 1 and Part 2
The overlap was rejected. I didn't like the angle, and I couldn't get a satisfactory rough draft--that sort of thing.

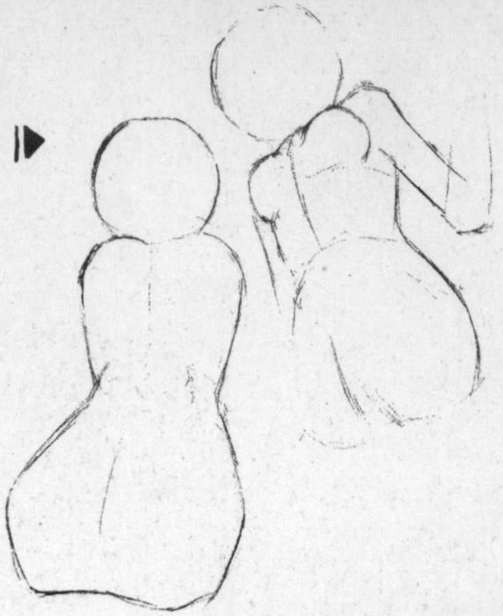

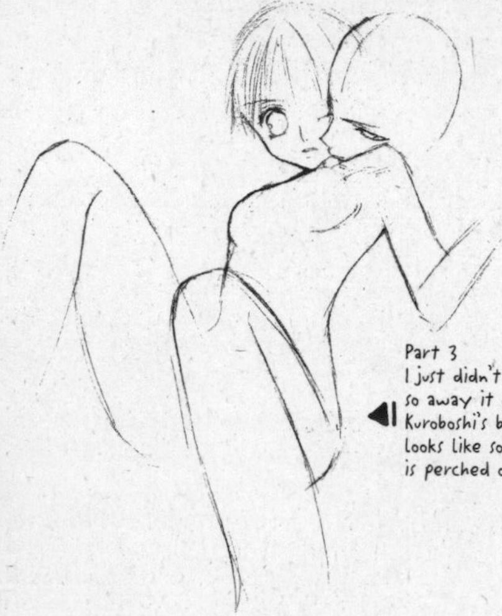

Part 3
I just didn't like it, so away it went. Kuroboshi's bald here. And it looks like some kind of mascot is perched on Kiyo's shoulder.

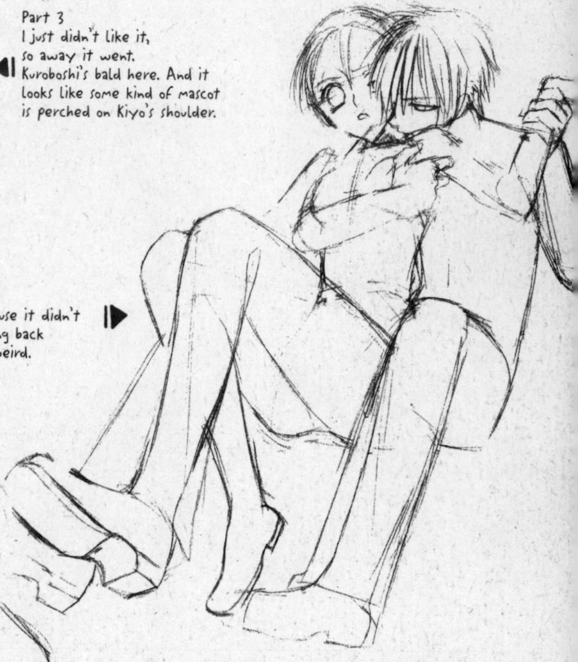

Part 4
I rejected this one because it didn't have much impact. Looking back on it, the leg angle is weird.

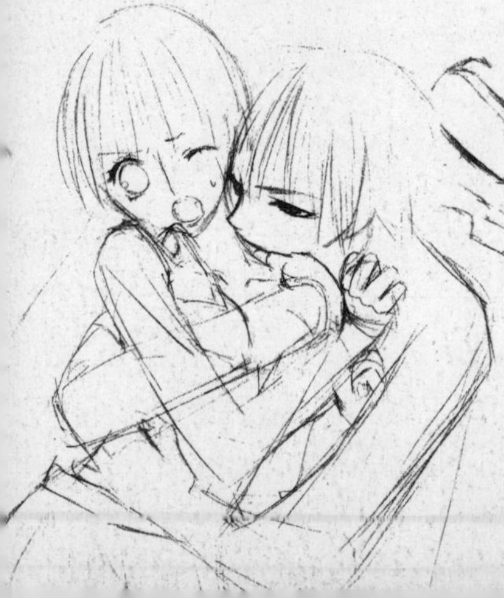

Part 5
This one's unnecessarily sexual. What the heck?

The total amount of time I spent perfecting page 68 was over 10 hours. Seriously, what's wrong with me?

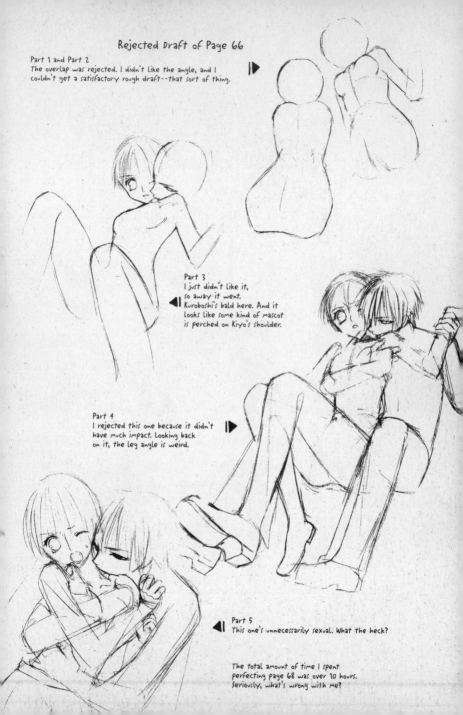

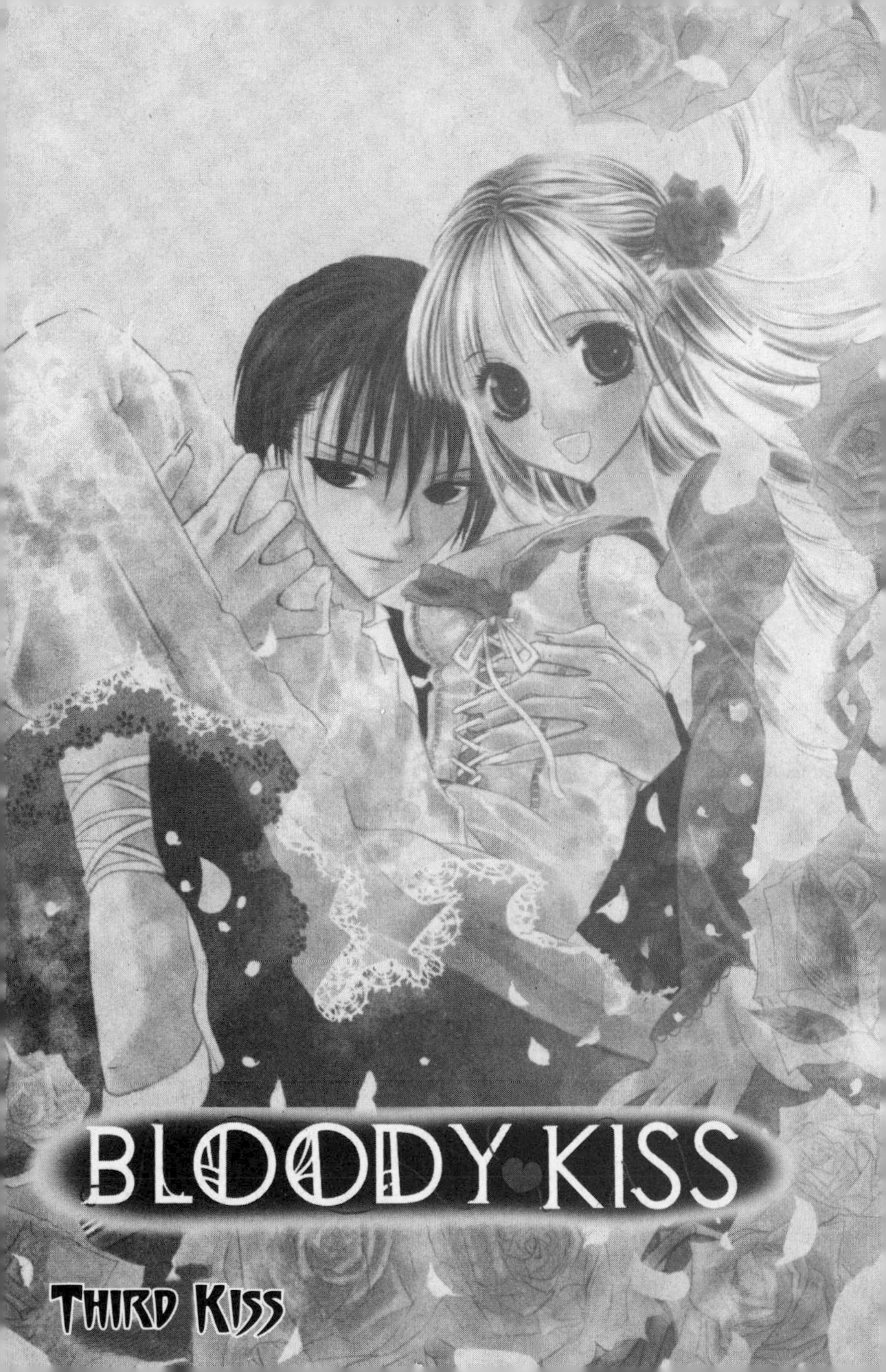
BLOODY KISS
THIRD KISS

Kiyo →♂ Kuroboshi →♀ gender switch version.
Kiyo's like a refreshing and honest honor roll student, I guess? Kuroboshi is a pretty, selfish girl who's prickly on the outside, but has a soft and gooey center. I think the male version of Kiyo is a bit boring. I kinda like the female version of Kuroboshi.

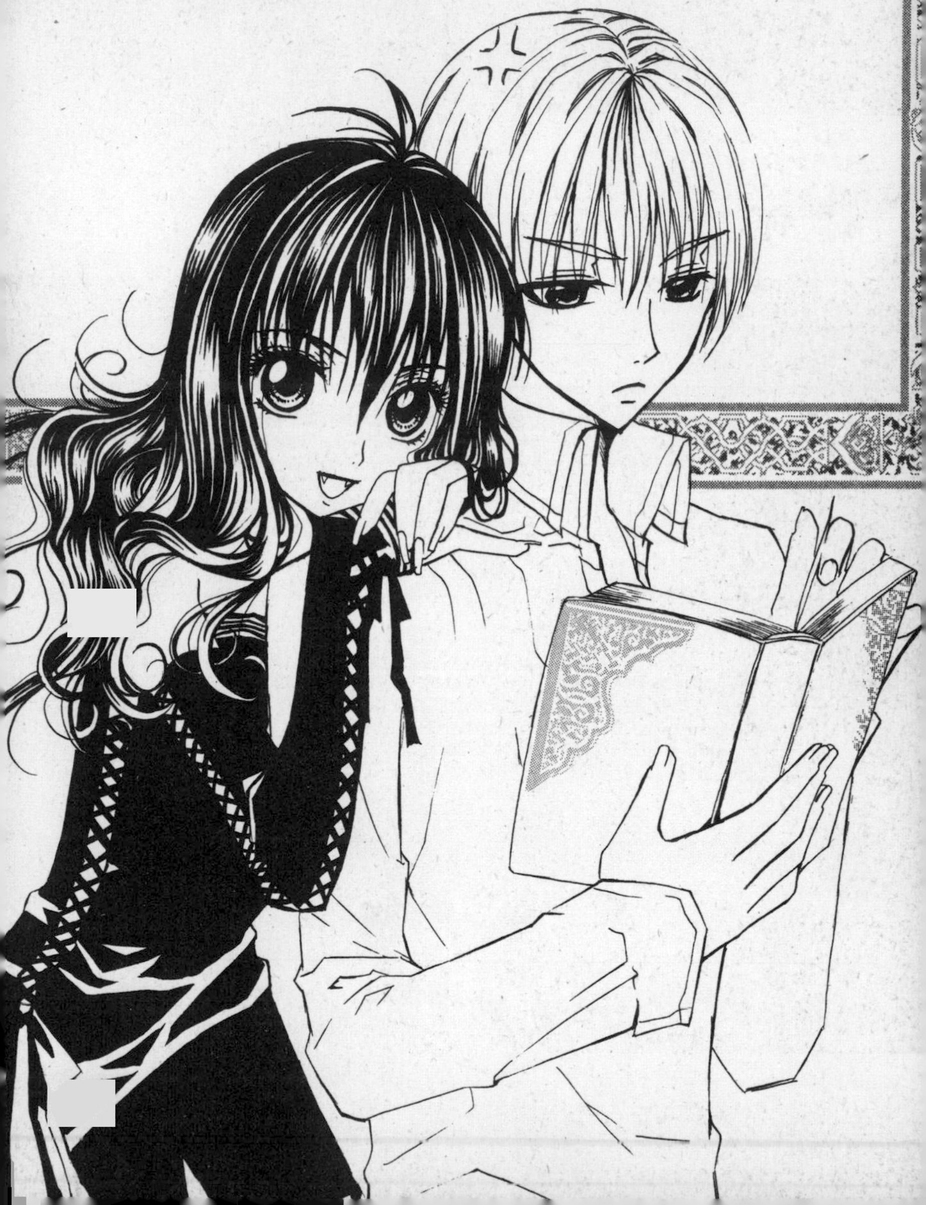

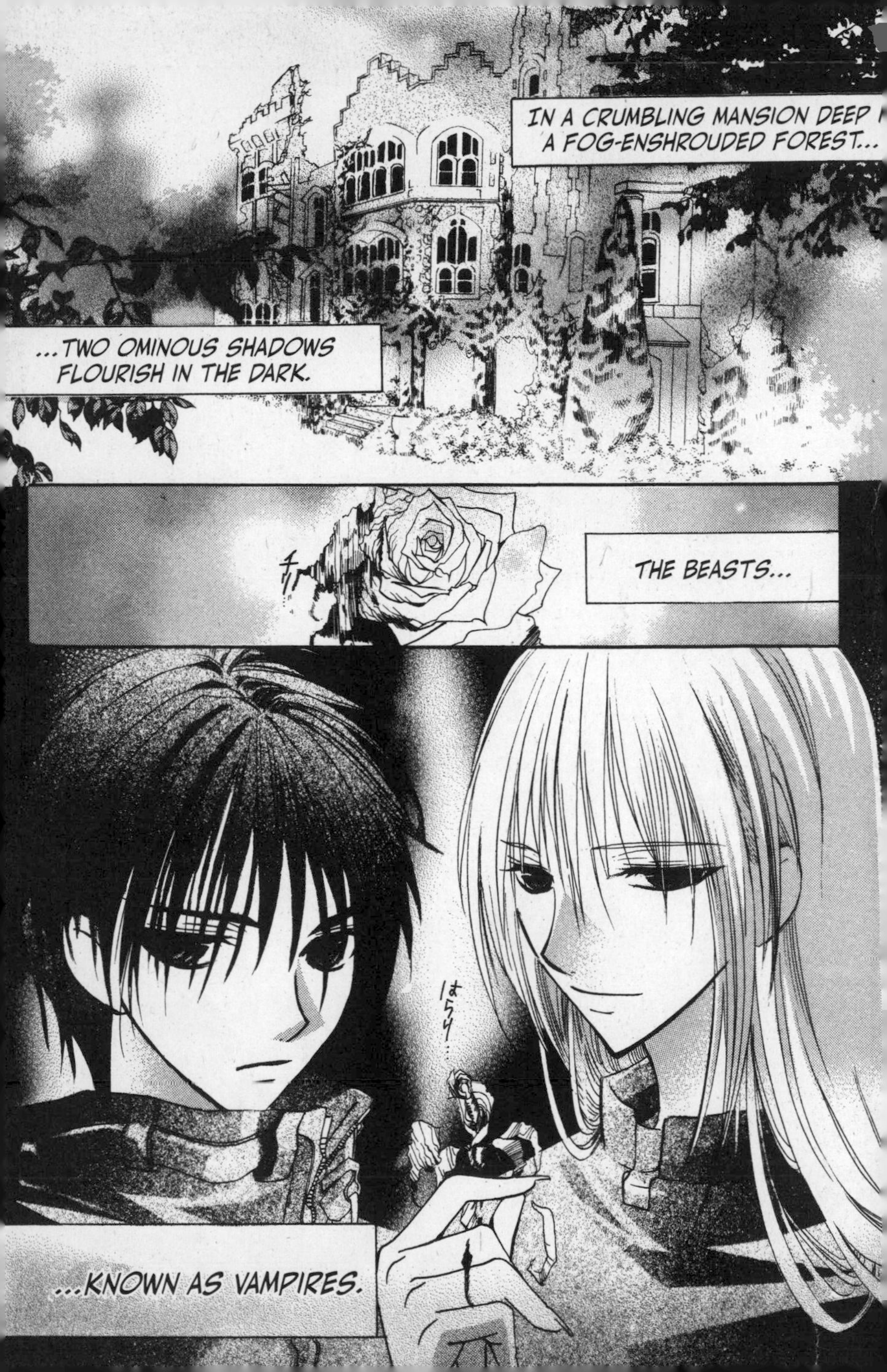
IN A CRUMBLING MANSION DEEP I
A FOG-ENSHROUDED FOREST...
...TWO OMINOUS SHADOWS FLOURISH IN THE DARK.
THE BEASTS...
...KNOWN AS VAMPIRES.

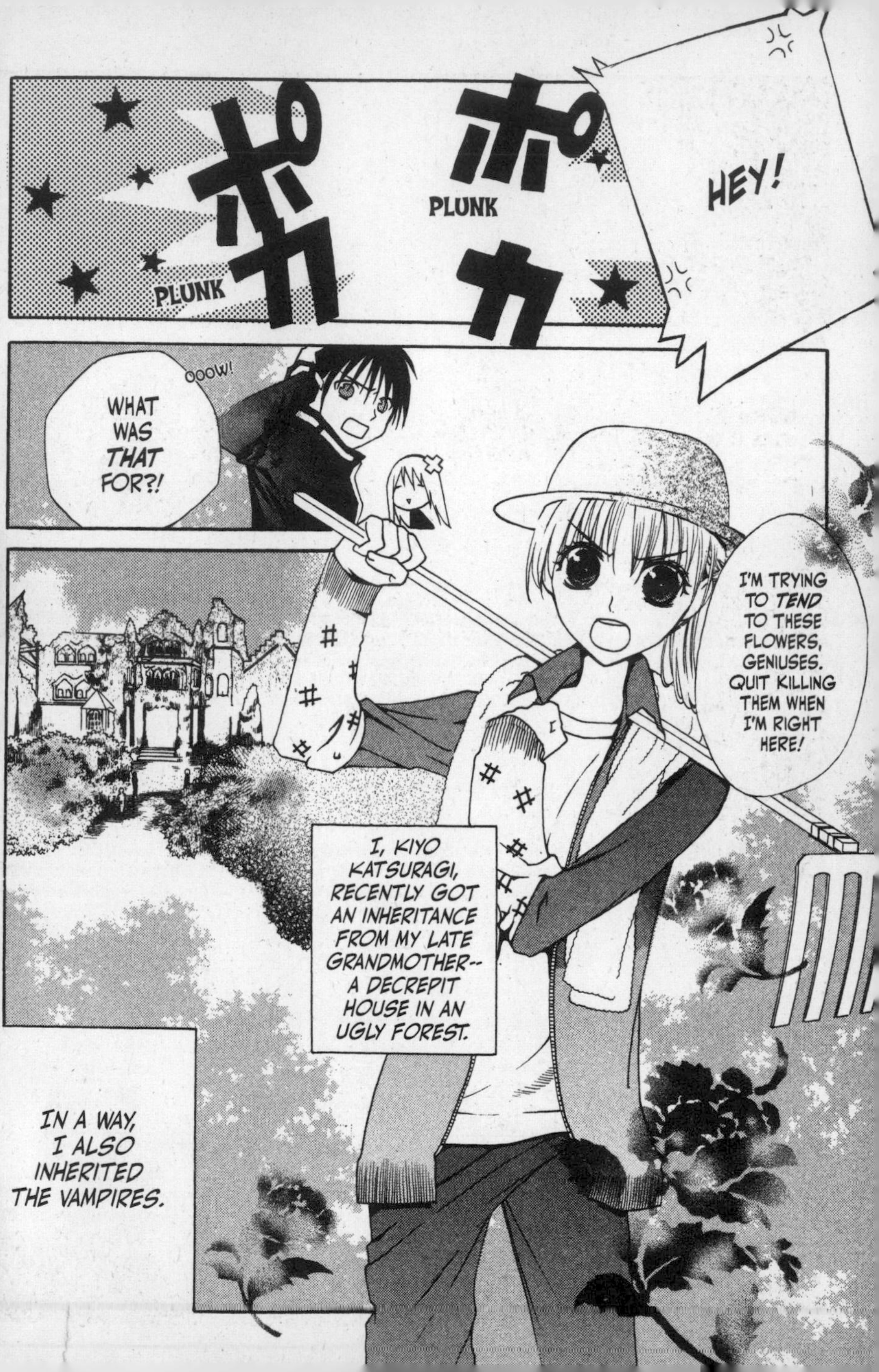
HEY!
ポカ
PLUNK
ポカ
PLUNK
OOOW!
WHAT WAS THAT FOR?!
I'M TRYING TO TEND TO THESE FLOWERS, GENIUSES. QUIT KILLING THEM WHEN I'M RIGHT HERE!
I, KIYO KATSURAGI, RECENTLY GOT AN INHERITANCE FROM MY LATE GRANDMOTHER-- A DECREPIT HOUSE IN AN UGLY FOREST.
IN A WAY, I ALSO INHERITED THE VAMPIRES.

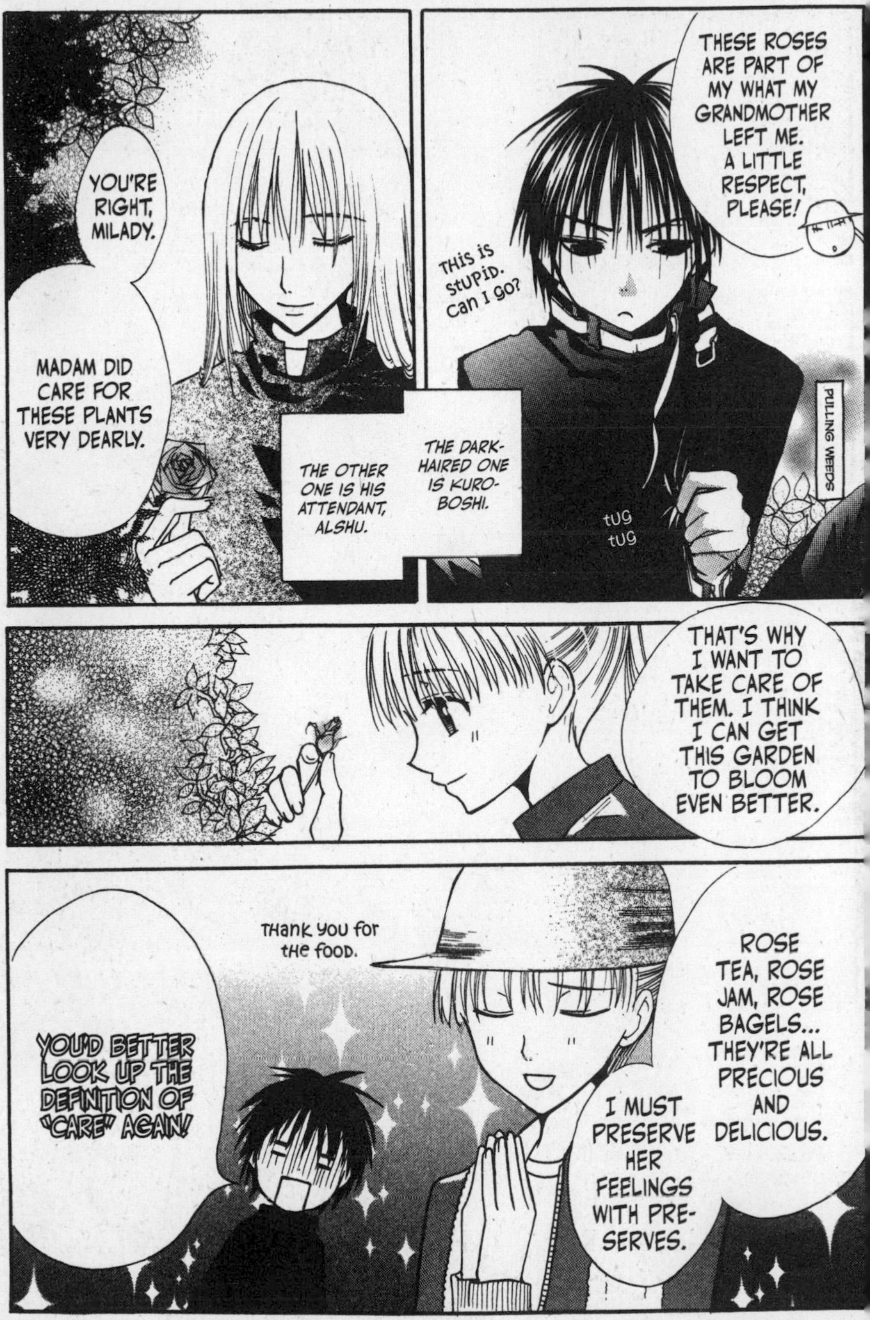
THESE ROSES ARE PART OF MY WHAT MY GRANDMOTHER LEFT ME. A LITTLE RESPECT, PLEASE!
PULLING WEEDS
THIS IS STUPID. CAN I GO?
TUG TUG
THE DARK-HAIRED ONE IS KURO-BOSHI.
THE OTHER ONE IS HIS ATTENDANT, ALSHU.
YOU'RE RIGHT, MILADY.
MADAM DID CARE FOR THESE PLANTS VERY DEARLY.
THAT'S WHY I WANT TO TAKE CARE OF THEM. I THINK I CAN GET THIS GARDEN TO BLOOM EVEN BETTER.
ROSE TEA, ROSE JAM, ROSE BAGELS... THEY'RE ALL PRECIOUS AND DELICIOUS.
I MUST PRESERVE HER FEELINGS WITH PRE-SERVES.
THANK YOU FOR THE FOOD.
YOU'D BETTER LOOK UP THE DEFINITION OF "CARE" AGAIN!

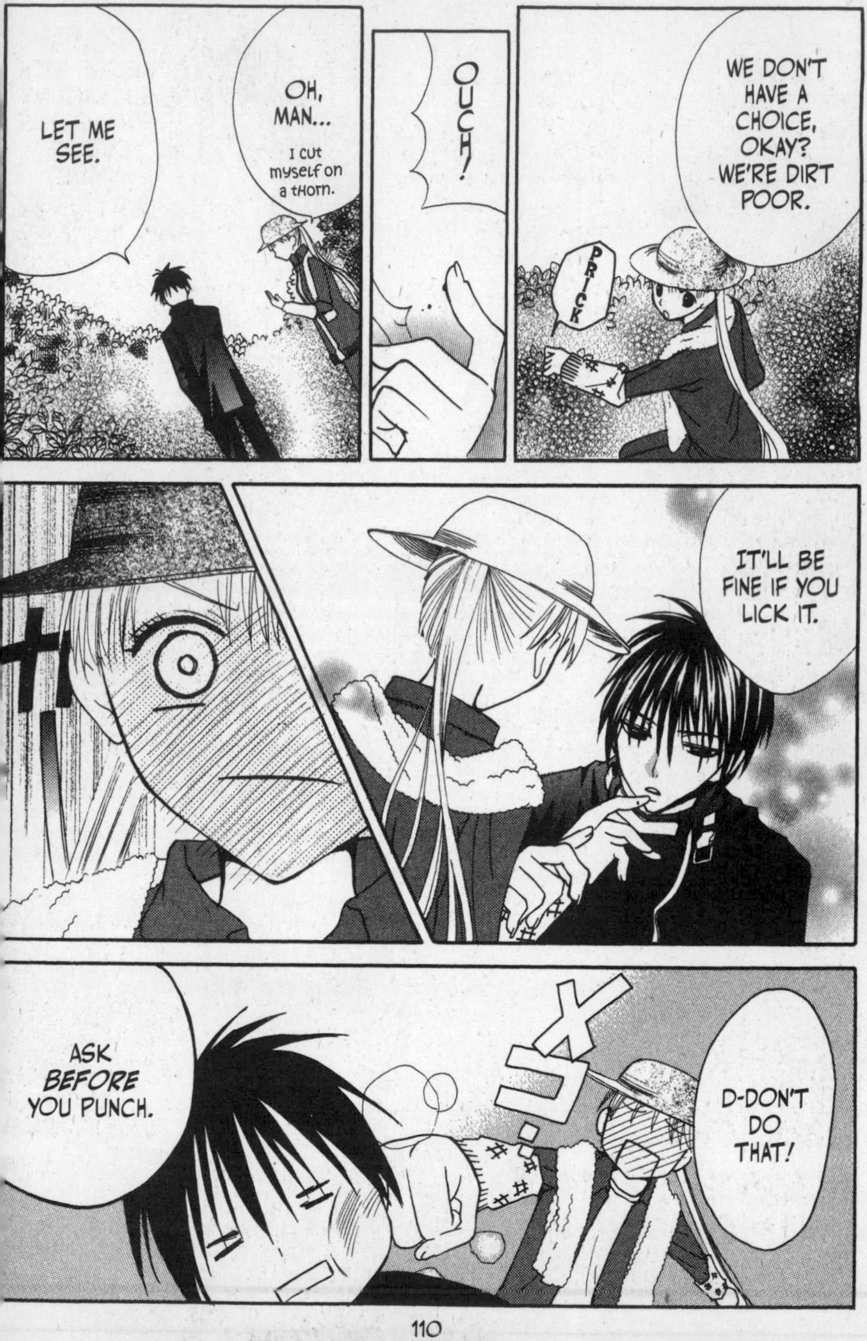
WE DON'T HAVE A CHOICE, OKAY? WE'RE DIRT POOR.
PRICK
OUCH!
OH, MAN...
I cut myself on a thorn.
LET ME SEE.
IT'LL BE FINE IF YOU LICK IT.
D-DON'T DO THAT!
ASK *BEFORE* YOU PUNCH.

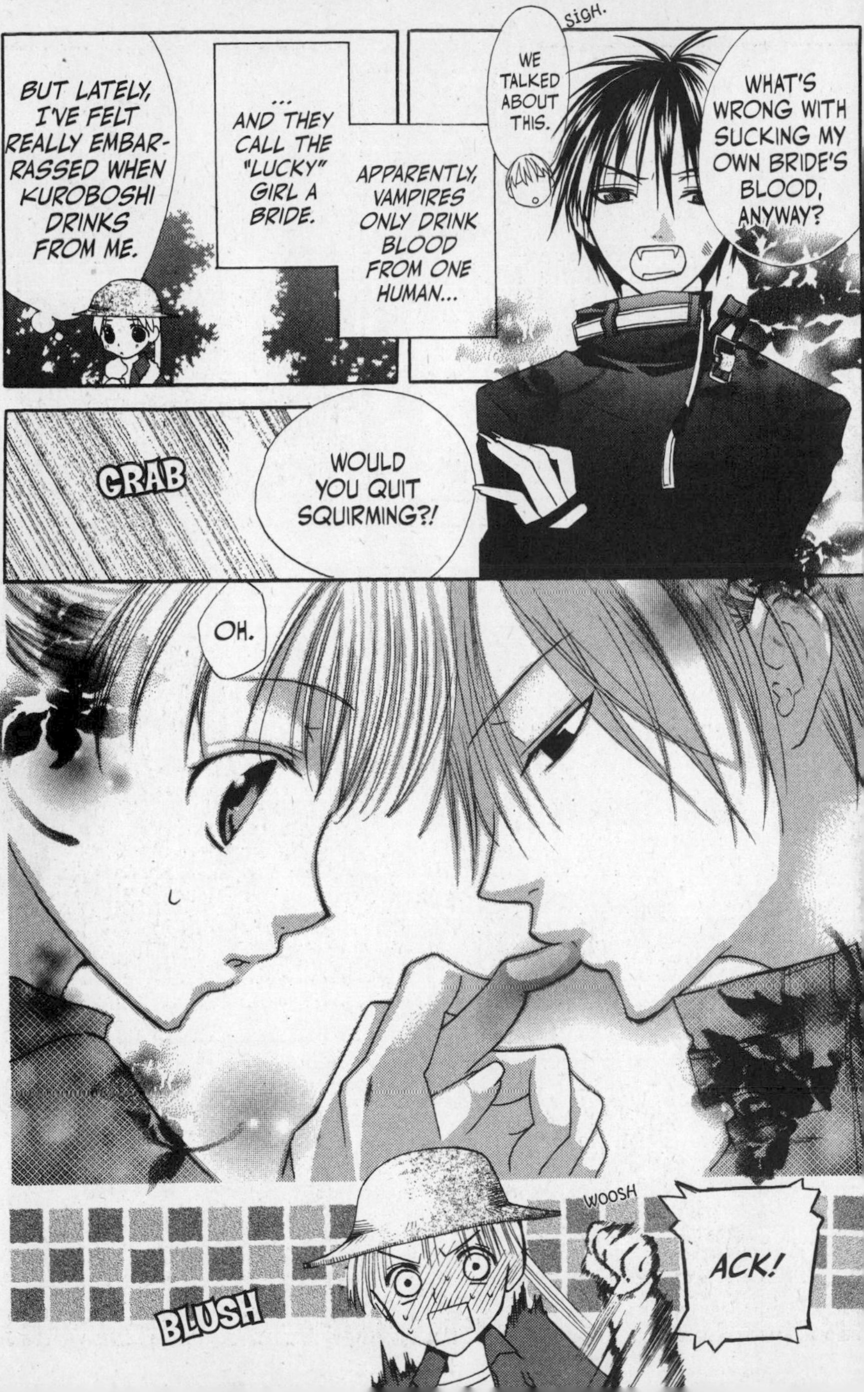
WHAT'S WRONG WITH SUCKING MY OWN BRIDE'S BLOOD, ANYWAY?
SIGH.
WE TALKED ABOUT THIS.
APPARENTLY, VAMPIRES ONLY DRINK BLOOD FROM ONE HUMAN...
... AND THEY CALL THE "LUCKY" GIRL A BRIDE.
BUT LATELY, I'VE FELT REALLY EMBARRASSED WHEN KUROBOSHI DRINKS FROM ME.
WOULD YOU QUIT SQUIRMING?!
GRAB
OH.
ACK!
WOOSH
BLUSH

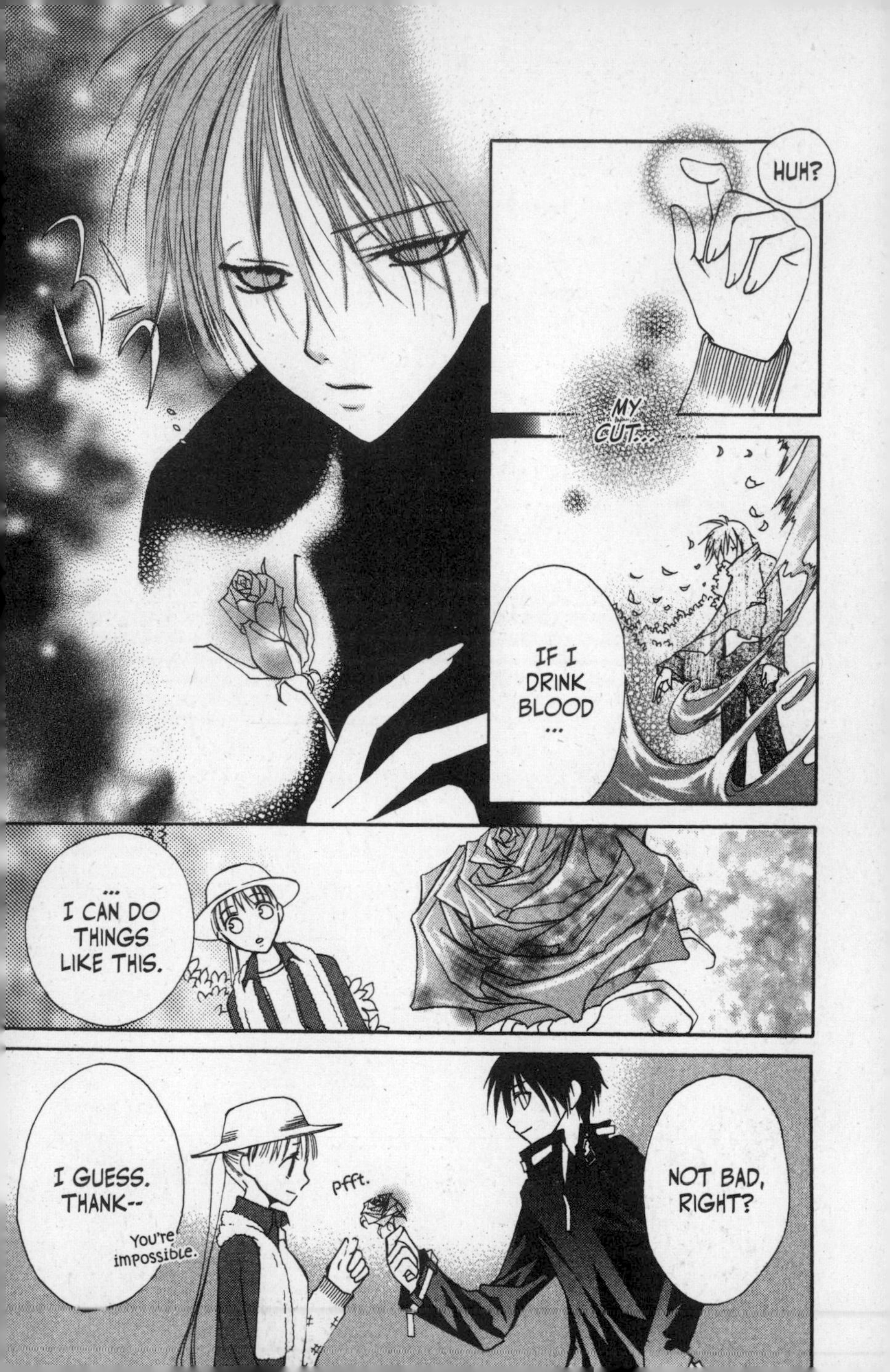
HUH?
MY CUT...
IF I DRINK BLOOD ...
... I CAN DO THINGS LIKE THIS.
NOT BAD, RIGHT?
pfft.
I GUESS. THANK--
You're impossible.

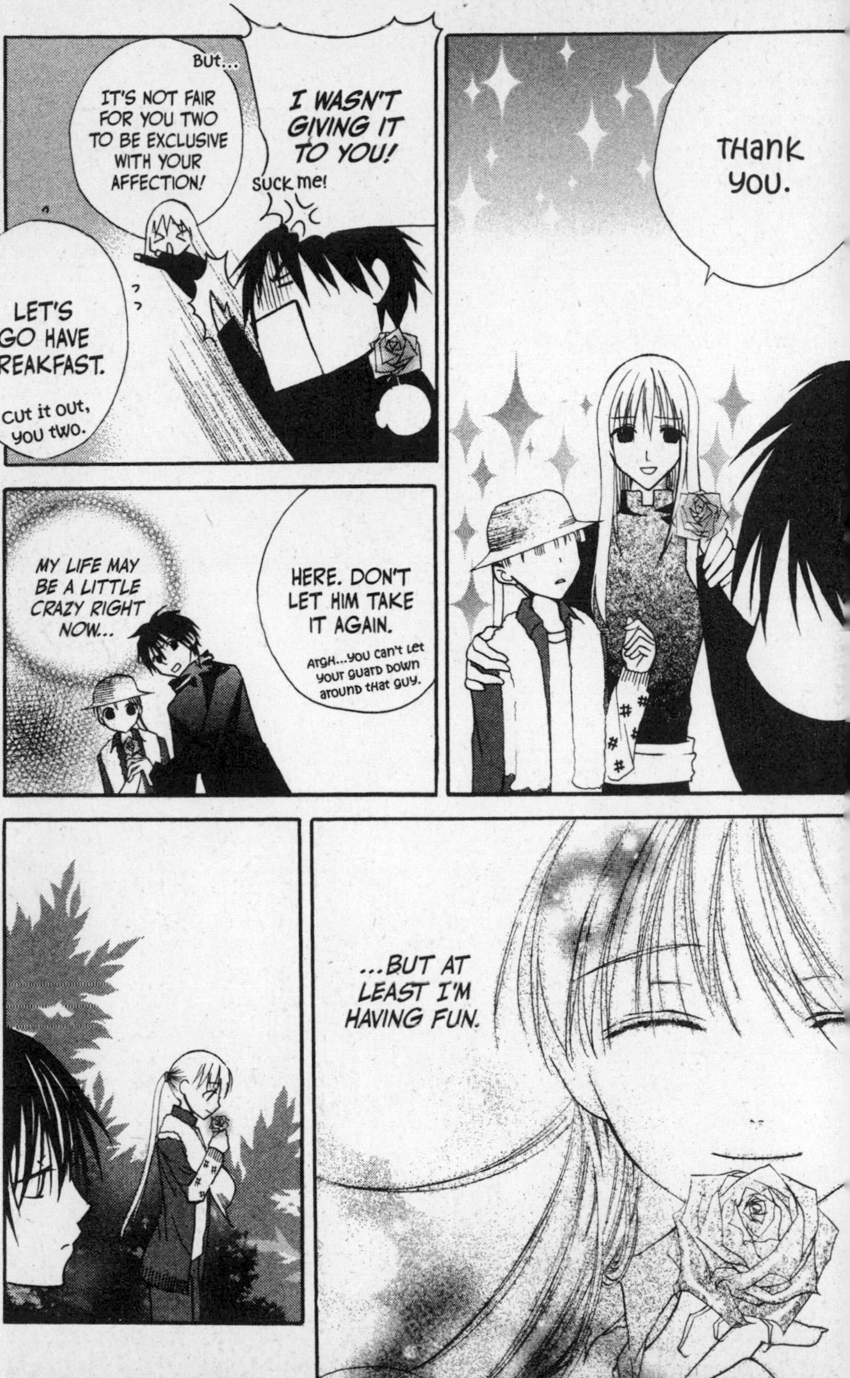
Thank you.
I WASN'T GIVING IT TO YOU!
Suck me!
But...
IT'S NOT FAIR FOR YOU TWO TO BE EXCLUSIVE WITH YOUR AFFECTION!
LET'S GO HAVE BREAKFAST.
Cut it out, you two.
HERE. DON'T LET HIM TAKE IT AGAIN.
Argh...you can't let your guard down around that guy.
MY LIFE MAY BE A LITTLE CRAZY RIGHT NOW...
...BUT AT LEAST I'M HAVING FUN.

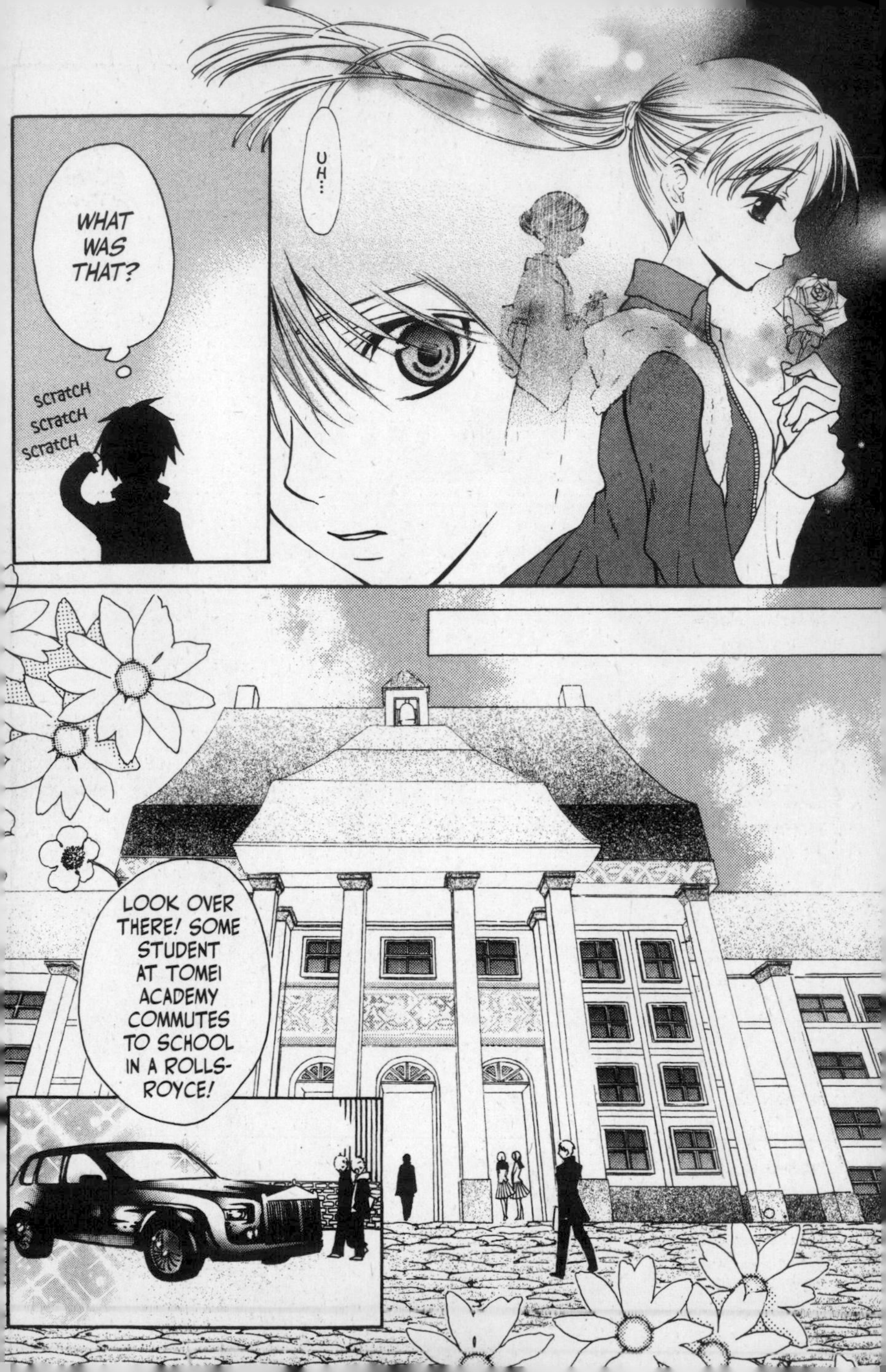
UH...
WHAT WAS THAT?
SCRATCH SCRATCH SCRATCH
LOOK OVER THERE! SOME STUDENT AT TOMEI ACADEMY COMMUTES TO SCHOOL IN A ROLLS-ROYCE!

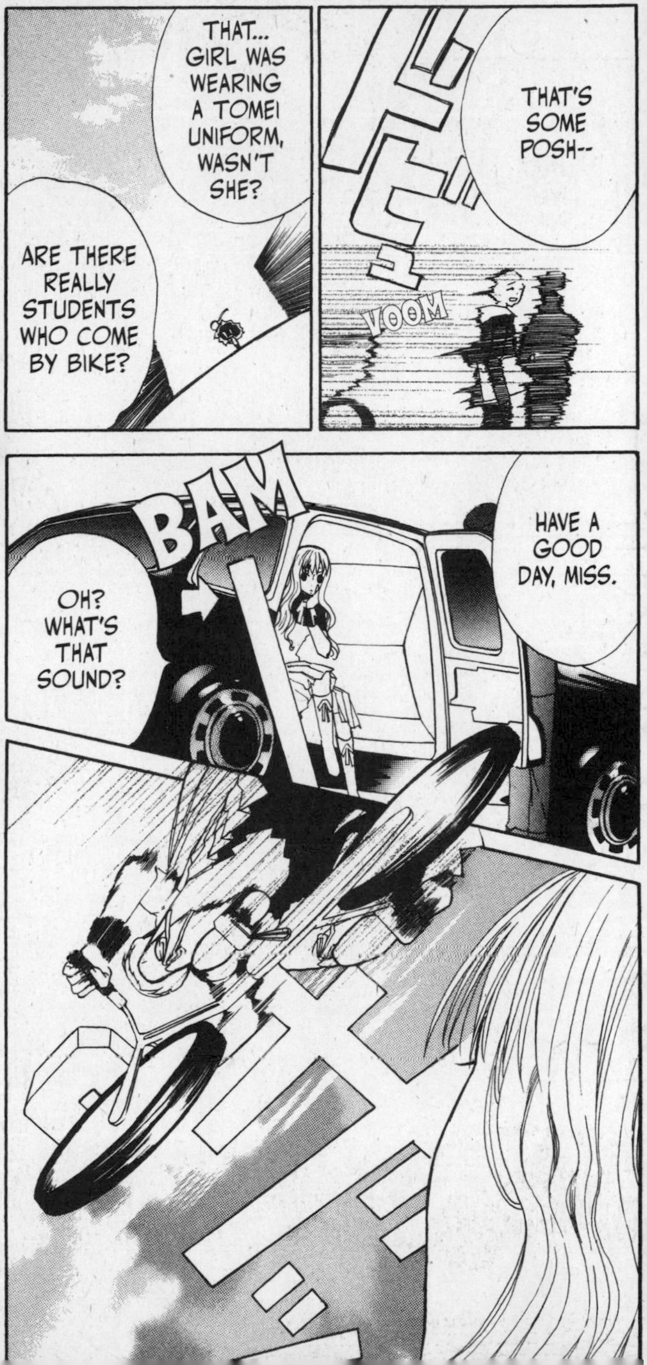
THAT'S SOME POSH--
VOOM
THAT... GIRL WAS WEARING A TOMEI UNIFORM, WASN'T SHE?
ARE THERE REALLY STUDENTS WHO COME BY BIKE?
HAVE A GOOD DAY, MISS.
BAM
OH? WHAT'S THAT SOUND?

Kuroboshi's image colors are red and black. Dab dab dab. H-hey...I think I've seen this before...could it be?!

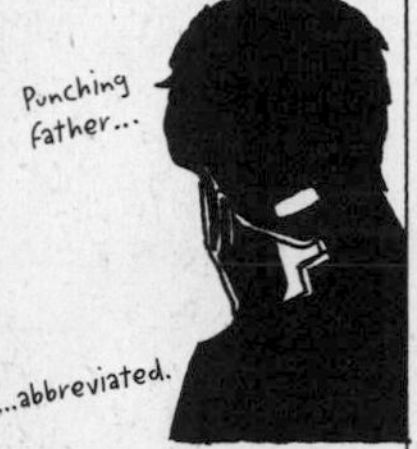
Punching father...
...abbreviated.

Why, he's wearing some realistic robot anime uniform! Kuroboshi transforms himself into a mobile suit pilot!

His memories playing SupaRobo* must still be fresh in his mind.

Anyway, I would be happy to read any comments you can offer me.

To: Kazuko Furumiya
Hana To Yume Editor's Desk
Hakusensha
2-2-2 Awaji City, Kanda
Chiyoda-ku, Tokyo
101-0063

OR

To: Kazuko Furumiya
TOKYOPOP
5900 Wilshire Blvd, #2000
Los Angeles, CA 90036

*Note: "SupaRobo" is the abbreviated name of the video game "Super Robot Taisen."

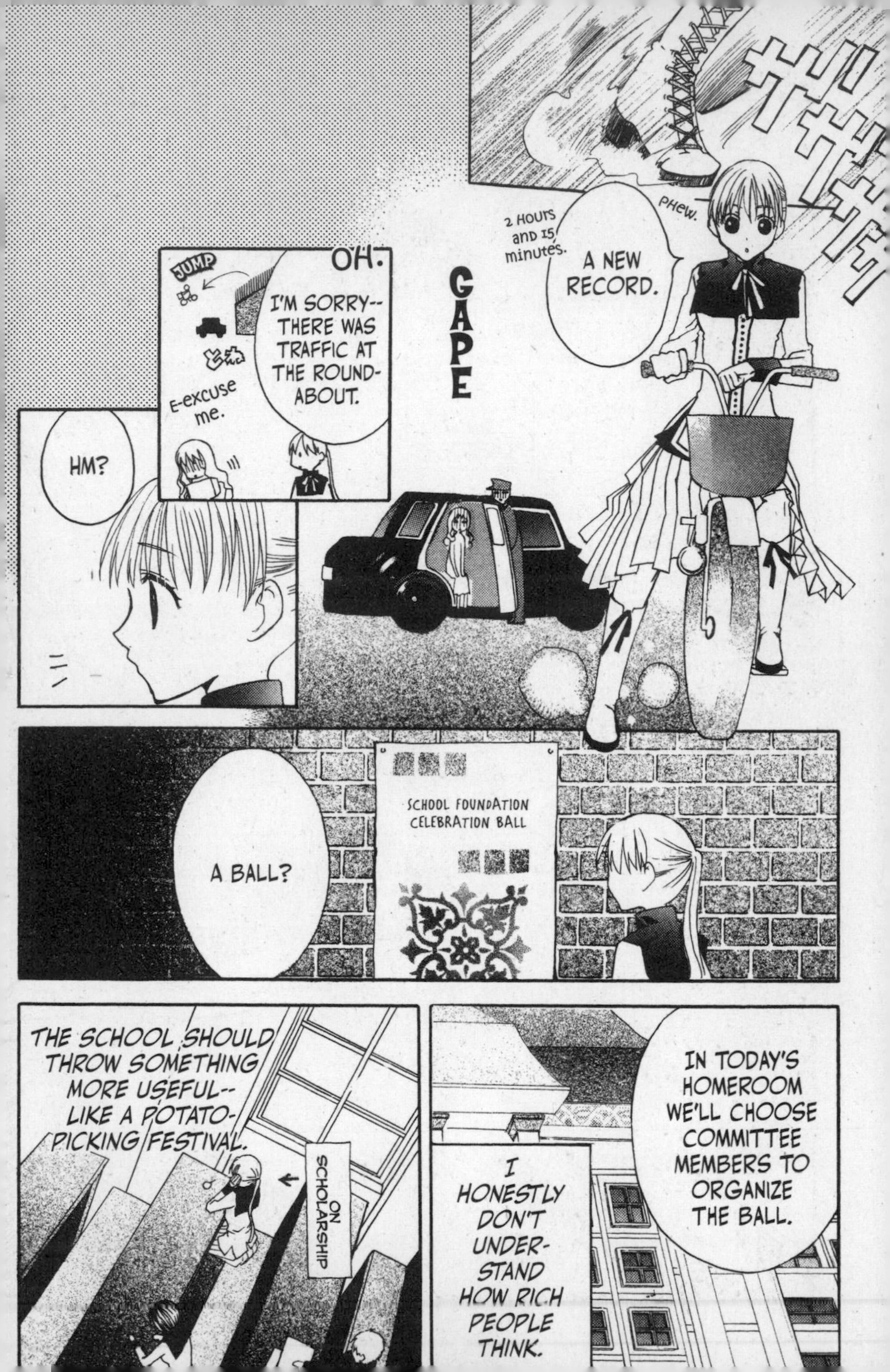

PHEW.
2 HOURS and 15 minutes.
A NEW RECORD.
GAPE
JUMP
OH.
I'M SORRY-- THERE WAS TRAFFIC AT THE ROUND-ABOUT.
E-excuse me.
HM?
SCHOOL FOUNDATION CELEBRATION BALL
A BALL?
IN TODAY'S HOMEROOM WE'LL CHOOSE COMMITTEE MEMBERS TO ORGANIZE THE BALL.
I HONESTLY DON'T UNDER-STAND HOW RICH PEOPLE THINK.
THE SCHOOL SHOULD THROW SOMETHING MORE USEFUL-- LIKE A POTATO-PICKING FESTIVAL.
ON SCHOLARSHIP

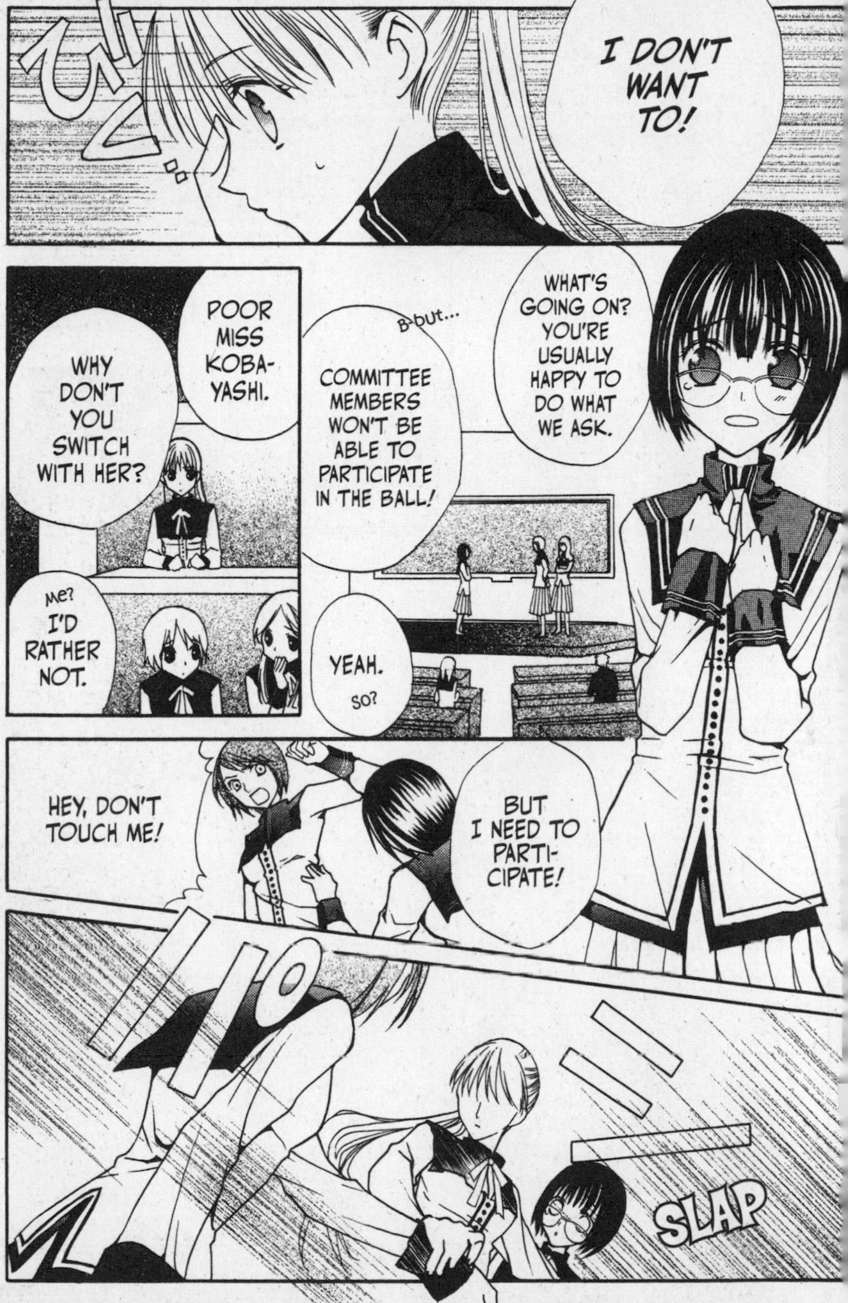
I DON'T WANT TO!
WHAT'S GOING ON? YOU'RE USUALLY HAPPY TO DO WHAT WE ASK.
B-but...
COMMITTEE MEMBERS WON'T BE ABLE TO PARTICIPATE IN THE BALL!
YEAH.
SO?
POOR MISS KOBA-YASHI.
WHY DON'T YOU SWITCH WITH HER?
Me? I'D RATHER NOT.
BUT I NEED TO PARTI-CIPATE!
HEY, DON'T TOUCH ME!
SLAP

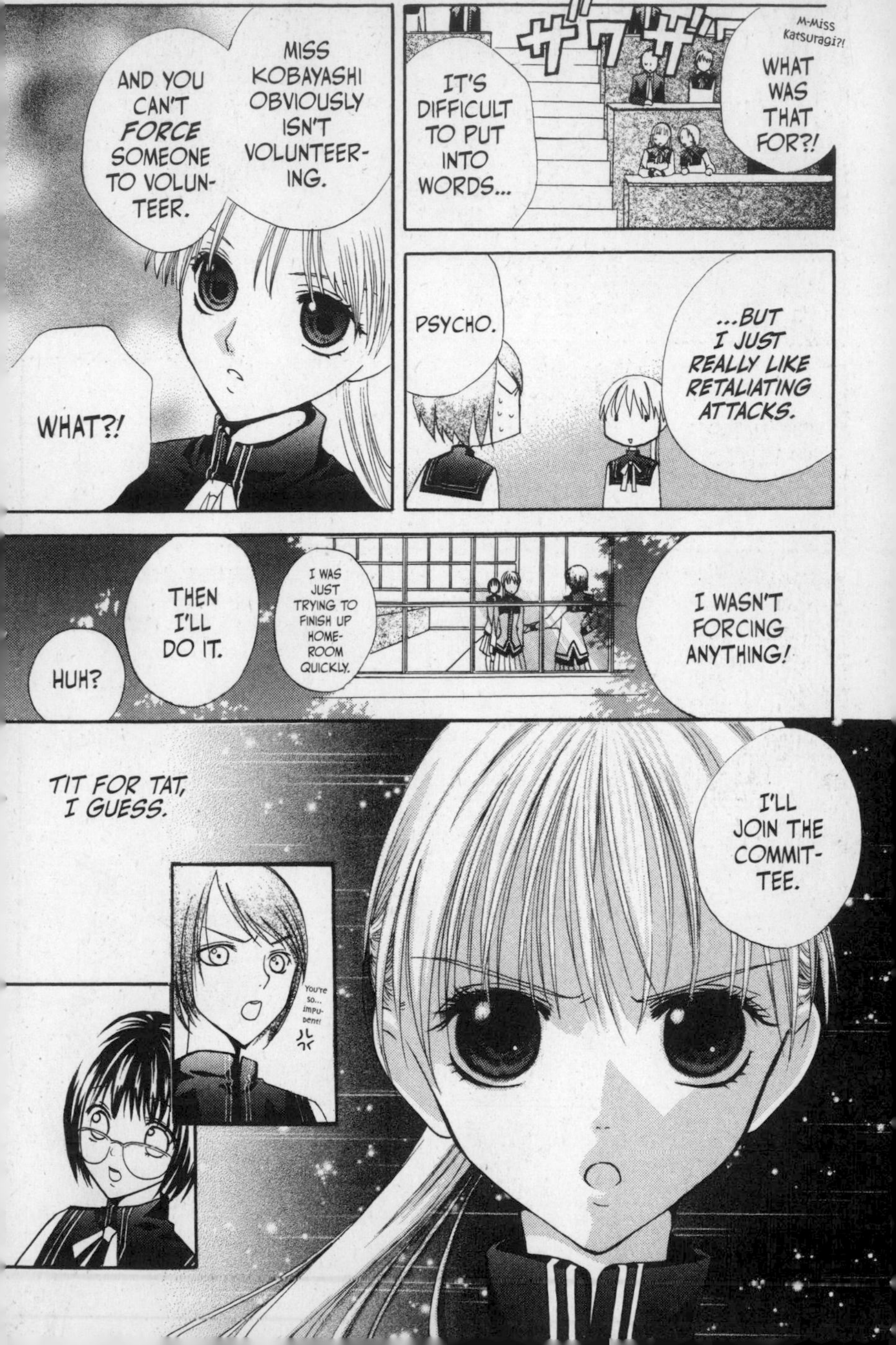
M-Miss Katsuragi?!
WHAT WAS THAT FOR?!
IT'S DIFFICULT TO PUT INTO WORDS...
...BUT I JUST REALLY LIKE RETALIATING ATTACKS.
PSYCHO.
MISS KOBAYASHI OBVIOUSLY ISN'T VOLUNTEER-ING.
AND YOU CAN'T FORCE SOMEONE TO VOLUN-TEER.
WHAT?!
I WASN'T FORCING ANYTHING!
I WAS JUST TRYING TO FINISH UP HOME-ROOM QUICKLY.
THEN I'LL DO IT.
HUH?
I'LL JOIN THE COMMIT-TEE.
TIT FOR TAT, I GUESS.
You're so... impu-dent!

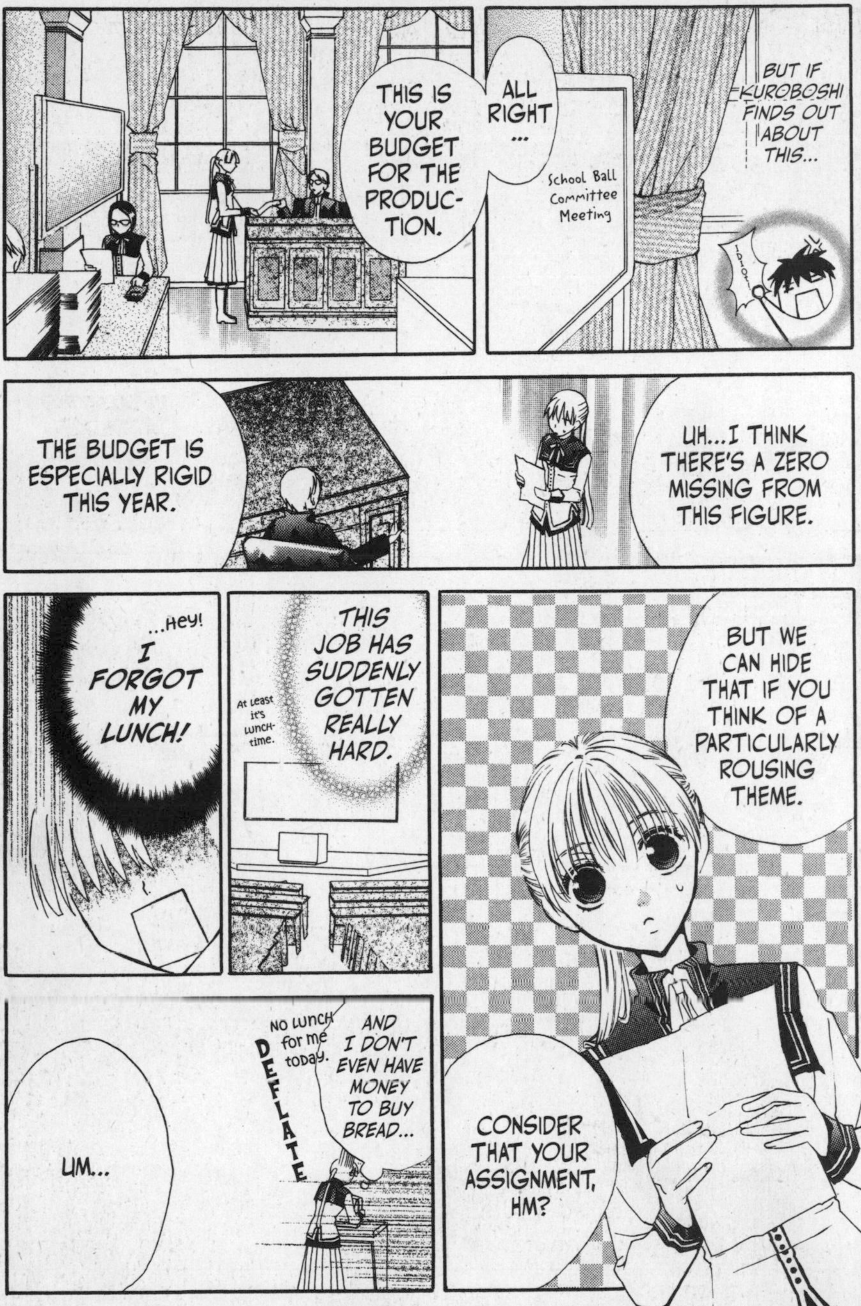
BUT IF KUROBOSHI FINDS OUT ABOUT THIS...
IDIOT!
ALL RIGHT...
School Ball Committee Meeting
THIS IS YOUR BUDGET FOR THE PRODUCTION.
UH...I THINK THERE'S A ZERO MISSING FROM THIS FIGURE.
THE BUDGET IS ESPECIALLY RIGID THIS YEAR.
BUT WE CAN HIDE THAT IF YOU THINK OF A PARTICULARLY ROUSING THEME.
CONSIDER THAT YOUR ASSIGNMENT, HM?
THIS JOB HAS SUDDENLY GOTTEN REALLY HARD.
At least it's lunch-time.
...Hey!
I FORGOT MY LUNCH!
AND I DON'T EVEN HAVE MONEY TO BUY BREAD...
No lunch for me today.
DEFLATE
UM...

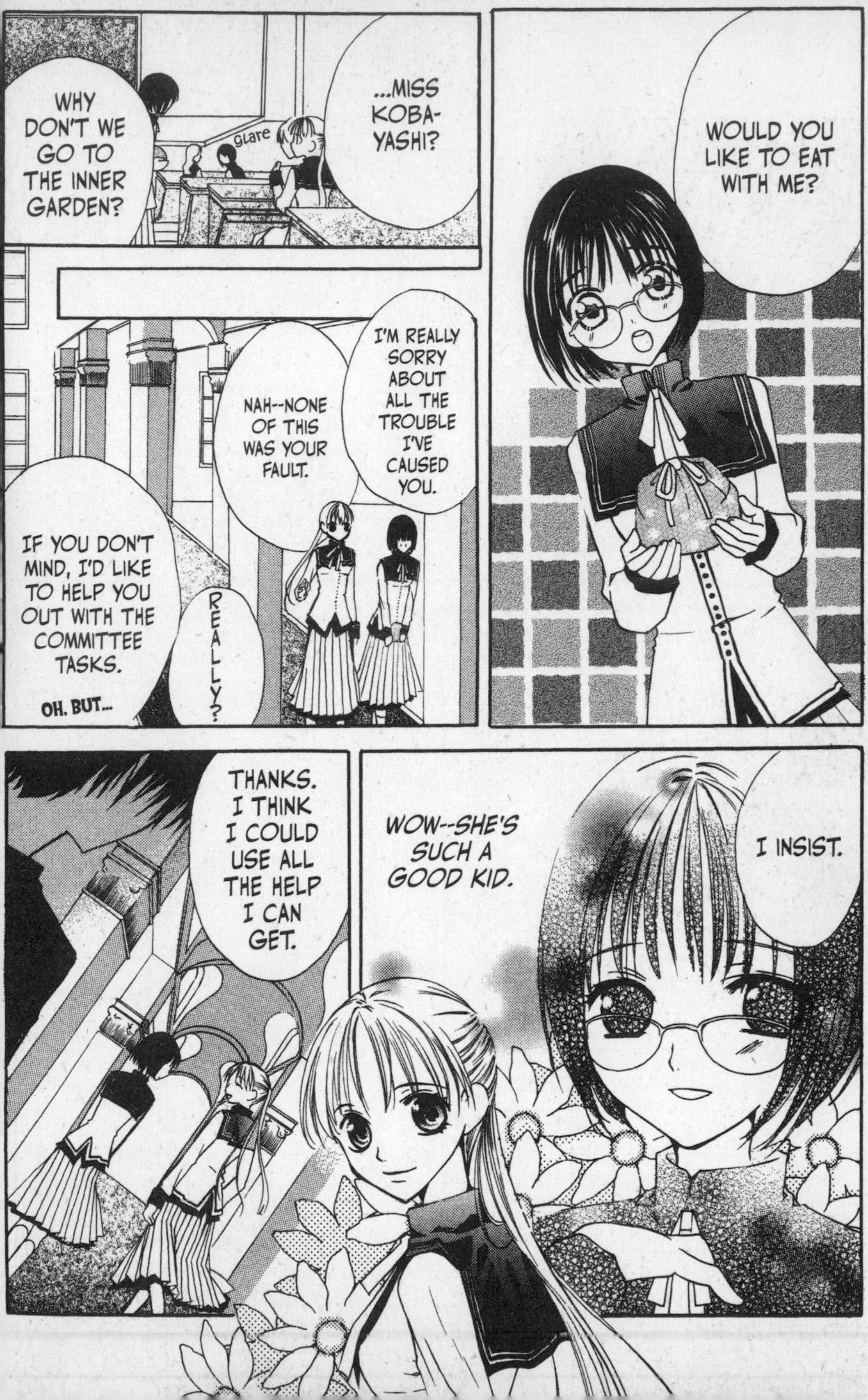
WOULD YOU LIKE TO EAT WITH ME?
...MISS KOBA-YASHI?
Glare
WHY DON'T WE GO TO THE INNER GARDEN?
I'M REALLY SORRY ABOUT ALL THE TROUBLE I'VE CAUSED YOU.
NAH--NONE OF THIS WAS YOUR FAULT.
REALLY?
IF YOU DON'T MIND, I'D LIKE TO HELP YOU OUT WITH THE COMMITTEE TASKS.
OH. BUT...
I INSIST.
WOW--SHE'S SUCH A GOOD KID.
THANKS. I THINK I COULD USE ALL THE HELP I CAN GET.

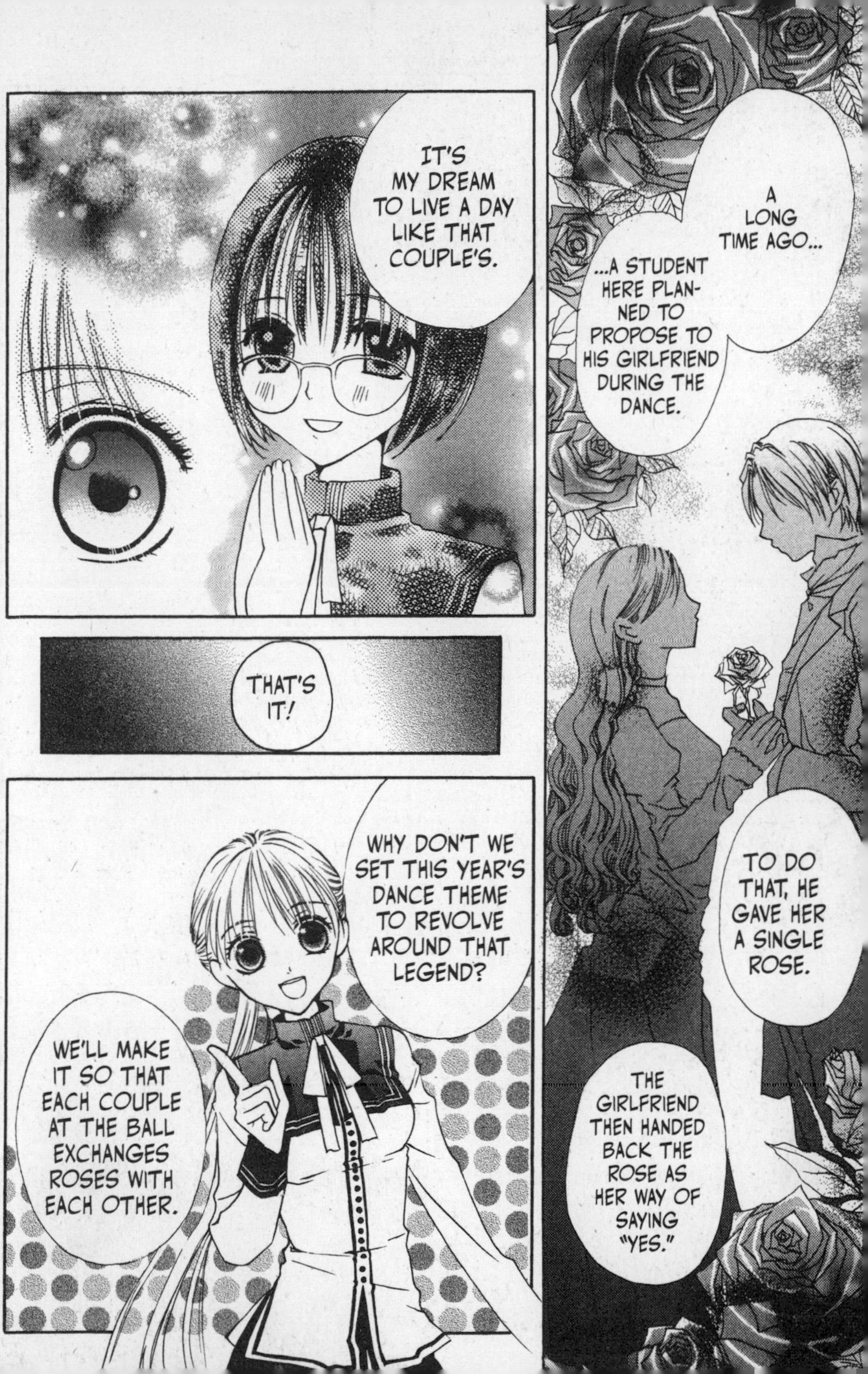

A LONG TIME AGO...
...A STUDENT HERE PLAN-NED TO PROPOSE TO HIS GIRLFRIEND DURING THE DANCE.
TO DO THAT, HE GAVE HER A SINGLE ROSE.
THE GIRLFRIEND THEN HANDED BACK THE ROSE AS HER WAY OF SAYING "YES."
IT'S MY DREAM TO LIVE A DAY LIKE THAT COUPLE'S.
THAT'S IT!
WHY DON'T WE SET THIS YEAR'S DANCE THEME TO REVOLVE AROUND THAT LEGEND?
WE'LL MAKE IT SO THAT EACH COUPLE AT THE BALL EXCHANGES ROSES WITH EACH OTHER.

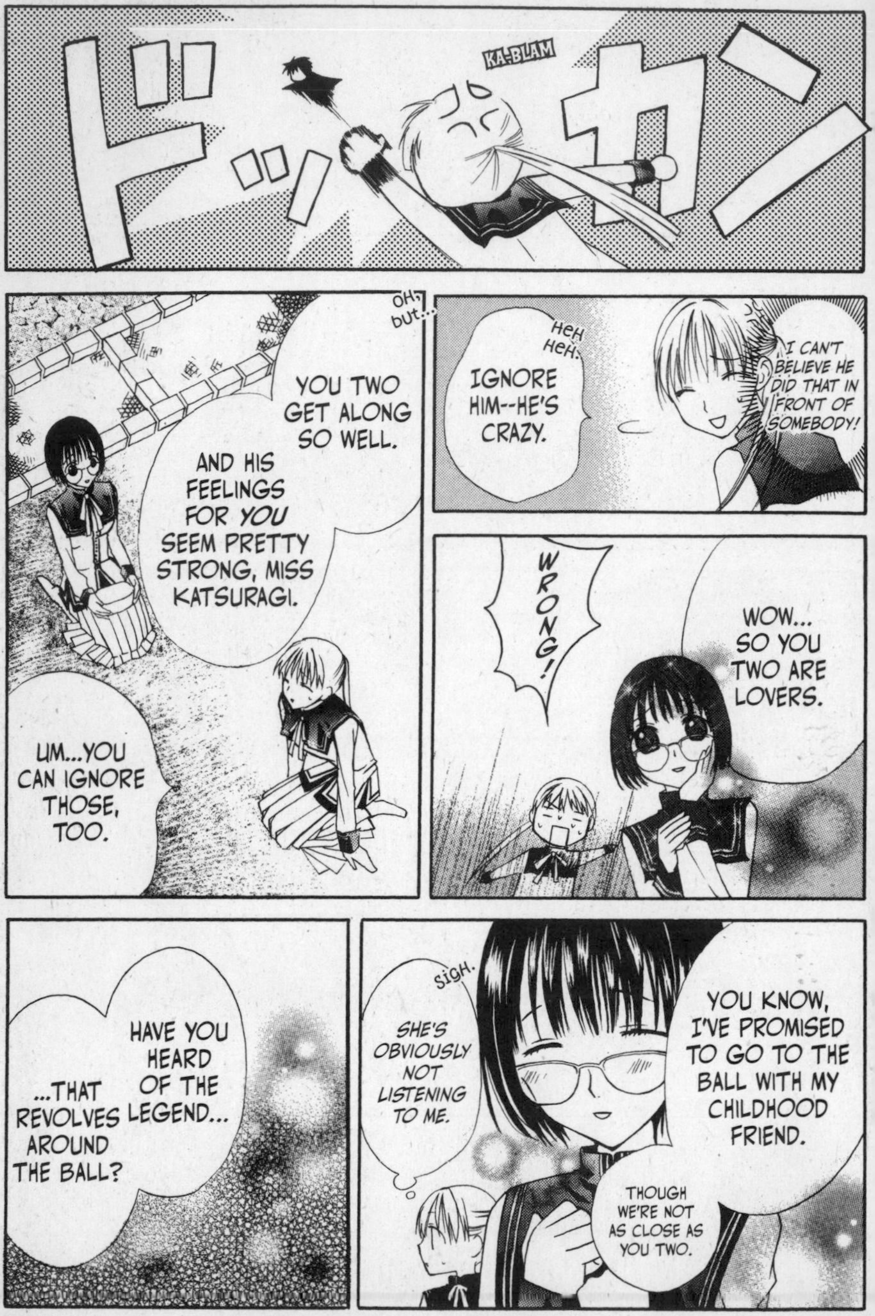
KA-BLAM
I CAN'T BELIEVE HE DID THAT IN FRONT OF SOMEBODY!
HEH HEH.
IGNORE HIM--HE'S CRAZY.
WOW... SO YOU TWO ARE LOVERS.
WRONG!
OH, but...
YOU TWO GET ALONG SO WELL.
AND HIS FEELINGS FOR *YOU* SEEM PRETTY STRONG, MISS KATSURAGI.
UM...YOU CAN IGNORE THOSE, TOO.
YOU KNOW, I'VE PROMISED TO GO TO THE BALL WITH MY CHILDHOOD FRIEND.
THOUGH WE'RE NOT AS CLOSE AS YOU TWO.
SIGH.
SHE'S OBVIOUSLY NOT LISTENING TO ME.
HAVE YOU HEARD OF THE LEGEND...
...THAT REVOLVES AROUND THE BALL?

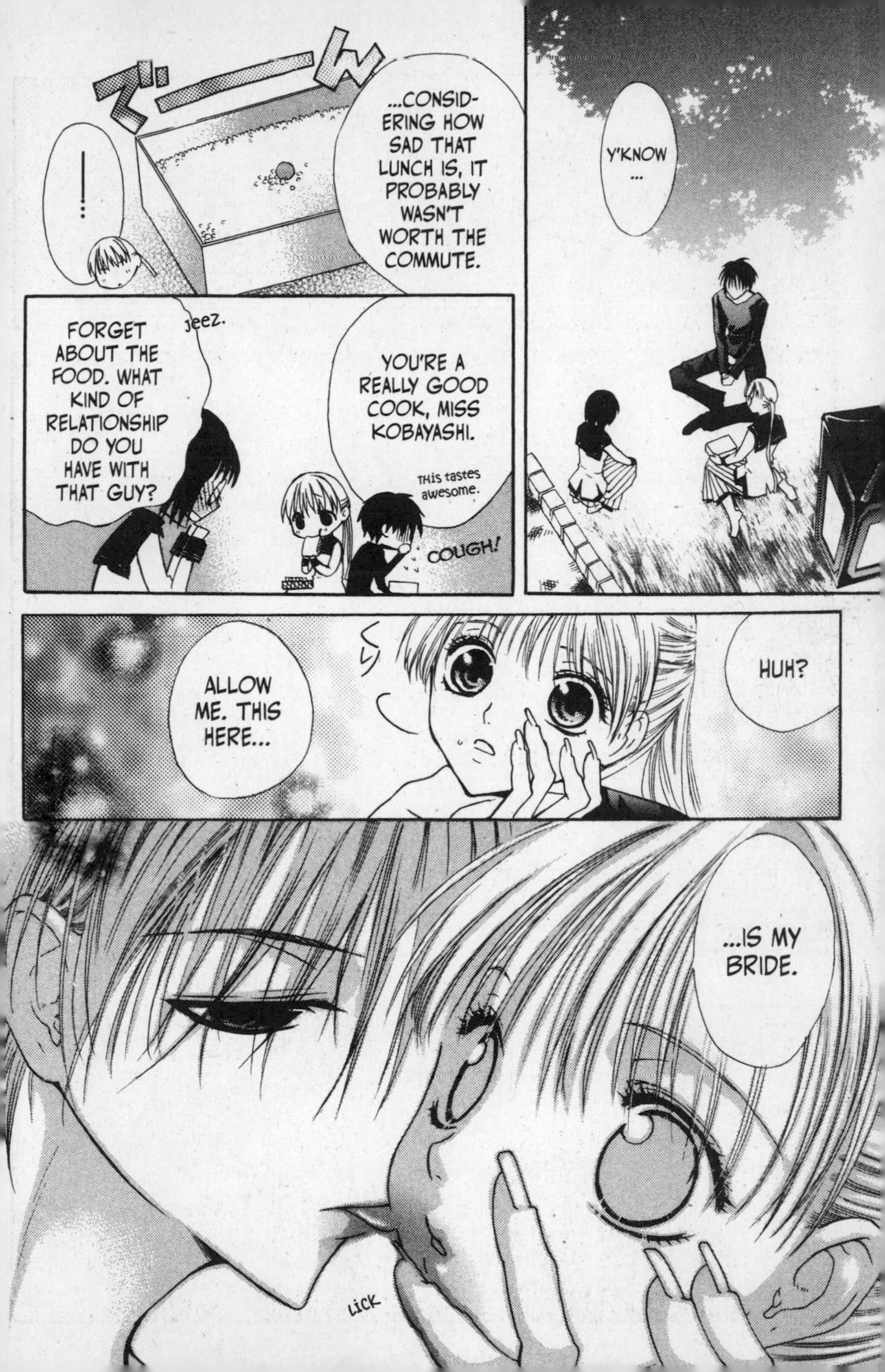
Y'KNOW ...
...CONSIDERING HOW SAD THAT LUNCH IS, IT PROBABLY WASN'T WORTH THE COMMUTE.
!...
YOU'RE A REALLY GOOD COOK, MISS KOBAYASHI.
THIS tastes awesome.
COUGH!
Jeez.
FORGET ABOUT THE FOOD. WHAT KIND OF RELATIONSHIP DO YOU HAVE WITH THAT GUY?
HUH?
ALLOW ME. THIS HERE...
...IS MY BRIDE.
LICK

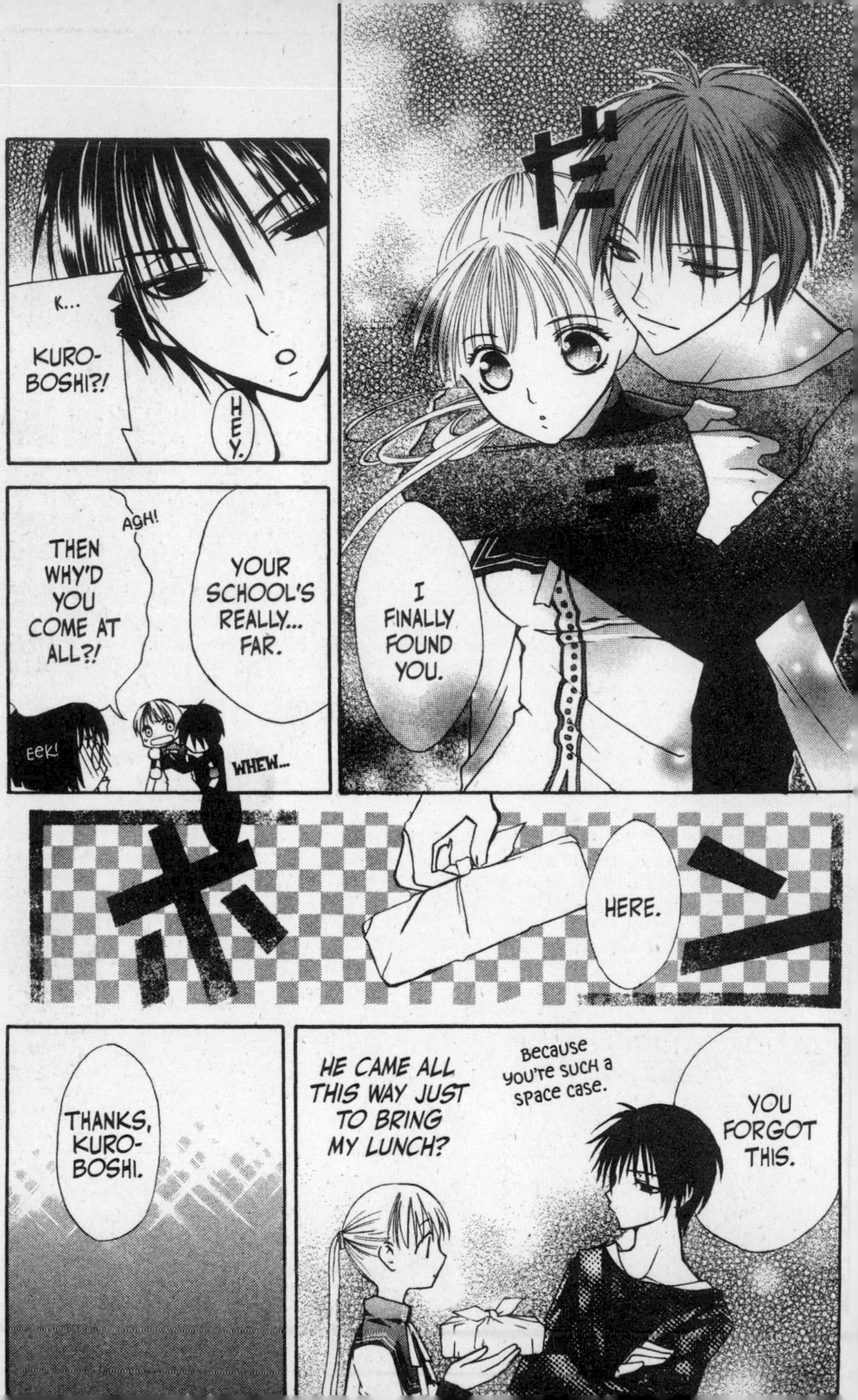
I FINALLY FOUND YOU.
HEY.
K...
KURO-BOSHI?!
YOUR SCHOOL'S REALLY... FAR.
AGH!
THEN WHY'D YOU COME AT ALL?!
WHEW...
EEK!
HERE.
YOU FORGOT THIS.
Because you're such a space case.
HE CAME ALL THIS WAY JUST TO BRING MY LUNCH?
THANKS, KURO-BOSHI.

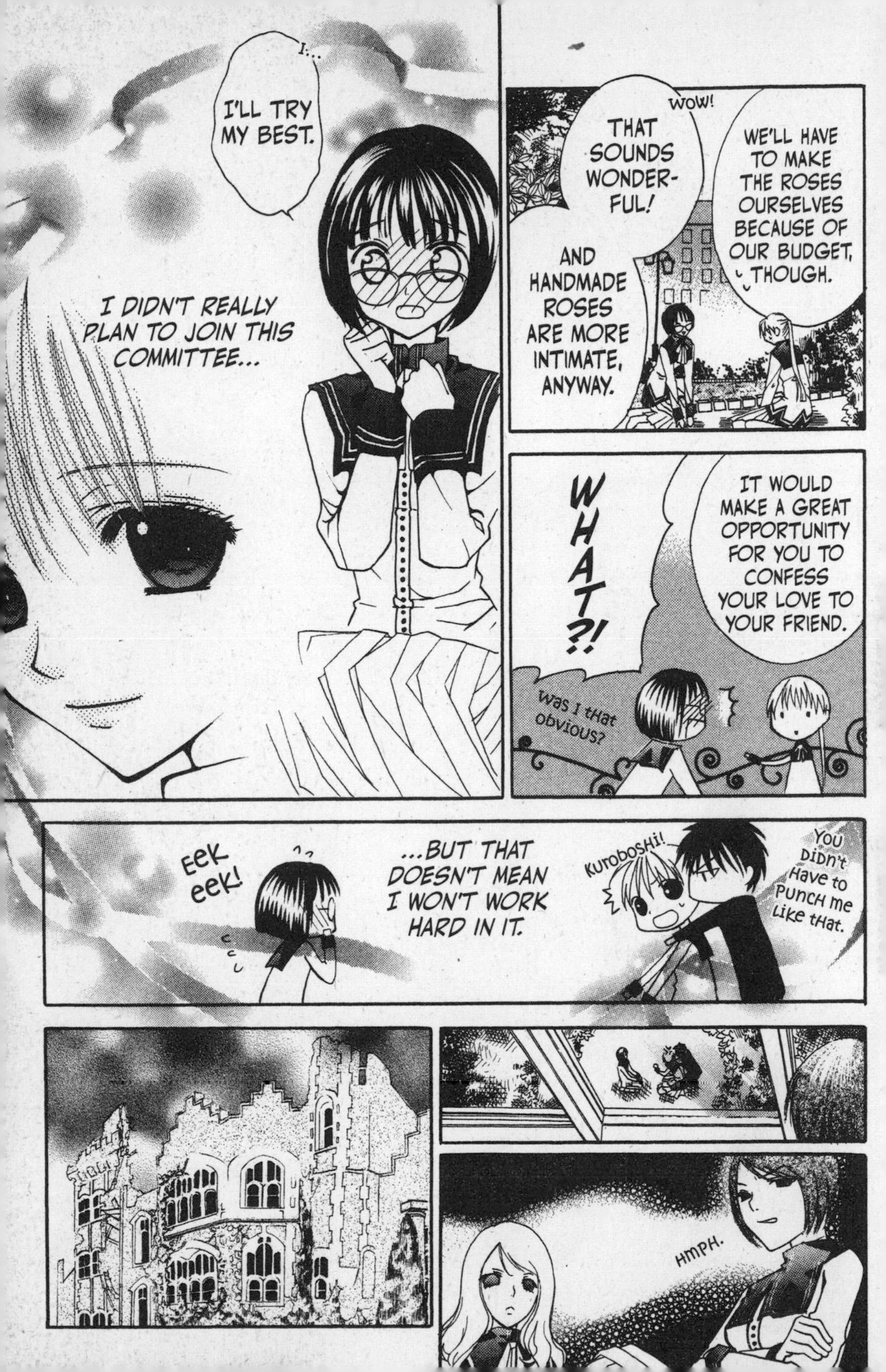
WE'LL HAVE TO MAKE THE ROSES OURSELVES BECAUSE OF OUR BUDGET, THOUGH.
WOW!
THAT SOUNDS WONDERFUL!
AND HANDMADE ROSES ARE MORE INTIMATE, ANYWAY.
IT WOULD MAKE A GREAT OPPORTUNITY FOR YOU TO CONFESS YOUR LOVE TO YOUR FRIEND.
WHAT?!
Was I that obvious?
I...
I'LL TRY MY BEST.
I DIDN'T REALLY PLAN TO JOIN THIS COMMITTEE...
You didn't have to punch me like that.
Kuroboshi!
...BUT THAT DOESN'T MEAN I WON'T WORK HARD IN IT.
Eek eek!
HMPH.

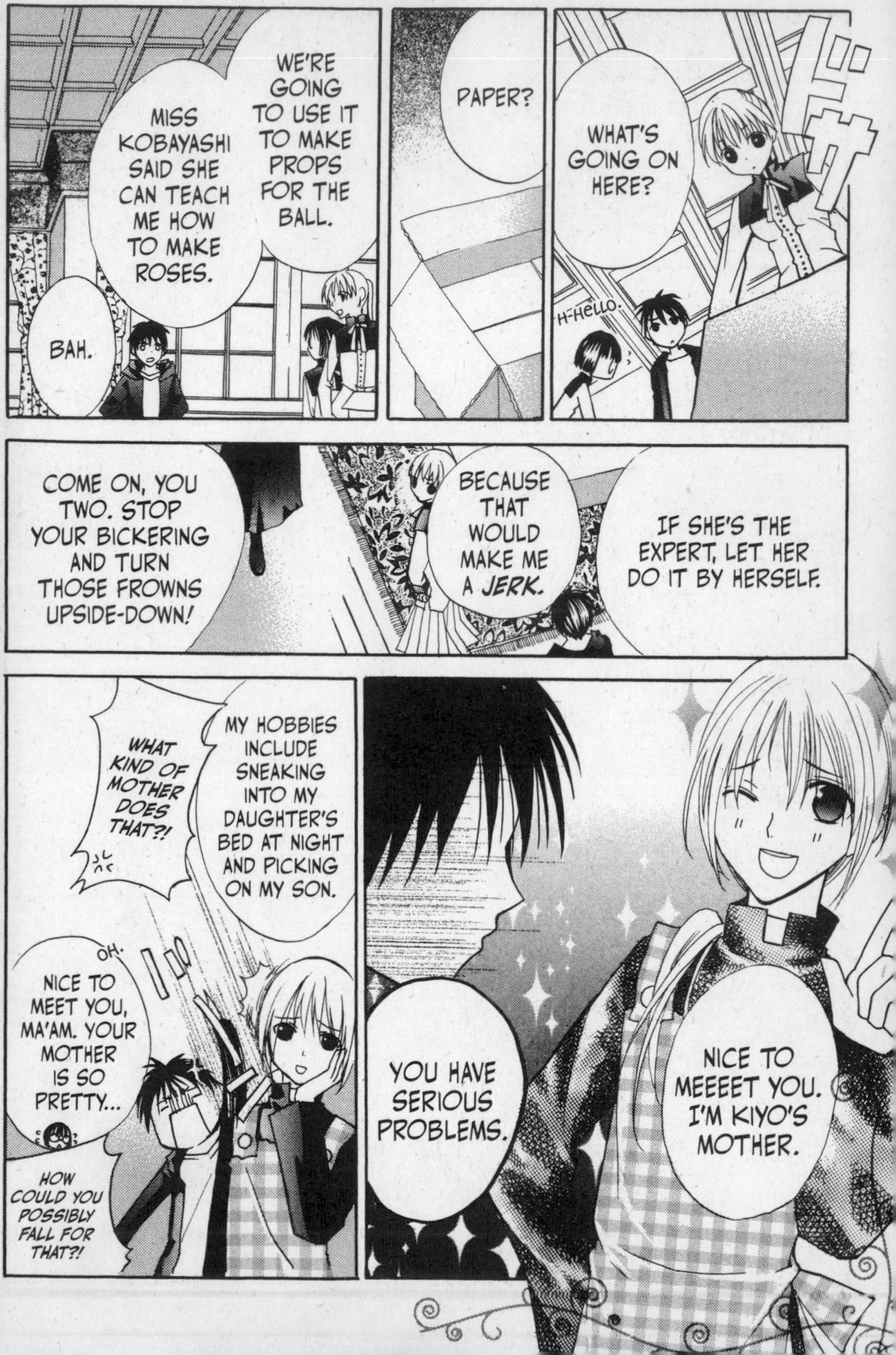
ドサ
WHAT'S GOING ON HERE?
H-HELLO.
PAPER?
WE'RE GOING TO USE IT TO MAKE PROPS FOR THE BALL.
MISS KOBAYASHI SAID SHE CAN TEACH ME HOW TO MAKE ROSES.
BAH.
IF SHE'S THE EXPERT, LET HER DO IT BY HERSELF.
BECAUSE THAT WOULD MAKE ME A *JERK.*
COME ON, YOU TWO. STOP YOUR BICKERING AND TURN THOSE FROWNS UPSIDE-DOWN!
NICE TO MEEEET YOU. I'M KIYO'S MOTHER.
YOU HAVE SERIOUS PROBLEMS.
MY HOBBIES INCLUDE SNEAKING INTO MY DAUGHTER'S BED AT NIGHT AND PICKING ON MY SON.
WHAT KIND OF MOTHER DOES THAT?!
OH.
NICE TO MEET YOU, MA'AM. YOUR MOTHER IS SO PRETTY...
HOW COULD YOU POSSIBLY FALL FOR THAT?!

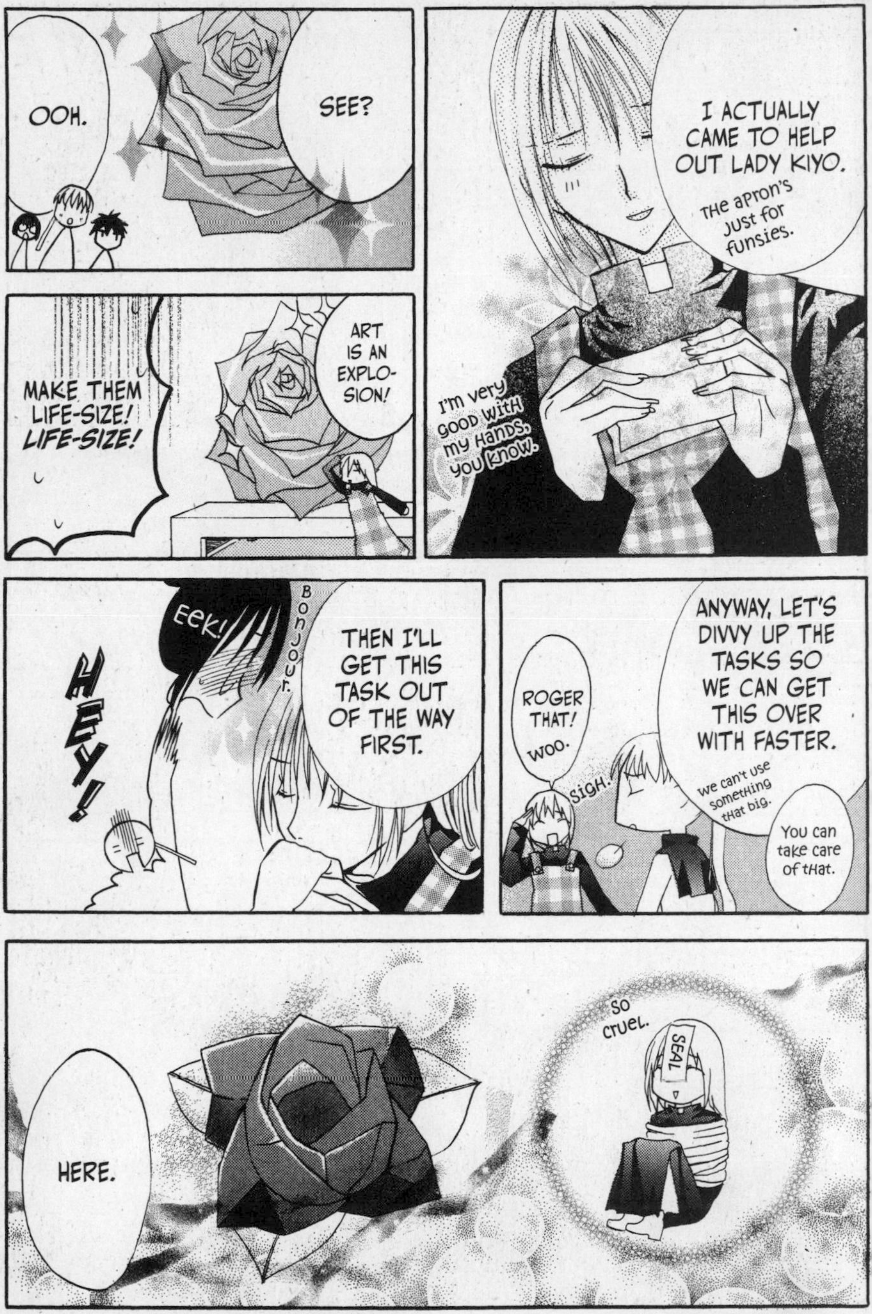
I ACTUALLY CAME TO HELP OUT LADY KIYO.
The apron's just for funsies.
I'm very good with my hands, you know.
SEE?
OOH.
ART IS AN EXPLOSION!
MAKE THEM LIFE-SIZE! LIFE-SIZE!
ANYWAY, LET'S DIVVY UP THE TASKS SO WE CAN GET THIS OVER WITH FASTER.
we can't use something that big.
You can take care of that.
ROGER THAT!
WOO.
SIGH.
Bonjour.
THEN I'LL GET THIS TASK OUT OF THE WAY FIRST.
Eek!
HEY!
So cruel.
SEAL
HERE.

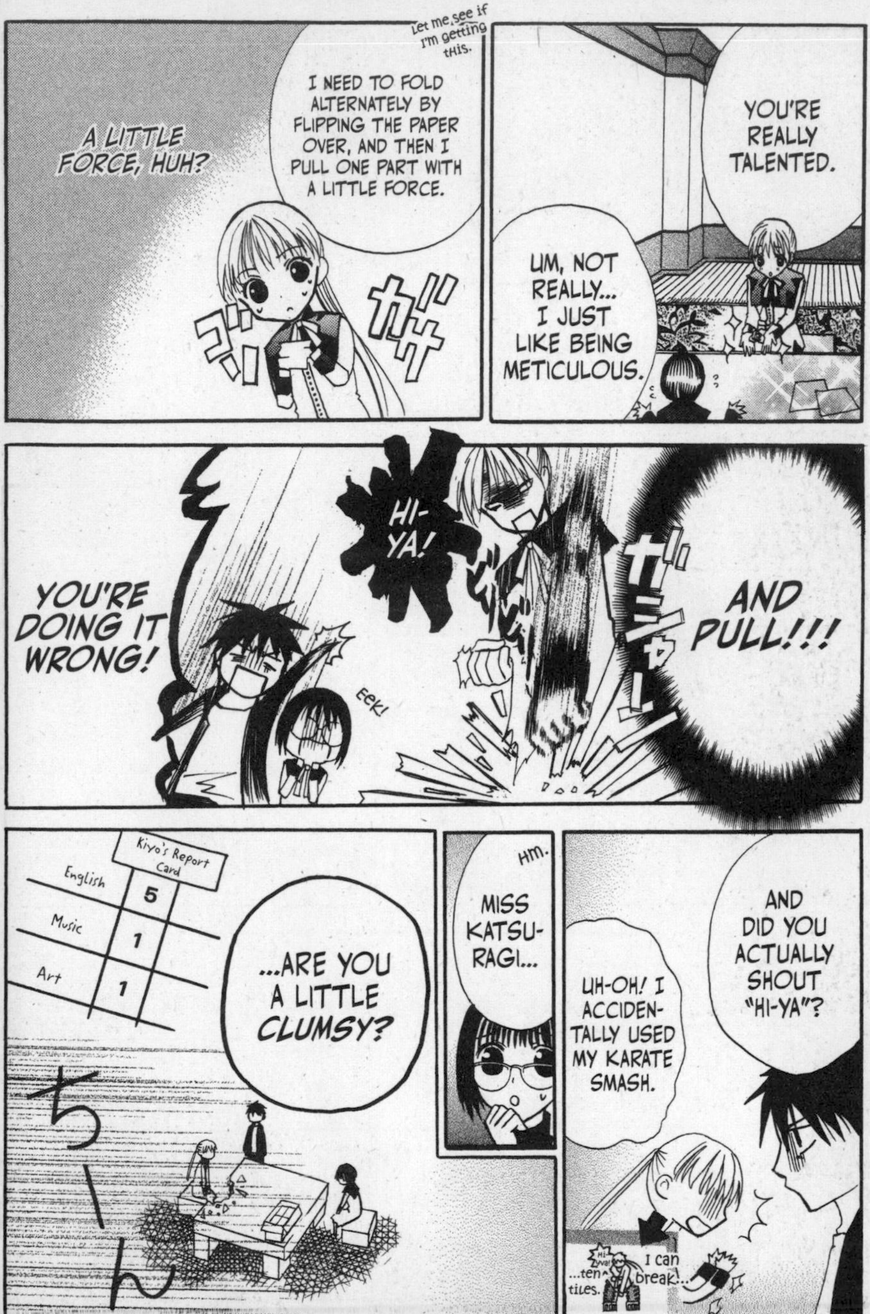
YOU'RE REALLY TALENTED.
UM, NOT REALLY... I JUST LIKE BEING METICULOUS.
Let me see if I'm getting this.
I NEED TO FOLD ALTERNATELY BY FLIPPING THE PAPER OVER, AND THEN I PULL ONE PART WITH A LITTLE FORCE.
A LITTLE FORCE, HUH?
AND PULL!!!
HI-YA!
YOU'RE DOING IT WRONG!
EEK!
AND DID YOU ACTUALLY SHOUT "HI-YA"?
UH-OH! I ACCIDENTALLY USED MY KARATE SMASH.
I can break...
Hi-ya!
...ten tiles.
HM.
MISS KATSURAGI...
...ARE YOU A LITTLE CLUMSY?
Kiyo's Report Card
English 5
Music 1
Art 1
ちーん

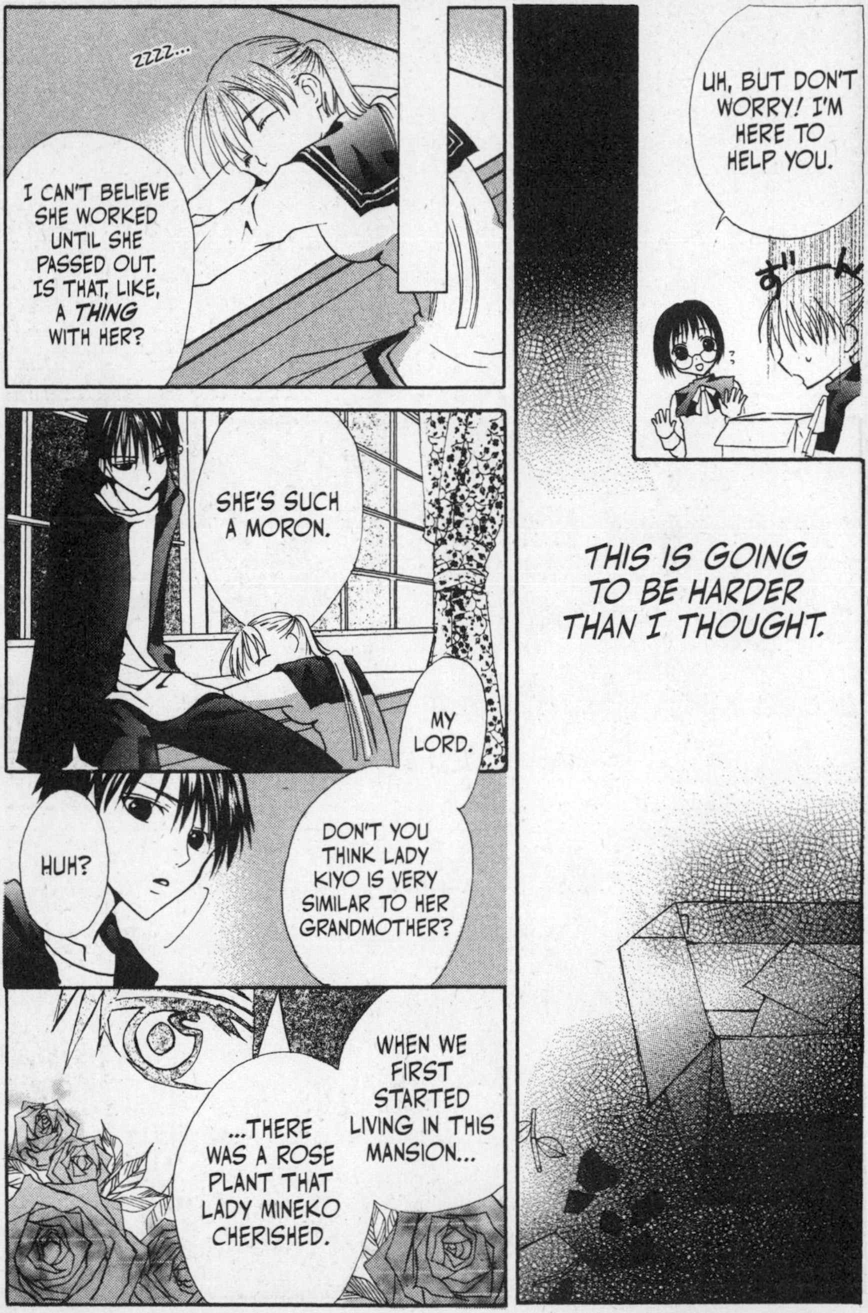
UH, BUT DON'T WORRY! I'M HERE TO HELP YOU.
ずーん
THIS IS GOING TO BE HARDER THAN I THOUGHT.
ZZZZ...
I CAN'T BELIEVE SHE WORKED UNTIL SHE PASSED OUT. IS THAT, LIKE, A *THING* WITH HER?
SHE'S SUCH A MORON.
MY LORD.
DON'T YOU THINK LADY KIYO IS VERY SIMILAR TO HER GRANDMOTHER?
HUH?
WHEN WE FIRST STARTED LIVING IN THIS MANSION...
...THERE WAS A ROSE PLANT THAT LADY MINEKO CHERISHED.

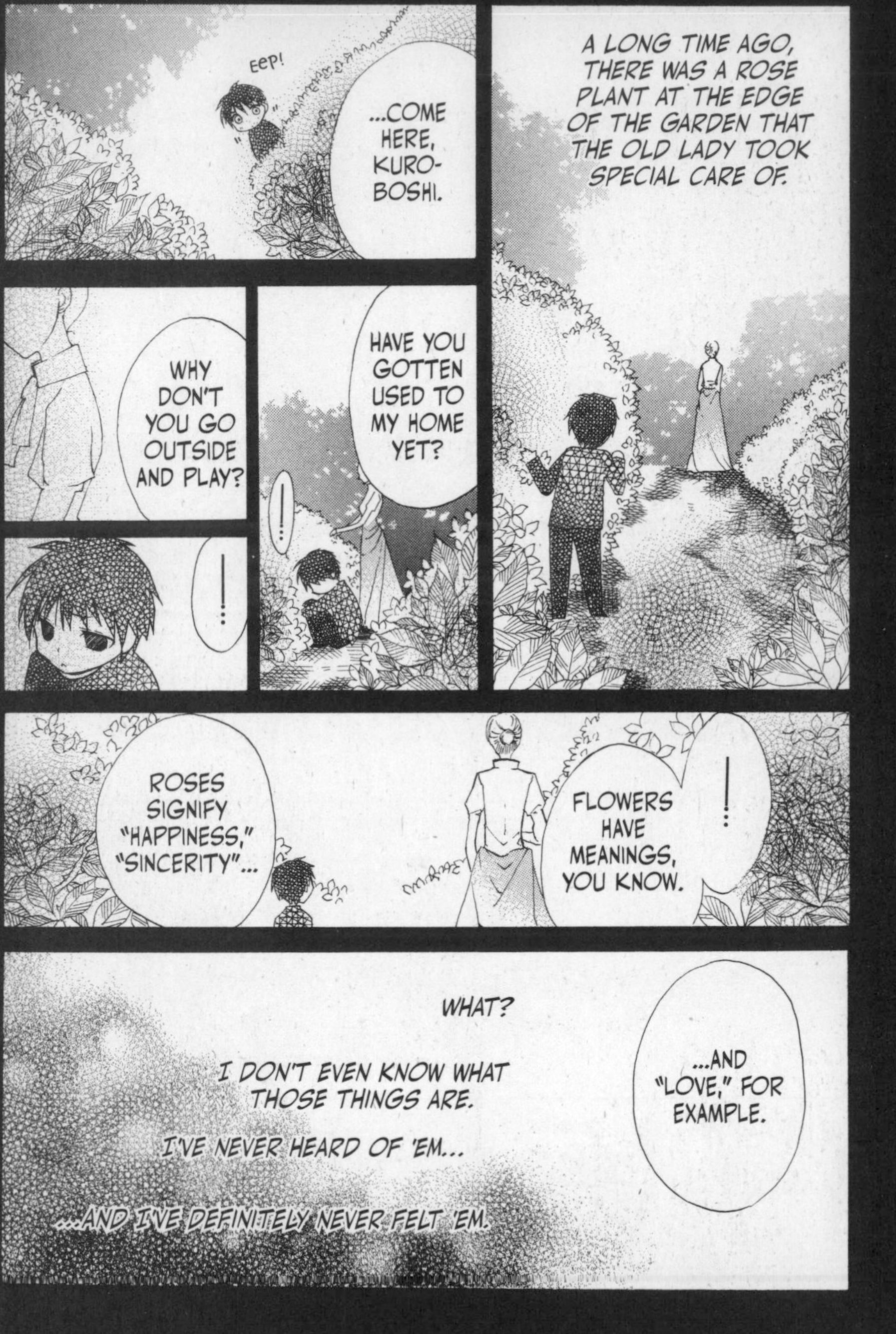
A LONG TIME AGO, THERE WAS A ROSE PLANT AT THE EDGE OF THE GARDEN THAT THE OLD LADY TOOK SPECIAL CARE OF.
...COME HERE, KURO-BOSHI.
EEP!
HAVE YOU GOTTEN USED TO MY HOME YET?
!
WHY DON'T YOU GO OUTSIDE AND PLAY?
!...
!...
FLOWERS HAVE MEANINGS, YOU KNOW.
ROSES SIGNIFY "HAPPINESS," "SINCERITY"...
...AND "LOVE," FOR EXAMPLE.
WHAT?
I DON'T EVEN KNOW WHAT THOSE THINGS ARE.
I'VE NEVER HEARD OF 'EM...
...AND I'VE DEFINITELY NEVER FELT 'EM.

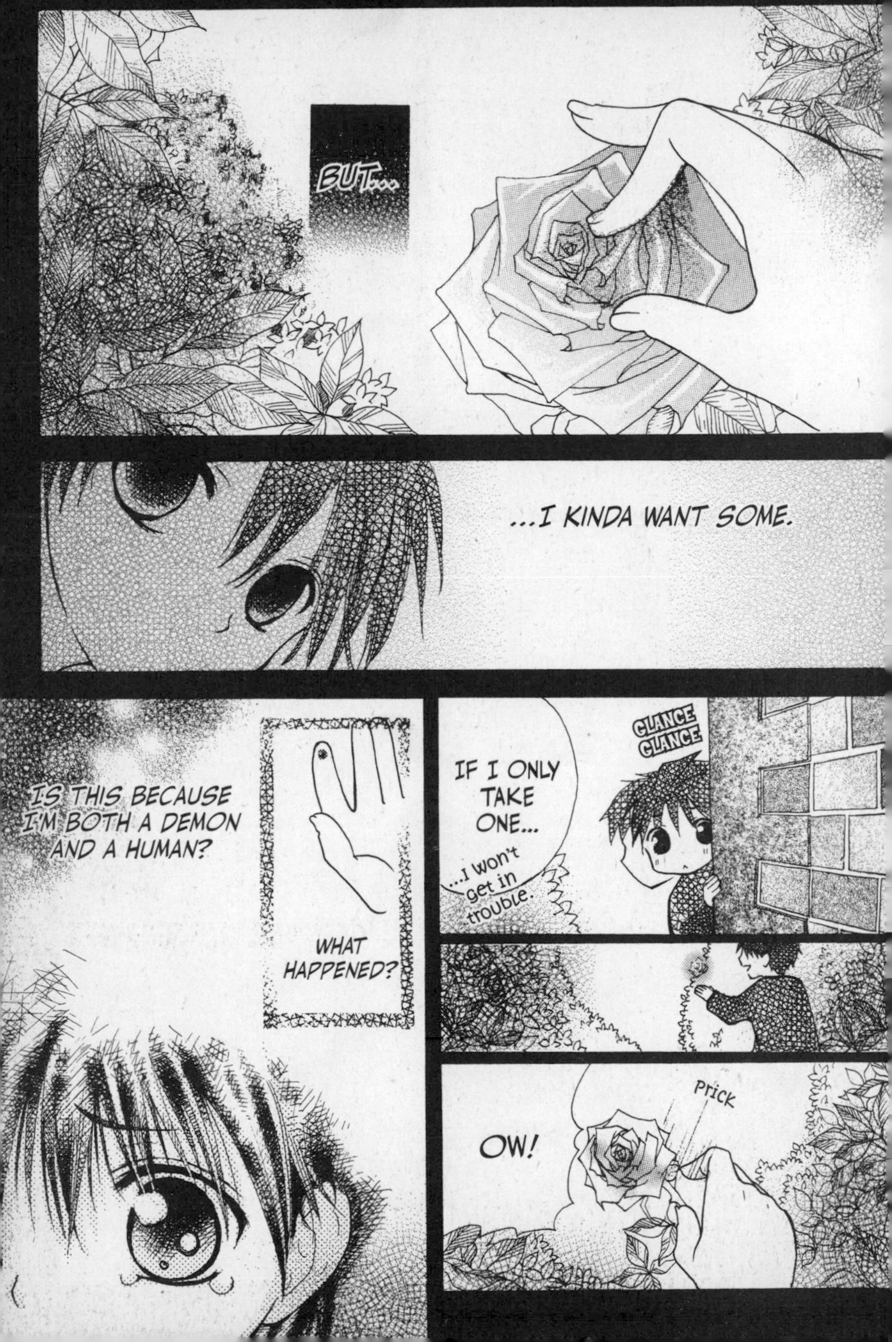
BUT...
...I KINDA WANT SOME.
GLANCE GLANCE
IF I ONLY TAKE ONE...
...I won't get in trouble.
Prick
OW!
WHAT HAPPENED?
IS THIS BECAUSE I'M BOTH A DEMON AND A HUMAN?

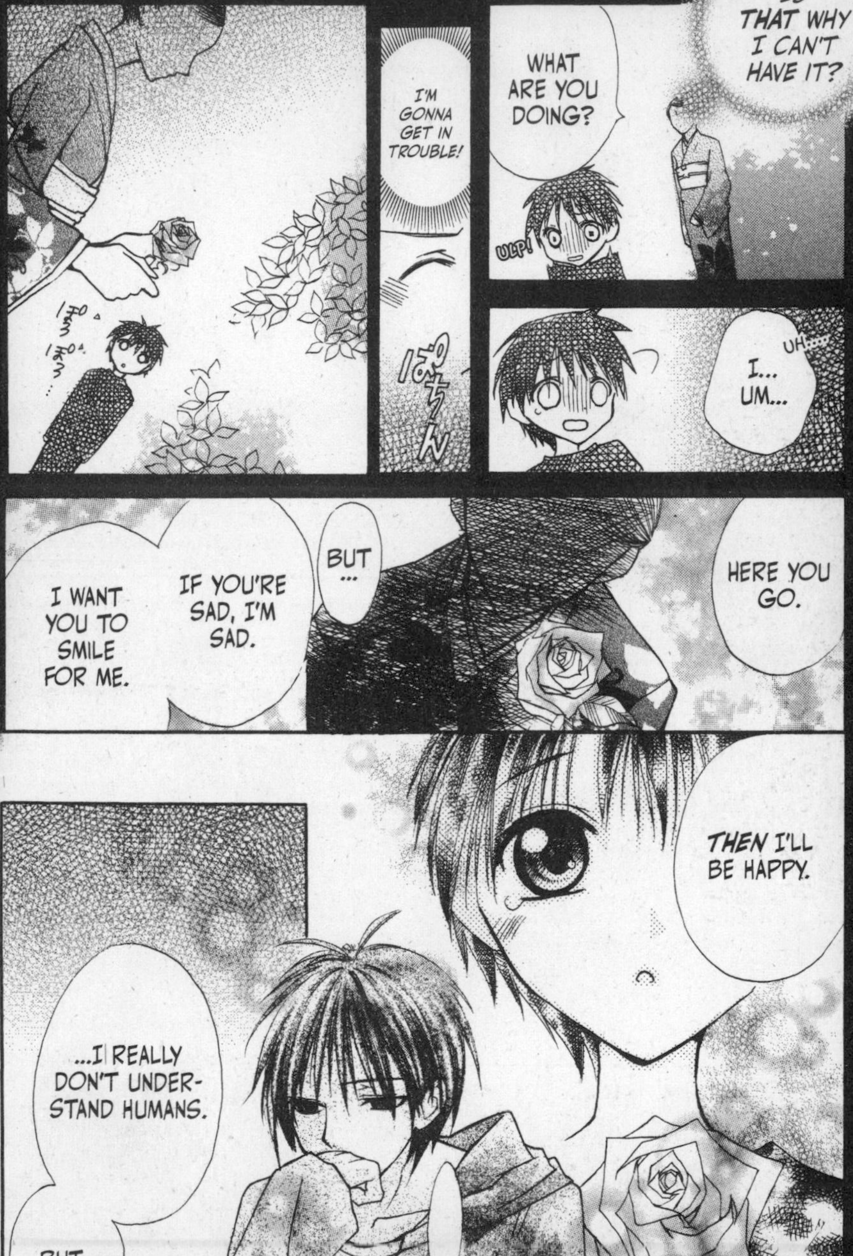
IS THAT WHY I CAN'T HAVE IT?
WHAT ARE YOU DOING?
ULP!
UH...
I... UM...
I'M GONNA GET IN TROUBLE!
HERE YOU GO.
BUT...
IF YOU'RE SAD, I'M SAD.
I WANT YOU TO SMILE FOR ME.
THEN I'LL BE HAPPY.
...I REALLY DON'T UNDER-STAND HUMANS.
BUT...

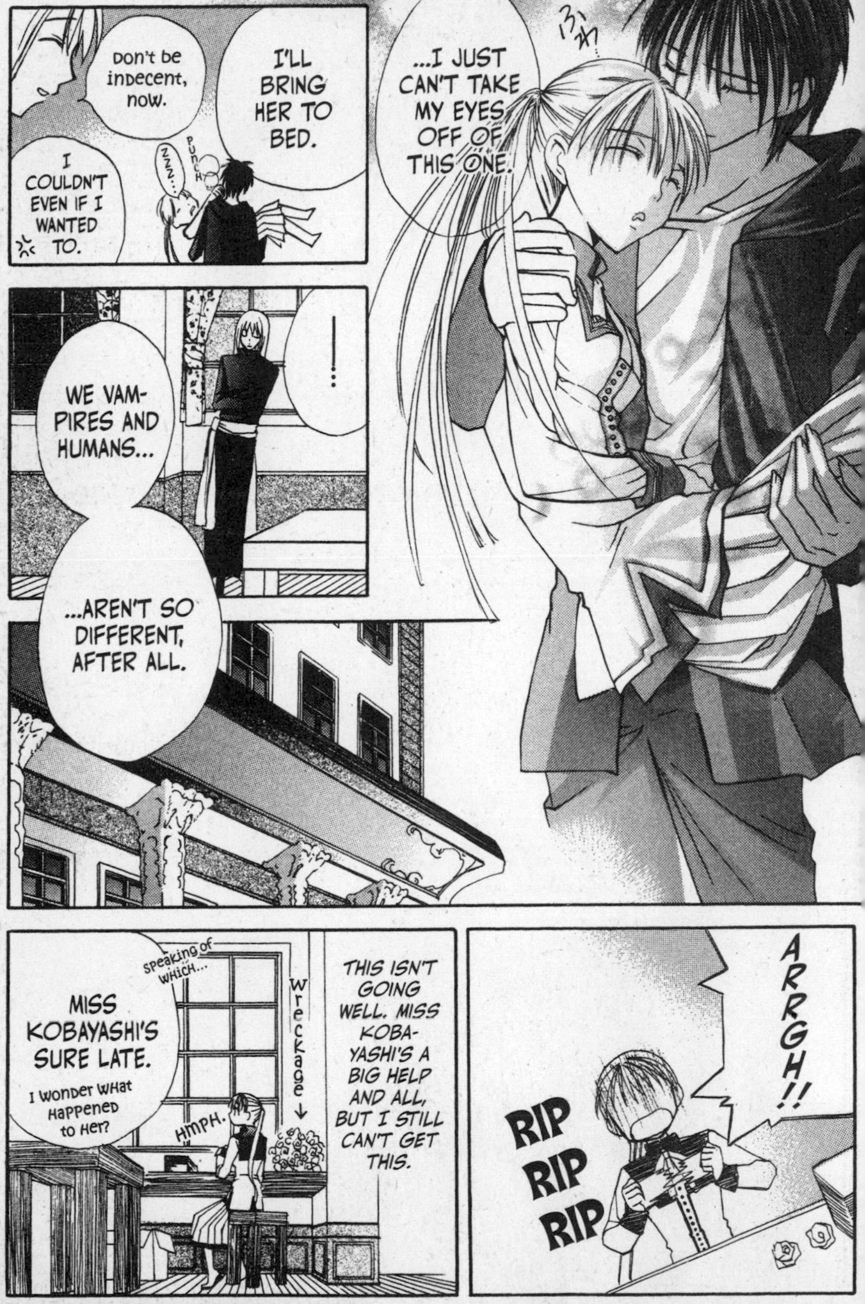
...I JUST CAN'T TAKE MY EYES OFF OF THIS ONE.
I'LL BRING HER TO BED.
Don't be indecent, now.
PUNCH
ZZZ...
I COULDN'T EVEN IF I WANTED TO.
...!
WE VAMPIRES AND HUMANS...
...AREN'T SO DIFFERENT, AFTER ALL.
ARRGH!!
RIP RIP RIP
THIS ISN'T GOING WELL. MISS KOBAYASHI'S A BIG HELP AND ALL, BUT I STILL CAN'T GET THIS.
Wreckage
Speaking of which...
MISS KOBAYASHI'S SURE LATE.
I wonder what happened to her?
HMPH.

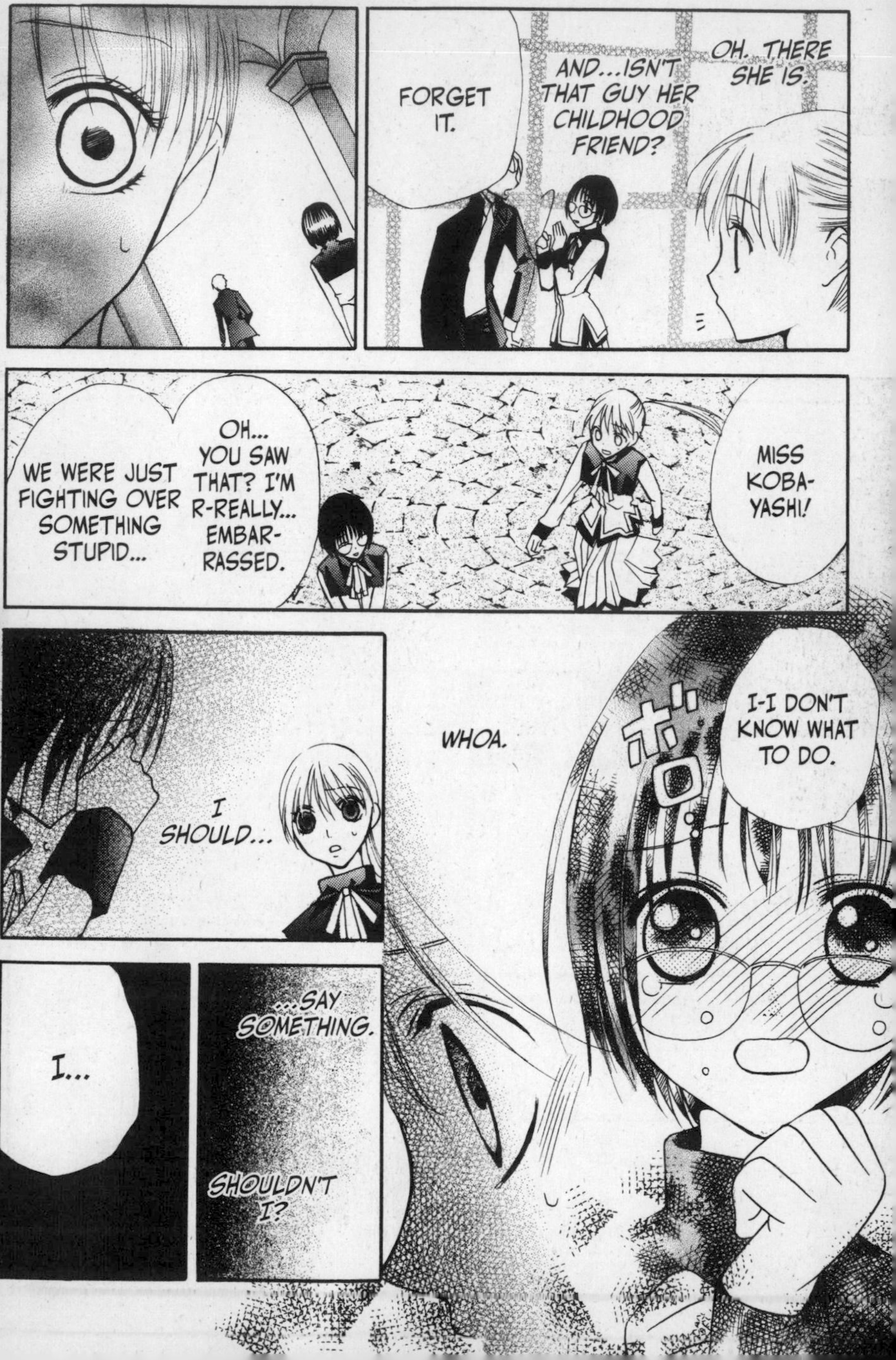
OH. THERE SHE IS.
AND...ISN'T THAT GUY HER CHILDHOOD FRIEND?
FORGET IT.
MISS KOBA-YASHI!
OH... YOU SAW THAT? I'M R-REALLY... EMBAR-RASSED.
WE WERE JUST FIGHTING OVER SOMETHING STUPID...
I-I DON'T KNOW WHAT TO DO.
WHOA.
I SHOULD...
...SAY SOMETHING.
SHOULDN'T I?
I...

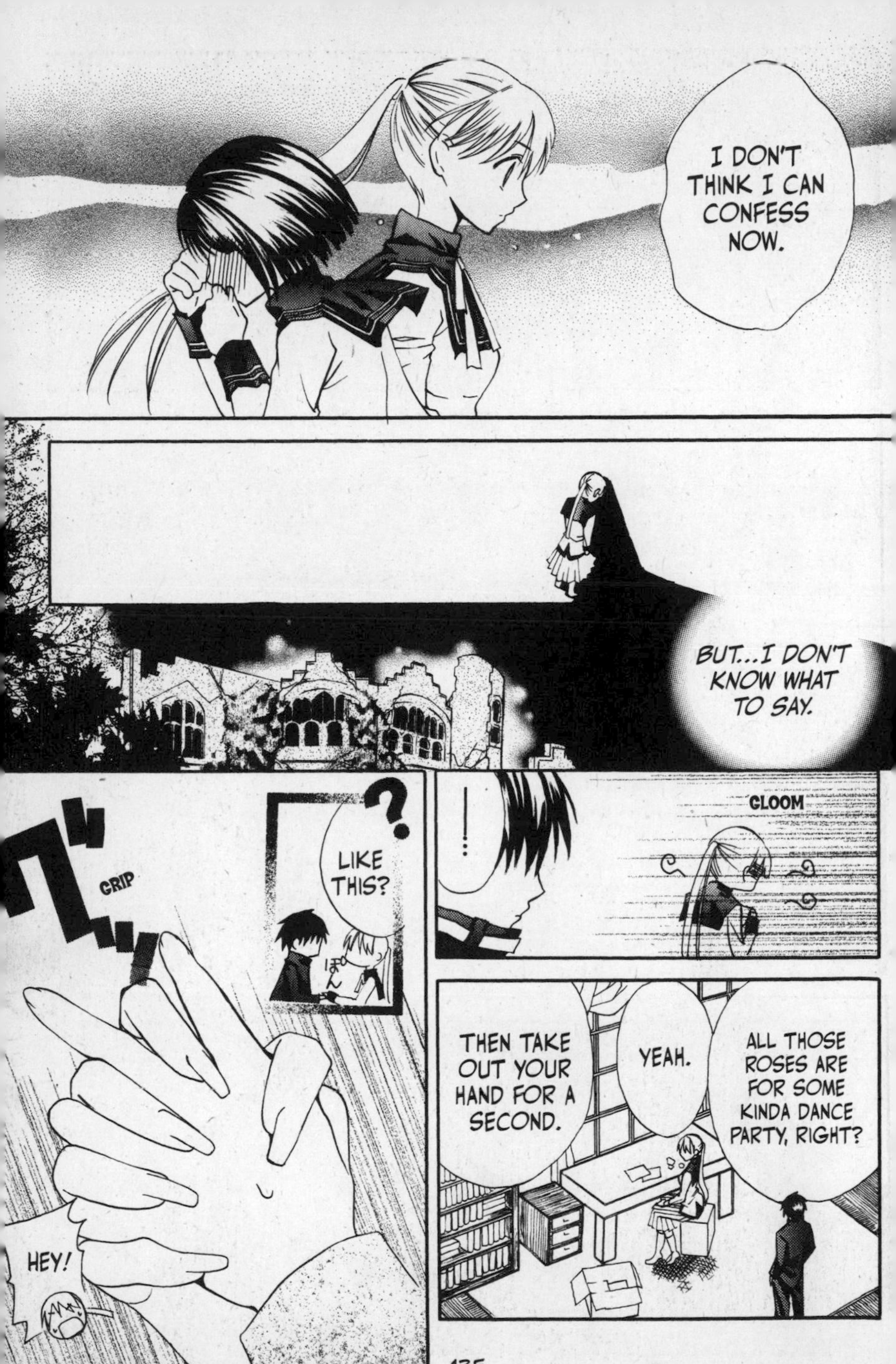
I DON'T THINK I CAN CONFESS NOW.
BUT...I DON'T KNOW WHAT TO SAY.
GLOOM
!...
ALL THOSE ROSES ARE FOR SOME KINDA DANCE PARTY, RIGHT?
YEAH.
THEN TAKE OUT YOUR HAND FOR A SECOND.
?
LIKE THIS?
ぽん
GRIP
HEY!

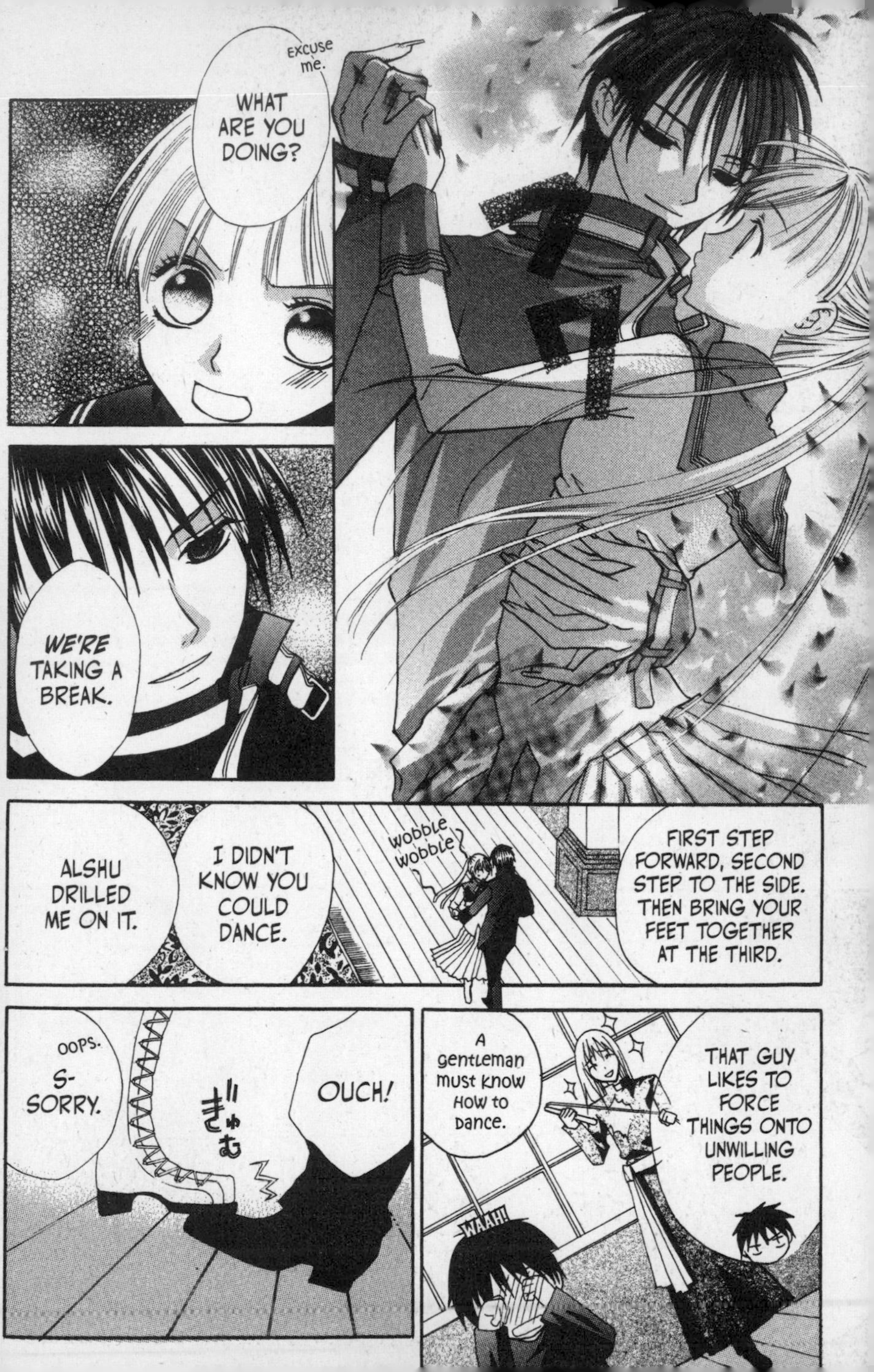
Excuse me.
WHAT ARE YOU DOING?
WE'RE TAKING A BREAK.
FIRST STEP FORWARD, SECOND STEP TO THE SIDE. THEN BRING YOUR FEET TOGETHER AT THE THIRD.
wobble wobble
I DIDN'T KNOW YOU COULD DANCE.
ALSHU DRILLED ME ON IT.
THAT GUY LIKES TO FORCE THINGS ONTO UNWILLING PEOPLE.
A gentleman must know how to dance.
WAAH!
OUCH!
ぎゅむ
OOPS.
S-SORRY.

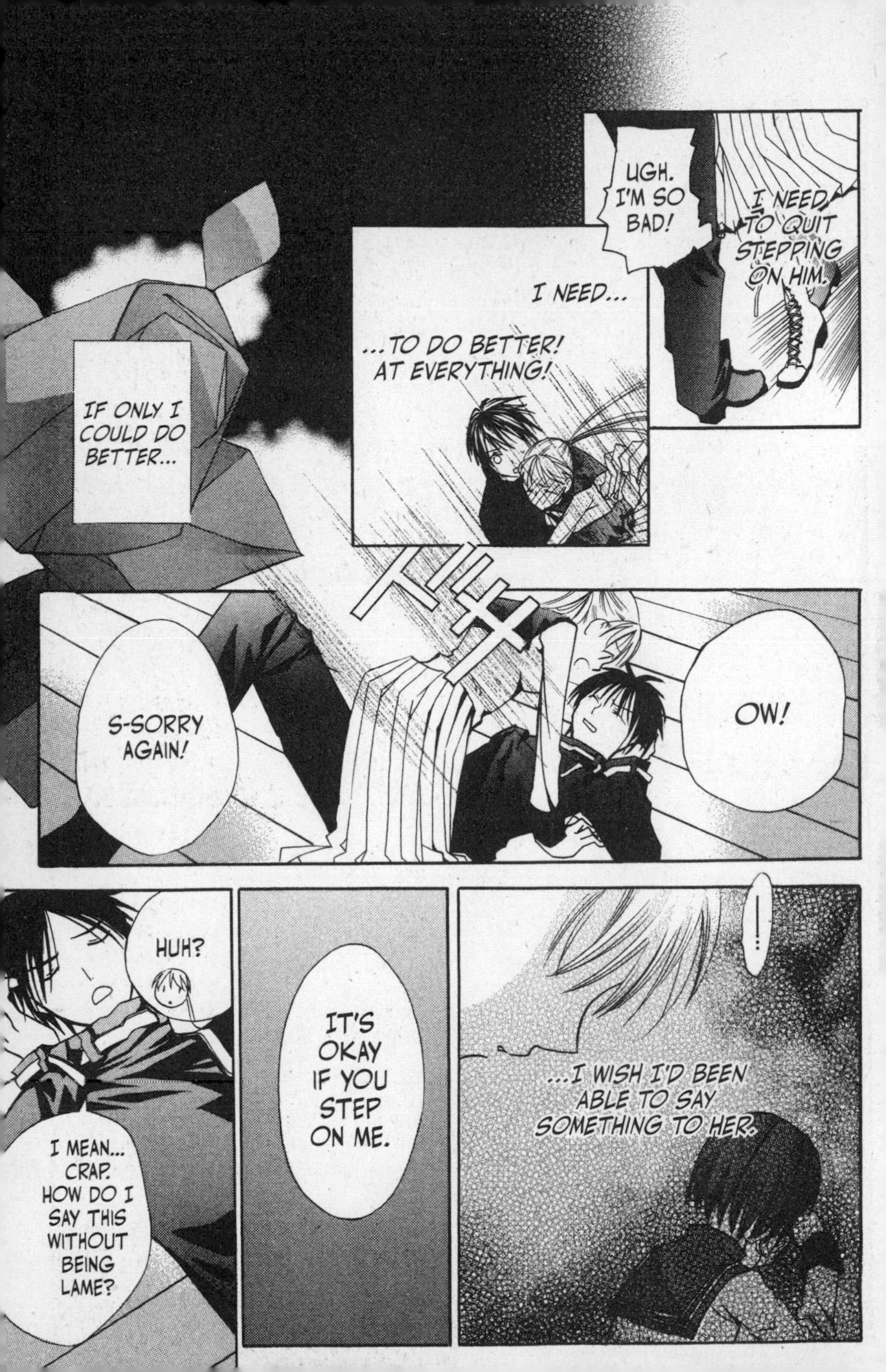
UGH. I'M SO BAD!
I NEED TO QUIT STEPPING ON HIM.
I NEED...
...TO DO BETTER! AT EVERYTHING!
IF ONLY I COULD DO BETTER...
OW!
S-SORRY AGAIN!
!
...I WISH I'D BEEN ABLE TO SAY SOMETHING TO HER.
IT'S OKAY IF YOU STEP ON ME.
HUH?
I MEAN... CRAP. HOW DO I SAY THIS WITHOUT BEING LAME?

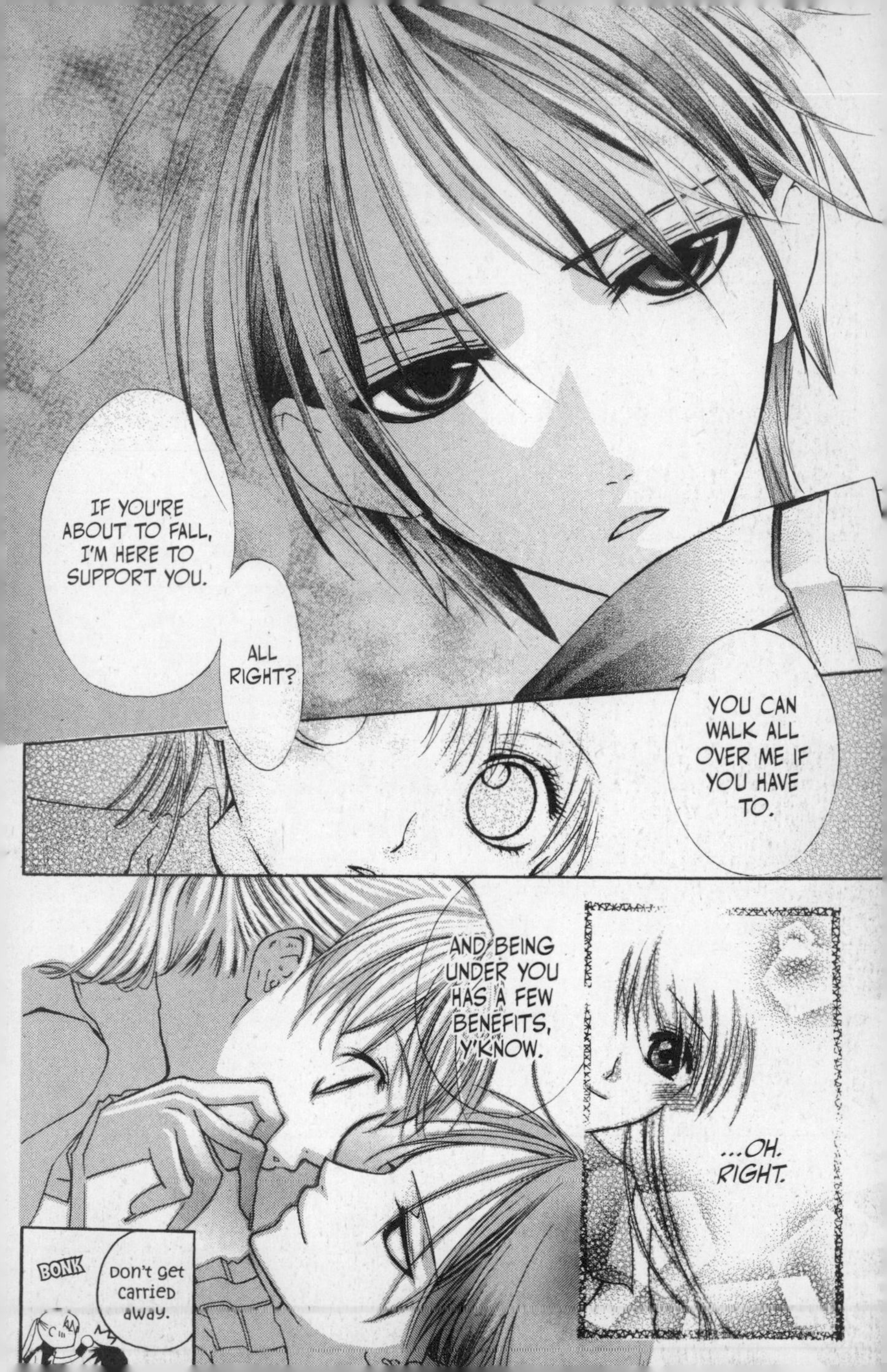
IF YOU'RE ABOUT TO FALL, I'M HERE TO SUPPORT YOU.
ALL RIGHT?
YOU CAN WALK ALL OVER ME IF YOU HAVE TO.
...OH. RIGHT.
AND BEING UNDER YOU HAS A FEW BENEFITS, Y'KNOW.
BONK
Don't get carried away.

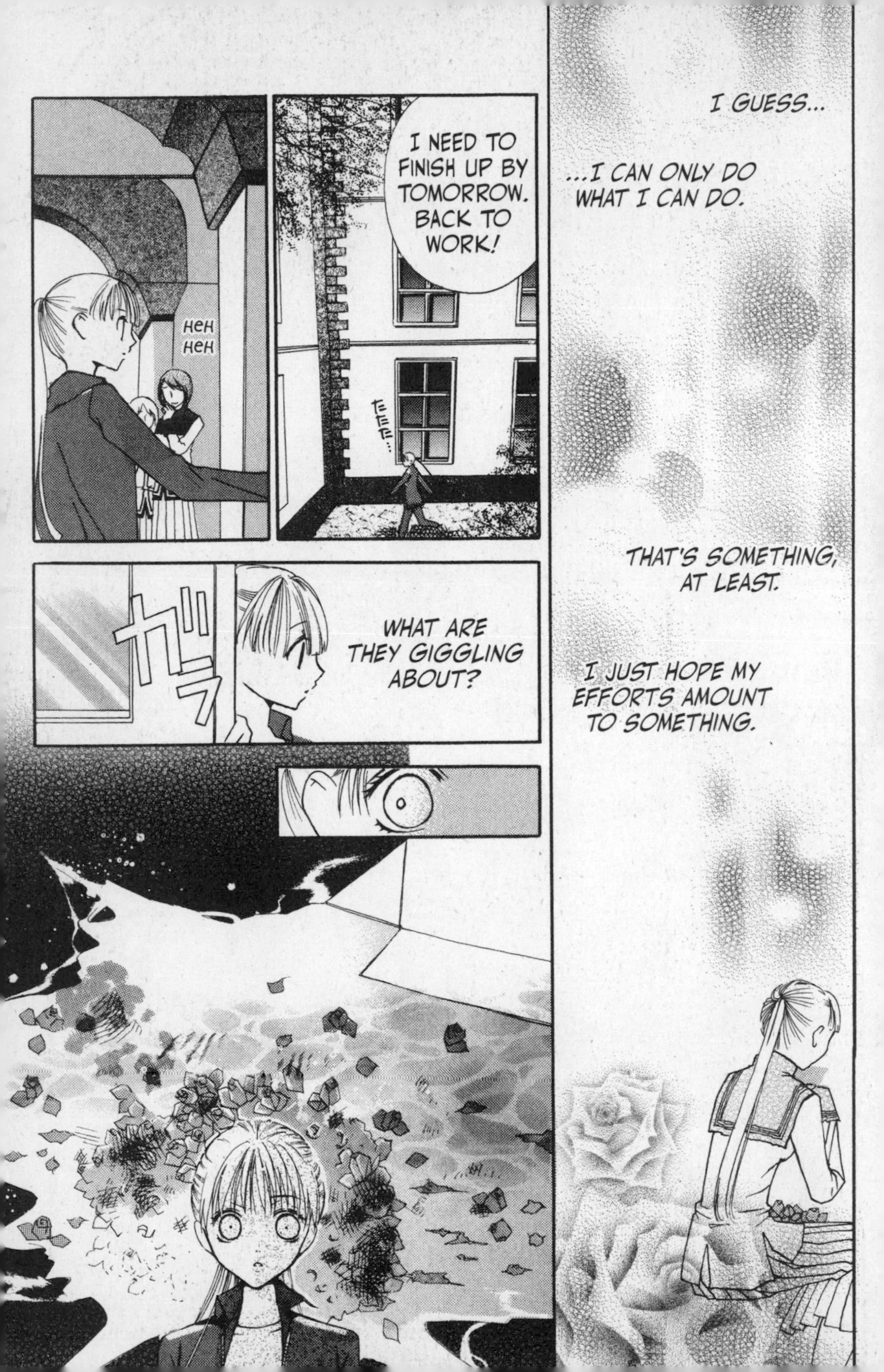
I GUESS...
...I CAN ONLY DO WHAT I CAN DO.
THAT'S SOMETHING, AT LEAST.
I JUST HOPE MY EFFORTS AMOUNT TO SOMETHING.
I NEED TO FINISH UP BY TOMORROW. BACK TO WORK!
たたた…
HEH HEH
ガラ
WHAT ARE THEY GIGGLING ABOUT?

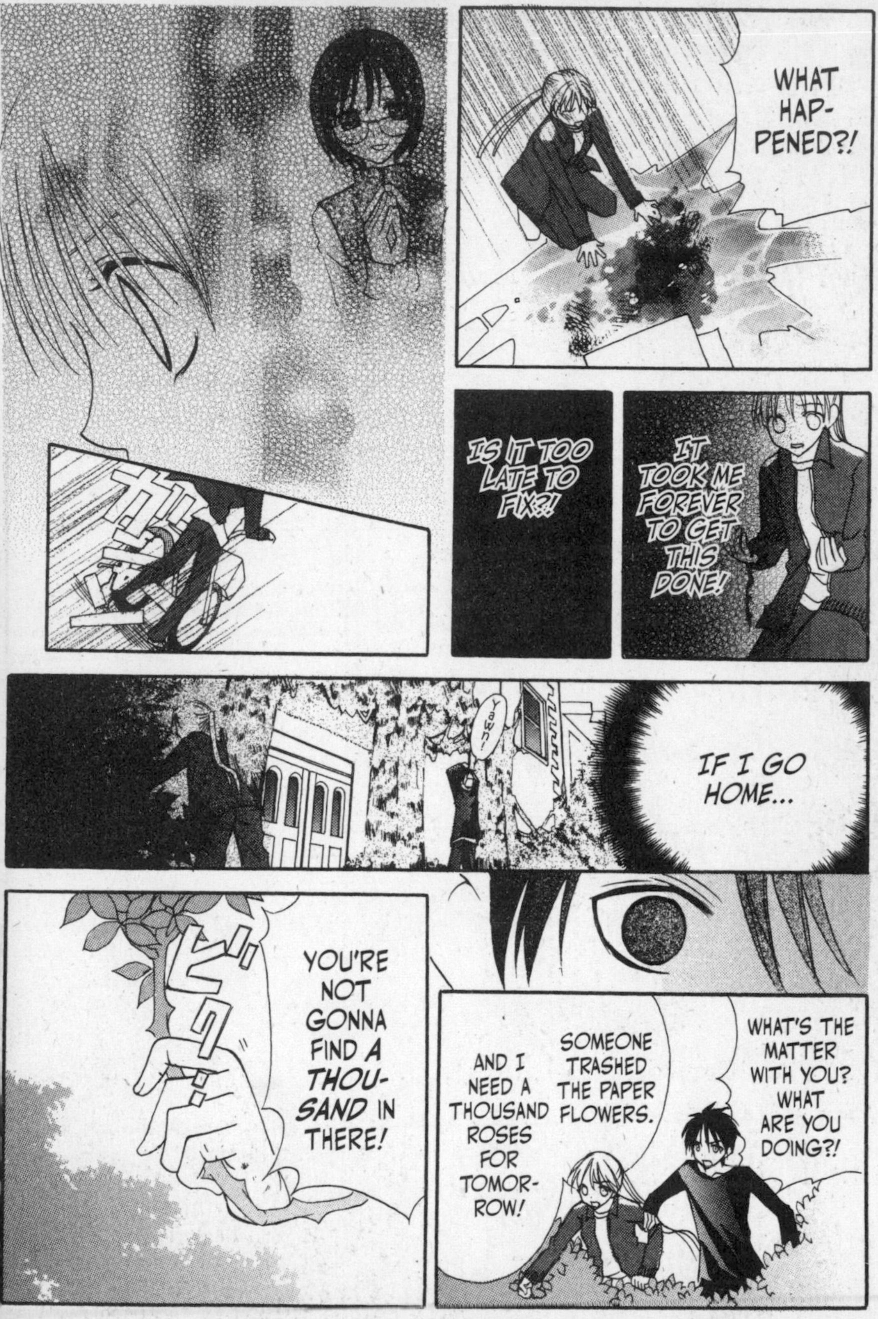
WHAT HAP-PENED?!
IT TOOK ME FOREVER TO GET THIS DONE!
IS IT TOO LATE TO FIX?!
IF I GO HOME...
Yawn!
WHAT'S THE MATTER WITH YOU? WHAT ARE YOU DOING?!
SOMEONE TRASHED THE PAPER FLOWERS.
AND I NEED A THOUSAND ROSES FOR TOMOR-ROW!
YOU'RE NOT GONNA FIND A *THOU-SAND* IN THERE!

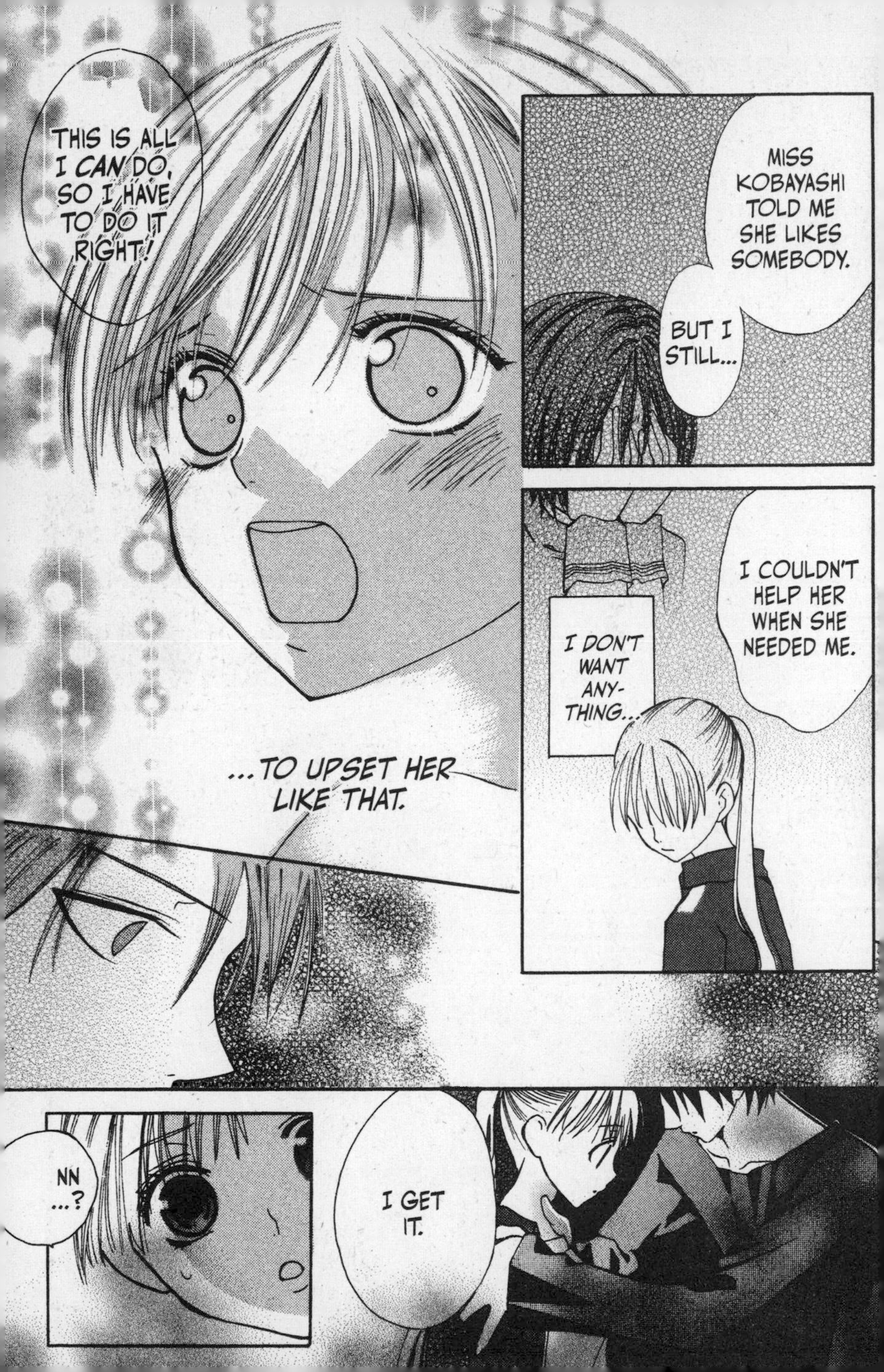
MISS KOBAYASHI TOLD ME SHE LIKES SOMEBODY.
BUT I STILL...
I COULDN'T HELP HER WHEN SHE NEEDED ME.
I DON'T WANT ANY-THING...
THIS IS ALL I CAN DO, SO I HAVE TO DO IT RIGHT!
...TO UPSET HER LIKE THAT.
I GET IT.
NN ...?

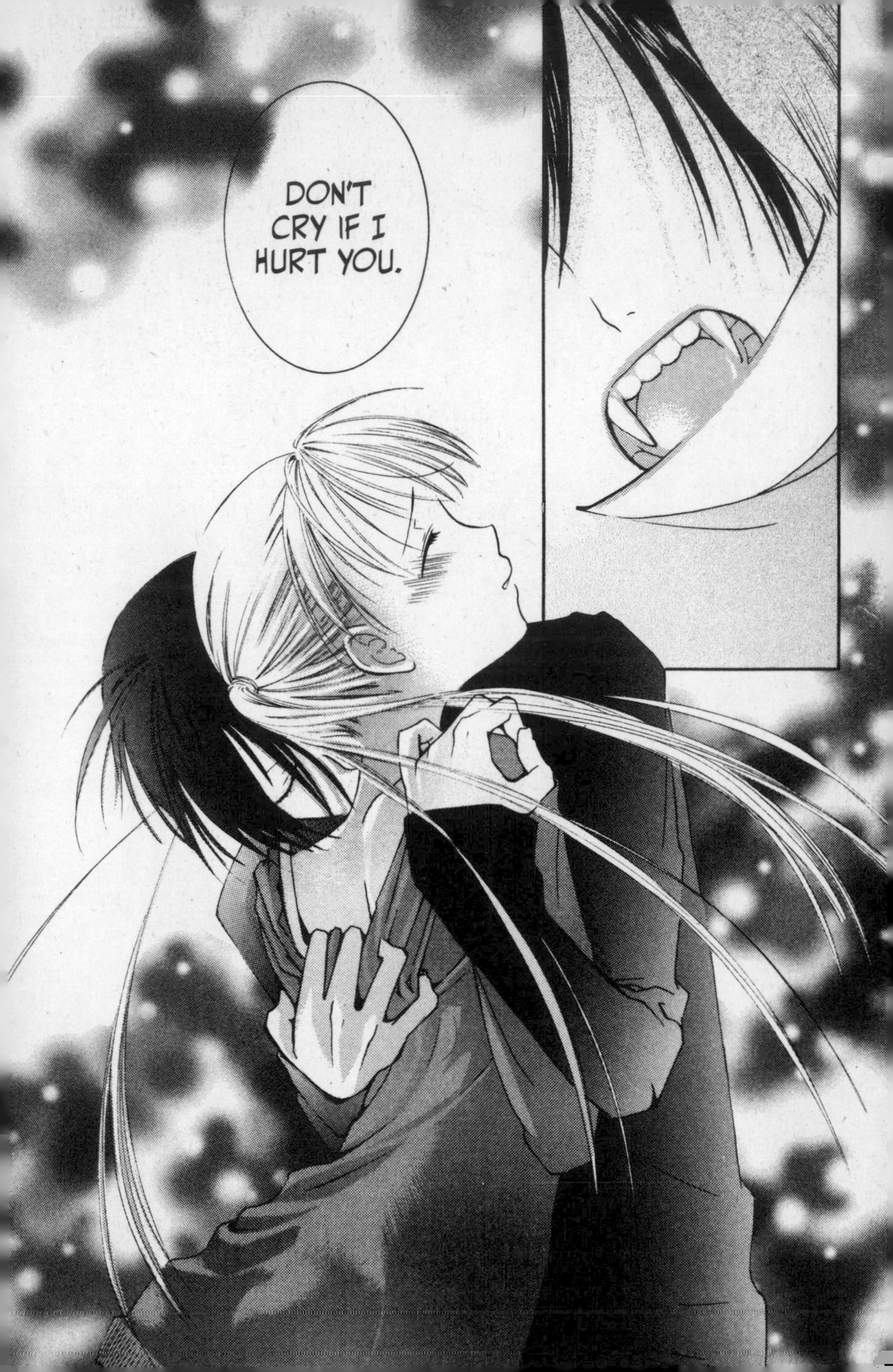
DON'T CRY IF I HURT YOU.

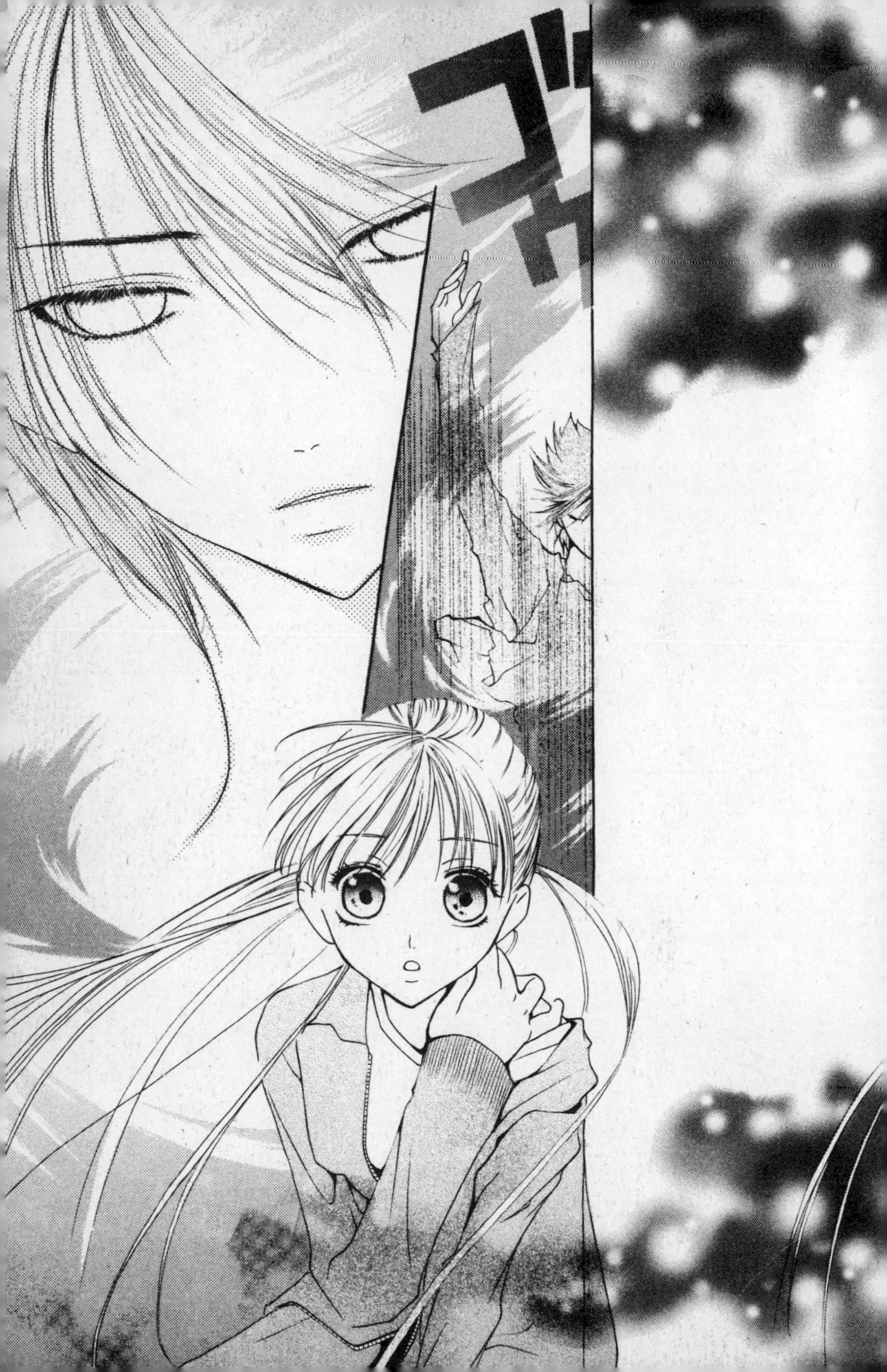
ゴ

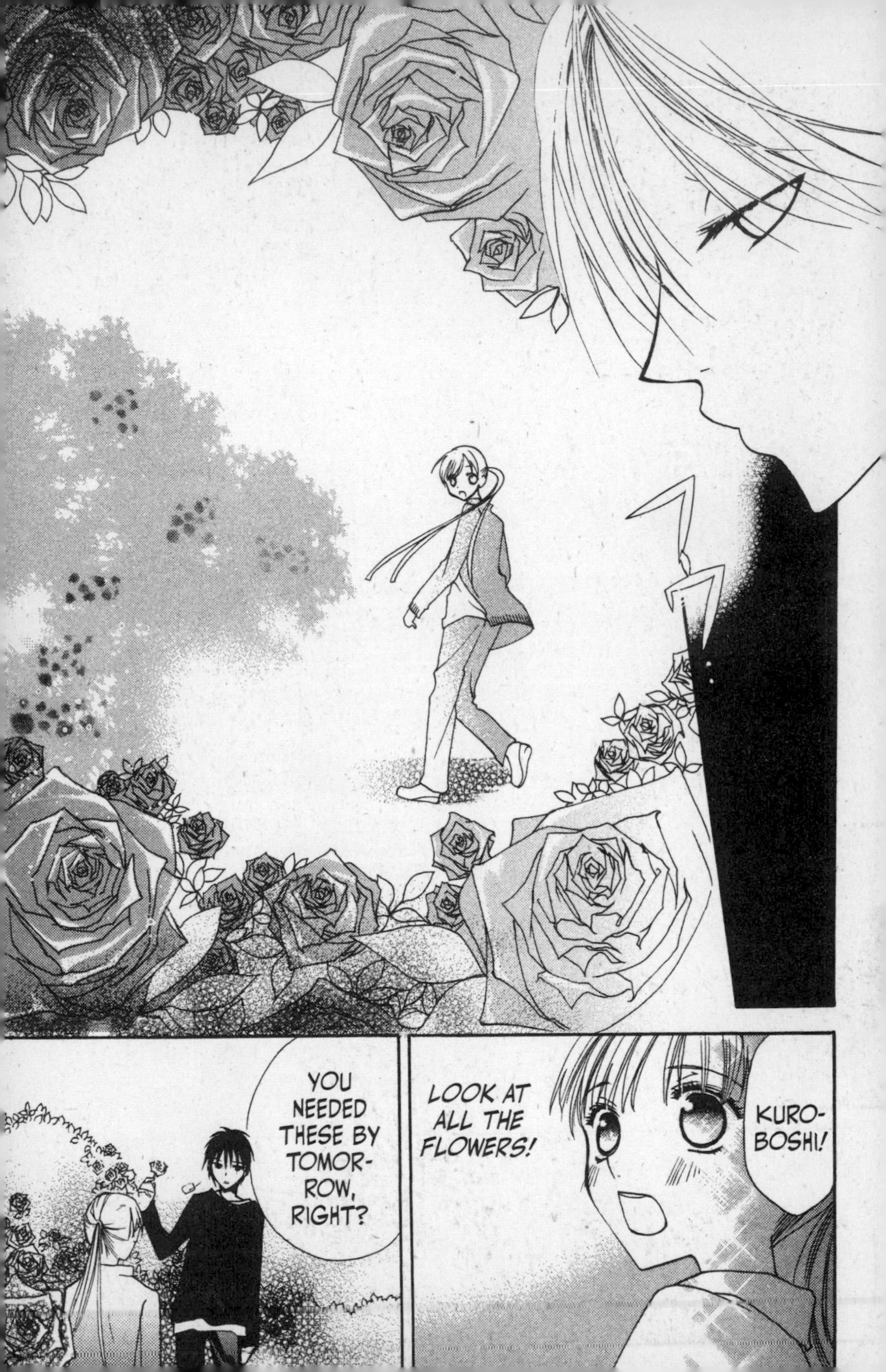
KURO-
BOSHI!
LOOK AT
ALL THE
FLOWERS!
YOU
NEEDED
THESE BY
TOMOR-
ROW,
RIGHT?

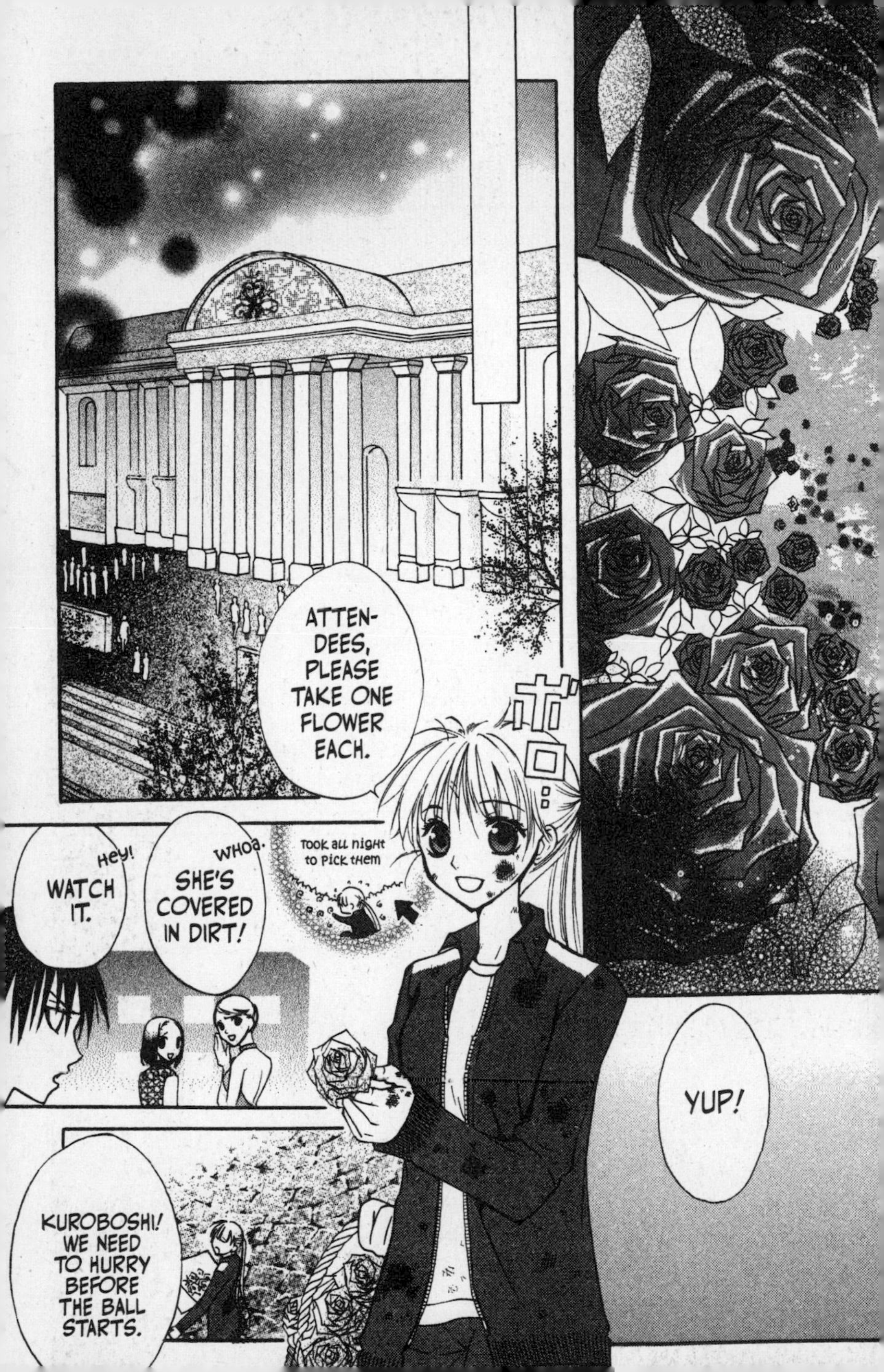
ATTEN-DEES, PLEASE TAKE ONE FLOWER EACH.
ボロ
YUP!
TOOK ALL NIGHT TO PICK THEM
WHOA. SHE'S COVERED IN DIRT!
HEY! WATCH IT.
KUROBOSHI! WE NEED TO HURRY BEFORE THE BALL STARTS.

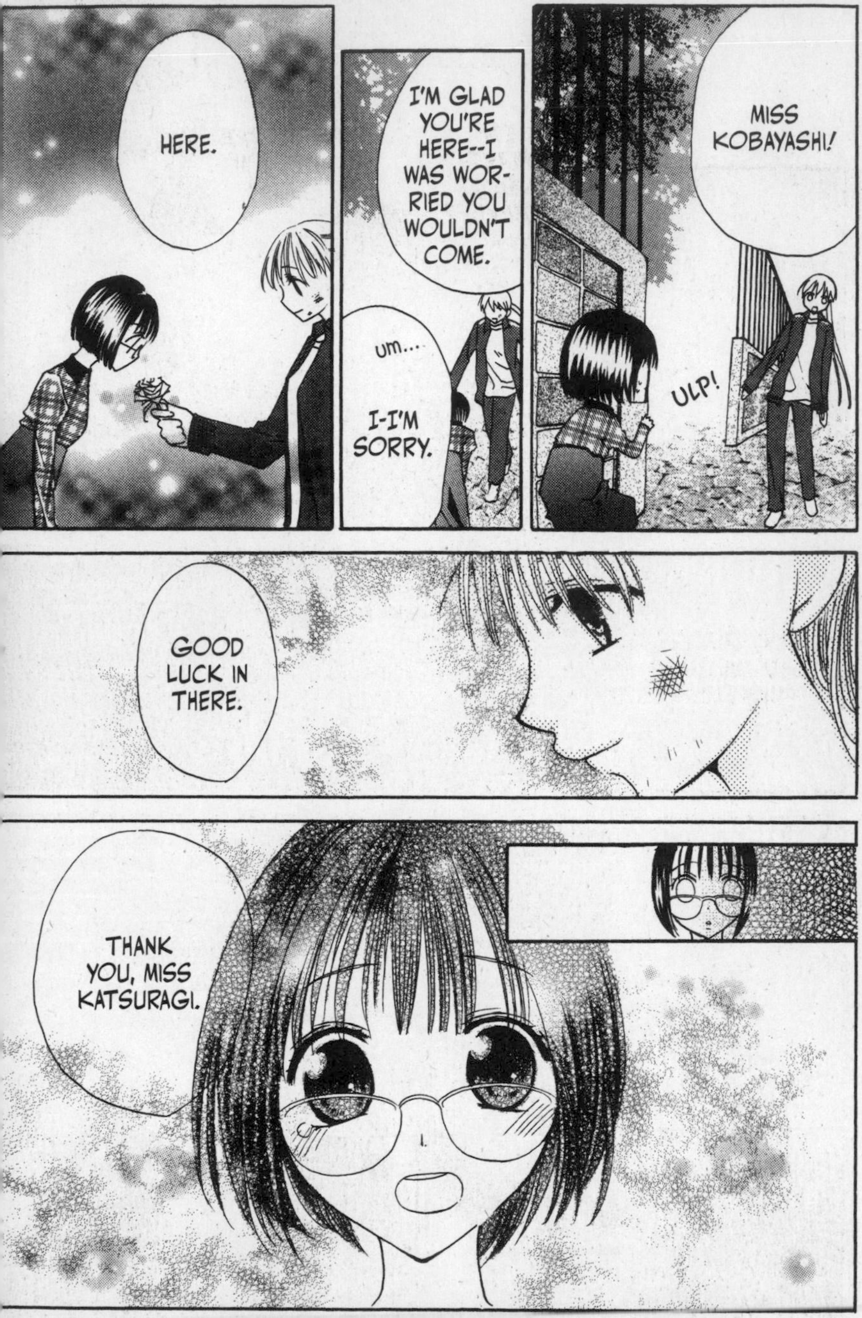
MISS KOBAYASHI!
ULP!
I'M GLAD YOU'RE HERE--I WAS WOR-RIED YOU WOULDN'T COME.
um...
I-I'M SORRY.
HERE.
GOOD LUCK IN THERE.
THANK YOU, MISS KATSURAGI.

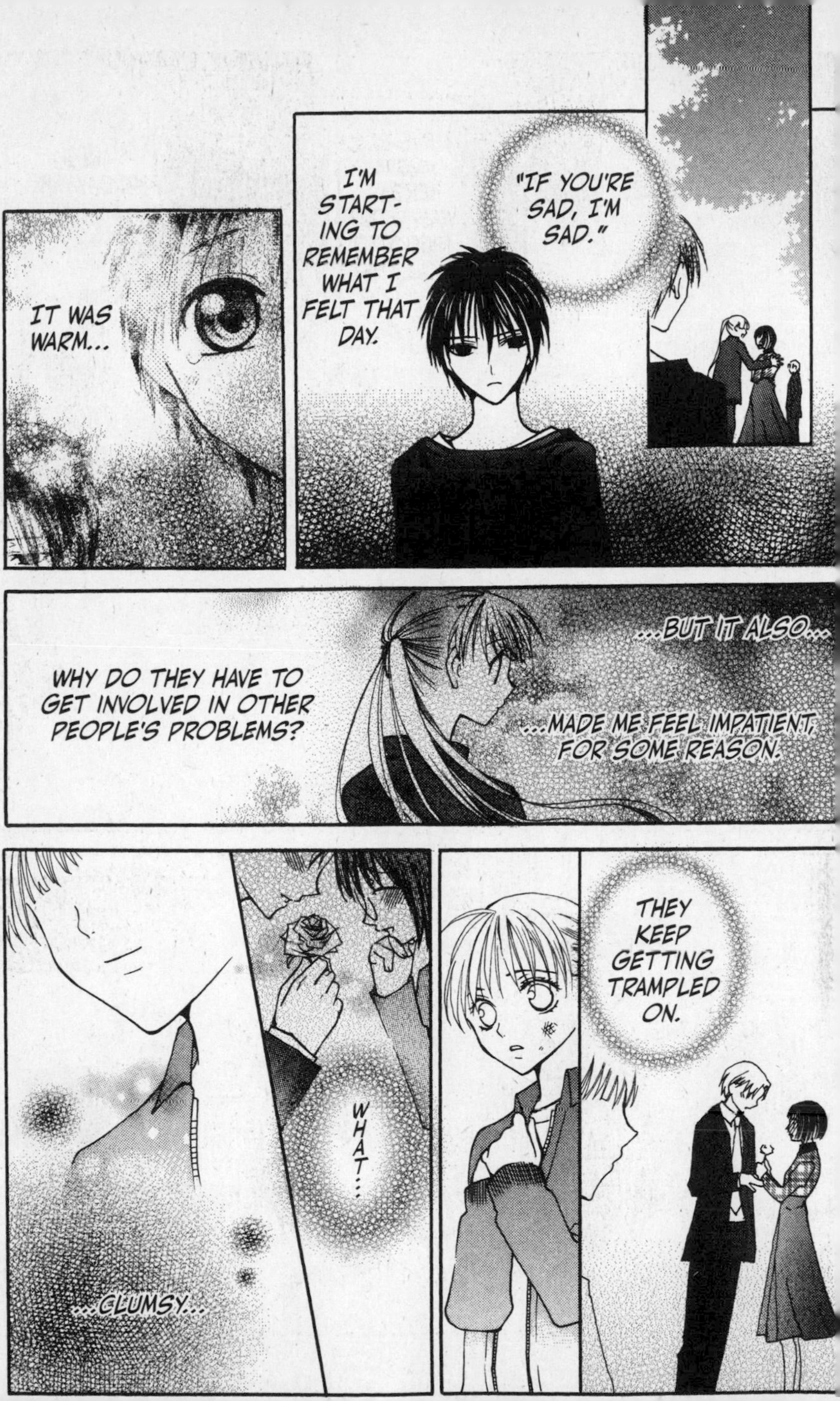
"IF YOU'RE SAD, I'M SAD."
I'M START-ING TO REMEMBER WHAT I FELT THAT DAY.
IT WAS WARM...
...BUT IT ALSO...
...MADE ME FEEL IMPATIENT, FOR SOME REASON.
WHY DO THEY HAVE TO GET INVOLVED IN OTHER PEOPLE'S PROBLEMS?
THEY KEEP GETTING TRAMPLED ON.
WHAT...
...CLUMSY...

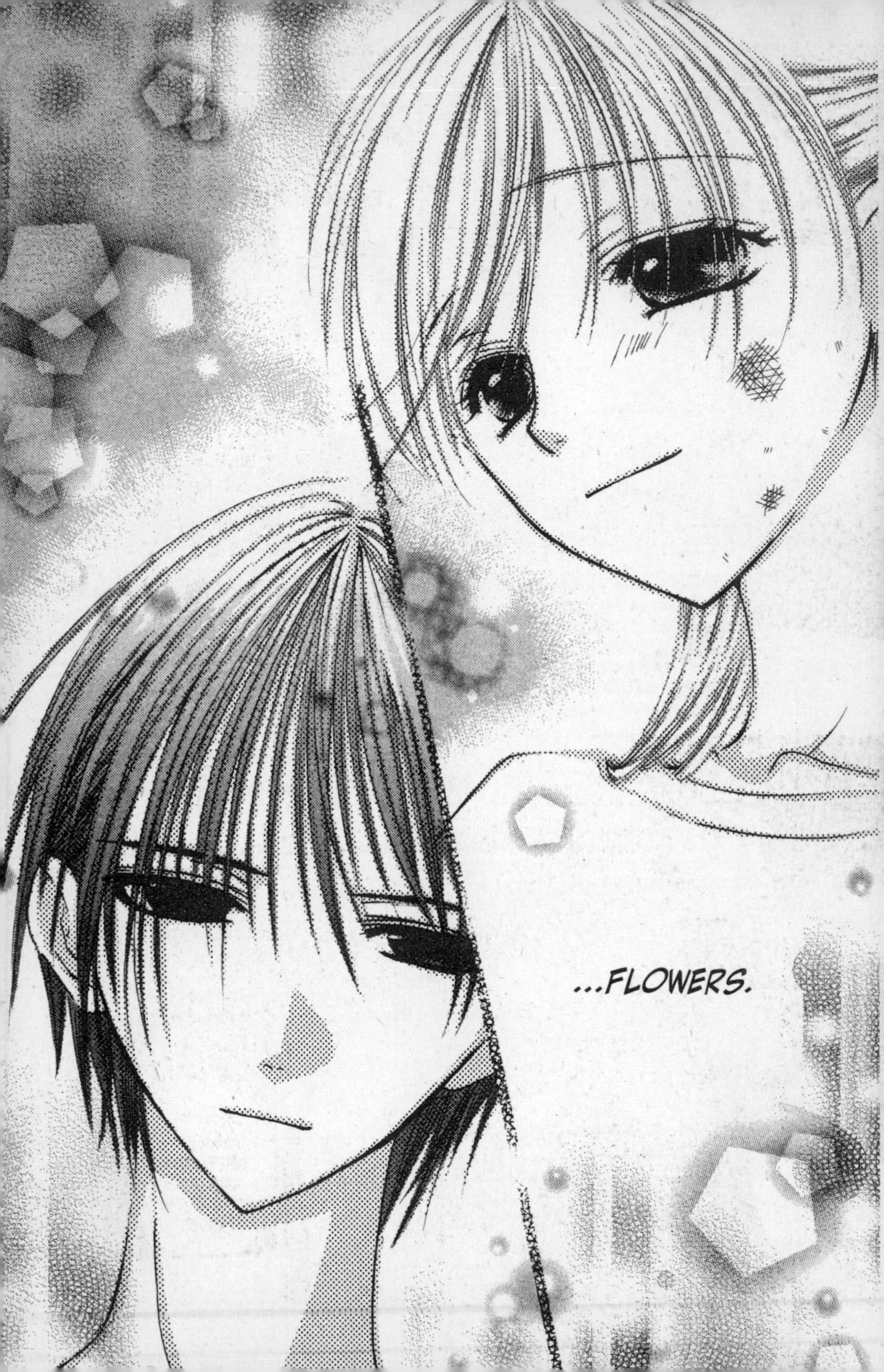
...FLOWERS.

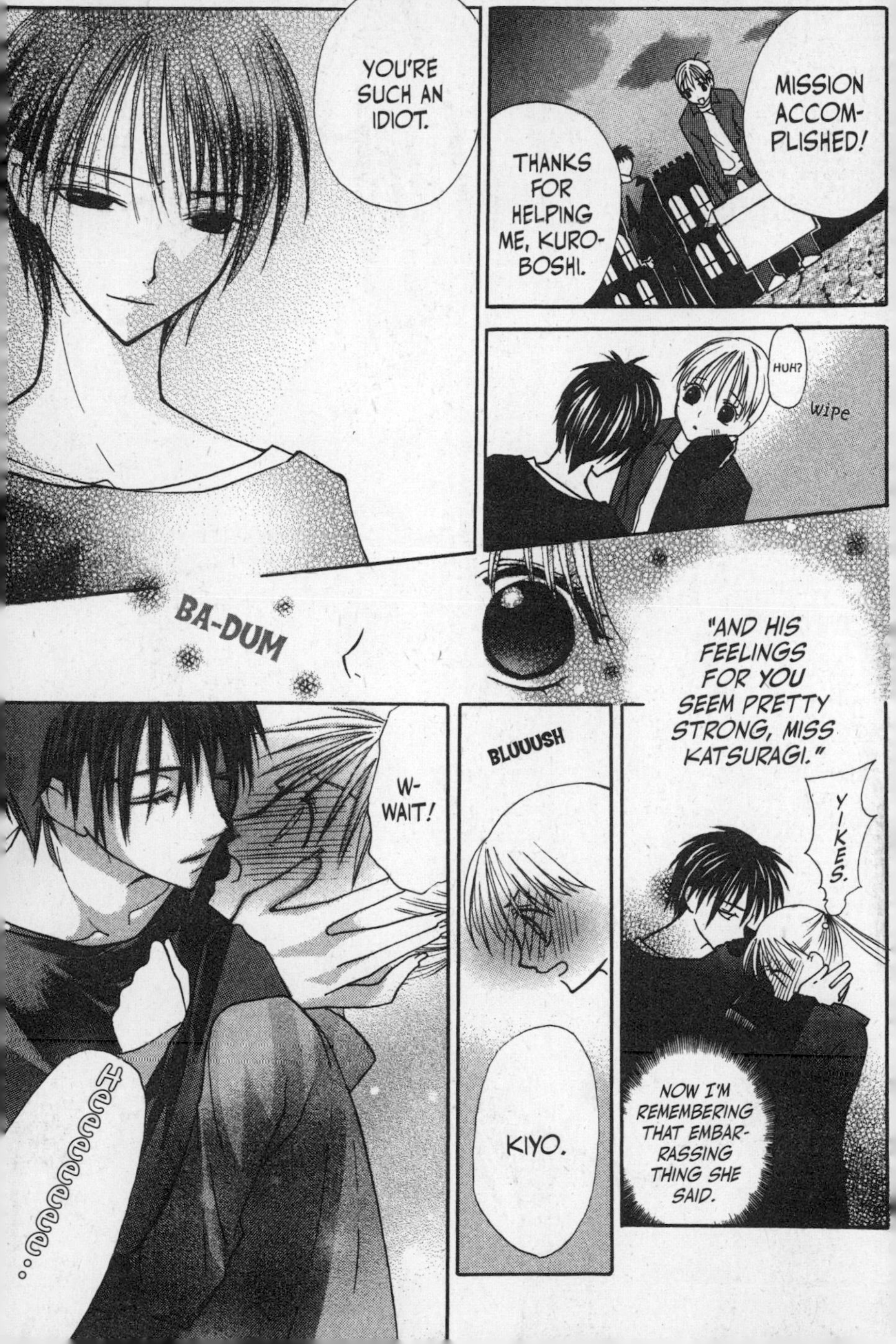
MISSION ACCOM-PLISHED!
THANKS FOR HELPING ME, KURO-BOSHI.
HUH?
wipe
YOU'RE SUCH AN IDIOT.
BA-DUM
"AND HIS FEELINGS FOR YOU SEEM PRETTY STRONG, MISS KATSURAGI."
YIKES.
NOW I'M REMEMBERING THAT EMBAR-RASSING THING SHE SAID.
BLUUUSH
KIYO.
W-WAIT!
Heeeeeeeeee..

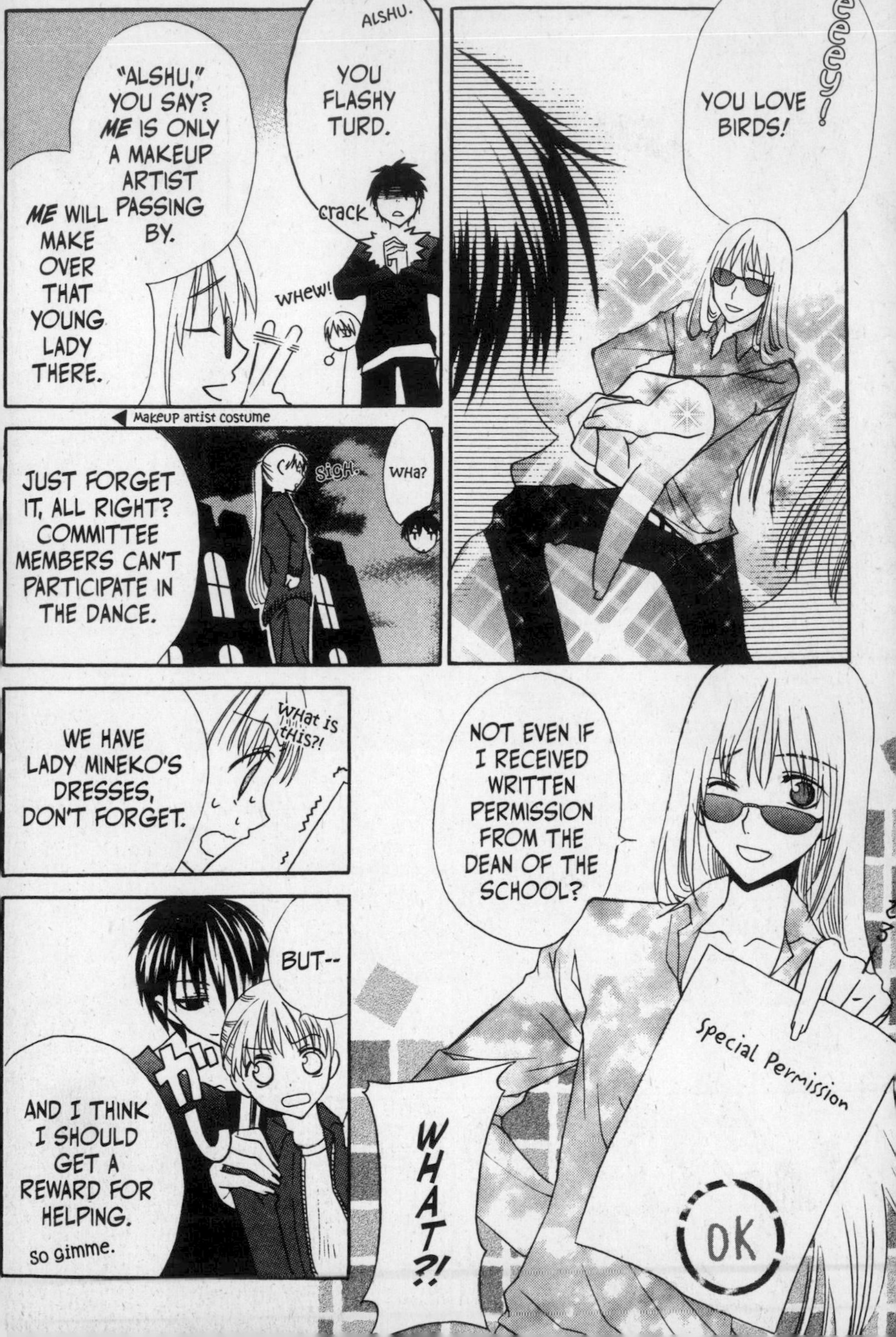
eeeey!
YOU LOVE BIRDS!
ALSHU.
YOU FLASHY TURD.
crack
"ALSHU," YOU SAY? ME IS ONLY A MAKEUP ARTIST PASSING BY.
ME WILL MAKE OVER THAT YOUNG LADY THERE.
WHEW!
Makeup artist costume
WHA?
SIGH.
JUST FORGET IT, ALL RIGHT? COMMITTEE MEMBERS CAN'T PARTICIPATE IN THE DANCE.
NOT EVEN IF I RECEIVED WRITTEN PERMISSION FROM THE DEAN OF THE SCHOOL?
Special Permission
OK
WHAT?!
What is this?!
WE HAVE LADY MINEKO'S DRESSES, DON'T FORGET.
BUT--
AND I THINK I SHOULD GET A REWARD FOR HELPING.
So gimme.

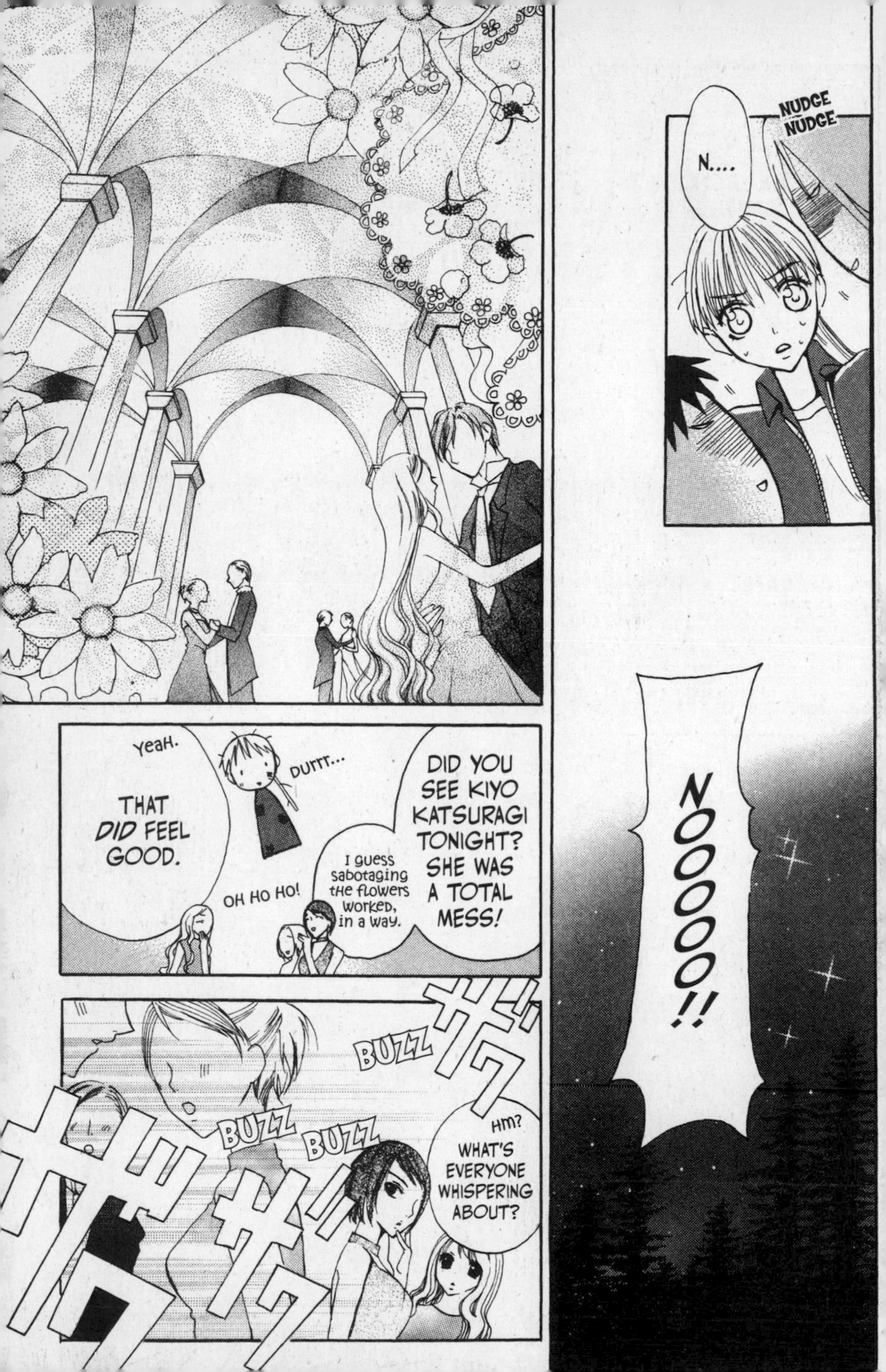
NUDGE NUDGE
N....
NOOOOOO!!
DID YOU SEE KIYO KATSURAGI TONIGHT? SHE WAS A TOTAL MESS!
Durrr...
I guess sabotaging the flowers worked, in a way.
OH HO HO!
Yeah.
THAT DID FEEL GOOD.
BUZZ
Hm? WHAT'S EVERYONE WHISPERING ABOUT?
BUZZ
BUZZ

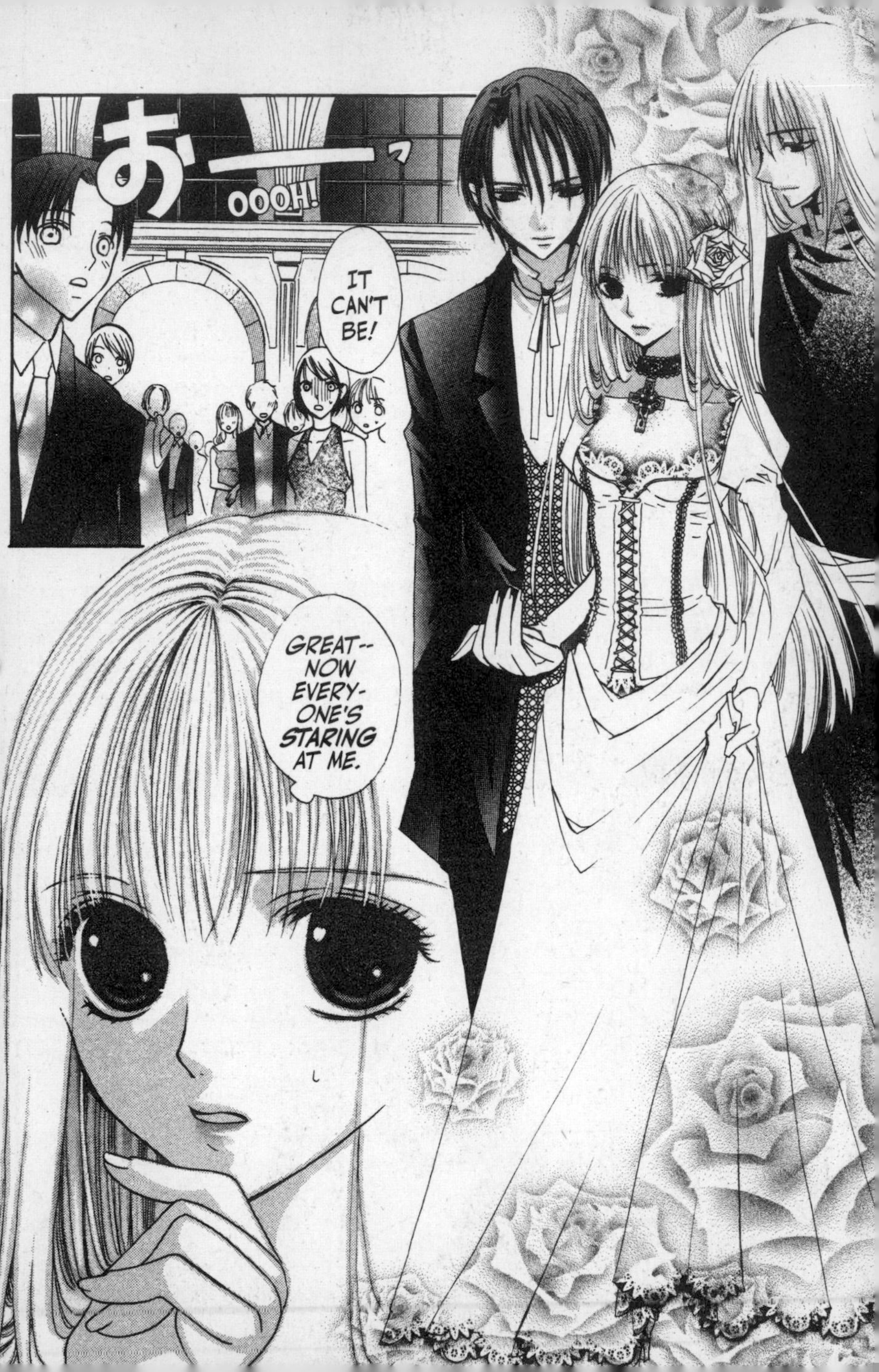
おーっ
OOOH!
IT CAN'T BE!
GREAT--NOW EVERY-ONE'S STARING AT ME.

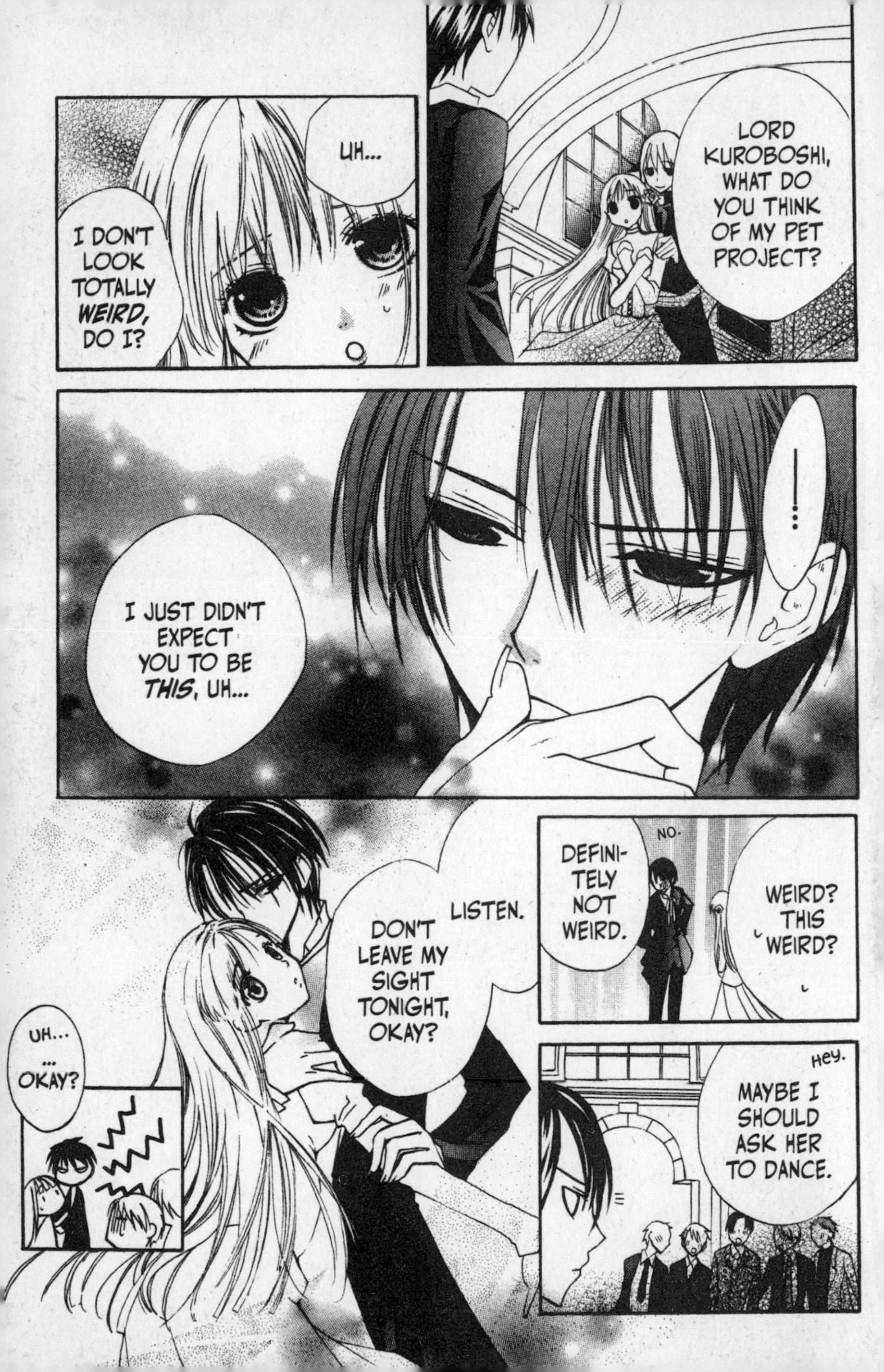
LORD KUROBOSHI, WHAT DO YOU THINK OF MY PET PROJECT?
UH...
I DON'T LOOK TOTALLY *WEIRD*, DO I?
!...
I JUST DIDN'T EXPECT YOU TO BE *THIS*, UH...
WEIRD? THIS WEIRD?
NO.
DEFINITELY NOT WEIRD.
Hey.
MAYBE I SHOULD ASK HER TO DANCE.
LISTEN.
DON'T LEAVE MY SIGHT TONIGHT, OKAY?
UH... ... OKAY?

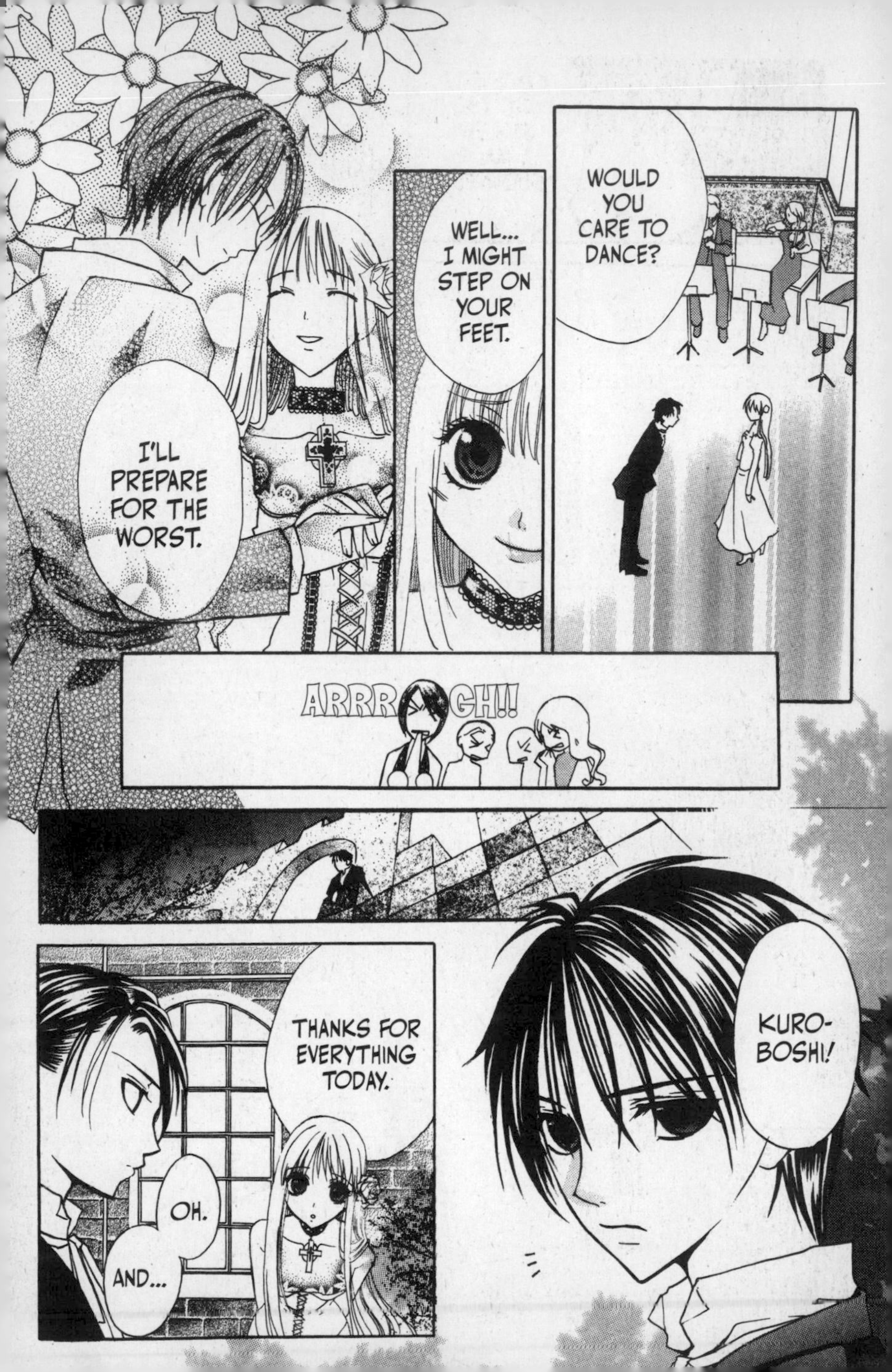
WOULD YOU CARE TO DANCE?
WELL... I MIGHT STEP ON YOUR FEET.
I'LL PREPARE FOR THE WORST.
ARRRGH!!
KURO-BOSHI!
THANKS FOR EVERYTHING TODAY.
OH.
AND...

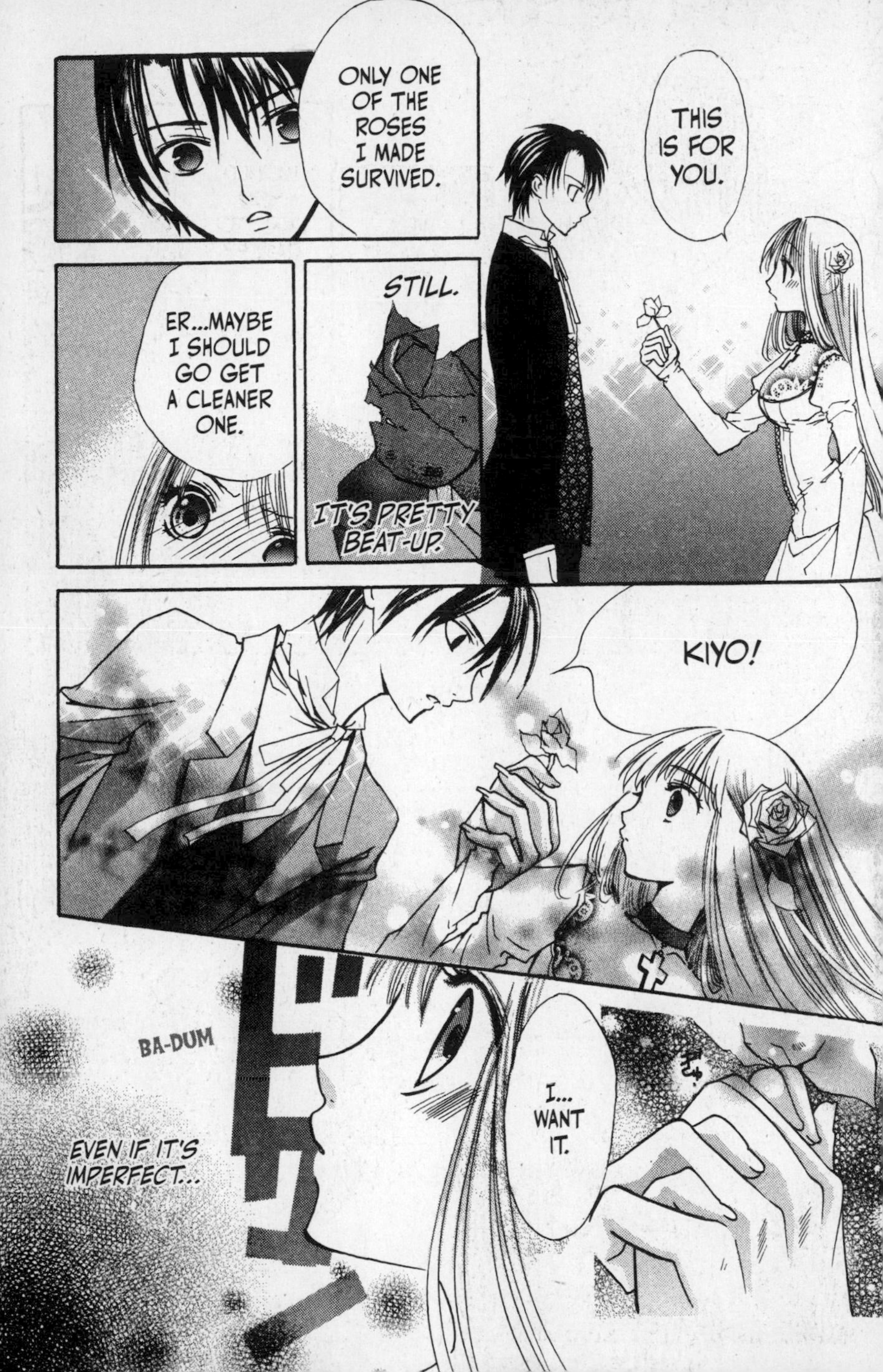
THIS IS FOR YOU.
ONLY ONE OF THE ROSES I MADE SURVIVED.
STILL.
IT'S PRETTY BEAT-UP.
ER...MAYBE I SHOULD GO GET A CLEANER ONE.
KIYO!
I... WANT IT.
BA-DUM
EVEN IF IT'S IMPERFECT...

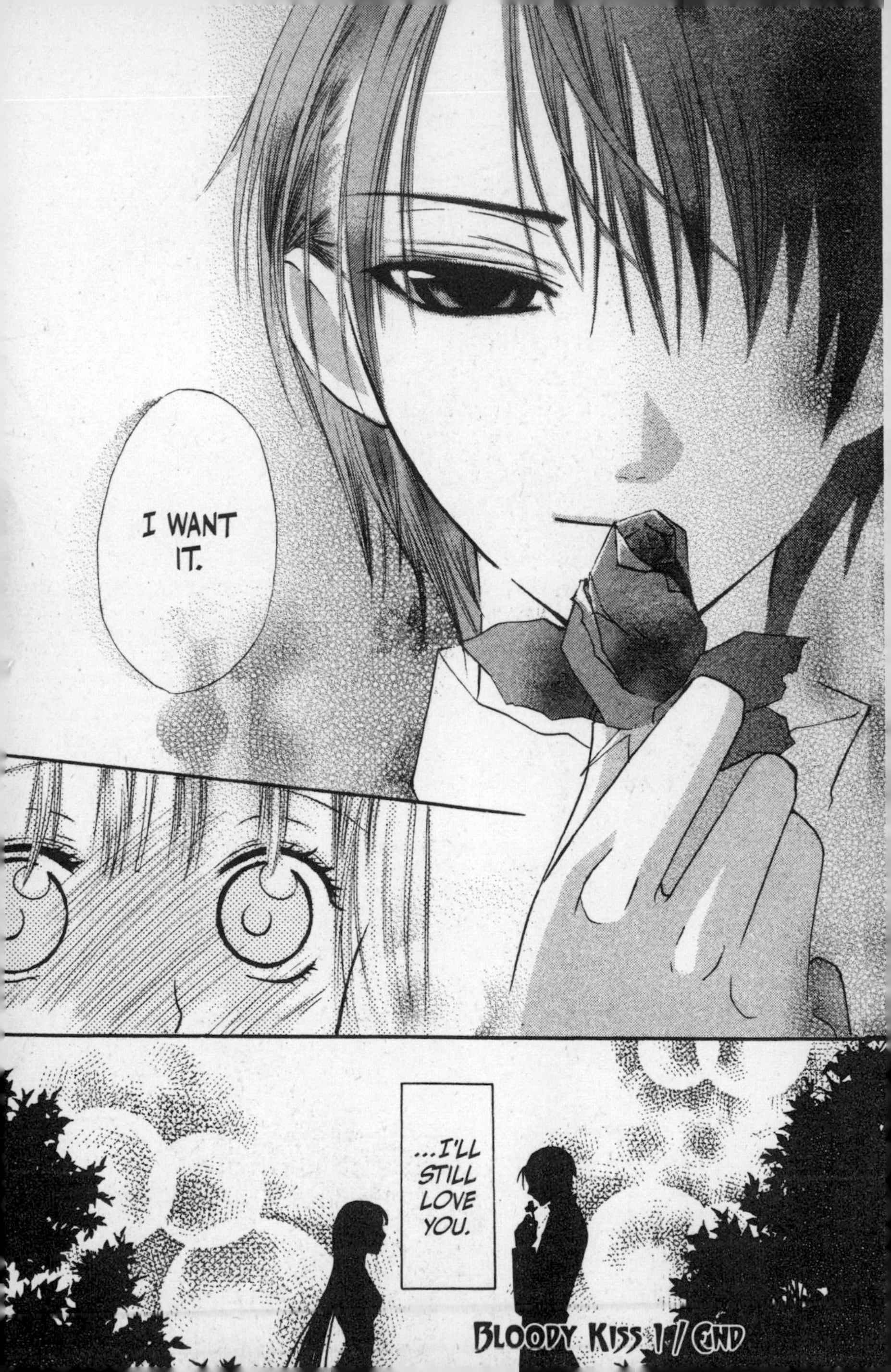
I WANT IT.
...I'LL STILL LOVE YOU.
BLOODY KISS 1 / END

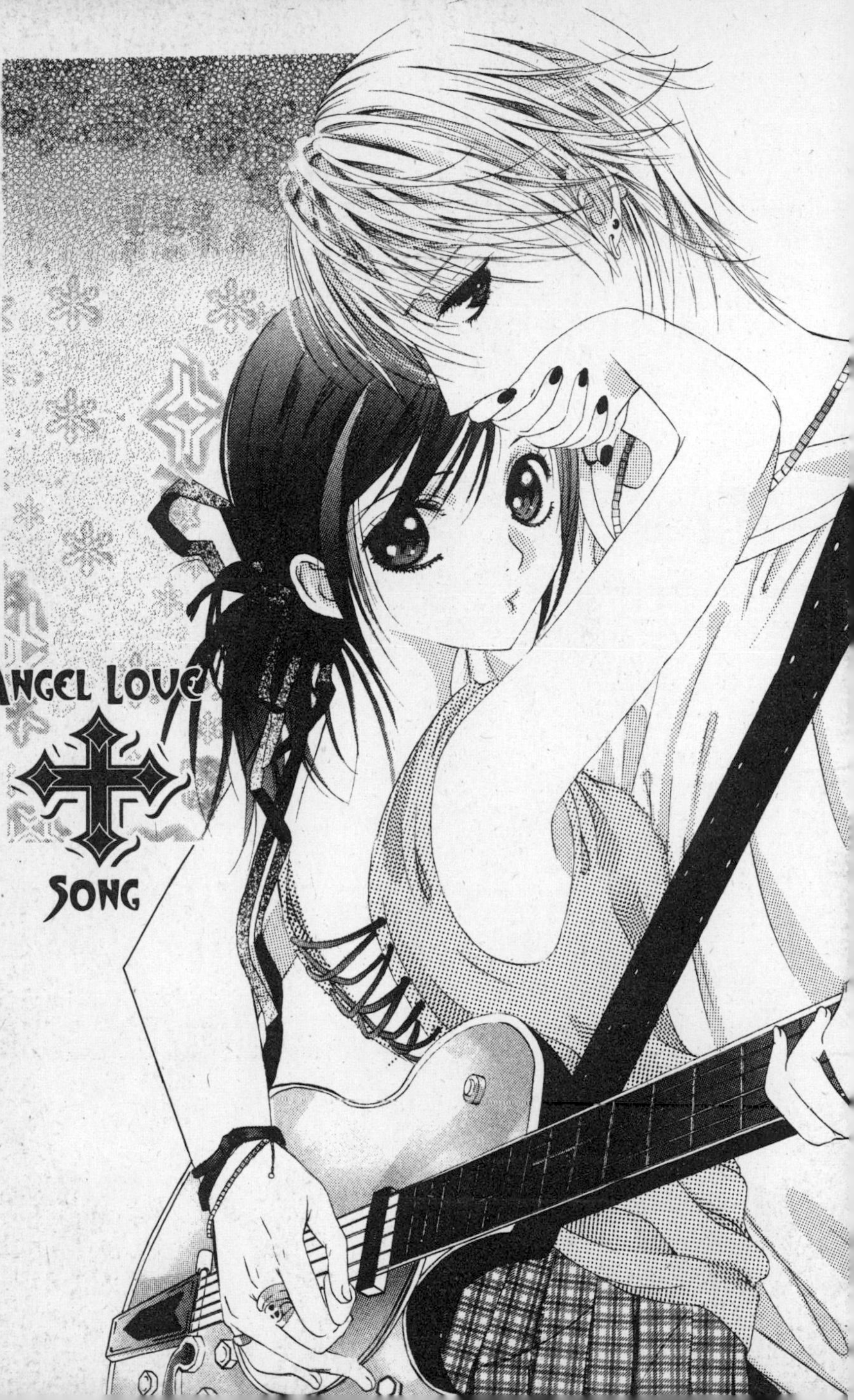
ANGEL LOVE
SONG

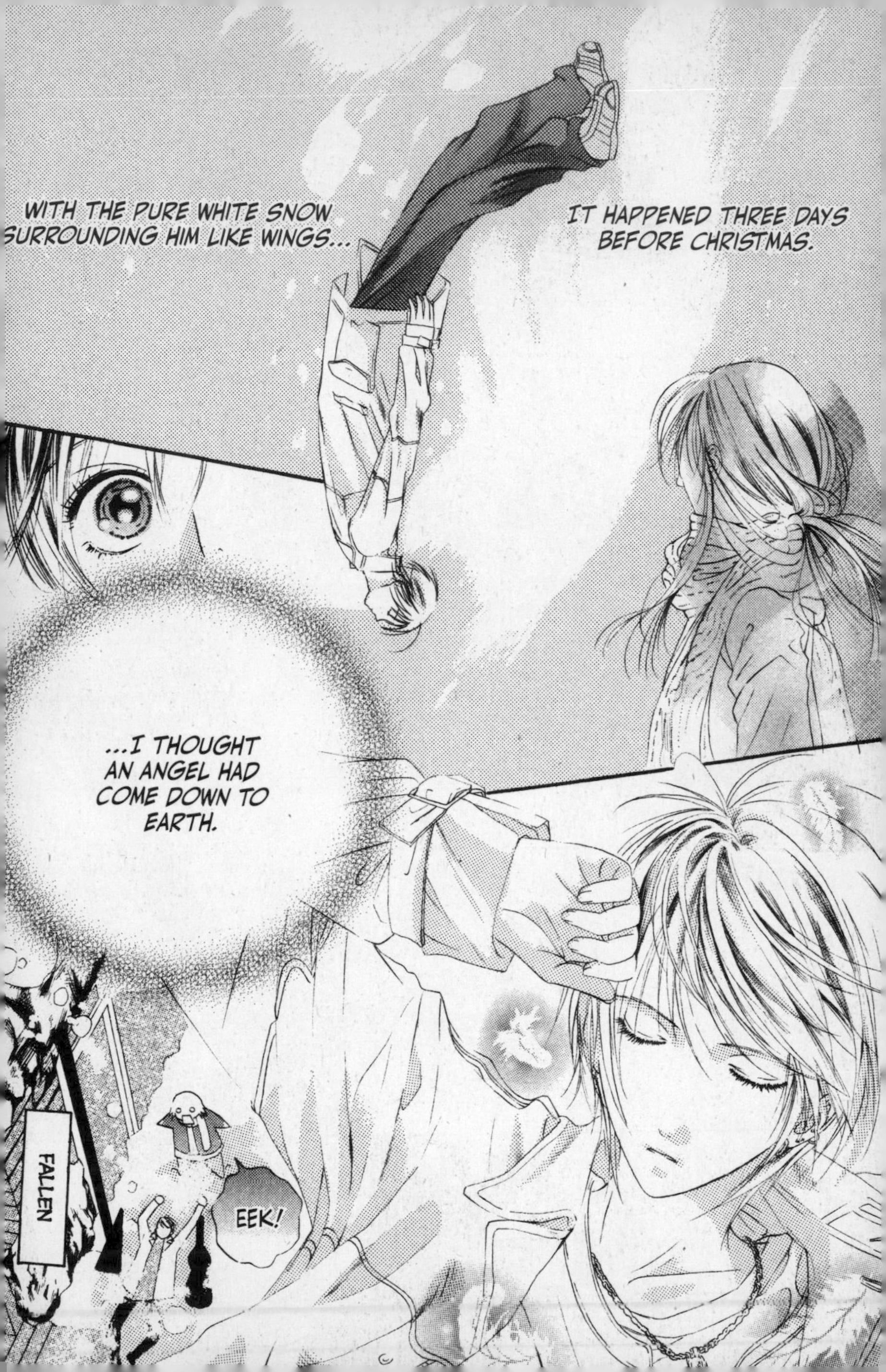
IT HAPPENED THREE DAYS BEFORE CHRISTMAS.
WITH THE PURE WHITE SNOW SURROUNDING HIM LIKE WINGS...
...I THOUGHT AN ANGEL HAD COME DOWN TO EARTH.
EEK!
FALLEN

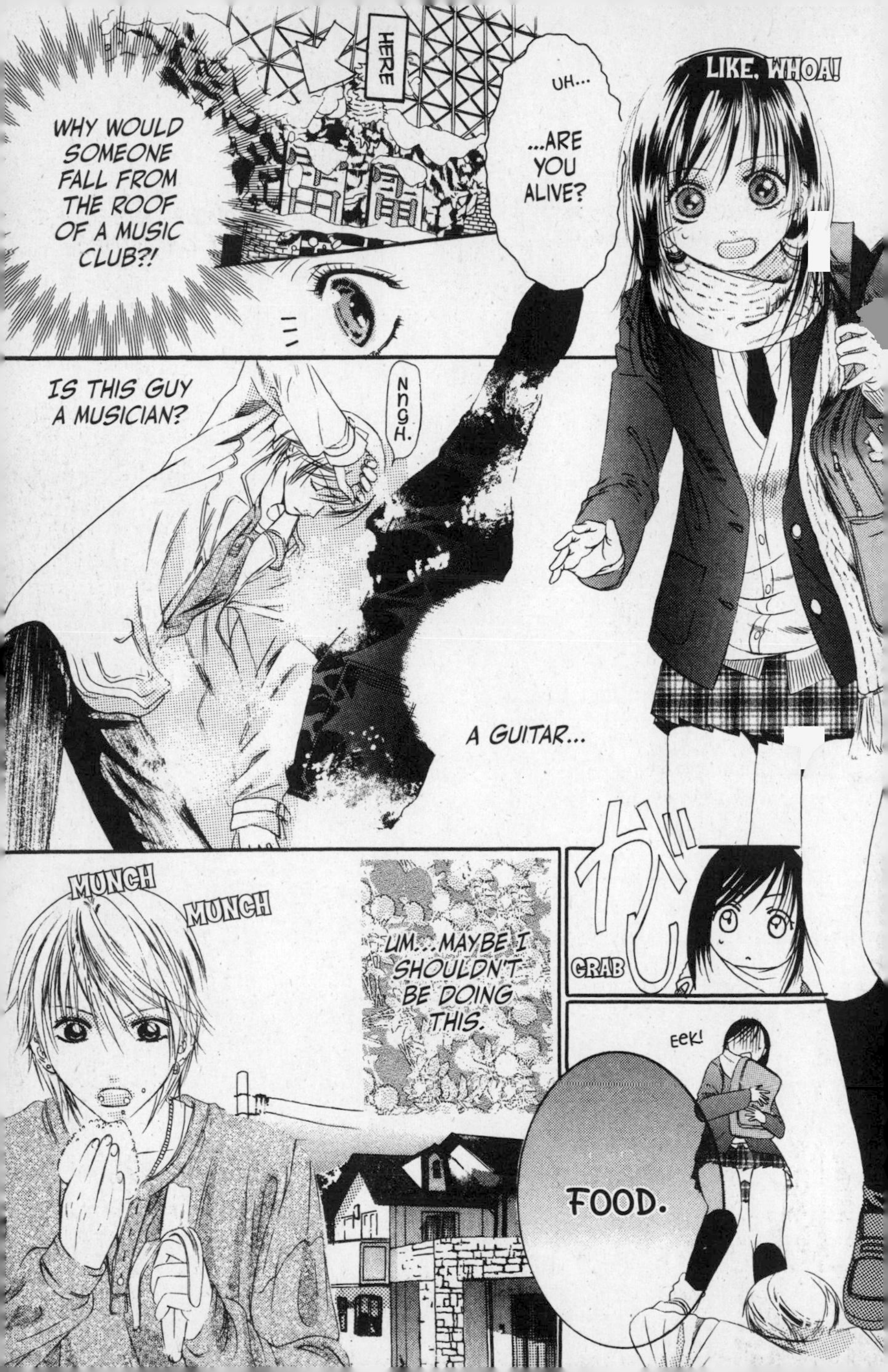
LIKE, WHOA!
UH...
...ARE YOU ALIVE?
HERE
WHY WOULD SOMEONE FALL FROM THE ROOF OF A MUSIC CLUB?!
NnGH.
IS THIS GUY A MUSICIAN?
A GUITAR...
GRAB
EEK!
FOOD.
UM... MAYBE I SHOULDN'T BE DOING THIS.
MUNCH
MUNCH

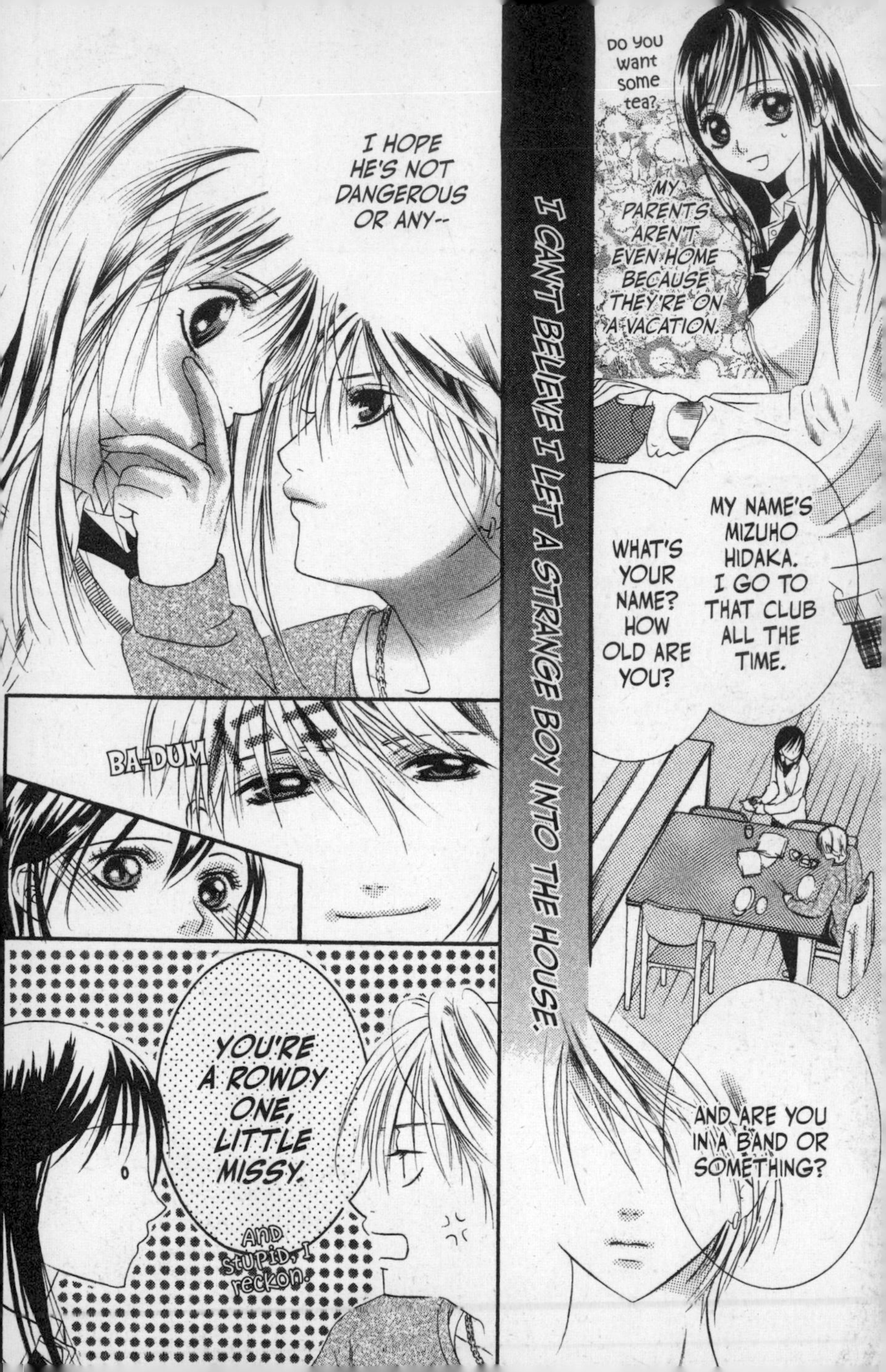
Do you want some tea?
MY PARENTS AREN'T EVEN HOME BECAUSE THEY'RE ON A VACATION.
MY NAME'S MIZUHO HIDAKA. I GO TO THAT CLUB ALL THE TIME.
WHAT'S YOUR NAME? HOW OLD ARE YOU?
AND ARE YOU IN A BAND OR SOMETHING?
I CAN'T BELIEVE I LET A STRANGE BOY INTO THE HOUSE.
I HOPE HE'S NOT DANGEROUS OR ANY--
BA-DUM
YOU'RE A ROWDY ONE, LITTLE MISSY.
AND STUPID, I RECKON.

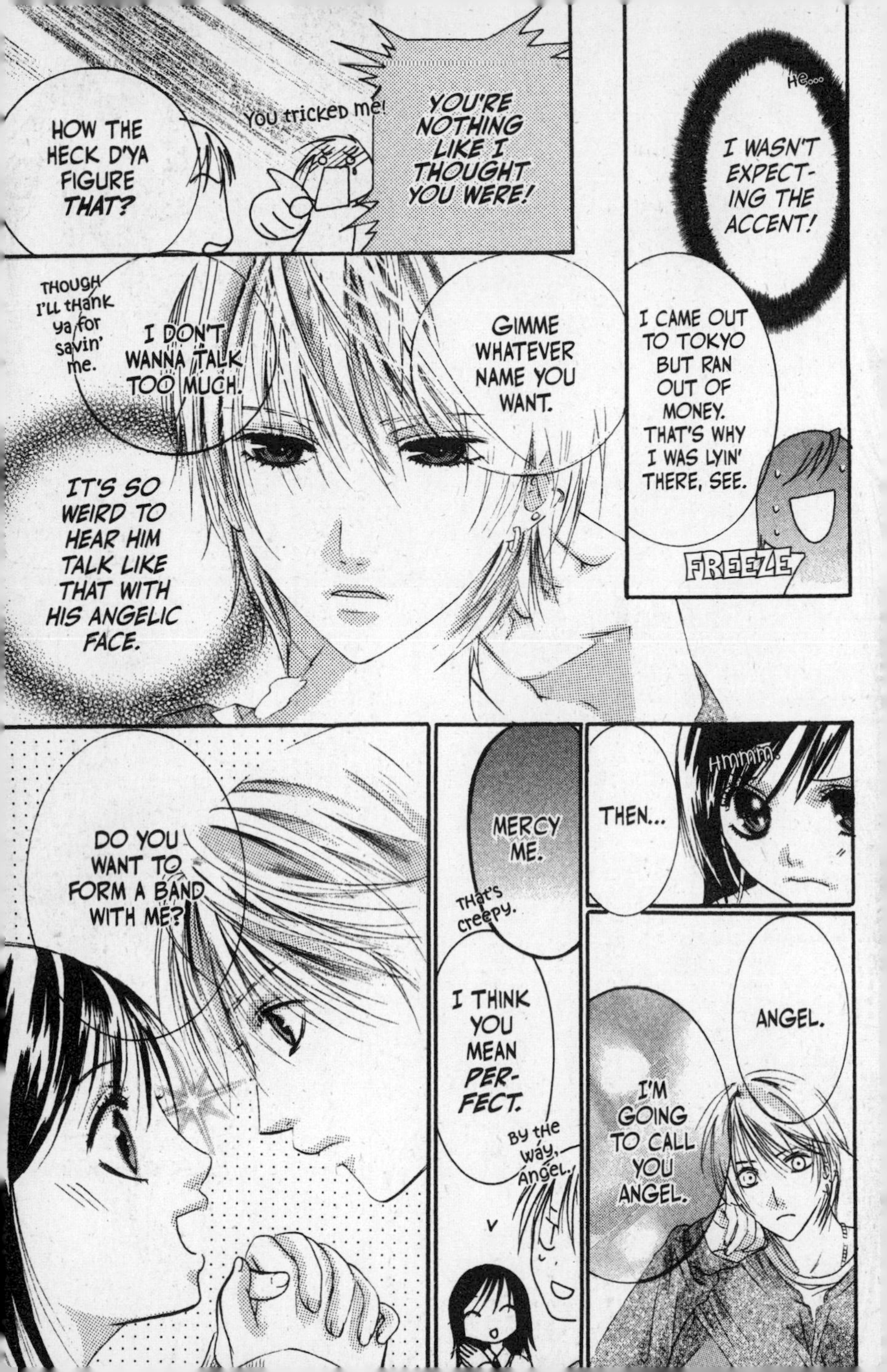
He...
I WASN'T EXPECTING THE ACCENT!
I CAME OUT TO TOKYO BUT RAN OUT OF MONEY. THAT'S WHY I WAS LYIN' THERE, SEE.
FREEZE
YOU'RE NOTHING LIKE I THOUGHT YOU WERE!
You tricked me!
HOW THE HECK D'YA FIGURE THAT?
GIMME WHATEVER NAME YOU WANT.
I DON'T WANNA TALK TOO MUCH.
THOUGH I'll thank ya for savin' me.
IT'S SO WEIRD TO HEAR HIM TALK LIKE THAT WITH HIS ANGELIC FACE.
Hmmm.
THEN...
ANGEL.
I'M GOING TO CALL YOU ANGEL.
MERCY ME.
That's creepy.
I THINK YOU MEAN PERFECT.
By the way, Angel.
DO YOU WANT TO FORM A BAND WITH ME?

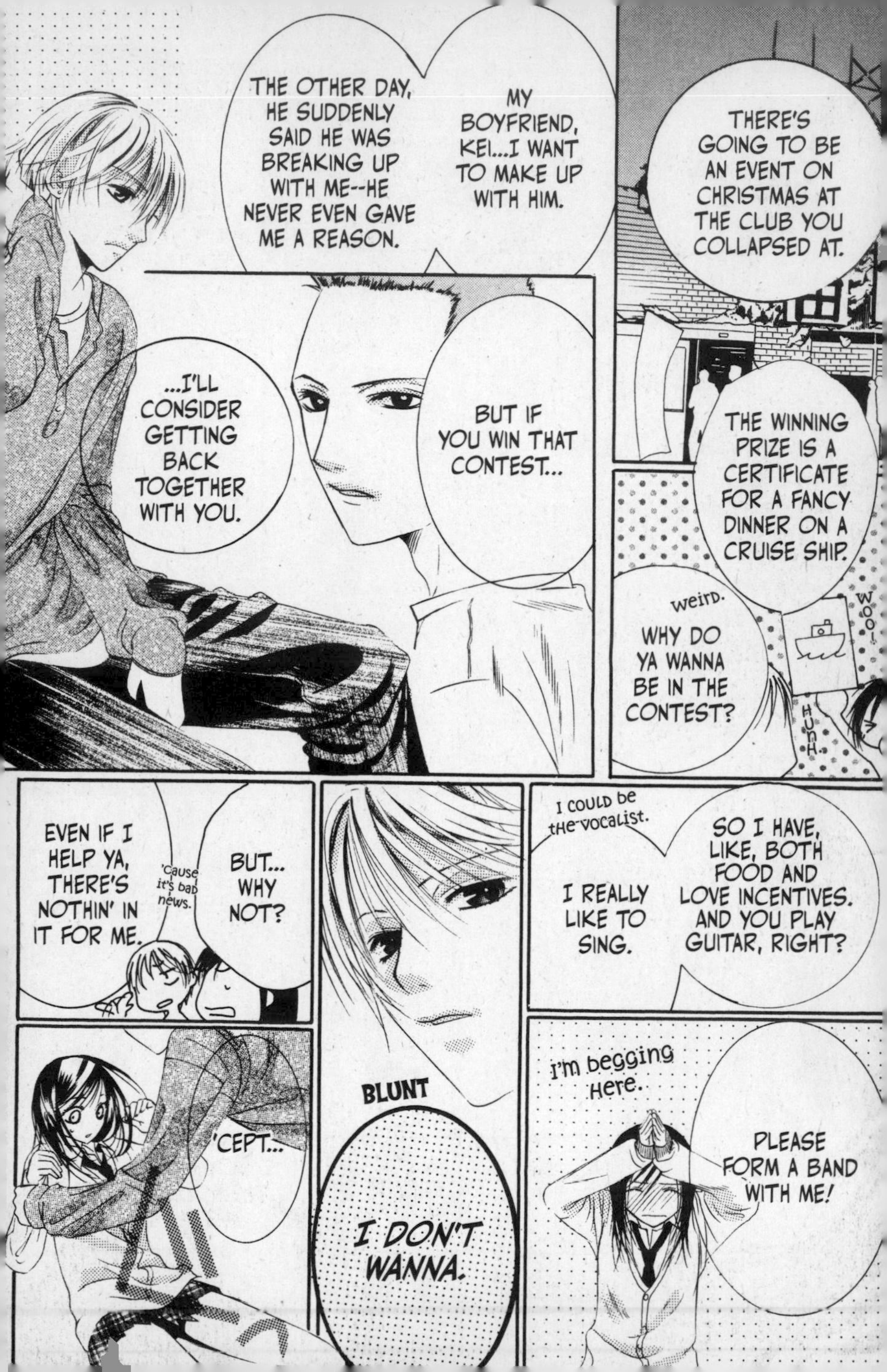
THERE'S GOING TO BE AN EVENT ON CHRISTMAS AT THE CLUB YOU COLLAPSED AT.
THE WINNING PRIZE IS A CERTIFICATE FOR A FANCY DINNER ON A CRUISE SHIP.
WOO!
Weird.
WHY DO YA WANNA BE IN THE CONTEST?
HUNH.
MY BOYFRIEND, KEI...I WANT TO MAKE UP WITH HIM.
THE OTHER DAY, HE SUDDENLY SAID HE WAS BREAKING UP WITH ME--HE NEVER EVEN GAVE ME A REASON.
BUT IF YOU WIN THAT CONTEST...
...I'LL CONSIDER GETTING BACK TOGETHER WITH YOU.
SO I HAVE, LIKE, BOTH FOOD AND LOVE INCENTIVES. AND YOU PLAY GUITAR, RIGHT?
I could be the vocalist.
I REALLY LIKE TO SING.
I'm begging here.
PLEASE FORM A BAND WITH ME!
BLUNT
I DON'T WANNA.
BUT... WHY NOT?
'Cause it's bad news.
EVEN IF I HELP YA, THERE'S NOTHIN' IN IT FOR ME.
'CEPT...

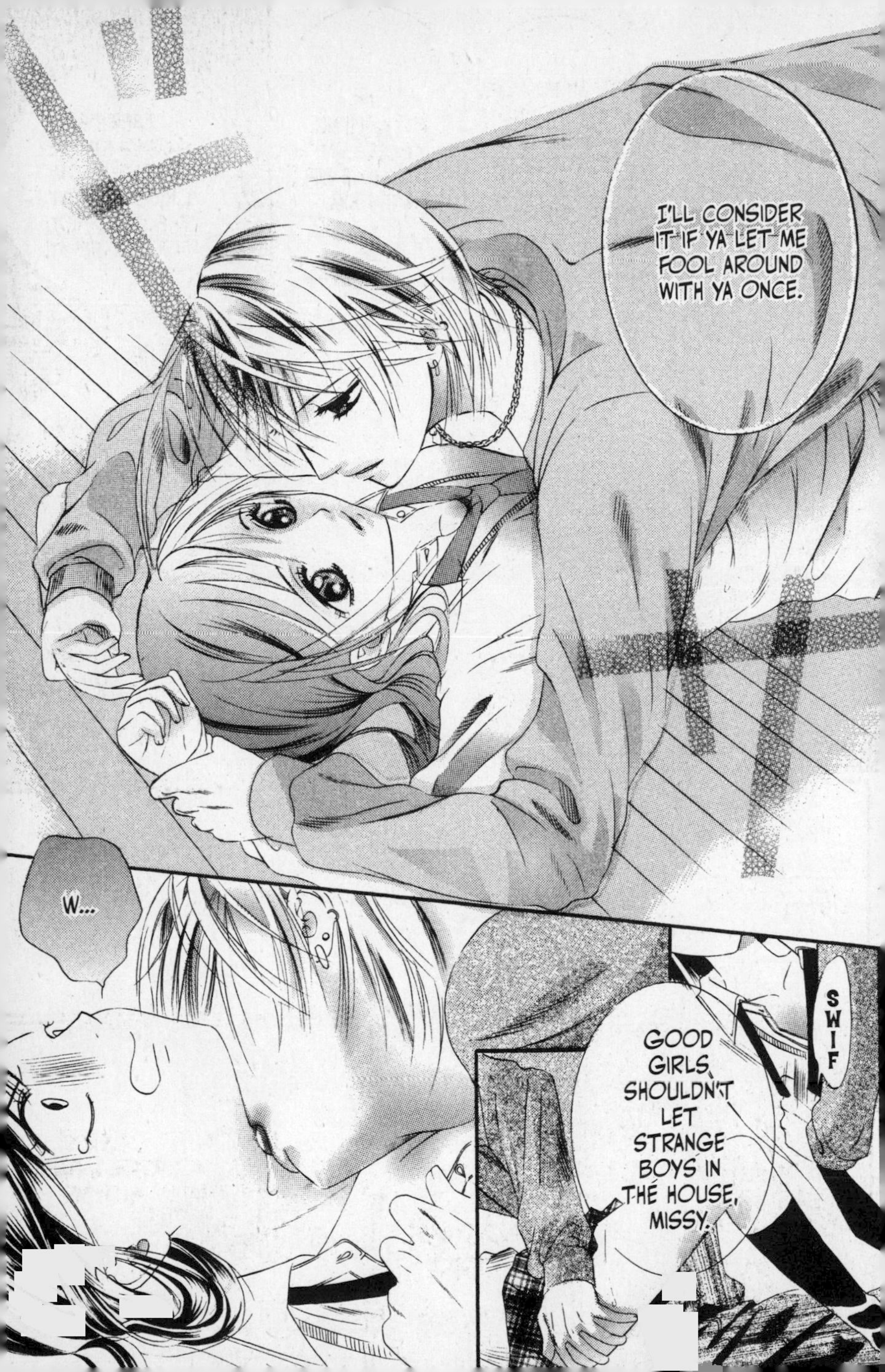
I'LL CONSIDER IT IF YA LET ME FOOL AROUND WITH YA ONCE.
SWIF
GOOD GIRLS SHOULDN'T LET STRANGE BOYS IN THE HOUSE, MISSY.
W...

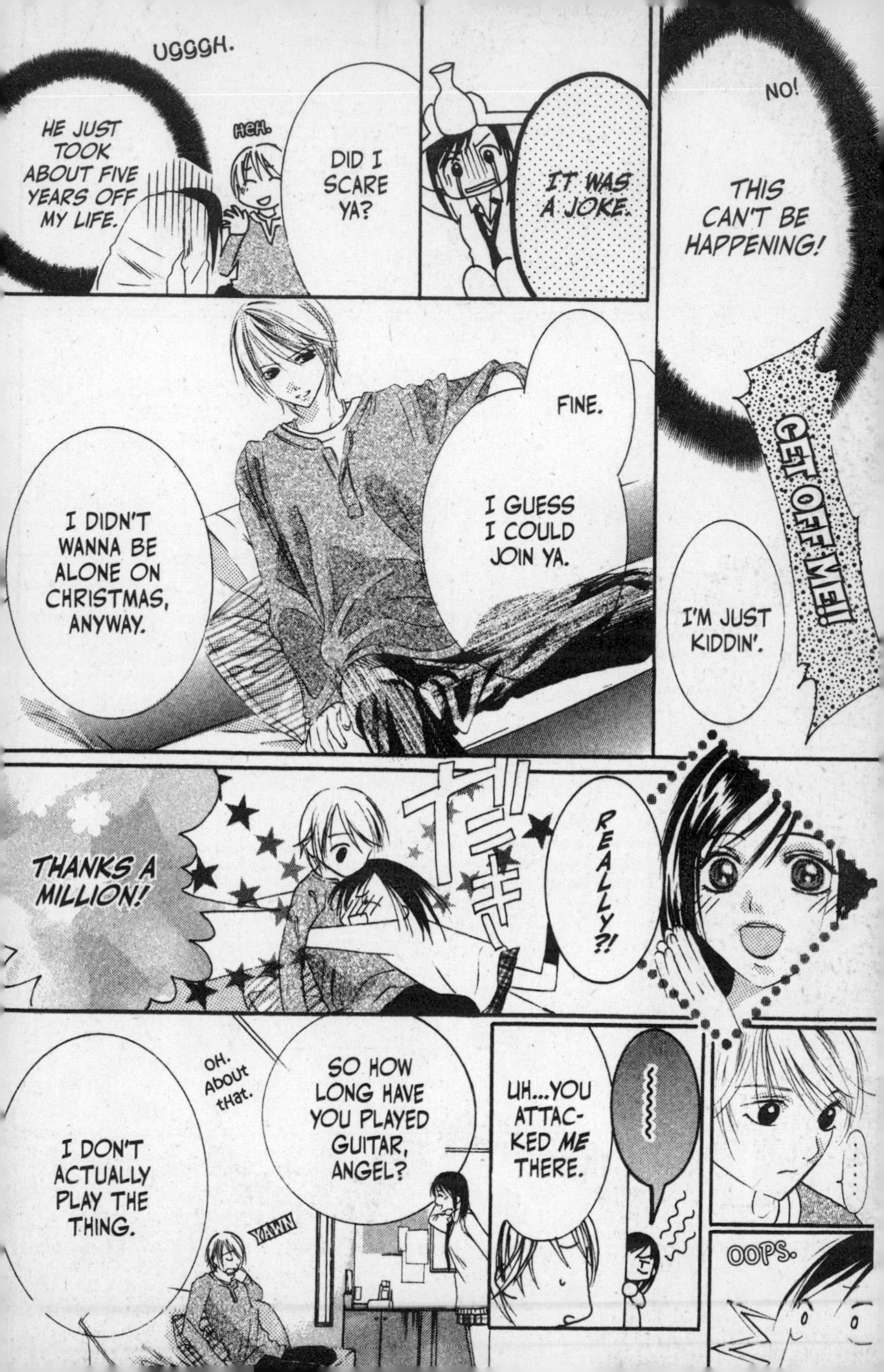
NO!
THIS CAN'T BE HAPPENING!
GET OFF ME!!
I'M JUST KIDDIN'.
IT WAS A JOKE.
DID I SCARE YA?
HEH.
UGGGH.
HE JUST TOOK ABOUT FIVE YEARS OFF MY LIFE.
FINE.
I GUESS I COULD JOIN YA.
I DIDN'T WANNA BE ALONE ON CHRISTMAS, ANYWAY.
REALLY?!
THANKS A MILLION!
OOPS.
UH...YOU ATTACKED ME THERE.
SO HOW LONG HAVE YOU PLAYED GUITAR, ANGEL?
OH. About that.
I DON'T ACTUALLY PLAY THE THING.
YAWN

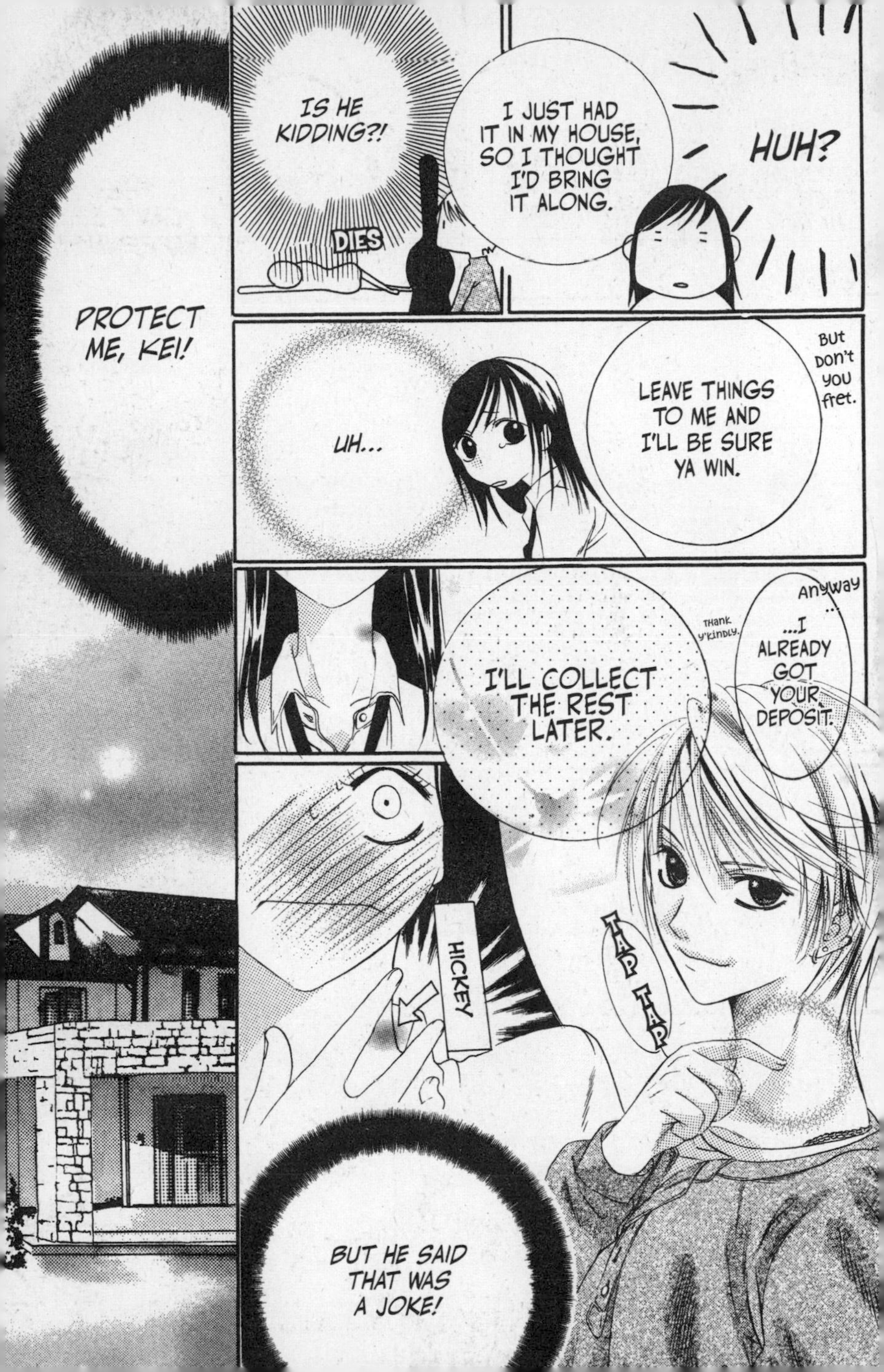
HUH?
I JUST HAD IT IN MY HOUSE, SO I THOUGHT I'D BRING IT ALONG.
IS HE KIDDING?!
DIES
But Don't you fret.
LEAVE THINGS TO ME AND I'LL BE SURE YA WIN.
UH...
Anyway...
...I ALREADY GOT YOUR DEPOSIT.
Thank y'kindly.
I'LL COLLECT THE REST LATER.
TAP TAP
HICKEY
BUT HE SAID THAT WAS A JOKE!
PROTECT ME, KEI!

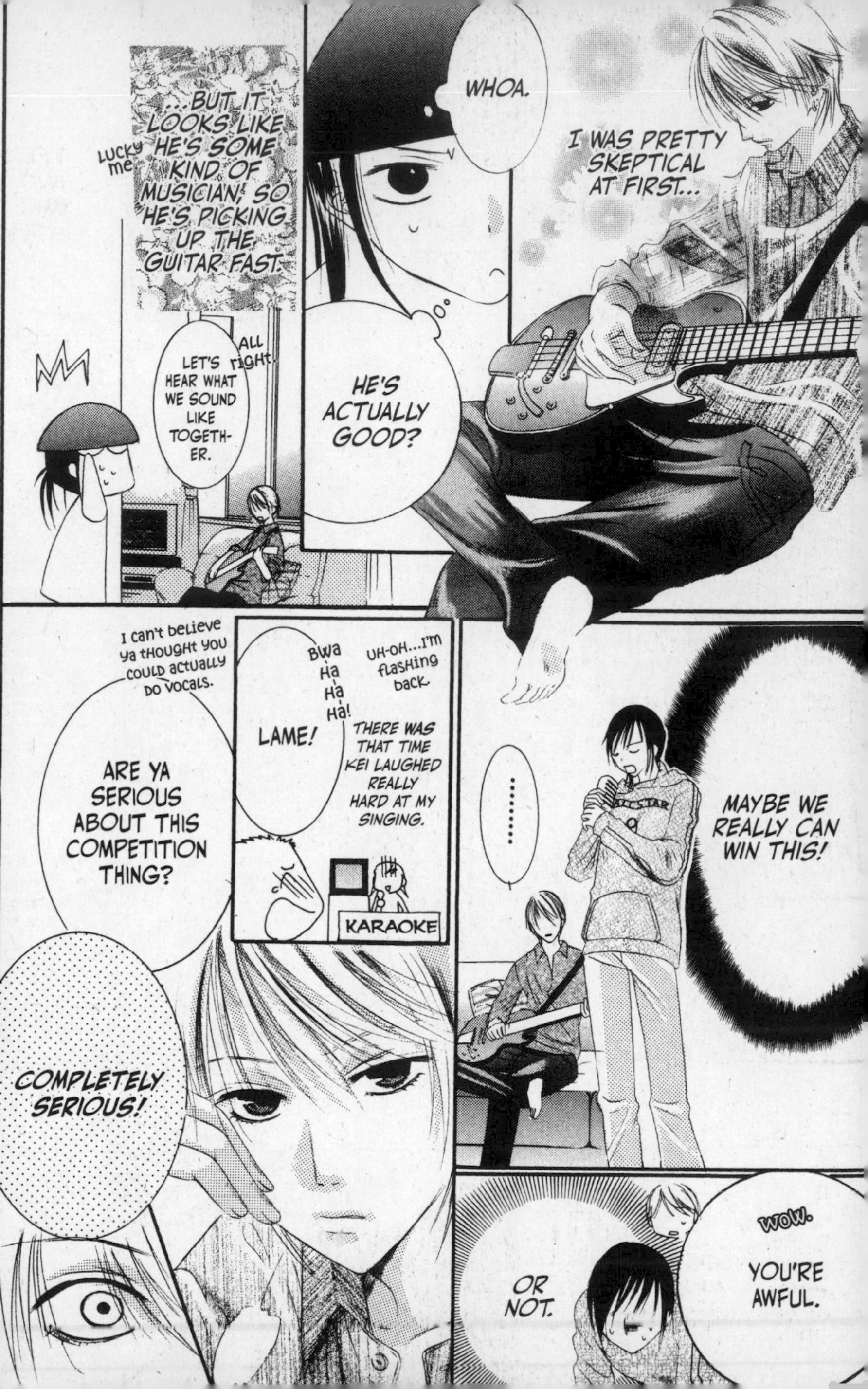
I WAS PRETTY SKEPTICAL AT FIRST...
WHOA.
HE'S ACTUALLY GOOD?
...BUT IT LOOKS LIKE HE'S SOME KIND OF MUSICIAN, SO HE'S PICKING UP THE GUITAR FAST.
Lucky me
All right.
LET'S HEAR WHAT WE SOUND LIKE TOGETH-ER.
MAYBE WE REALLY CAN WIN THIS!
......
WOW.
YOU'RE AWFUL.
OR NOT.
UH-OH...I'M flashing back.
THERE WAS THAT TIME KEI LAUGHED REALLY HARD AT MY SINGING.
Bwa Ha Ha Ha!
LAME!
KARAOKE
I can't believe ya thought you could actually do vocals.
ARE YA SERIOUS ABOUT THIS COMPETITION THING?
COMPLETELY SERIOUS!

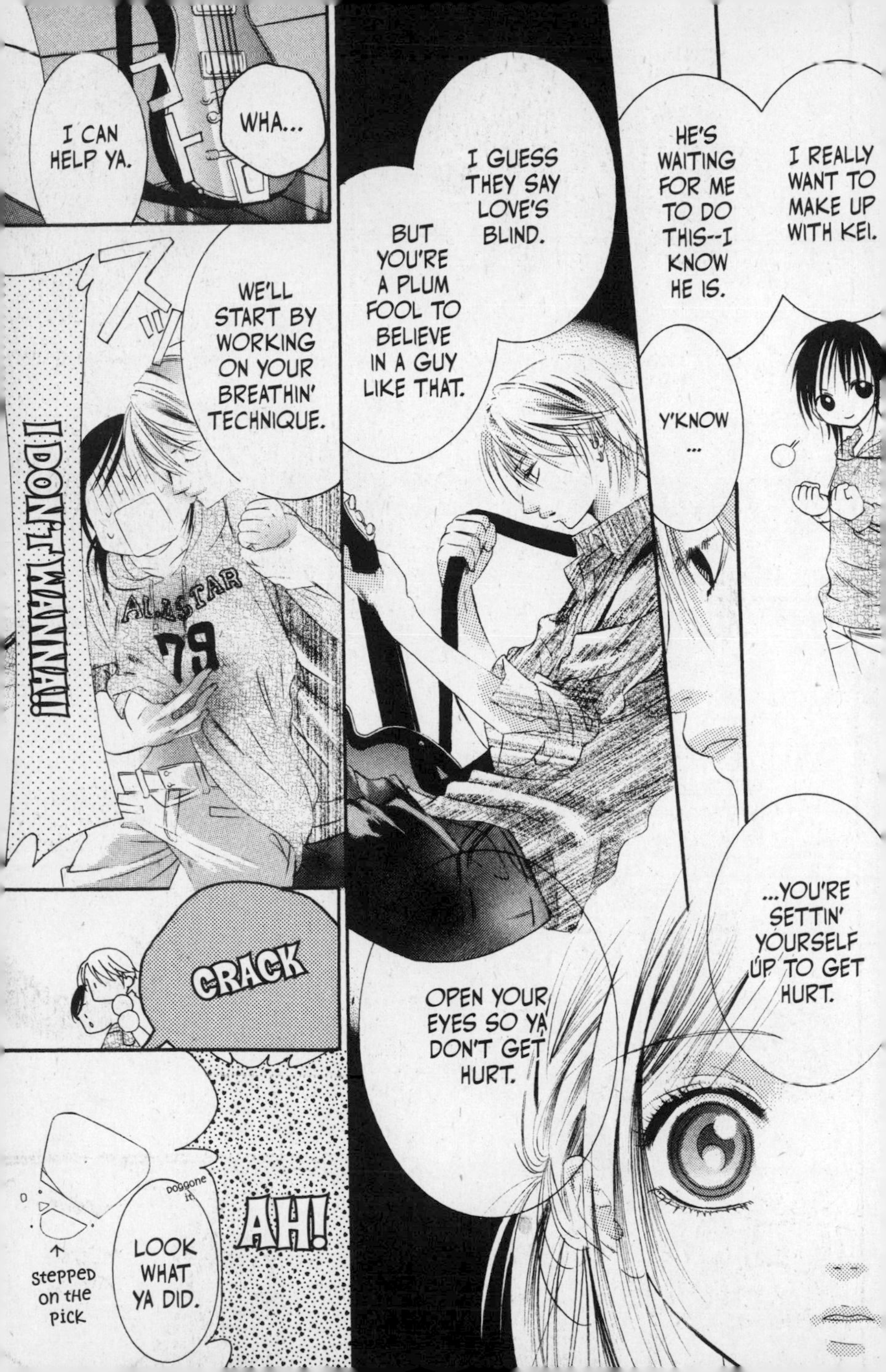
I REALLY WANT TO MAKE UP WITH KEI.
HE'S WAITING FOR ME TO DO THIS--I KNOW HE IS.
Y'KNOW ...
...YOU'RE SETTIN' YOURSELF UP TO GET HURT.
I GUESS THEY SAY LOVE'S BLIND.
BUT YOU'RE A PLUM FOOL TO BELIEVE IN A GUY LIKE THAT.
OPEN YOUR EYES SO YA DON'T GET HURT.
WHA...
I CAN HELP YA.
WE'LL START BY WORKING ON YOUR BREATHIN' TECHNIQUE.
I DON'T WANNA!!
ALLSTAR 79
CRACK
AH!
doggone it
LOOK WHAT YA DID.
stepped on the pick

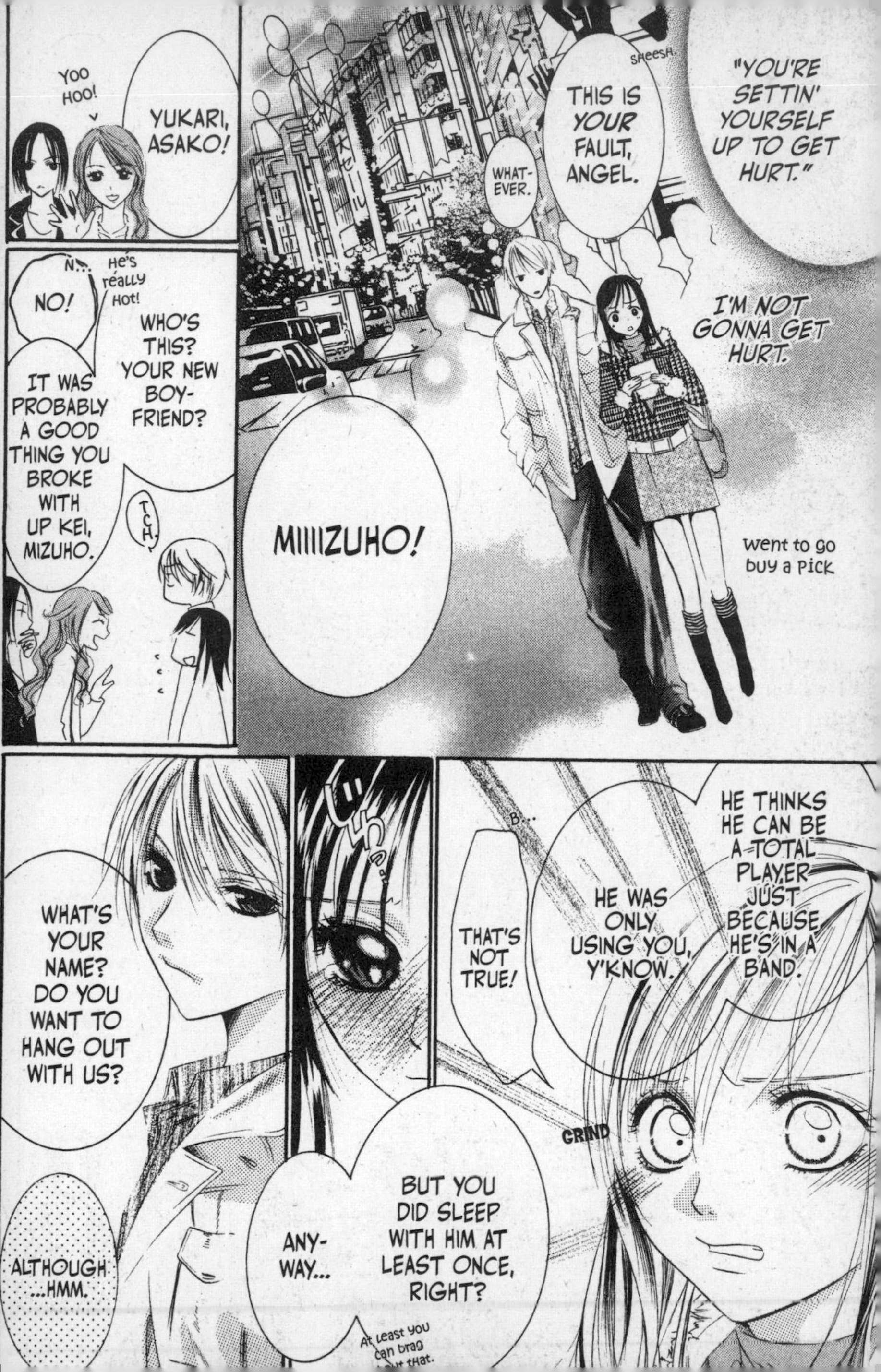
"YOU'RE SETTIN' YOURSELF UP TO GET HURT."
SHEESH.
THIS IS YOUR FAULT, ANGEL.
WHAT-EVER.
I'M NOT GONNA GET HURT.
went to go buy a pick
MIIIIZUHO!
YUKARI, ASAKO!
YOO HOO!
WHO'S THIS? YOUR NEW BOY-FRIEND?
He's really Hot!
N... NO!
IT WAS PROBABLY A GOOD THING YOU BROKE UP WITH KEI, MIZUHO.
TCH.
HE THINKS HE CAN BE A TOTAL PLAYER JUST BECAUSE HE'S IN A BAND.
HE WAS ONLY USING YOU, Y'KNOW.
B...
THAT'S NOT TRUE!
GRIND
BUT YOU DID SLEEP WITH HIM AT LEAST ONCE, RIGHT?
ANY-WAY...
At least you can brag
WHAT'S YOUR NAME? DO YOU WANT TO HANG OUT WITH US?
ALTHOUGH ...HMM.

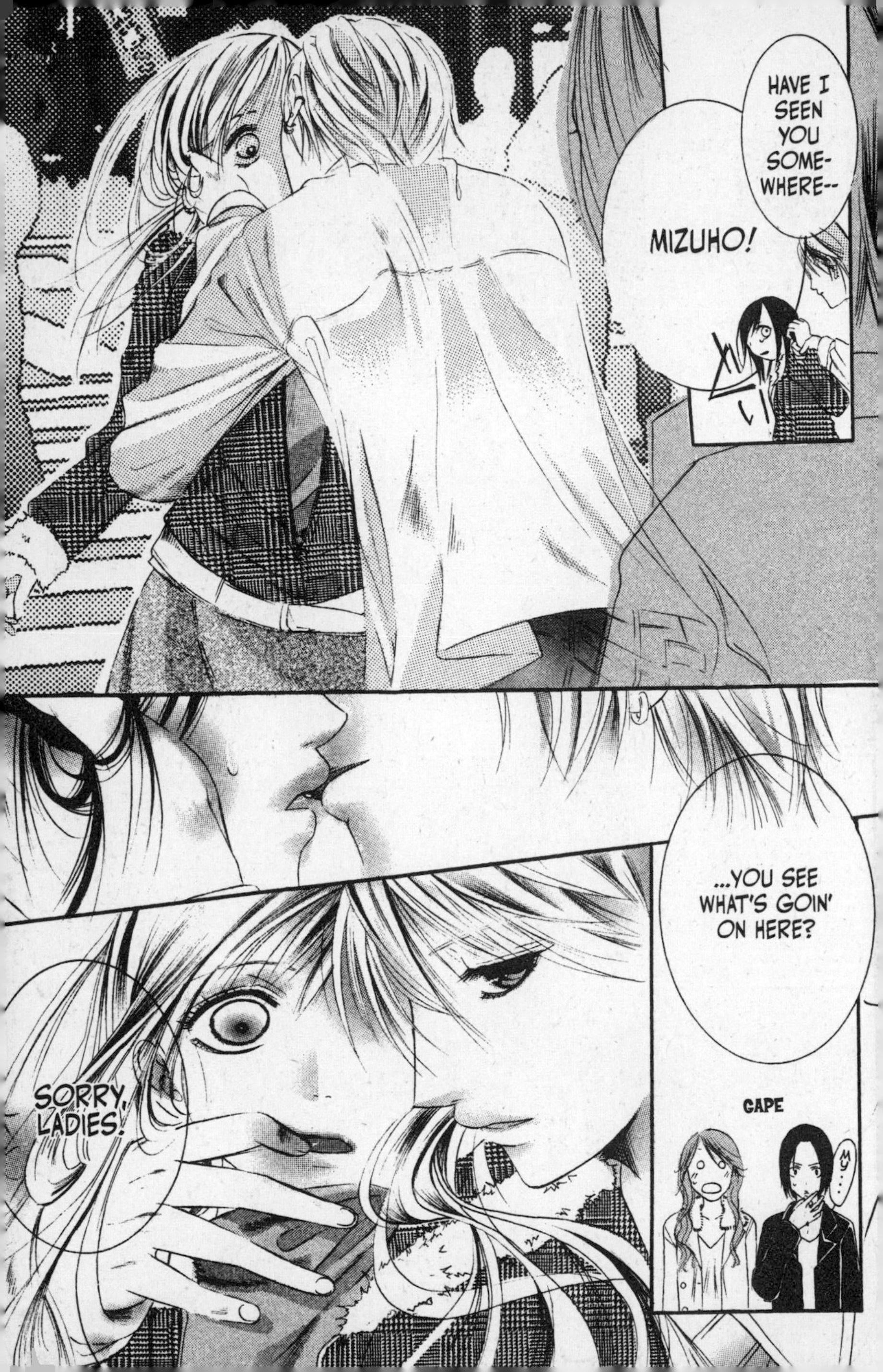
HAVE I SEEN YOU SOME-WHERE--
MIZUHO!
...YOU SEE WHAT'S GOIN' ON HERE?
GAPE
MY...
SORRY, LADIES!

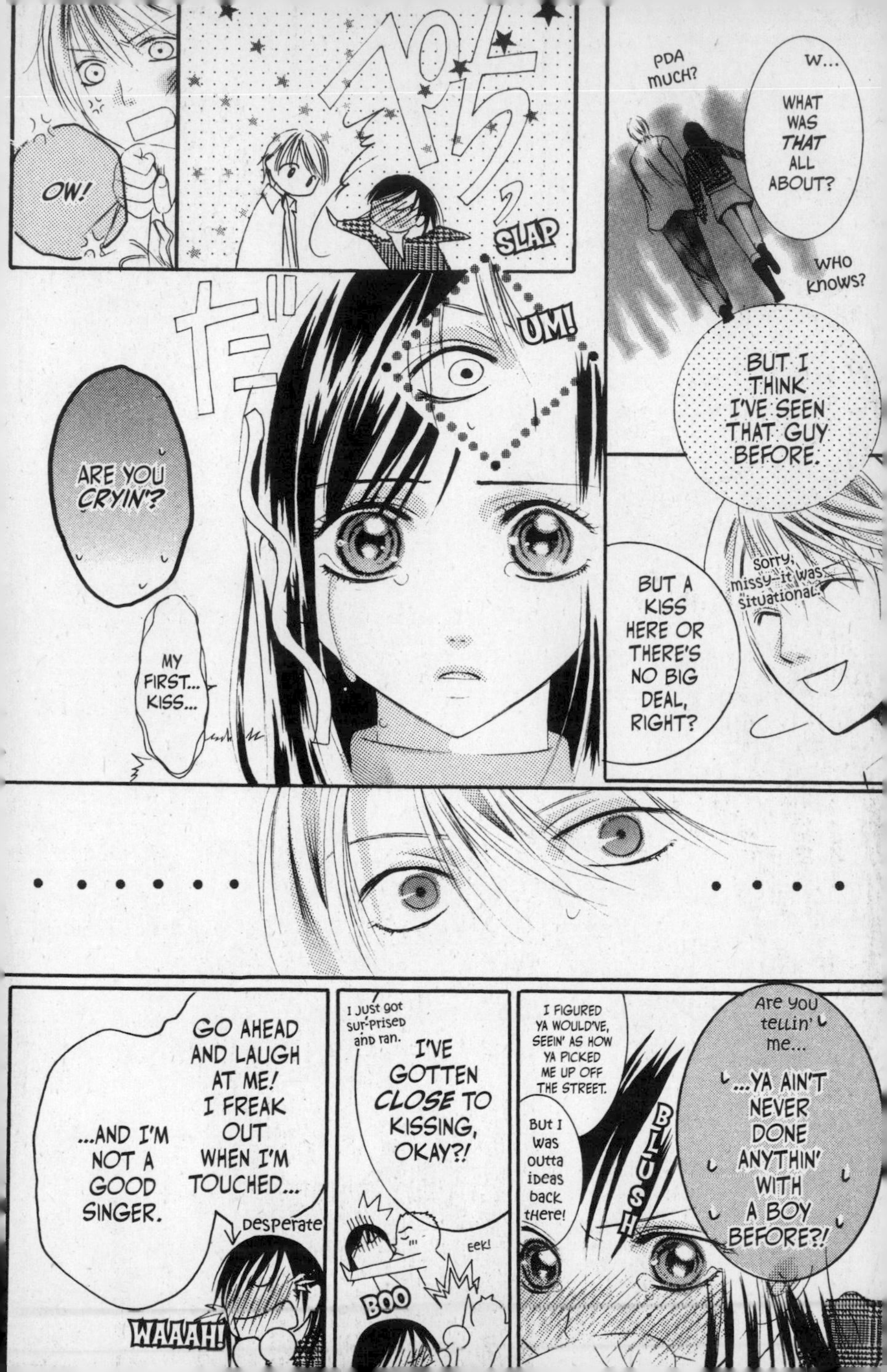
W...
WHAT WAS THAT ALL ABOUT?
PDA MUCH?
WHO KNOWS?
SLAP
OW!
BUT I THINK I'VE SEEN THAT GUY BEFORE.
UM!
BUT A KISS HERE OR THERE'S NO BIG DEAL, RIGHT?
Sorry, missy–it was situational.
ARE YOU CRYIN'?
MY FIRST... KISS...
Are you tellin' me...
...YA AIN'T NEVER DONE ANYTHIN' WITH A BOY BEFORE?!
BLUSH
I FIGURED YA WOULD'VE, SEEIN' AS HOW YA PICKED ME UP OFF THE STREET.
But I was outta ideas back there!
I'VE GOTTEN CLOSE TO KISSING, OKAY?!
I just got sur-prised and ran.
EEK!
BOO
GO AHEAD AND LAUGH AT ME! I FREAK OUT WHEN I'M TOUCHED...
...AND I'M NOT A GOOD SINGER.
Desperate
WAAAH!

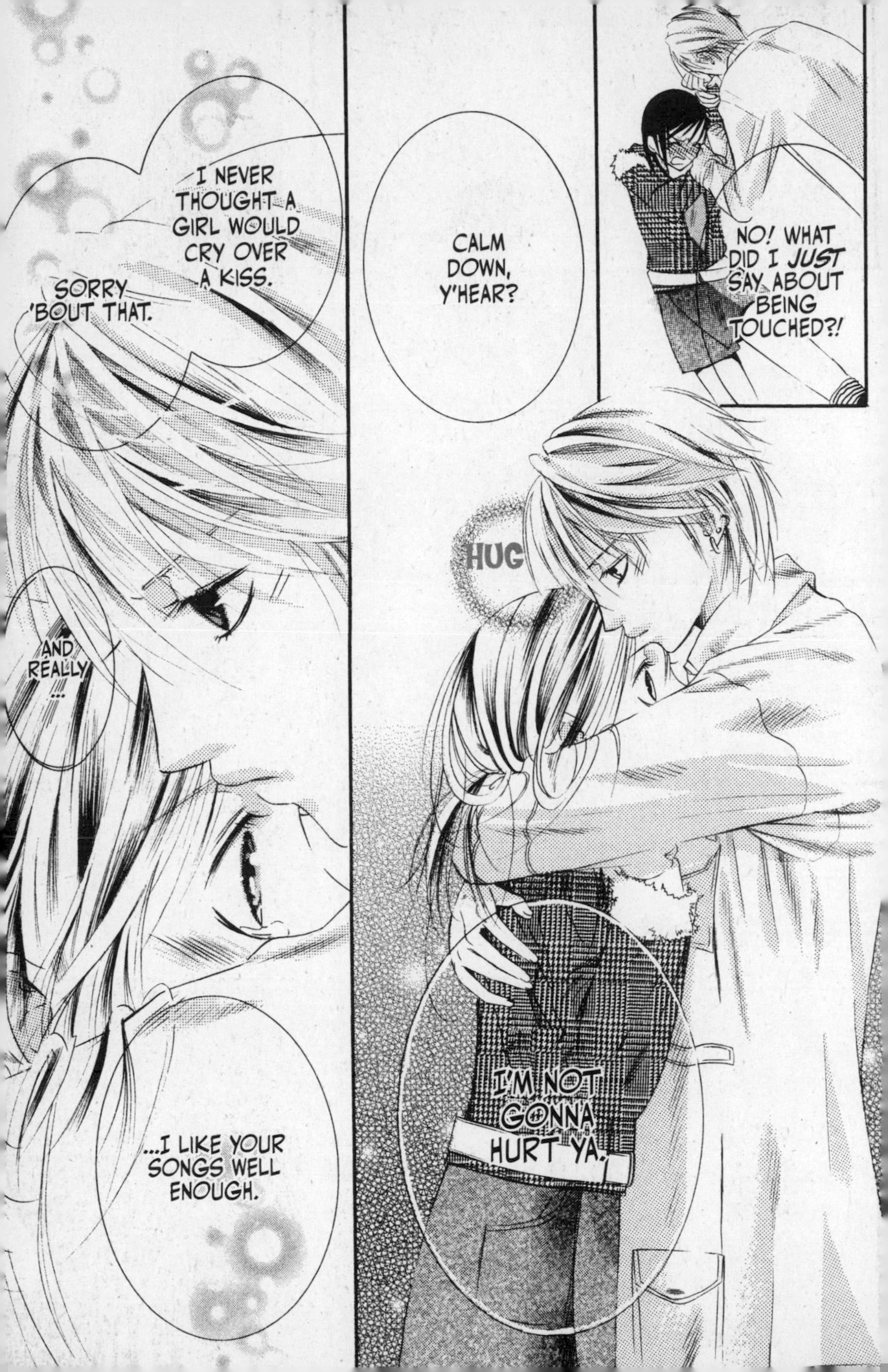
NO! WHAT DID I *JUST* SAY ABOUT BEING TOUCHED?!
CALM DOWN, Y'HEAR?
HUG
I'M NOT GONNA HURT YA.
I NEVER THOUGHT A GIRL WOULD CRY OVER A KISS.
SORRY 'BOUT THAT.
AND REALLY ...
...I LIKE YOUR SONGS WELL ENOUGH.

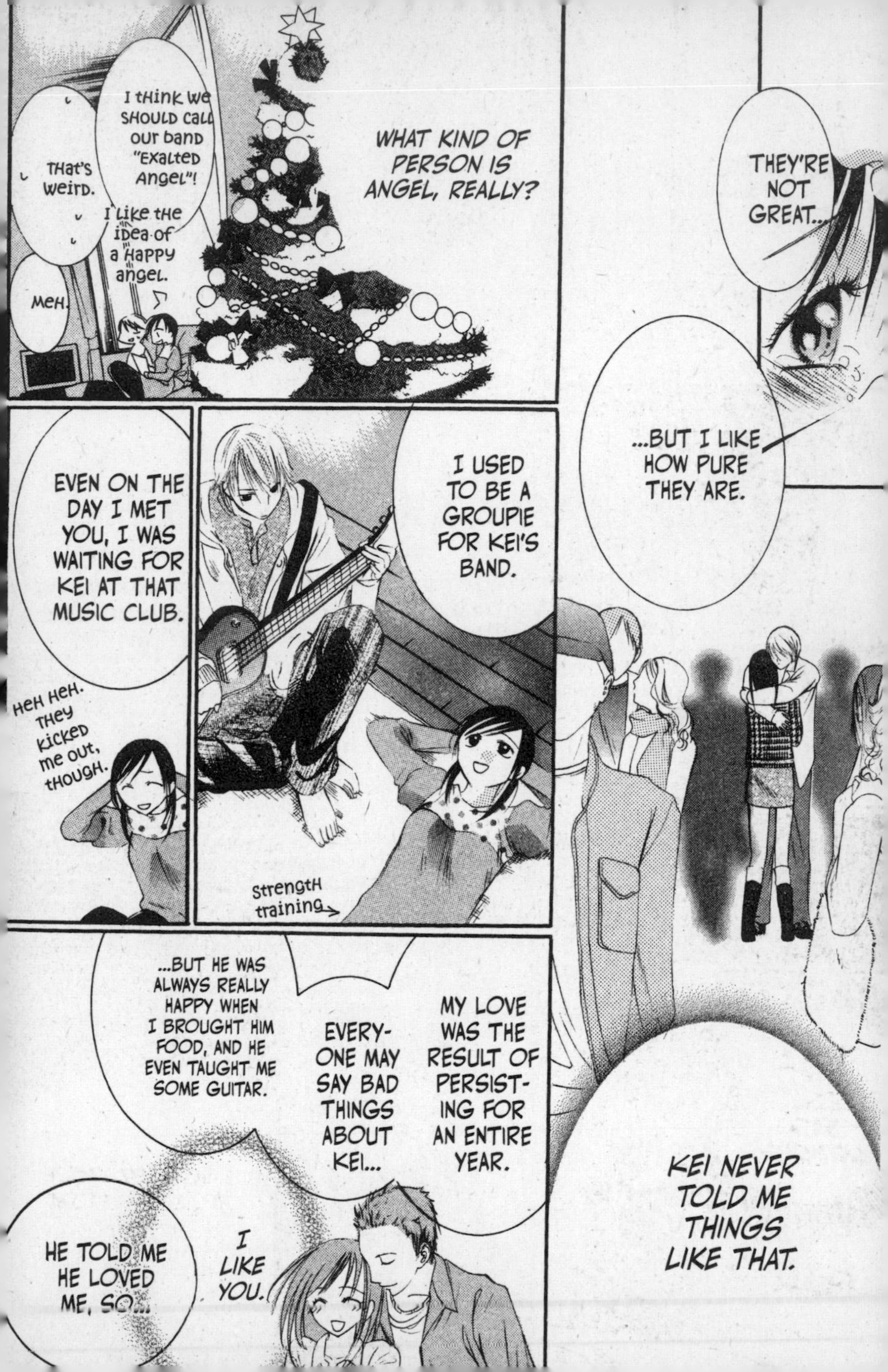
THEY'RE NOT GREAT...
...BUT I LIKE HOW PURE THEY ARE.
WHAT KIND OF PERSON IS ANGEL, REALLY?
I think we should call our band "Exalted Angel"!
I like the idea of a happy angel.
That's weird.
Meh.
I USED TO BE A GROUPIE FOR KEI'S BAND.
Strength training
EVEN ON THE DAY I MET YOU, I WAS WAITING FOR KEI AT THAT MUSIC CLUB.
Heh heh. They kicked me out, though.
MY LOVE WAS THE RESULT OF PERSIST-ING FOR AN ENTIRE YEAR.
EVERY-ONE MAY SAY BAD THINGS ABOUT KEI...
...BUT HE WAS ALWAYS REALLY HAPPY WHEN I BROUGHT HIM FOOD, AND HE EVEN TAUGHT ME SOME GUITAR.
I LIKE YOU.
HE TOLD ME HE LOVED ME, SO...
KEI NEVER TOLD ME THINGS LIKE THAT.

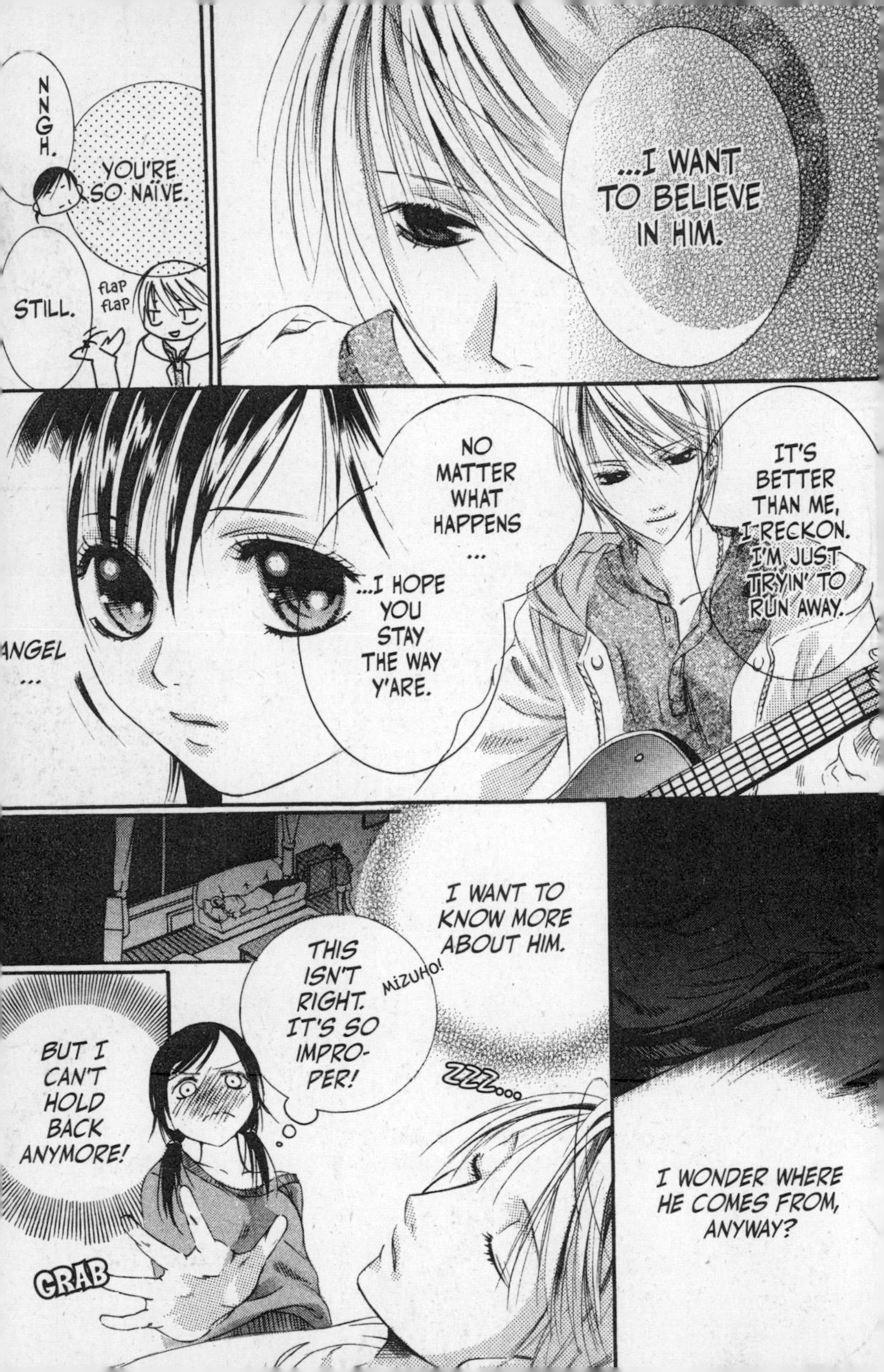
...I WANT TO BELIEVE IN HIM.
YOU'RE SO NAÏVE.
NNGH.
flap flap
STILL.
IT'S BETTER THAN ME, I RECKON. I'M JUST TRYIN' TO RUN AWAY.
NO MATTER WHAT HAPPENS ...
...I HOPE YOU STAY THE WAY Y'ARE.
ANGEL ...
I WANT TO KNOW MORE ABOUT HIM.
ZZZ...
I WONDER WHERE HE COMES FROM, ANYWAY?
THIS ISN'T RIGHT. IT'S SO IMPRO-PER!
MIZUHO!
BUT I CAN'T HOLD BACK ANYMORE!
GRAB

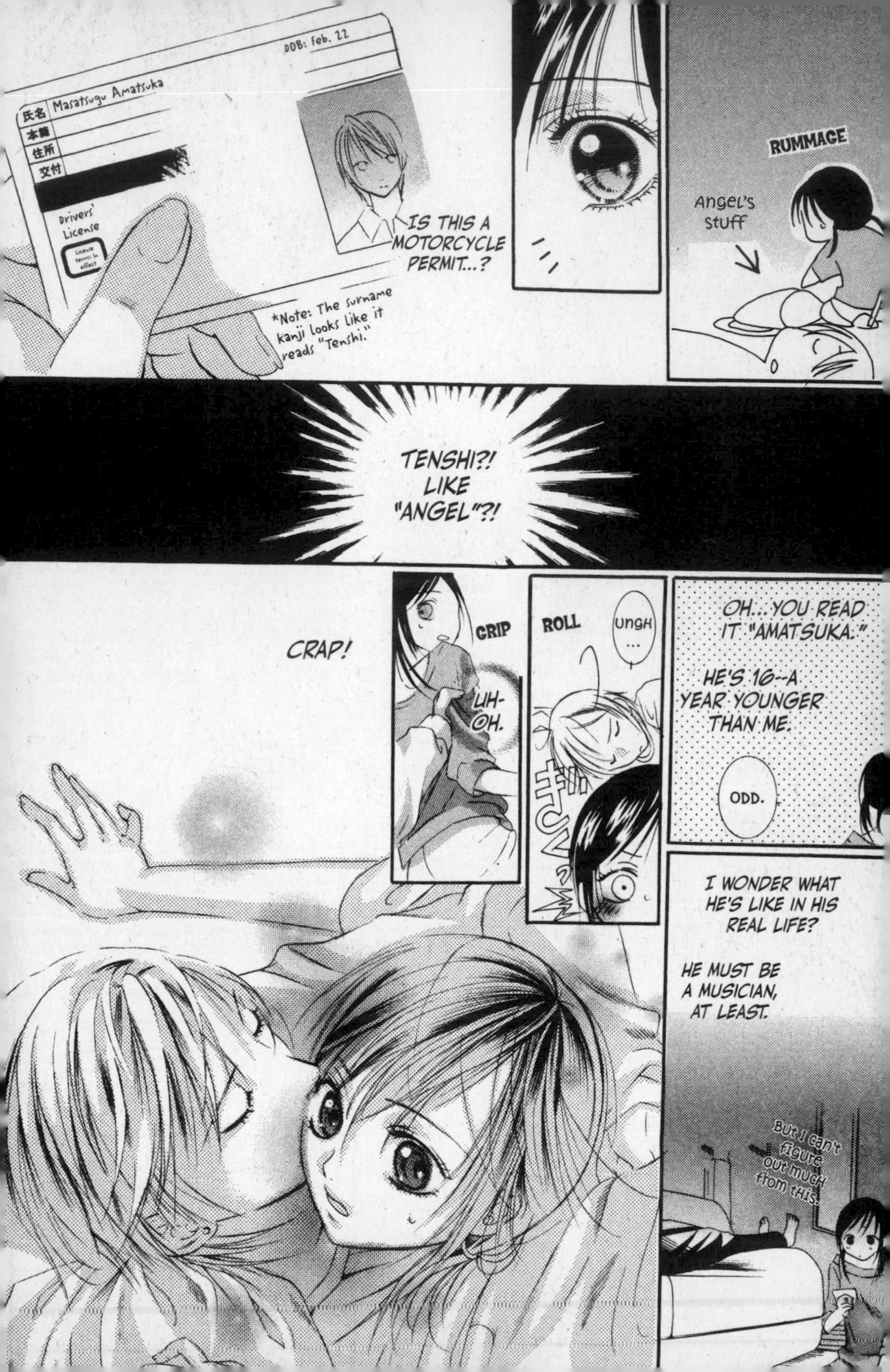
RUMMAGE
Angel's stuff
IS THIS A MOTORCYCLE PERMIT...?
DOB: Feb. 22
氏名 Masatsugu Amatsuka
本籍
住所
交付
Drivers' License
License terms in effect
*Note: The surname kanji looks like it reads "Tenshi."
TENSHI?! LIKE "ANGEL"?!
OH... YOU READ IT "AMATSUKA."
HE'S 16--A YEAR YOUNGER THAN ME.
ODD.
I WONDER WHAT HE'S LIKE IN HIS REAL LIFE?
HE MUST BE A MUSICIAN, AT LEAST.
But I can't figure out much from this.
UNGH...
ROLL
GRIP
UH-OH.
CRAP!

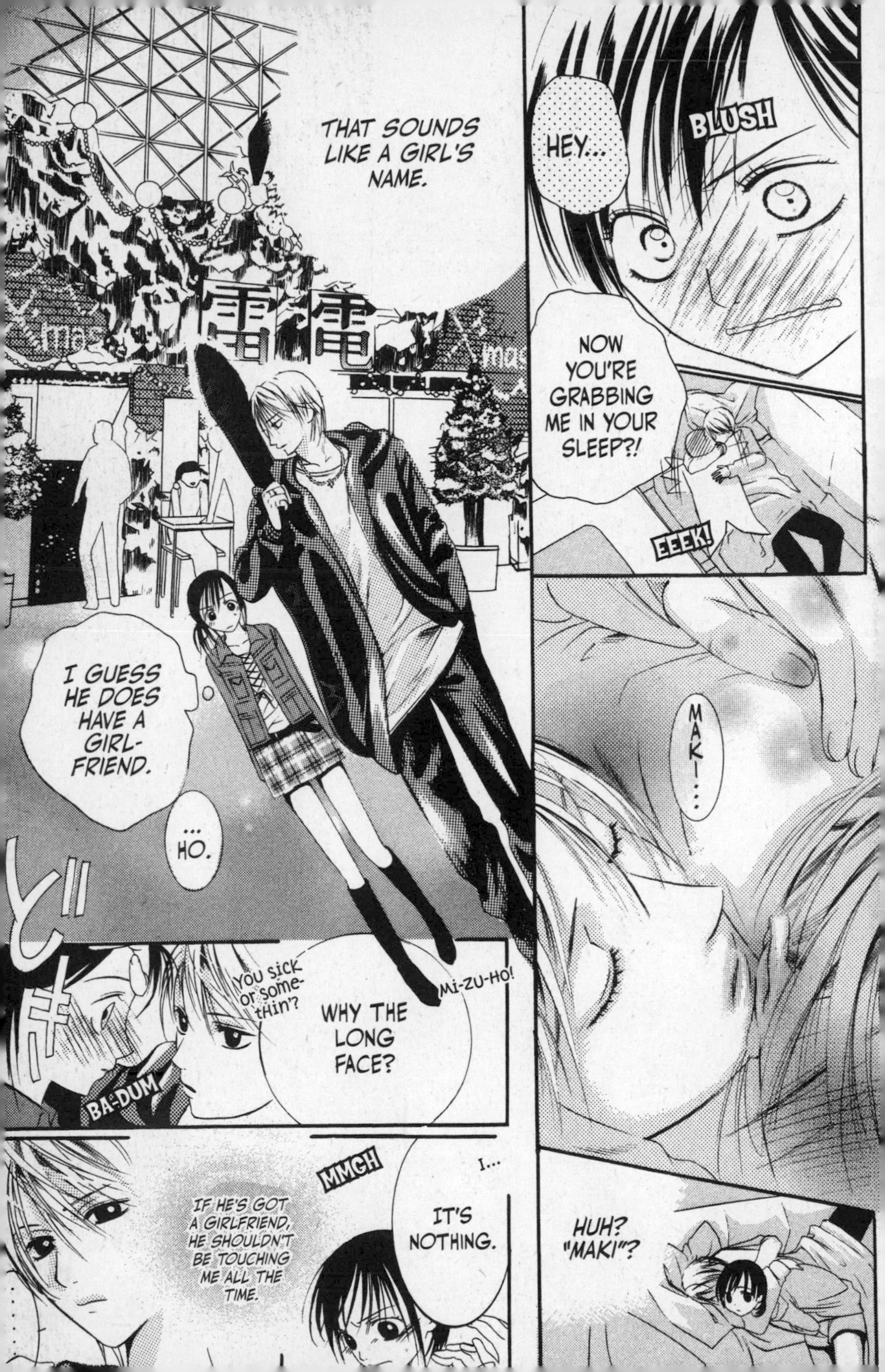
HEY...
BLUSH
NOW YOU'RE GRABBING ME IN YOUR SLEEP?!
EEEK!
MAKI...
HUH? "MAKI"?
THAT SOUNDS LIKE A GIRL'S NAME.
I GUESS HE DOES HAVE A GIRL-FRIEND.
...HO.
どき
MI-ZU-HO!
WHY THE LONG FACE?
YOU SICK OR SOME-THIN'?
BA-DUM
I...
IT'S NOTHING.
MMGH
IF HE'S GOT A GIRLFRIEND, HE SHOULDN'T BE TOUCHING ME ALL THE TIME.

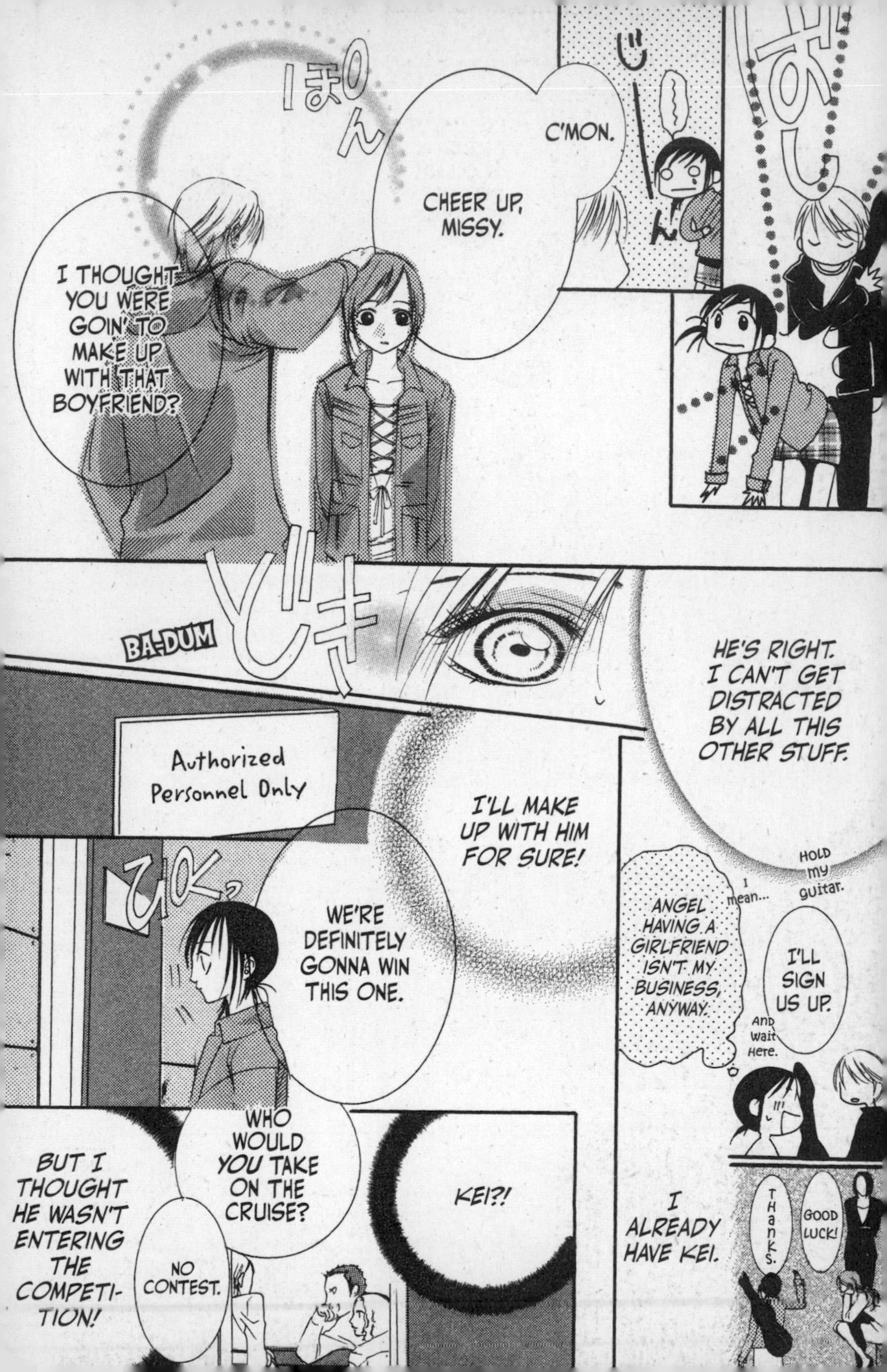
ずし
じ～ん
ぽん
C'MON.
CHEER UP, MISSY.
I THOUGHT YOU WERE GOIN' TO MAKE UP WITH THAT BOYFRIEND?
BA-DUM
どき
HE'S RIGHT. I CAN'T GET DISTRACTED BY ALL THIS OTHER STUFF.
HOLD my guitar.
I'LL SIGN US UP.
And wait Here.
I mean...
ANGEL HAVING A GIRLFRIEND ISN'T MY BUSINESS, ANYWAY.
Thanks.
GOOD LUCK!
Authorized Personnel Only
I'LL MAKE UP WITH HIM FOR SURE!
ひょこっ
WE'RE DEFINITELY GONNA WIN THIS ONE.
WHO WOULD YOU TAKE ON THE CRUISE?
NO CONTEST.
I ALREADY HAVE KEI.
KEI?!
BUT I THOUGHT HE WASN'T ENTERING THE COMPETITION!

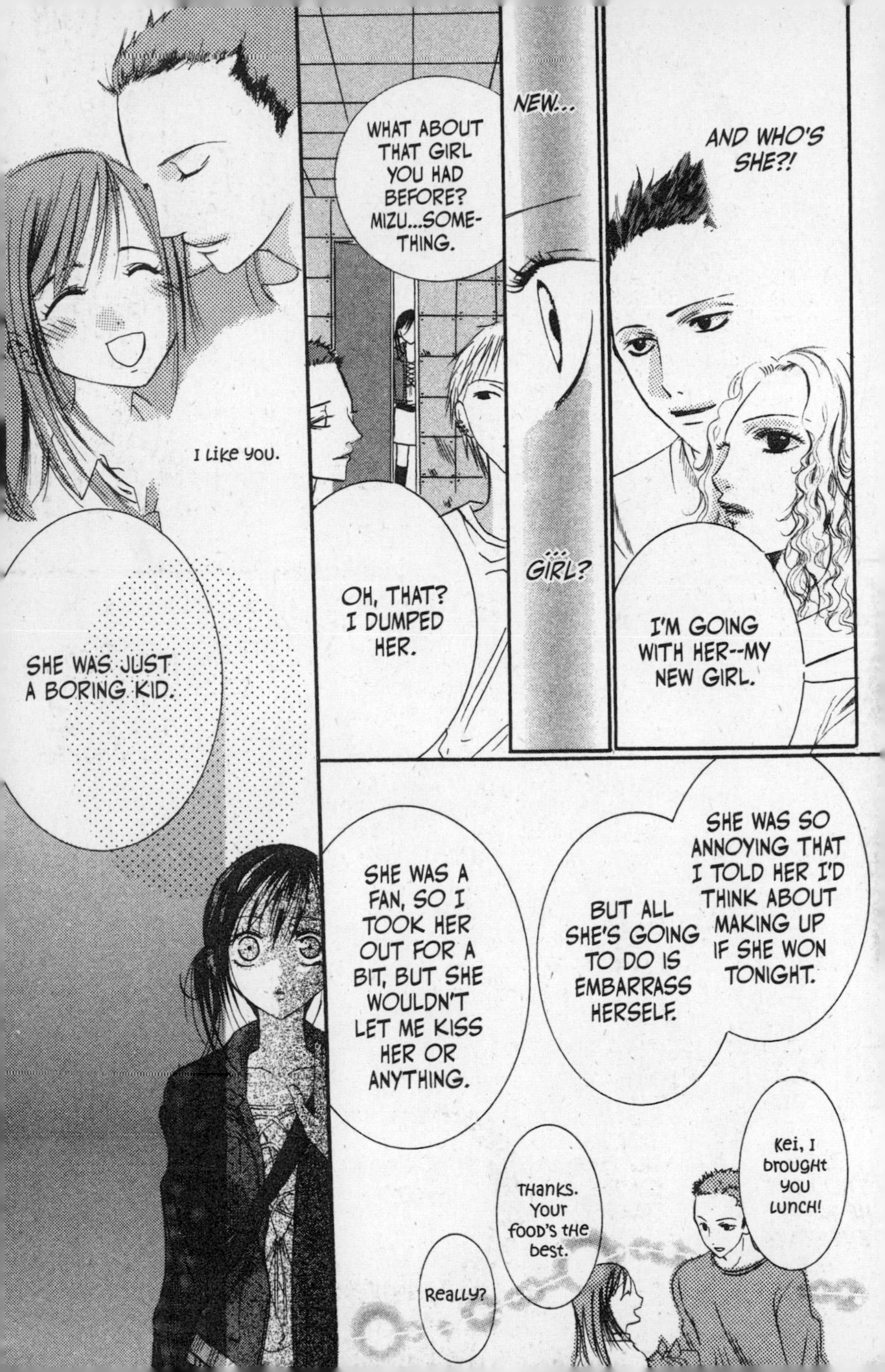
AND WHO'S SHE?!
I'M GOING WITH HER--MY NEW GIRL.
NEW...
...GIRL?
WHAT ABOUT THAT GIRL YOU HAD BEFORE? MIZU...SOME-THING.
OH, THAT? I DUMPED HER.
SHE WAS SO ANNOYING THAT I TOLD HER I'D THINK ABOUT MAKING UP IF SHE WON TONIGHT.
BUT ALL SHE'S GOING TO DO IS EMBARRASS HERSELF.
SHE WAS A FAN, SO I TOOK HER OUT FOR A BIT, BUT SHE WOULDN'T LET ME KISS HER OR ANYTHING.
Kei, I brought you lunch!
Thanks. Your food's the best.
Really?
I like you.
SHE WAS JUST A BORING KID.

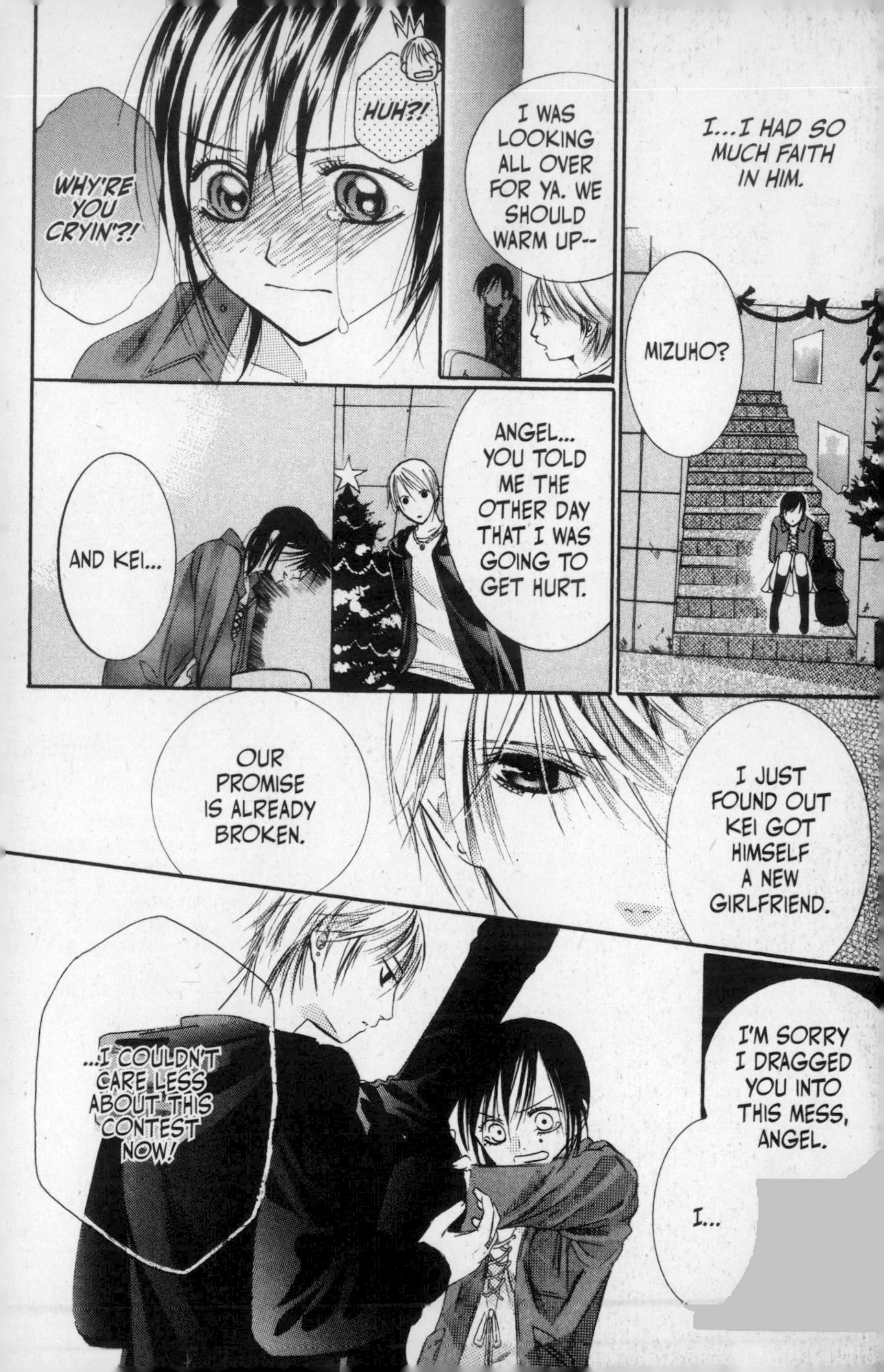
I...I HAD SO MUCH FAITH IN HIM.
MIZUHO?
I WAS LOOKING ALL OVER FOR YA. WE SHOULD WARM UP--
HUH?!
WHY'RE YOU CRYIN'?!
ANGEL... YOU TOLD ME THE OTHER DAY THAT I WAS GOING TO GET HURT.
AND KEI...
I JUST FOUND OUT KEI GOT HIMSELF A NEW GIRLFRIEND.
OUR PROMISE IS ALREADY BROKEN.
I'M SORRY I DRAGGED YOU INTO THIS MESS, ANGEL.
I...
...I COULDN'T CARE LESS ABOUT THIS CONTEST NOW!

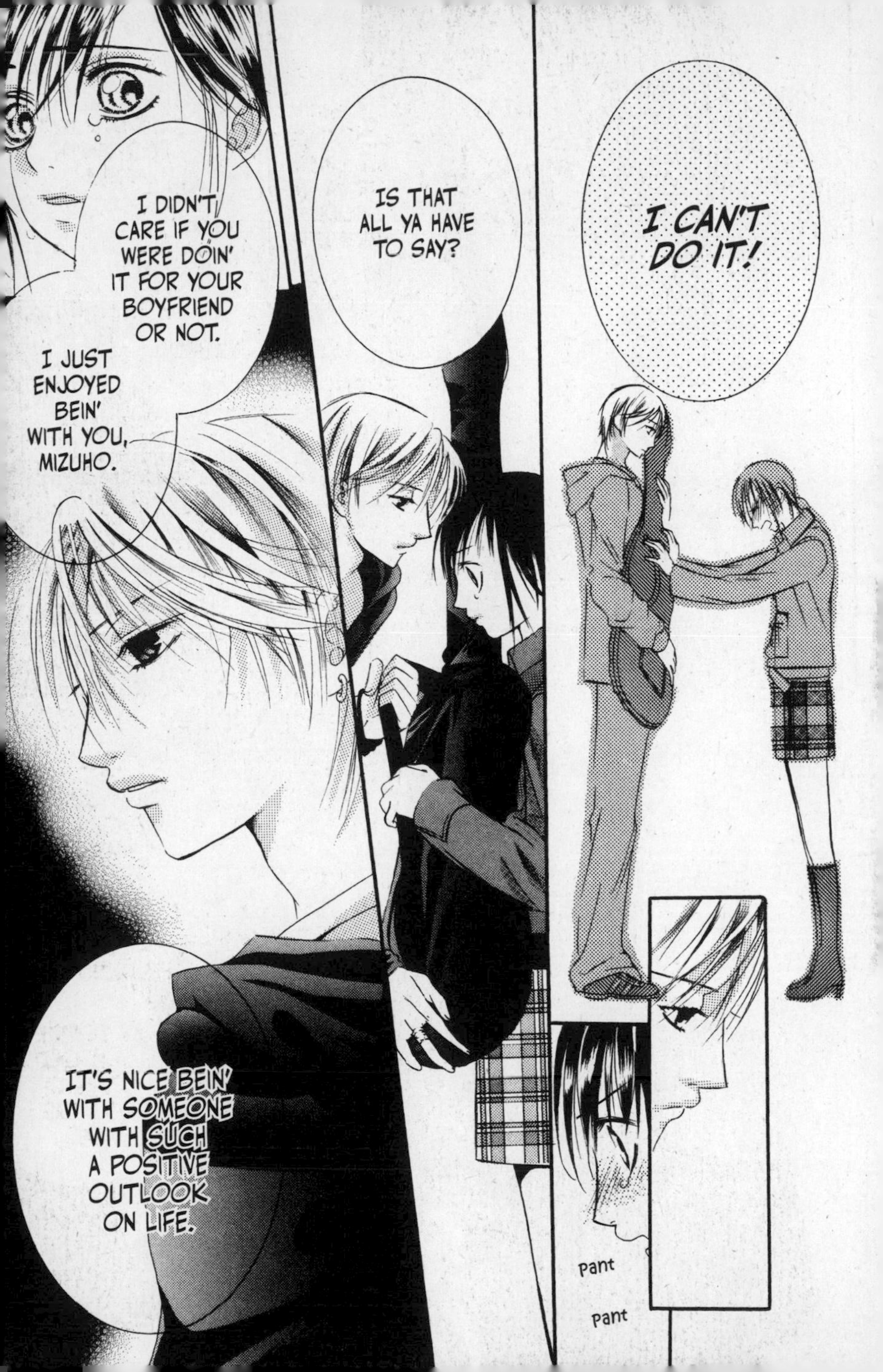
I CAN'T DO IT!
Pant
Pant
IS THAT ALL YA HAVE TO SAY?
I DIDN'T CARE IF YOU WERE DOIN' IT FOR YOUR BOYFRIEND OR NOT.
I JUST ENJOYED BEIN' WITH YOU, MIZUHO.
IT'S NICE BEIN' WITH SOMEONE WITH SUCH A POSITIVE OUTLOOK ON LIFE.

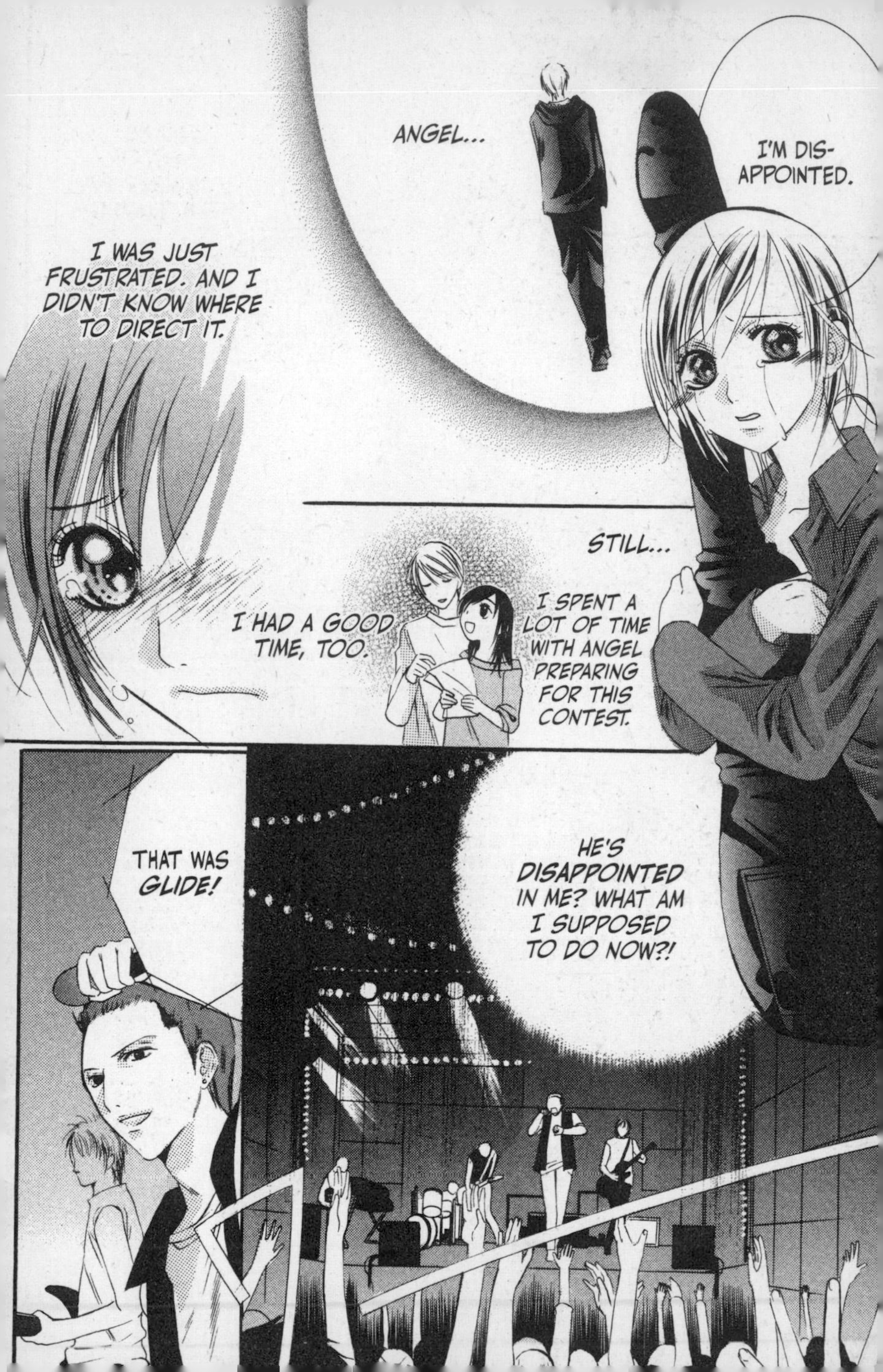
I'M DIS-APPOINTED.
ANGEL...
I WAS JUST FRUSTRATED. AND I DIDN'T KNOW WHERE TO DIRECT IT.
STILL...
I SPENT A LOT OF TIME WITH ANGEL PREPARING FOR THIS CONTEST.
I HAD A GOOD TIME, TOO.
HE'S DISAPPOINTED IN ME? WHAT AM I SUPPOSED TO DO NOW?!
THAT WAS GLIDE!

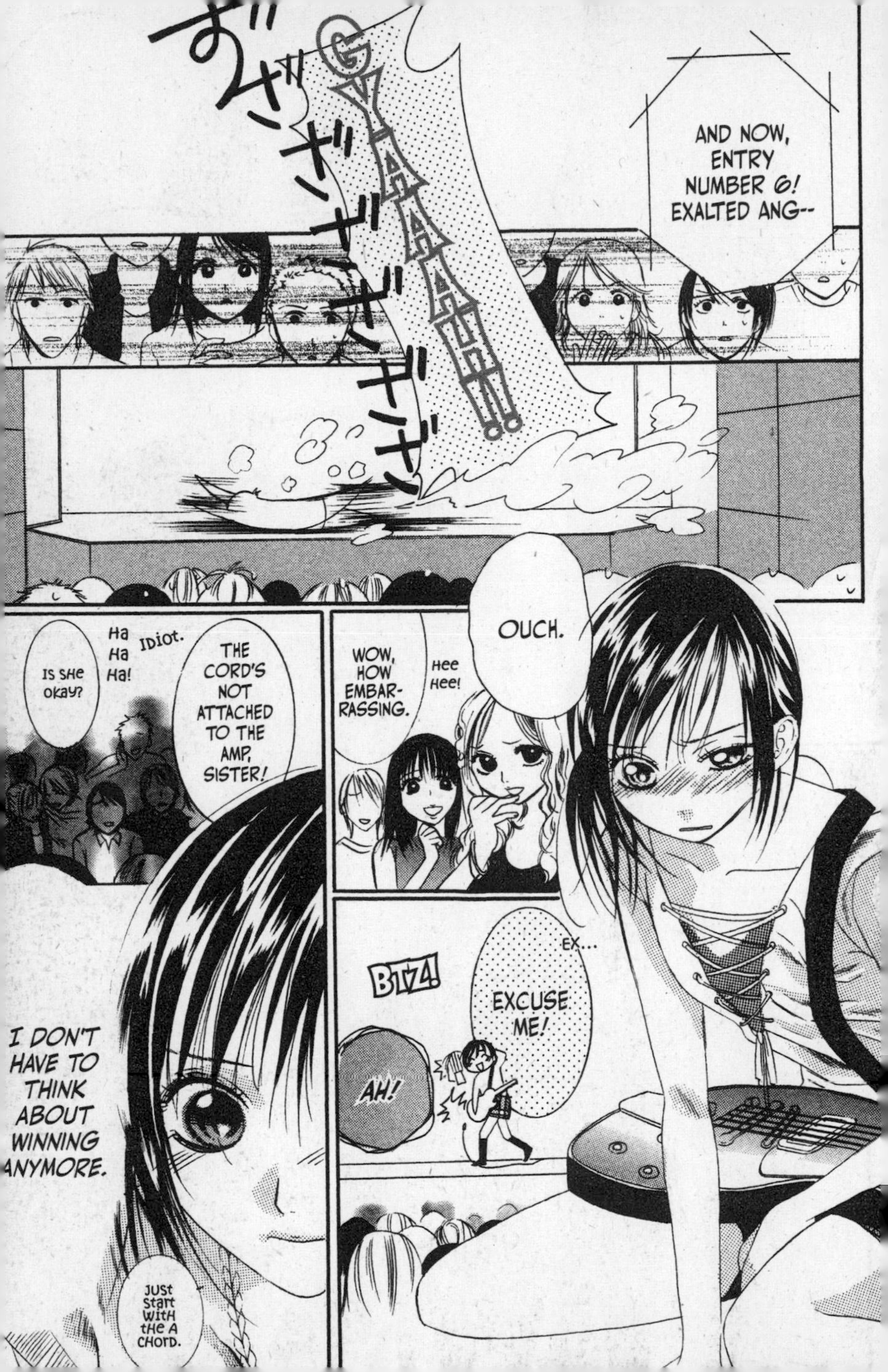
AND NOW, ENTRY NUMBER 6! EXALTED ANG--
OUCH.
WOW, HOW EMBARRASSING.
Hee hee!
THE CORD'S NOT ATTACHED TO THE AMP, SISTER!
Idiot.
Ha Ha Ha!
Is she okay?
Ex...
EXCUSE ME!
BTZ!
AH!
I DON'T HAVE TO THINK ABOUT WINNING ANYMORE.
Just start with the A chord.

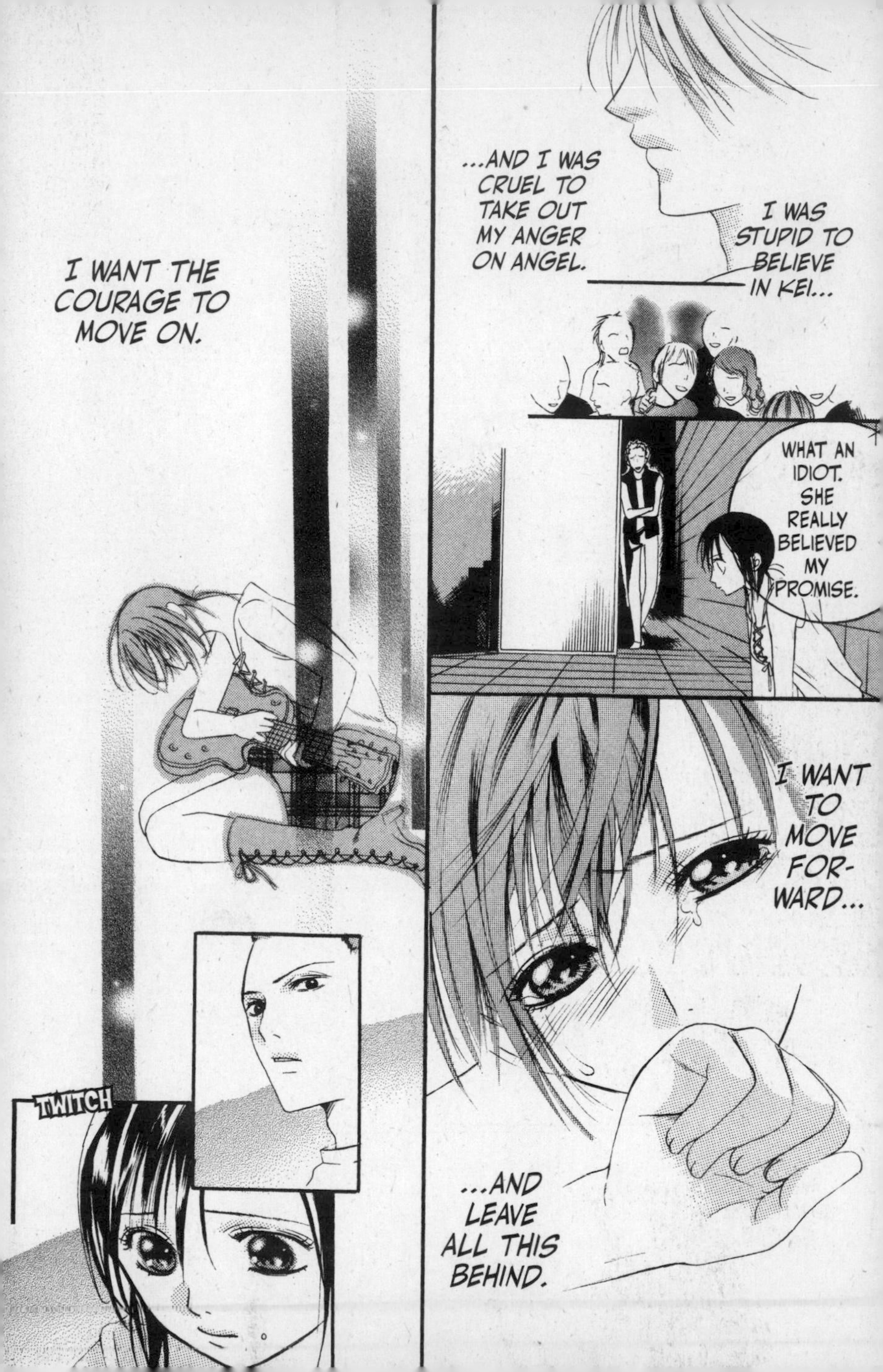
I WAS STUPID TO BELIEVE IN KEI...
...AND I WAS CRUEL TO TAKE OUT MY ANGER ON ANGEL.
WHAT AN IDIOT. SHE REALLY BELIEVED MY PROMISE.
I WANT TO MOVE FOR-WARD...
...AND LEAVE ALL THIS BEHIND.
I WANT THE COURAGE TO MOVE ON.
TWITCH

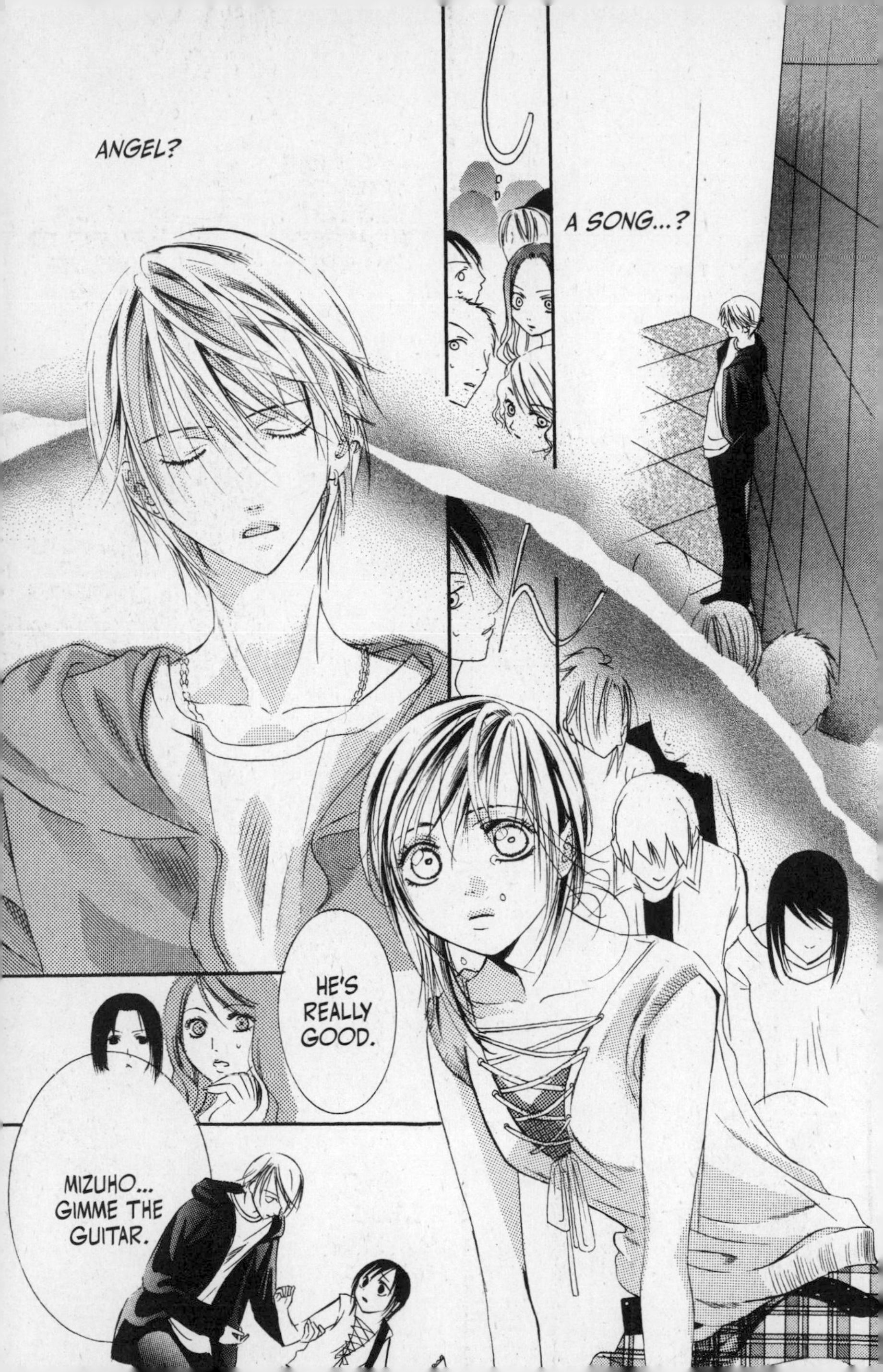
A SONG...?
ANGEL?
HE'S REALLY GOOD.
MIZUHO... GIMME THE GUITAR.

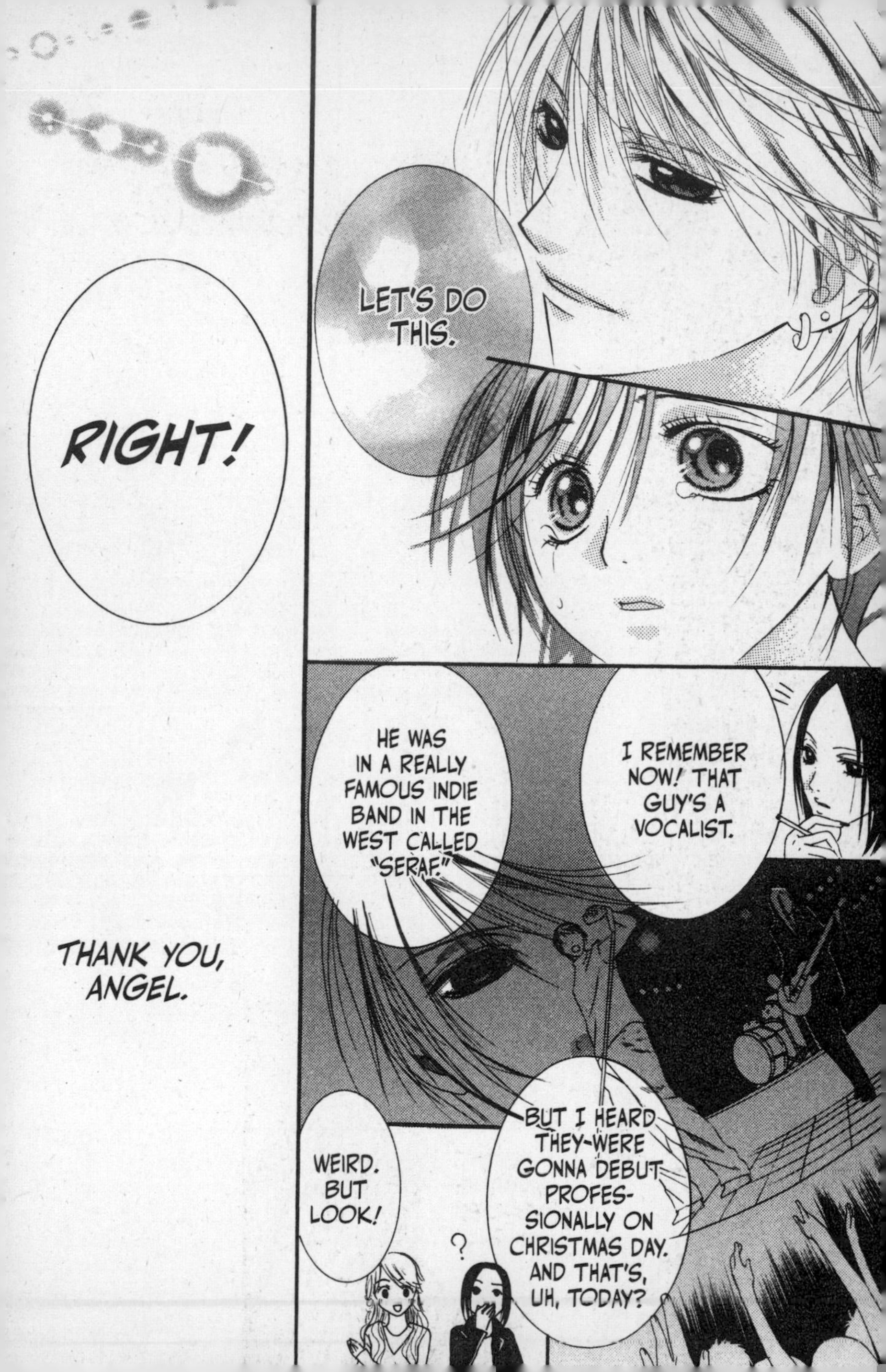
LET'S DO THIS.
I REMEMBER NOW! THAT GUY'S A VOCALIST.
HE WAS IN A REALLY FAMOUS INDIE BAND IN THE WEST CALLED "SERAF."
BUT I HEARD THEY WERE GONNA DEBUT PROFES-SIONALLY ON CHRISTMAS DAY. AND THAT'S, UH, TODAY?
WEIRD. BUT LOOK!
?
RIGHT!
THANK YOU, ANGEL.

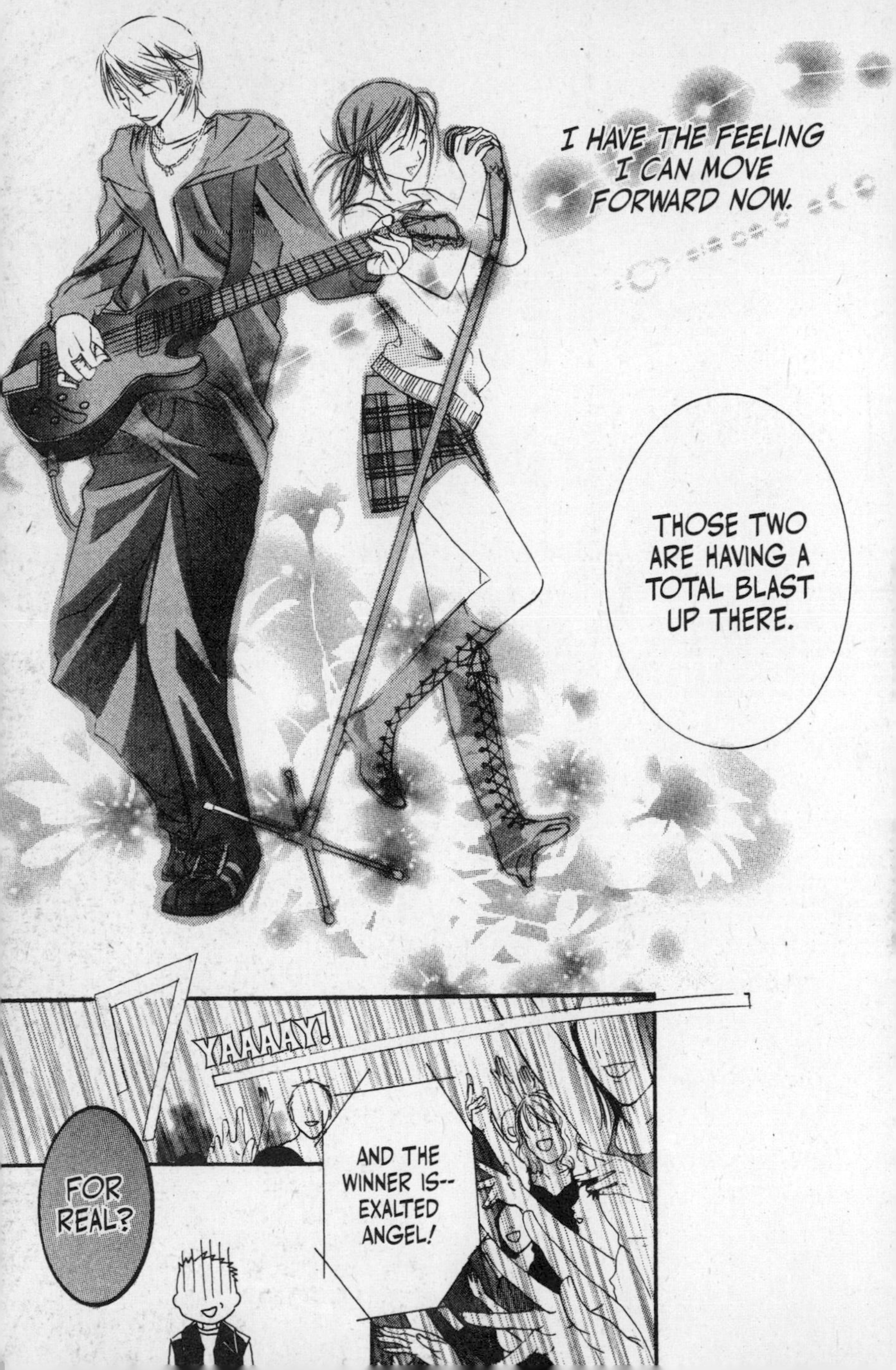
I HAVE THE FEELING I CAN MOVE FORWARD NOW.
THOSE TWO ARE HAVING A TOTAL BLAST UP THERE.
YAAAAY!
AND THE WINNER IS-- EXALTED ANGEL!
FOR REAL?

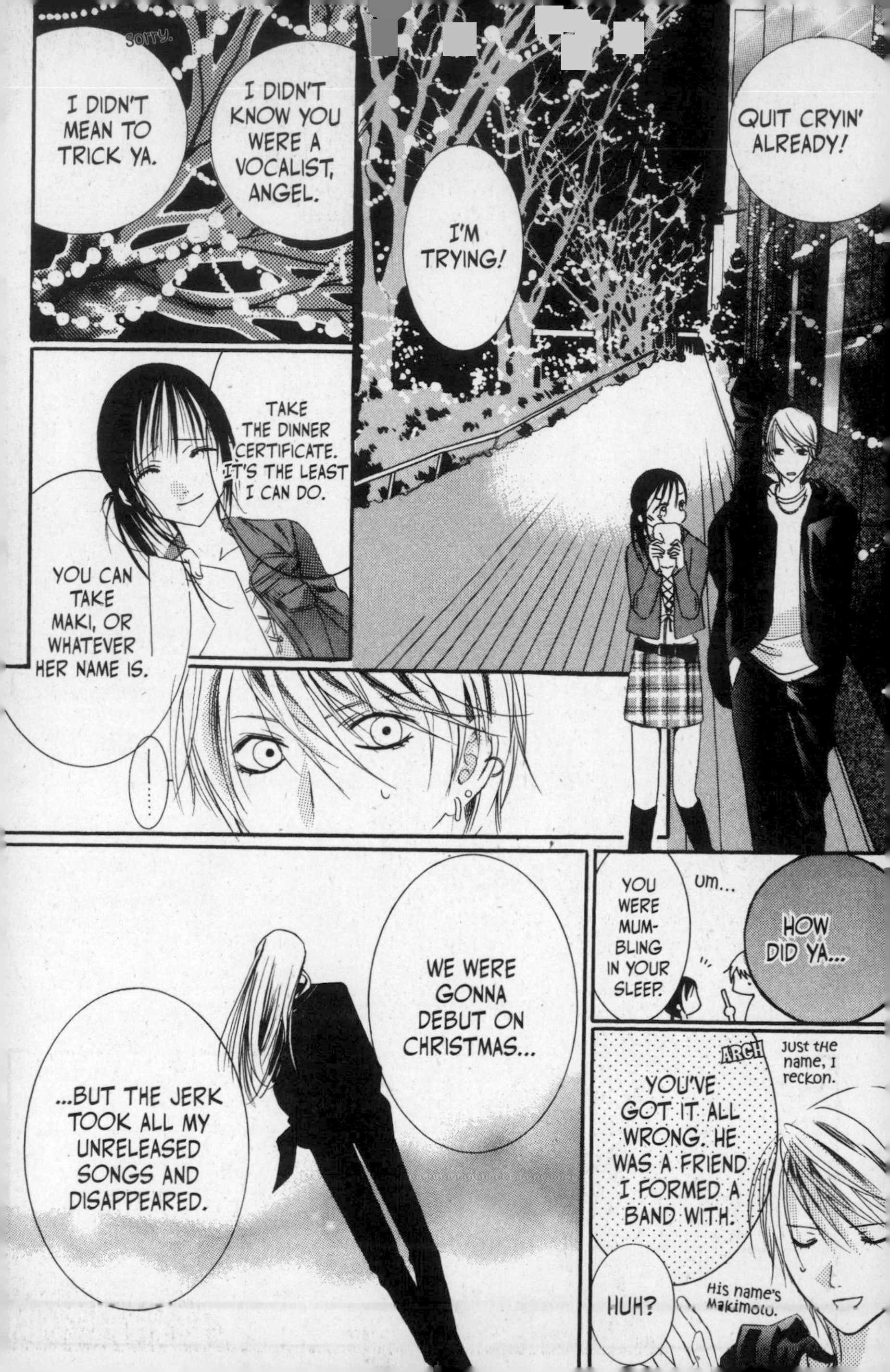
QUIT CRYIN' ALREADY!
I'M TRYING!
I DIDN'T KNOW YOU WERE A VOCALIST, ANGEL.
sorry.
I DIDN'T MEAN TO TRICK YA.
TAKE THE DINNER CERTIFICATE. IT'S THE LEAST I CAN DO.
YOU CAN TAKE MAKI, OR WHATEVER HER NAME IS.
!......
HOW DID YA...
um...
YOU WERE MUM-BLING IN YOUR SLEEP.
Just the name, I reckon.
ARGH
YOU'VE GOT IT ALL WRONG. HE WAS A FRIEND I FORMED A BAND WITH.
His name's Makimoto.
HUH?
WE WERE GONNA DEBUT ON CHRISTMAS...
...BUT THE JERK TOOK ALL MY UNRELEASED SONGS AND DISAPPEARED.

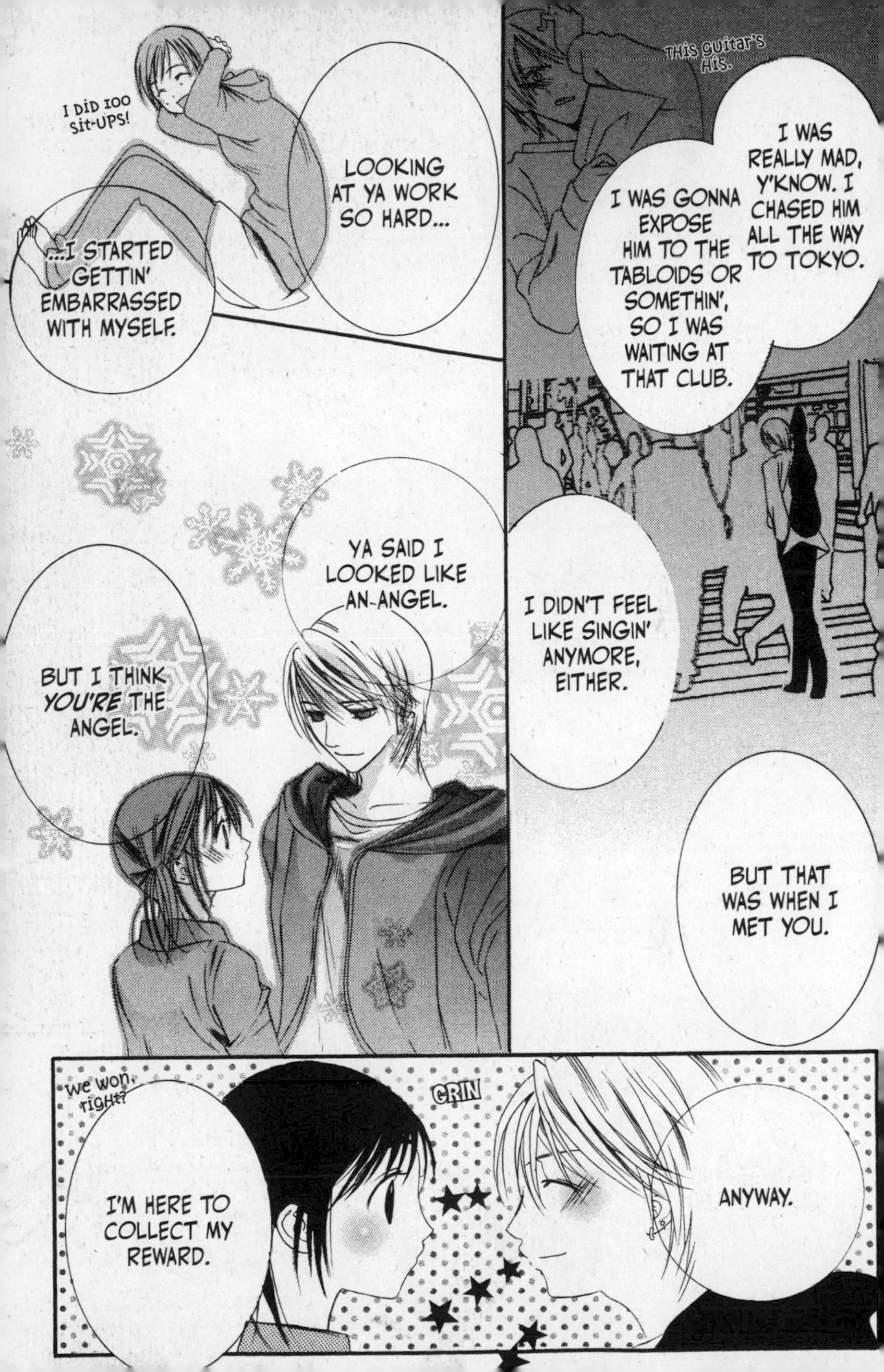

THIS GUITAR'S HIS.
I WAS REALLY MAD, Y'KNOW. I CHASED HIM ALL THE WAY TO TOKYO.
I WAS GONNA EXPOSE HIM TO THE TABLOIDS OR SOMETHIN', SO I WAS WAITING AT THAT CLUB.
I DIDN'T FEEL LIKE SINGIN' ANYMORE, EITHER.
BUT THAT WAS WHEN I MET YOU.
LOOKING AT YA WORK SO HARD...
I DID 100 SIT-UPS!
...I STARTED GETTIN' EMBARRASSED WITH MYSELF.
YA SAID I LOOKED LIKE AN ANGEL.
BUT I THINK *YOU'RE* THE ANGEL.
ANYWAY.
GRIN
WE WON, RIGHT?
I'M HERE TO COLLECT MY REWARD.

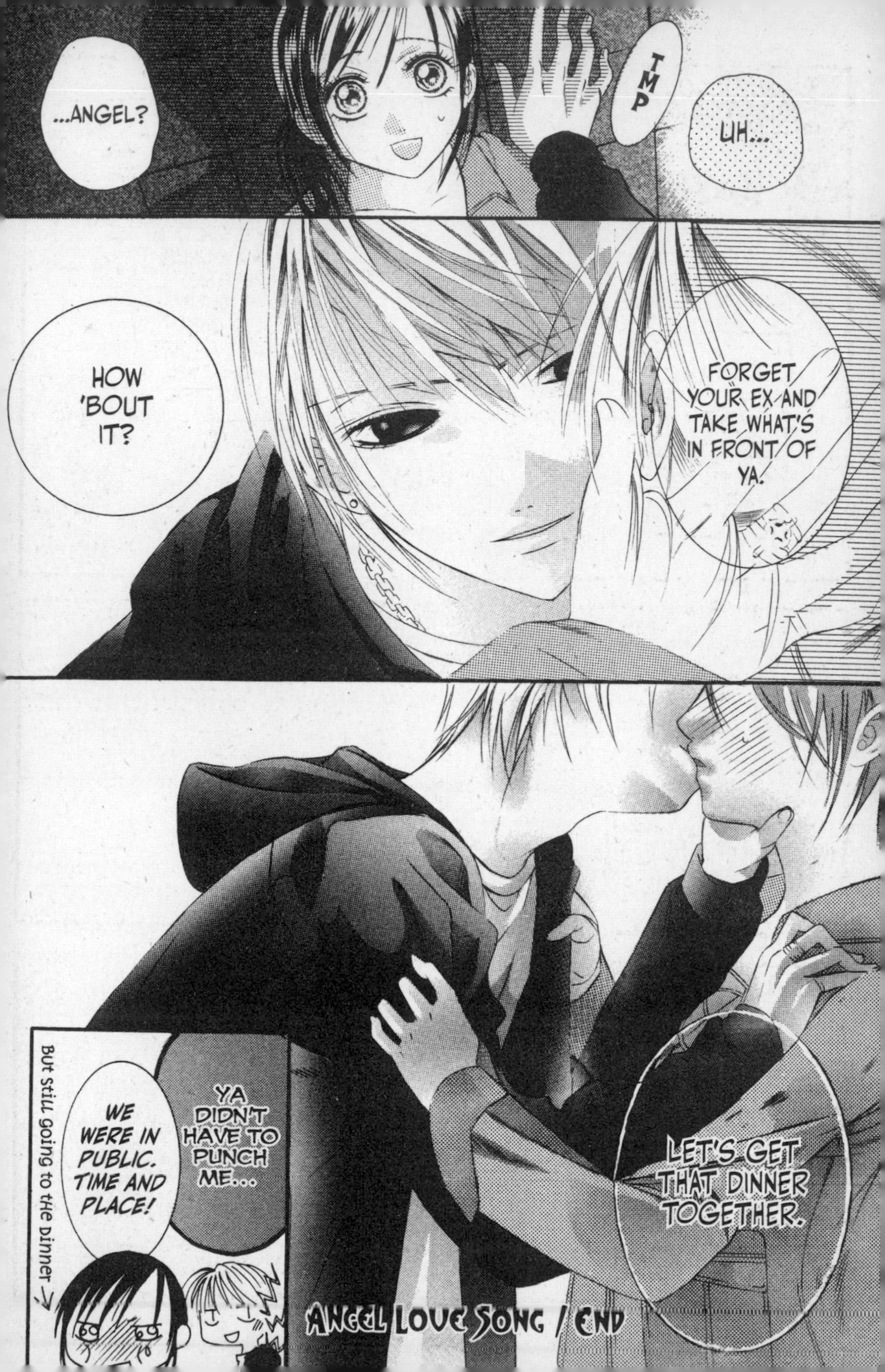
UH...
TMP
...ANGEL?
FORGET YOUR EX AND TAKE WHAT'S IN FRONT OF YA.
HOW 'BOUT IT?
LET'S GET THAT DINNER TOGETHER.
YA DIDN'T HAVE TO PUNCH ME...
WE WERE IN PUBLIC. TIME AND PLACE!
But still going to the dinner →
Angel Love Song / End

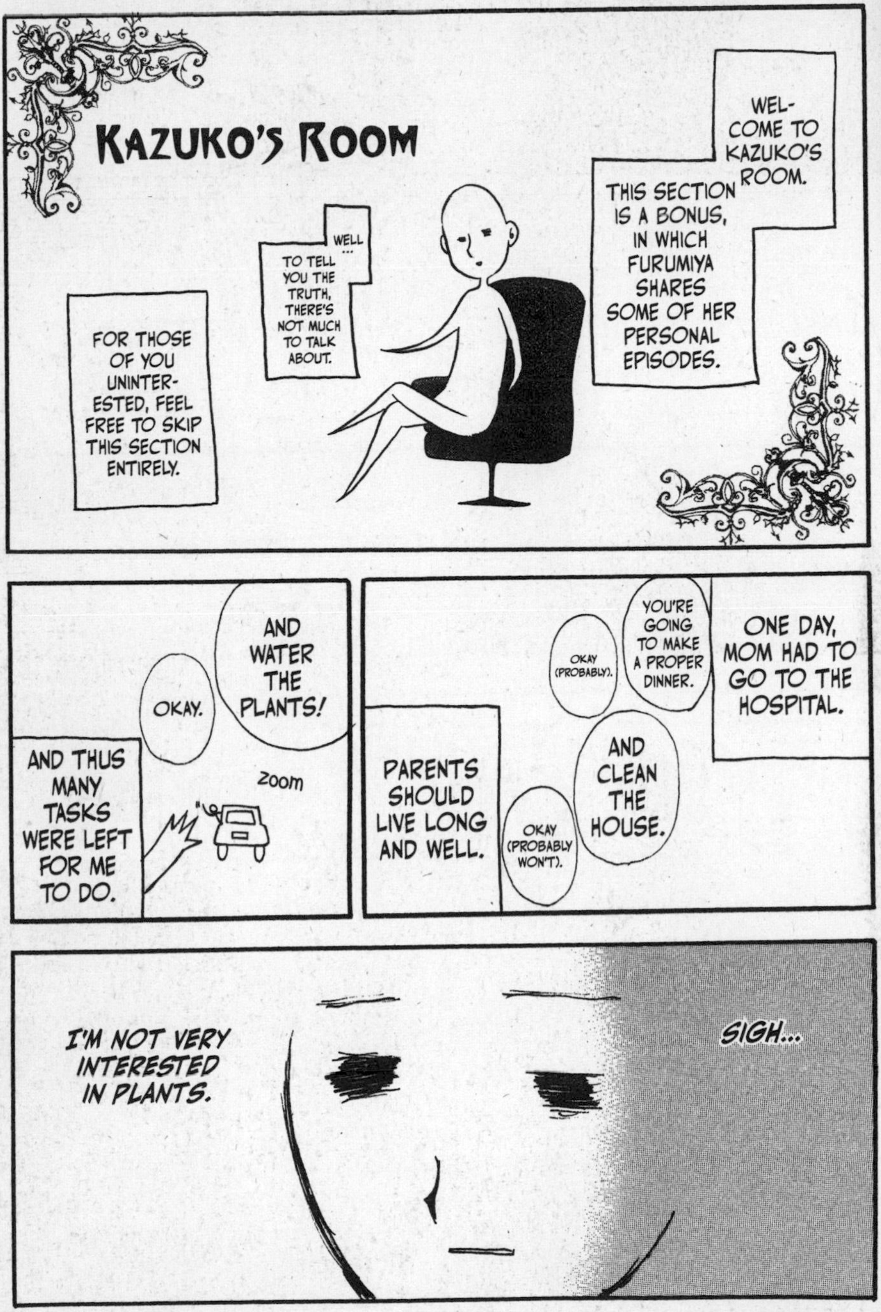
KAZUKO'S ROOM
WELCOME TO KAZUKO'S ROOM.
THIS SECTION IS A BONUS, IN WHICH FURUMIYA SHARES SOME OF HER PERSONAL EPISODES.
WELL...
TO TELL YOU THE TRUTH, THERE'S NOT MUCH TO TALK ABOUT.
FOR THOSE OF YOU UNINTERESTED, FEEL FREE TO SKIP THIS SECTION ENTIRELY.
ONE DAY, MOM HAD TO GO TO THE HOSPITAL.
YOU'RE GOING TO MAKE A PROPER DINNER.
OKAY (PROBABLY).
AND CLEAN THE HOUSE.
OKAY (PROBABLY WON'T).
PARENTS SHOULD LIVE LONG AND WELL.
AND WATER THE PLANTS!
OKAY.
zoom
AND THUS MANY TASKS WERE LEFT FOR ME TO DO.
SIGH...
I'M NOT VERY INTERESTED IN PLANTS.

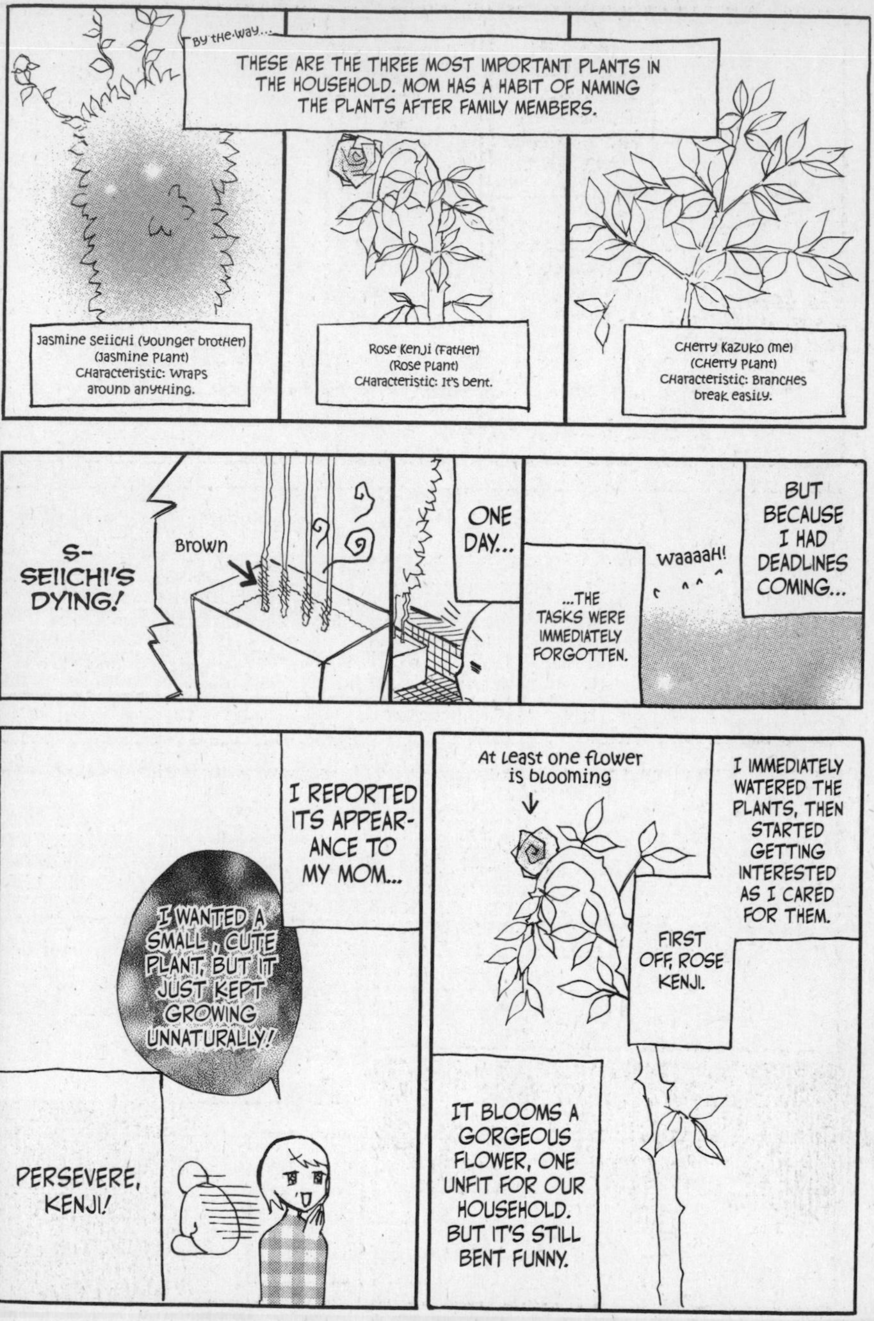
By the way...
THESE ARE THE THREE MOST IMPORTANT PLANTS IN THE HOUSEHOLD. MOM HAS A HABIT OF NAMING THE PLANTS AFTER FAMILY MEMBERS.
Cherry Kazuko (me) (Cherry Plant) Characteristic: Branches break easily.
Rose Kenji (Father) (Rose Plant) Characteristic: It's bent.
Jasmine Seiichi (younger brother) (Jasmine Plant) Characteristic: Wraps around anything.
BUT BECAUSE I HAD DEADLINES COMING...
Waaaah!
...THE TASKS WERE IMMEDIATELY FORGOTTEN.
ONE DAY...
Brown
S-SEIICHI'S DYING!
I IMMEDIATELY WATERED THE PLANTS, THEN STARTED GETTING INTERESTED AS I CARED FOR THEM.
At least one flower is blooming
FIRST OFF, ROSE KENJI.
IT BLOOMS A GORGEOUS FLOWER, ONE UNFIT FOR OUR HOUSEHOLD. BUT IT'S STILL BENT FUNNY.
I REPORTED ITS APPEARANCE TO MY MOM...
I WANTED A SMALL, CUTE PLANT, BUT IT JUST KEPT GROWING UNNATURALLY!
PERSEVERE, KENJI!

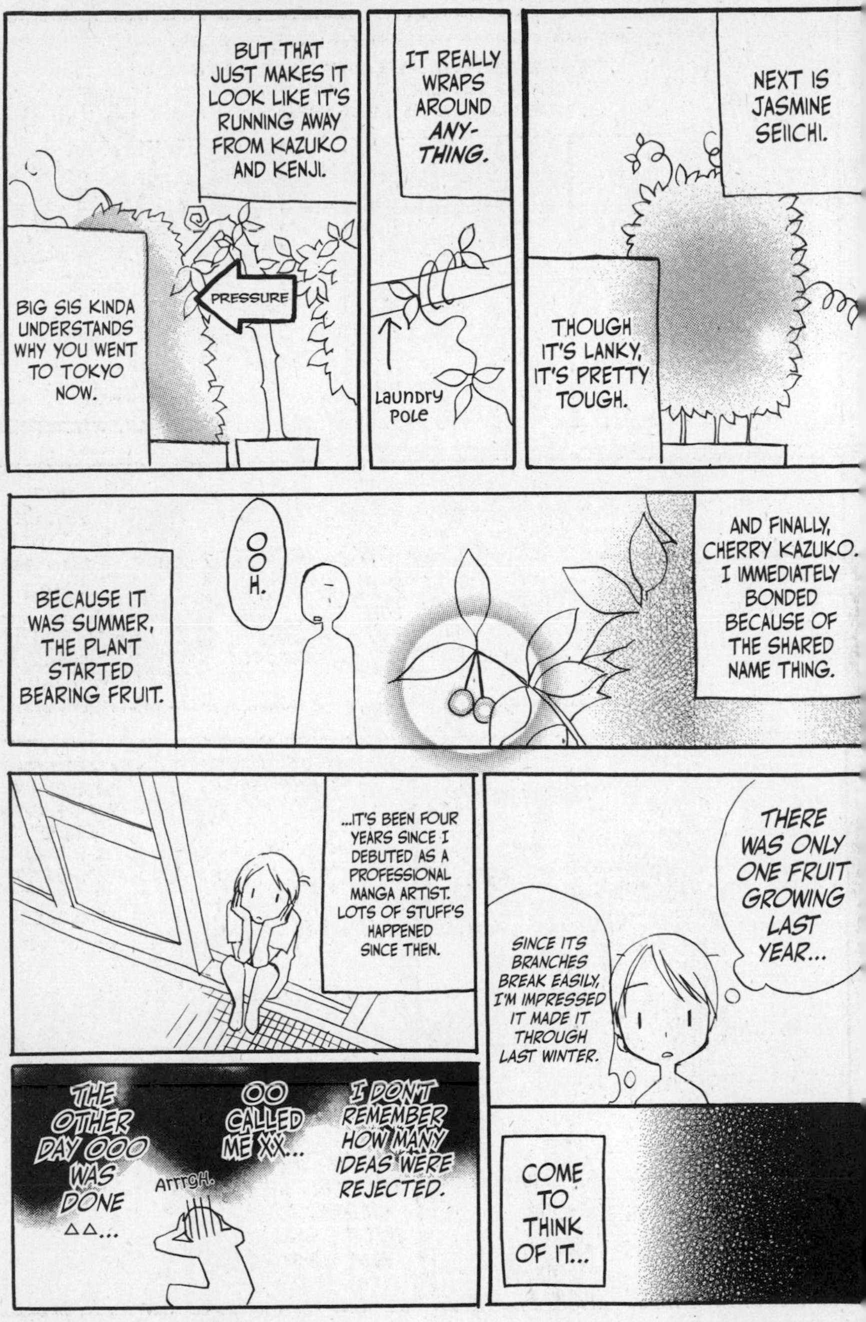
NEXT IS JASMINE SEIICHI.
THOUGH IT'S LANKY, IT'S PRETTY TOUGH.
IT REALLY WRAPS AROUND ANY-THING.
Laundry Pole
BUT THAT JUST MAKES IT LOOK LIKE IT'S RUNNING AWAY FROM KAZUKO AND KENJI.
PRESSURE
BIG SIS KINDA UNDERSTANDS WHY YOU WENT TO TOKYO NOW.
AND FINALLY, CHERRY KAZUKO. I IMMEDIATELY BONDED BECAUSE OF THE SHARED NAME THING.
OOH.
BECAUSE IT WAS SUMMER, THE PLANT STARTED BEARING FRUIT.
THERE WAS ONLY ONE FRUIT GROWING LAST YEAR...
SINCE ITS BRANCHES BREAK EASILY, I'M IMPRESSED IT MADE IT THROUGH LAST WINTER.
COME TO THINK OF IT...
...IT'S BEEN FOUR YEARS SINCE I DEBUTED AS A PROFESSIONAL MANGA ARTIST. LOTS OF STUFF'S HAPPENED SINCE THEN.
I DON'T REMEMBER HOW MANY IDEAS WERE REJECTED.
OO CALLED ME XX...
THE OTHER DAY OOO WAS DONE △△...
Arrrgh.

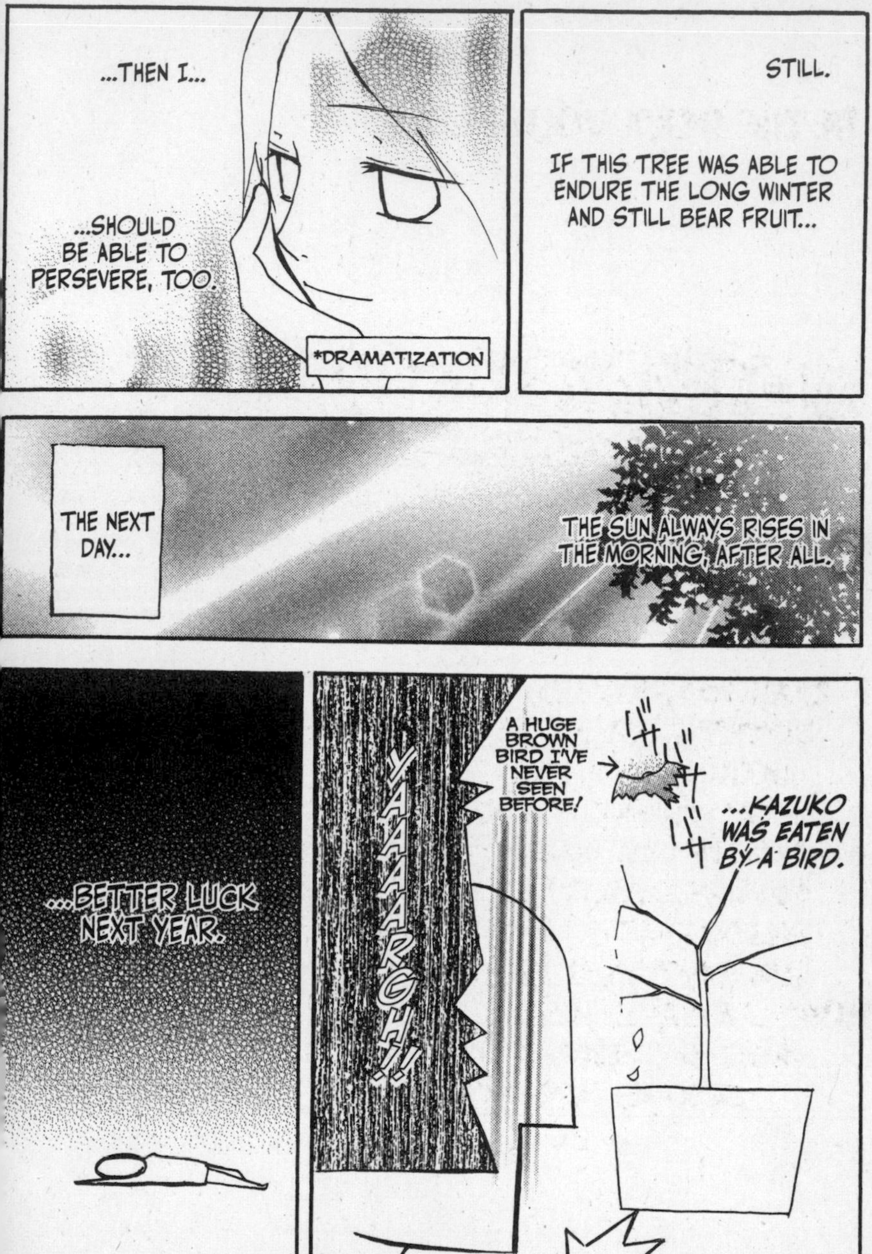
STILL.
IF THIS TREE WAS ABLE TO ENDURE THE LONG WINTER AND STILL BEAR FRUIT...
...THEN I...
...SHOULD BE ABLE TO PERSEVERE, TOO.
*DRAMATIZATION
THE SUN ALWAYS RISES IN THE MORNING, AFTER ALL.
THE NEXT DAY...
A HUGE BROWN BIRD I'VE NEVER SEEN BEFORE!
YAAAAARGH!!
...KAZUKO WAS EATEN BY A BIRD.
...BETTER LUCK NEXT YEAR.

KAZUKO'S ROOM / END

IN THE NEXT VOLUME OF

BLOODY KISS

MUCH TO KIYO'S DISMAY, KUROBOSHI AND ALSHU BEGIN ATTENDING HER SCHOOL, AND OF COURSE, KUROBOSHI BECOMES AN IMMEDIATE HIT WITH ALL THE YOUNG FEMALE STUDENTS. KIYO'S NOT THE ONLY ONE ANNOYED WITH THE NEW ARRIVAL, THOUGH. ANOTHER STUDENT, FUJIWARA, DOESN'T LIKE SHARING THE SPOTLIGHT AND CHALLENGES KIYO TO A TENNIS MATCH. IF KIYO LOSES... KUROBOSHI HAS TO LEAVE! PROBLEM SOLVED, RIGHT? BUT WHEN KIYO REALIZES HER FEELINGS FOR KUROBOSHI MIGHT BE STRONGER THAN SHE FIRST THOUGHT, SHE BECOMES DETERMINED TO WIN THE MATCH!

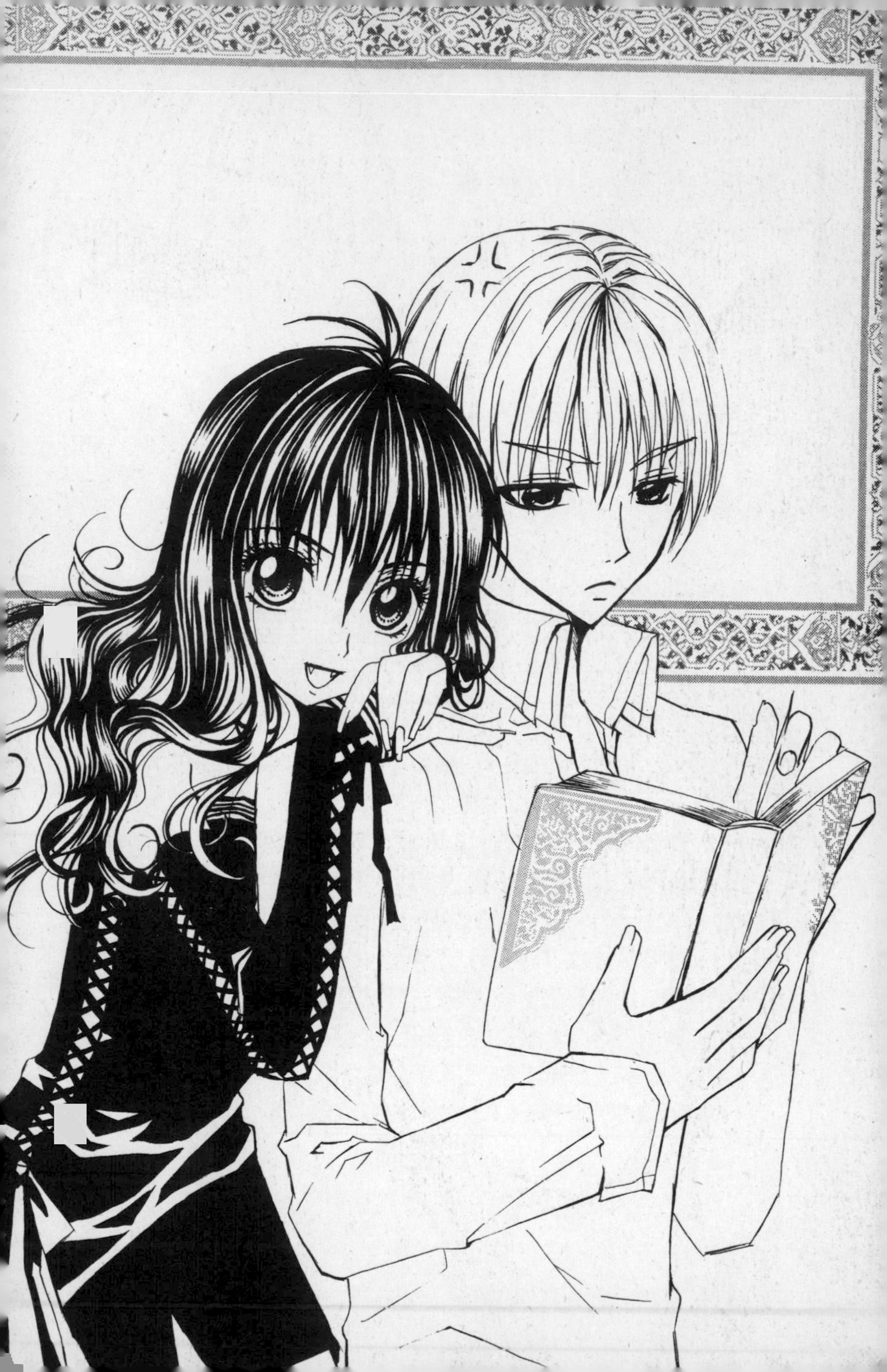

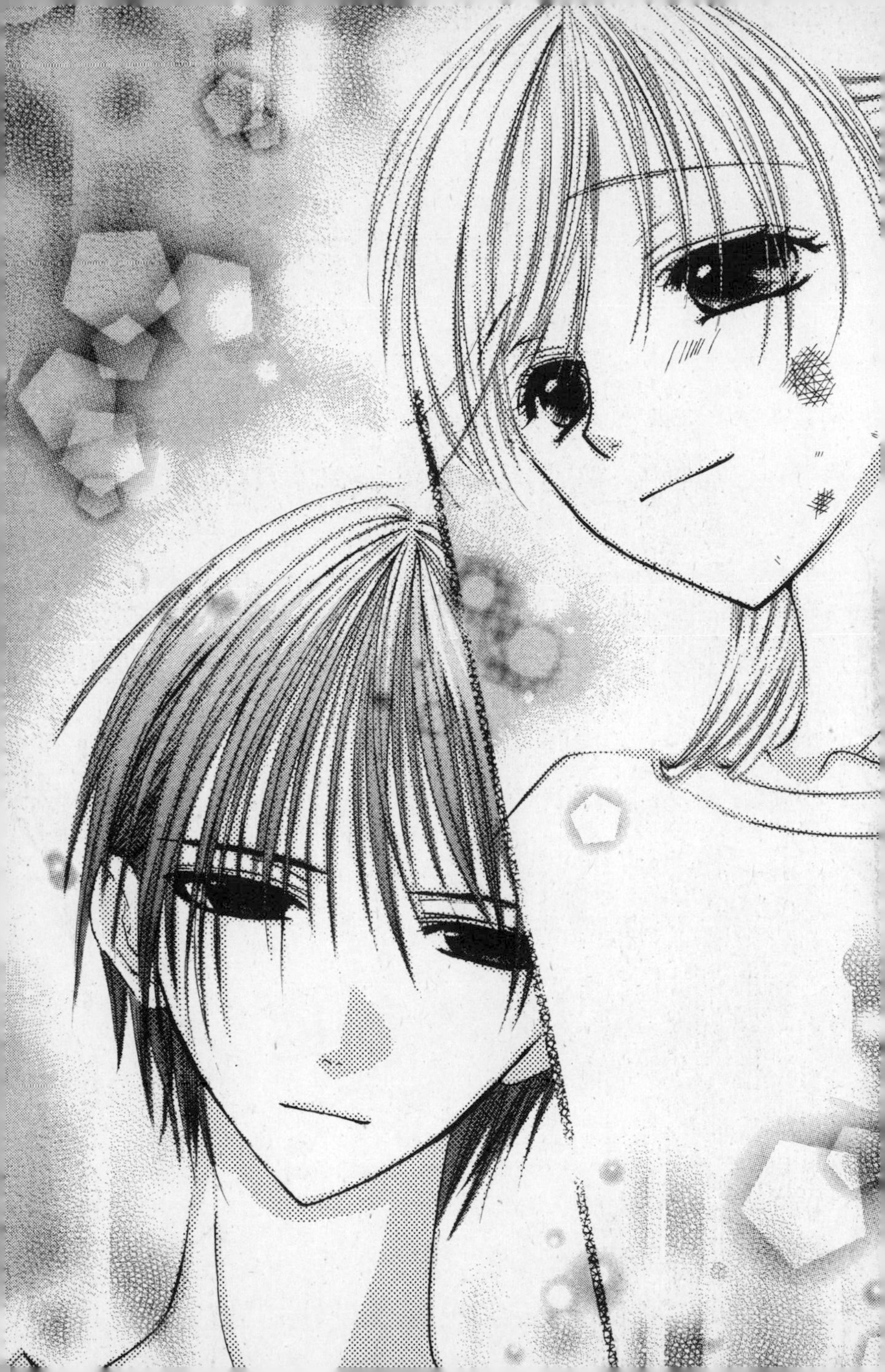

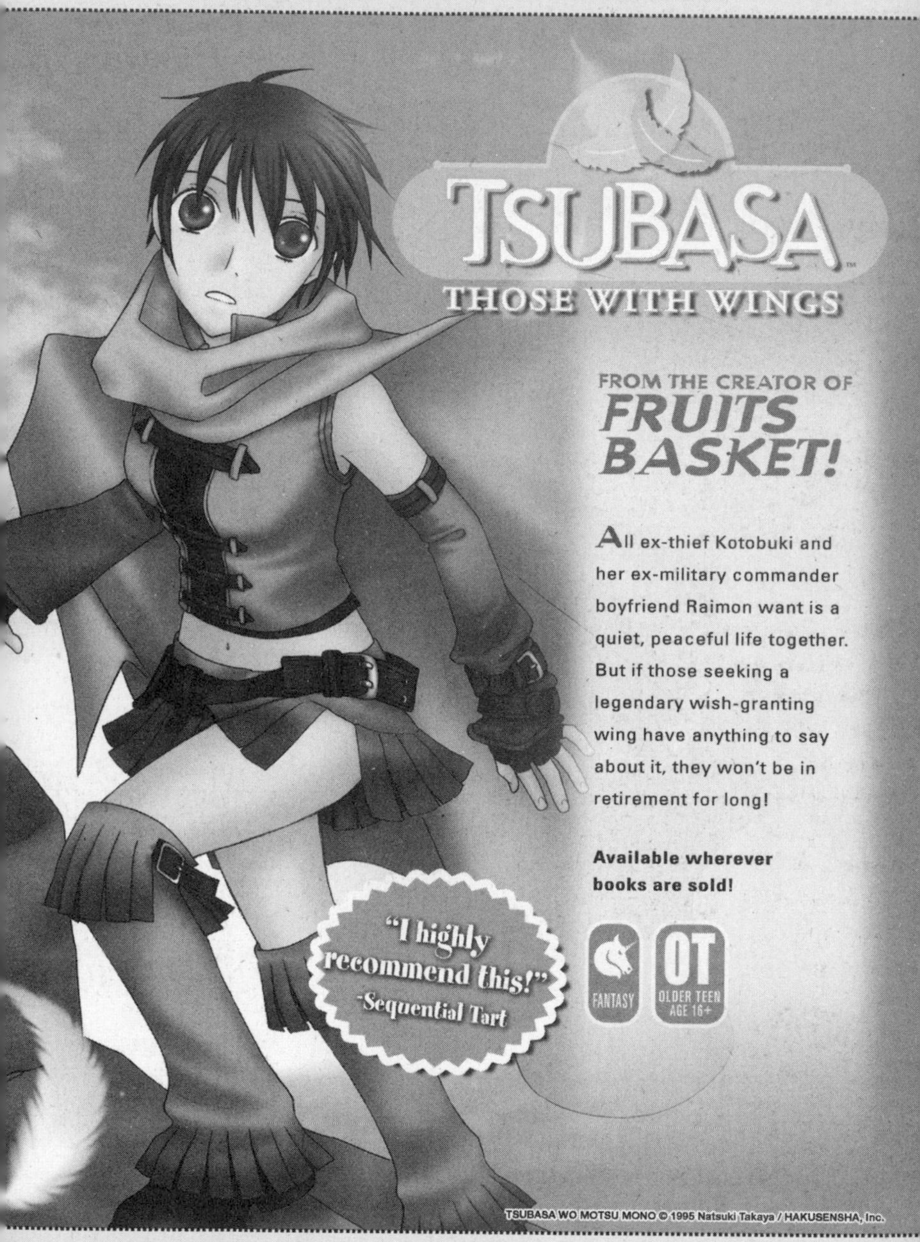
TSUBASA™
THOSE WITH WINGS
FROM THE CREATOR OF
FRUITS BASKET!
All ex-thief Kotobuki and her ex-military commander boyfriend Raimon want is a quiet, peaceful life together. But if those seeking a legendary wish-granting wing have anything to say about it, they won't be in retirement for long!
Available wherever books are sold!
"I highly recommend this!" -Sequential Tart
FANTASY
OT
OLDER TEEN AGE 16+
TSUBASA WO MOTSU MONO © 1995 Natsuki Takaya / HAKUSENSHA, Inc.

Discover Why Fruits Basket

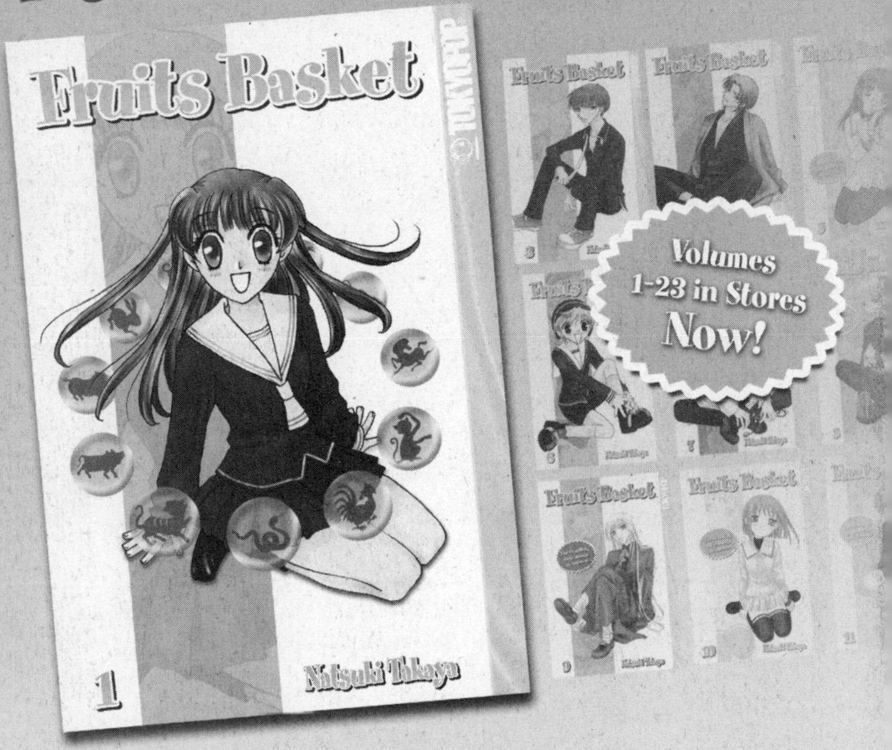
Fruits Basket
TOKYOPOP
1
Natsuki Takaya
Volumes
1-23 in Stores
Now!

A family with an ancient curse... And the girl who will change their lives forever... Tohru Honda was an orphan with no place to go until the mysterious Sohma family offered her a place to call home. Now her ordinary high school life is turned upside down as she's introduced to the Sohma's world of magical curses and family secrets. Discover for yourself the Secret of the Zodiac, and find out why *Fruits Basket* has won the hearts of readers the world over!

ROMANCE

T TEEN AGE 13+

READ *FRUITS BASKET* AND OTHER MANGA AT WWW.TOKYOPOP.COM/OnlineManga

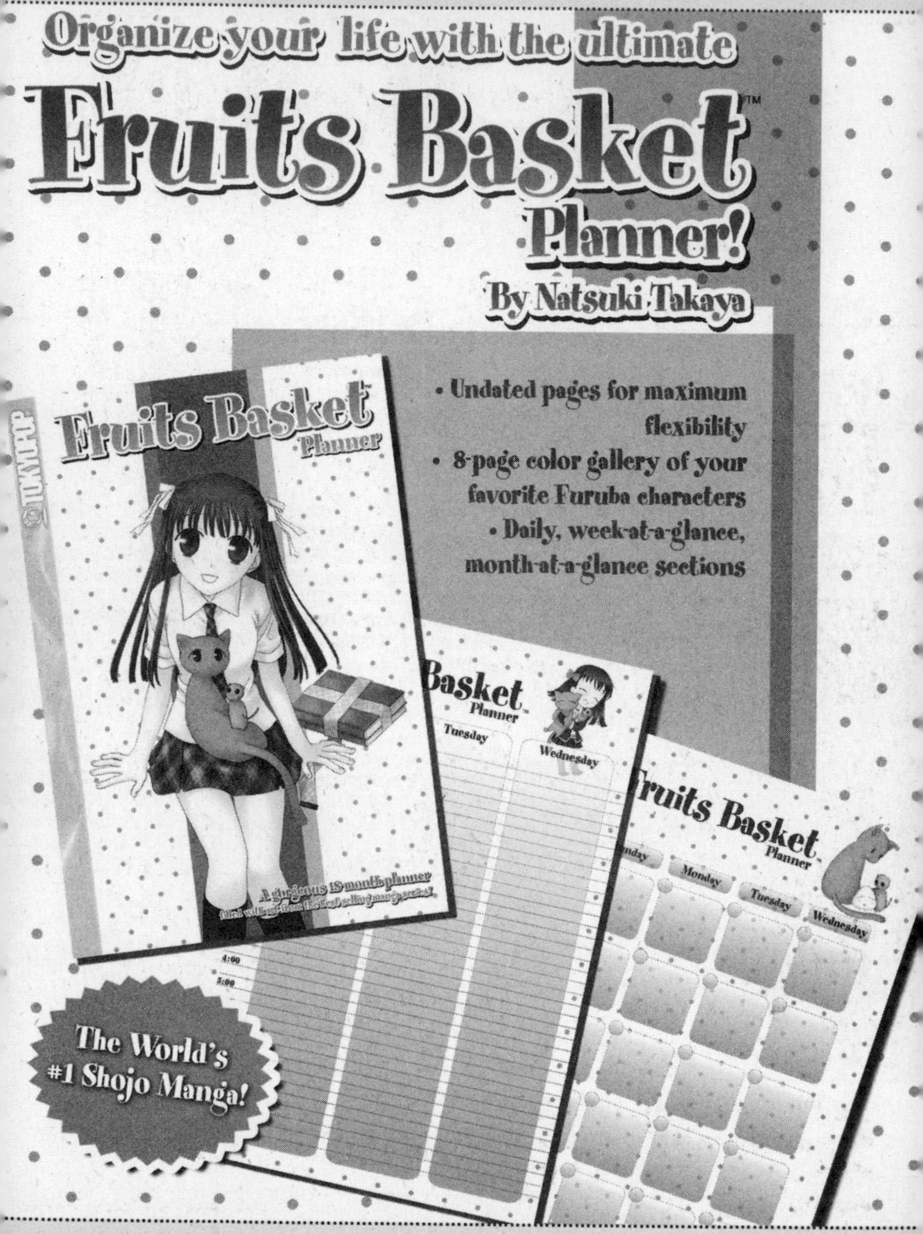

BUY IT AT WWW.TOKYOPOP.COM/SHOP

The class president has a little secret she's keeping from the sexy bad boy in school...

It's love at first fight in this shojo romantic comedy—with a hilarious spin on geek culture and... student government?!

As President of the Student Council, the overachieving feminist Misaki really socks it to the boys in an attempt to make the former all-boys' school attract a more female student body. But what will she do when the hottest boy in class finds out Misaki's after-school gig is in a maid café?!

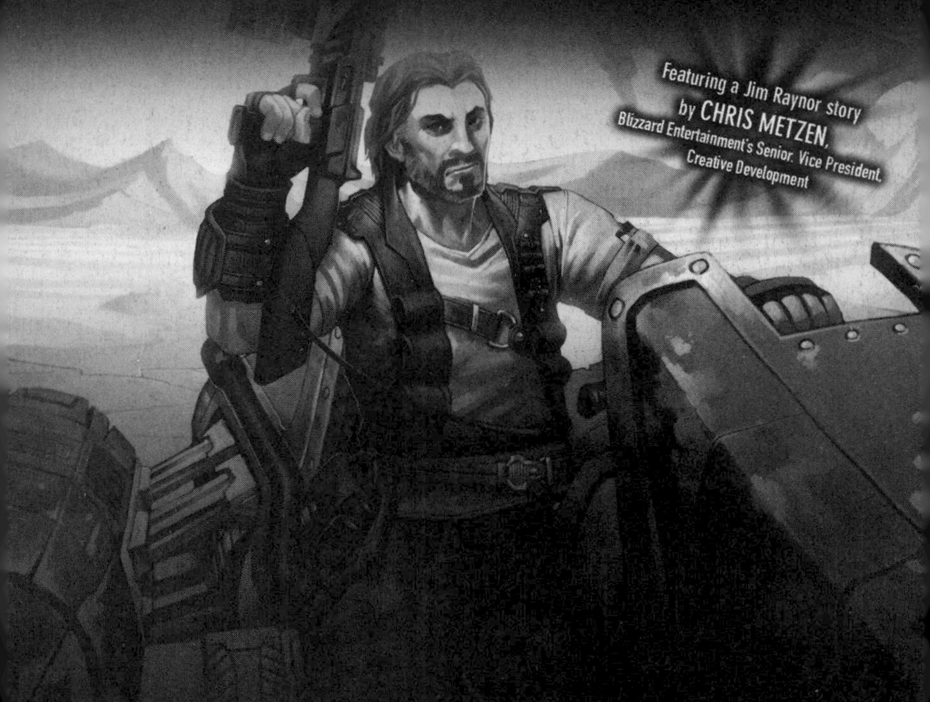
Featuring a Jim Raynor story
by CHRIS METZEN,
Blizzard Entertainment's Senior Vice President,
Creative Development

STOP!

This is the back of the book.
You wouldn't want to spoil a great ending!

This book is printed "manga-style," in the authentic Japanese right-to-left format. Since none of the artwork has been flipped or altered, readers get to experience the story just as the creator intended. You've been asking for it, so TOKYOPOP® delivered: authentic, hot-off-the-press, and far more fun!

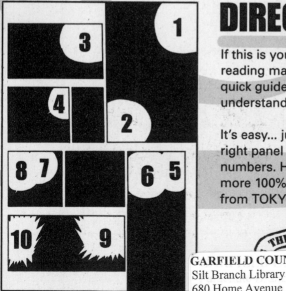

DIRECTIONS

If this is your first time reading manga-style, here's a quick guide to help you understand how it works.

It's easy... just start in the top right panel and follow the numbers. Have fun, and look for more 100% authentic manga from TOKYOPOP®!